SPIRITUALITY

**The Journey of Character Formation
Toward Christlikeness**

ALEXANDER F. VENTER

Published by ALEXANDER F. VENTER – KINGDOM TREASURES
Website: www.alexanderventer.com
Email: Shop@alexanderventer.com

Text © Alexander Venter 2019

First Edition 2019
Second Edition 2020

The Scripture quotations in this publication are taken from:
NIV – THE HOLY BIBLE, NEW INTERNATIONAL VERSION
© 1973, 1978, 1984, 2010 International Bible Society. Used by permission.
King James Version (KJV) © 1984, 1977 by Thomas Nelson, Inc.
New Revised Standard Version (NRSV) © 1989, Division of Christian Education of the National Council of the Churches of Christ in the USA, Zondervan Publishing House, Grand Rapids. Used by permission.

All rights reserved. No part of this publication may be reproduced, stored in a retrieval system, or transmitted, in any form or by any means, electronic, mechanical, photocopying, recording or otherwise, without the prior permission of the author.

Cover by Zelda Pringle
Cover image from www.dreamstime.com
Icons from www.flaticon.com

ISBN: 978-1-797-63935-2

DEDICATION AND ACKNOWLEDGEMENTS

The desert fox. A true brother and faithful friend ever since we first met, empowering my life way more than you know. I am eternally grateful. The roadrunner.

The Field community, with whom our family lived for 22 years. I learnt much with regard to spiritual living, not least that actions of loving care far outweigh words.

Following Jesus, the Vineyard church I have led since 2012, during which time I wrote the major portion of this book between all the responsibilities as senior pastor and travelling teacher. I thank the leaders and people for this opportunity.

To my many mentors in the spiritual life within the historical and contemporary community of God's people – too many to name – not least my wife, Gilli, and our two adult children, who have been primary in my spiritual formation.

Thanks to Gilli, Robin, Graham, Mike, Derek, Zelda and Rhonda – all who have contributed in meaningful ways to make this book a reality.

And to Dallas Willard. When I began to work on *Doing Spirituality*, I asked him if he would write a foreword. He graciously agreed. After writing the first two chapters, I had to put this project on hold. Then, sadly, Dallas died. I wrote a tribute to him, and consequently was honoured by invitations to speak at various meetings on his life and legacy. Therefore, instead of his foreword, I share my tribute in his memory.

PERSONAL TRIBUTE TO DALLAS WILLARD (1935-2013)

By Alexander Venter, Ascension Day 2013

A great man of God – in the truest sense of the words – has passed into the kingdom of the heavens. After a protracted struggle with cancer, Dallas Albert Willard entered the fullness of God's presence yesterday, 8 May 2013. He is now at home in the arms of the Father, Son and Spirit – and those of his extended family and friends, in the communion of saints. Our prayers are with his wife, Jane, and their children, John and Becky (with her husband Bill and daughter Karissa).

Like many others, I was honoured to have Dallas as a most influential mentor and friend. I first met him through a colleague, Trevor Hudson, at a pastors' retreat in South Africa in 1987. (Dallas came to South Africa on five ministry visits, leaving a rich legacy of spiritual formation in our nation.) He taught on the "The Spirit of the Disciplines", and then gave me a copy of his typed manuscript of the yet unpublished book. It was just before my marriage to Gill, so the manuscript became our reading on honeymoon (not as inappropriate as you may think!). I mention this story to say that it was the new start of an intentional journey of spiritual formation toward Christlikeness – because we were so inspired by Dallas' soft heart, gentle character, profoundly insightful mind, and diligent apprenticeship to Jesus.

Having Dallas stay in our home on some subsequent visits and travelling with him to Cape Town on a ministry trip, was an absolute privilege. He was genuinely interested in my (and others') wellbeing.

He listened deeply and loved truly. His sense of humor – understated yet witty and playful – was delightful. His capacity to talk about Jesus, scripture and shared-life in God's kingdom, was unending. More impressive was his humility and restraint, and his self-knowledge of his need for God's intimate presence, seen in his regular withdrawal to his room for solitude. The sheer spiritual substance or "weight of glory" (as C.S. Lewis called it) that rested on Dallas spoke louder than all his words.

He was generous and caring, always giving away the honorarium soon after it was given to him – at least on his trips to South Africa. He posted me a spiral-bound copy of his A4-typed manuscript of *Divine Conspiracy* (a massive parcel). I hungrily ploughed my way through it – not that I understood it all – but I felt stuff shift deep inside me as I read. After every couple of sentences, I had to pause and think and pray. Without fail, Dallas' writings leave me with a groaning for God's increased presence in my life, not to mention the unseen spiritual and mental formation that takes place. He also sent *Renovation of the Heart* and *Knowing Christ Today* as they became available – a faithful friend and mentor!

God has used a remarkable human being to leave an even more remarkable legacy of spiritual formation: the "with-God-life" of God's kingdom. Our best tribute to Dallas is to model and impart this kind of life: transformational apprenticeship to Jesus. The last two words he spoke before he went into the heavens were so appropriate to his life and character, "Thank you." No, thank *you*, Dallas, and thank *you*, Father, for the gift of Dallas Albert Willard.

CONTENTS

Preface	8
Part One: INTRODUCTION	19
1. Story: Travel Notes from My Spiritual Journey	20
2. Definitions: Understanding Spirituality	46
3. Overview: Four Christian Spiritual Traditions	69
Part Two: THEOLOGY	93
4. Theology: God's Kingdom and Jesus' Spirituality	94
5. Synoptic Tradition I: Kingdom Discipleship	122
6. Synoptic Tradition II: The Great Commandment	146
7. Johannine Tradition: Life in Union with Father	173
8. Pauline Tradition: Sanctification in Kingdom Tension	204
Part Three: PRAXIS	242
9. Church Tradition: The Trinitarian Spiritual Path	243
10. Transformation: The Spirit of the Disciplines	285
11. Practices I: Disciplines of Engagement – The Already	314
12. Practices II: Disciplines of Abstinence – The Not Yet	338
13. Practices III: Other Classic Tools for Spiritual Living	364
14. Conclusion: Living the Integrated Spiritual Life	388

Appendices:
Appendix 1: Understanding Gnosticism and Spirituality   411
Appendix 2: Comparing Cataphatic and Apophatic Approaches 419
Appendix 3: Ministry Planning Template   420
Appendix 4: Fowler's Faith Development Theory   423

Bibliography of Sources Consulted   426

Endorsements   441

Table of Diagrams:
Figure 1.   Church History Timeline   74
Figure 2.   Overview of Christian Spirituality   76
Figure 3.   Our Experience of God (and Excess)   87
Figure 4.   The Framework of the Kingdom of God   106
Figure 5.   Missional Implications of the Kingdom   112
Figure 6.   The Framework of Discipleship   144
Figure 7.   Circles in the Dance of Love   194
Figure 8.   Paul's Eschatological Framework   216
Figure 9.   Eschatological Salvation   219
Figure 10. "SF" Actions and the Whole Person   297
Figure 11. Golden Triangle of Transformation   301
Figure 12. Gnostic Dualism   413

PREFACE

"...only one thing is needed. Mary has chosen..."
Jesus – Lk 10:42

"...to be conformed to the likeness of his Son..."
Paul – Rom 8:29

All people and all religions, almost without exception, recognize the historical Jesus as a good person. His spirituality is universally respected, even admired. People are once again turning to his life and teachings to find the secret of his spirituality. Who was he, really? What made him such a good person? How can we emulate him?

Mary sat at Jesus' feet looking up, learning from him. Her stressed-out sister complained that she had left her to do all the work. Jesus defended and commended Mary's undistracted devotion, her single-minded contemplation of him, her choice to do the "only one thing (that) is needed". As Soren Kierkegaard said: "Purity of heart is to will one thing."[1] Ultimately, only one thing in life is needed, and that is, in the words of Paul, to be conformed to the likeness of God's Son, Jesus Christ. *Doing Spirituality* is an invitation to do just that, to choose a journey of becoming more like Jesus, to will this one thing. I am convinced that nothing else will satisfy our deepest human longing in life, our yearning for love, our search for spirituality.

Spirituality has become *the* buzzword in our postmodern era. Everyone is into "it", almost without exception. The search for spirituality is a global phenomenon, an explosion of spiritual awareness and hunger. Some pursue it as the latest best spiritual commodity to be procured,

---

1   Cited by Willard in *Renovation of the Heart*, 153.

while others see it as another passing historical fad. There are those who say it is the most hopeful development that has taken place in centuries, possibly since the origin of humanity. That is saying something!

Could the global emergence of this "new spirituality" be the most significant shift in the history of human consciousness? Many believe so, saying we are coming of age: humanity began as truly spiritual, but then religion – religious beliefs – came along and divided us. However, the new spirituality is now once again uniting humanity in a transcendent universal consciousness that will birth the utopian age. It's an emerging post-Christian, post-religious, post-war, postmodern spirituality. And so we shall be saved, planet earth included… they say!

Is this true? Is it *really* the case?

The answer depends on what we mean by spiritual consciousness or spirituality. It means different things to different people: anything from good vibes to esoteric experiences, to developing spiritual awareness, to experiencing God, to being a good person. *As a preliminary definition,* spirituality is the person or character we have (and will) become due to our relationship with spirit – either God and/or gods. Whoever or whatever we follow, believe and give ultimate value to in our lives, spiritually forms us over time into its image.

For Christians, it's about spiritual formation into Christ's likeness: Jesus, the quintessential human being, who came to reveal the Creator-God. Practically, it means formation of moral character, knowing right from wrong, and routinely and naturally doing what is good and right in love of God and others. The question is: have people in general, and leaders in particular, come of age in *this* regard?

In my view *the* most serious issue underlying *all* others in our world today is that of spirituality, which is *a crisis of character.* The authenticity of our experience and intimate knowing of God is seen in character transformation, in lived life as a good, godly person. There is the shameful failure of spiritual leaders, as in sexual abuse in the Catholic priesthood with the cover-ups and abuse of power – not that Evangelicals are much better! It is a mirror of the crisis in political and business leadership. Corrupt, autocratic, immoral and post-truth leaders are not only accepted but celebrated in our day. Living in Africa, I see it daily, explaining why Africa is the way it is. Not that the West is much different! The capacity for extreme evil in the human heart says we have *not* "come of age"! We are worse than our flawed forefathers. There is no evidence to suggest that leaders and people are changing for the better by means of the new emerging universal spiritual consciousness. If anything, the trend is toward greater self-deception and character degradation.

Be that as it may, we *can* say that *the unprecedented search for spirituality* is a desperate cry for meaning and purpose in a confused and meaningless world. It is "the silent sigh of human anguish"[2] for ultimate salvation, an expression of profound disillusionment with scientific explanations and technological inventions, a growing hunger for mystery, for ultimate (spiritual) reality.

What effect has this had on Christianity? Negatively, the explosion in spirituality has drawn some circles of Christianity deeper into New Age Gnostic beliefs and practices. Positively, there is a tremendous resurgence across most denominations of interest in classic Christian spirituality – exemplified in Jesus and his first followers, and the best of the spiritual masters in the Christian tradition.

Research into the historical Jesus is fueling this fire, producing a new vision of Jesus, with a passion to become like him. Also, there is a new openness to dialogue with and learn from other Christian traditions, other religions, beliefs and spiritualities, for the common good of humanity *and* care for our planet. This does not mean we suspend discernment and evangelism – both will be much needed and *humbly used* in the growing inter-spiritual encounter and conversation that is taking place in our fast-shrinking global village.

---

2   From Abraham Heschel. *The Prophets*, xiii.

The purpose and title of the book

This is a textbook on spirituality, specifically *Christian* spirituality. We can call it a 101 Course on Christian Spirituality – a storied, theological and practical text for spiritual growth. Thus, I have written from an overview perspective: a concise but comprehensive discussion on the personal, historical, biblical, theological, practical and experiential dimensions of Christian spirituality.

My aim is to help the reader understand and practise spirituality as Jesus did: to be captivated by him and his spirituality, to walk in his way and become like him, following him in his kingdom. Why Jesus? Because we believe he was both human and divine: he modelled what it means to be truly human as God's image, *and* he was God incarnate, revealing God to us. Jesus is indeed *The Way* to God.

The metaphors of "walk" or "journey" are apt, because the spiritual life is a step-by-step walk with God, a journey into God's Person and presence. It involves and evolves the whole of who we are for the rest of our lives, till we die. And beyond into eternity. Never to end. Our lives on earth are but a breath, a split-second in light of eternity. We need to take our split-second journey seriously, because the person we will have become when we die is the person we will be in eternity!

Leading travellers on this road, especially biblical characters, are authoritative guides on our journey. Church fathers and mothers who have gone before us are companions via their spiritual writings. But as Theophan the Recluse says (Russian Orthodox bishop, died 1894), we cannot think we have understood the spiritual life by reading the "travel notes" of spiritual fathers and mothers *without* experiencing it ourselves: "Only those can understand such notes as are following the path of that kind of life. For those who have not entered this path it [the spiritual life] is quite an unknown science."[3] Those who are interested in the spiritual journey, for whatever reason, *but are not committed to it by personal*

---

3   Kadloubovsky & Palmer, *Writings from the Philokalia: On Prayer of the Heart*, 14.

practice in accountability to spiritual leadership, are mere observers of the journey of others. They may even gain a fairly good idea of those foreign lands but have no desire – let alone commitment – to travel those distant roads. They may admire the travellers but will struggle to understand or relate to their spiritual writings – seeming strange, otherworldly, even fanatical.

The point is: it's about practice. Doing it. Personal experience. The longer we *actually* journey *with* Jesus, the more the Bible and the spiritual writings of the church mothers and fathers open themselves to us. The writings do not change, we change. We come inwardly into a space or place, an attitude of heart, where we can hear and receive their guidance and instruction and be transformed by it. Similarly with this book: it will benefit you little to read it merely as information. It's not *Studying Spirituality*. It is *Doing Spirituality*. We learn by doing. Knowledge that is life-changing is interactive – it comes by hearing, applying and obeying. Jesus contrasted those who hear and do *not* obey (thus building their lives on shifting sands) with those who hear and obey (thus building their lives on solid rock, Matt 7:24–27). My hope is that the more you seek to practise spirituality, the more you will appreciate this book as a trustworthy travel companion to help you in your life journey.

Doing Spirituality is the fourth in my *Doing* series.[4] The books have grown out of my life experience in terms of a particular biblical understanding of the kingdom of God – called Enacted Inaugurated Eschatology (explained in chapter 4).[5] Eschatology means "the study of the end" of this age, when God's kingdom comes to earth. In a certain decisive sense *that has taken place* in Jesus. He *inaugurated* God's

---

4　*Doing Church, Doing Reconciliation*, and *Doing Healing* (see the Bibliography).
5　Articulated in Derek Morphew's series on kingdom theology in my Bibliography. It's the distinctive paradigm of "Empowered Evangelicals" (which includes Vineyard churches) in contrast to conservative evangelicals who do not embrace a kingdom theology of the Spirit power-gifts in ministry and mission – a Charismatic/Pentecostal practice of church life. See Rich Nathan & Ken Wilson, *Empowered Evangelicals*, and my *Doing Church*, 36–45.

kingdom in fulfilment of the Hebrew prophets by *enacting* its presence and power in his ministry and miracles, death and resurrection. Yet it did not bring this present evil age to an end – we await that at the Second Coming of Jesus. Hence the mystery of the "already" and "not yet" of God's kingdom in Jesus (I drop the quotation marks in subsequent use of this phrase). This is the theological worldview behind each of my *Doing* books on church/leadership, on reconciliation/justice, on healing/Spirit-ministry, and now spirituality/discipleship.

The subtitle, *The Journey of Character Formation toward Christlikeness,* defines spirituality as being conformed to the likeness of Christ. The broader context in which this takes place is *Following Jesus in His Kingdom,* the alternate subtitle I wrestled with. It defines doing spirituality in the bigger picture of Jesus and his kingdom. However, I eventually settled on the former due to its focus on Christlikeness. Be that as it may, Christian spirituality is the journey of following Jesus of Nazareth in his revelation of God, in his vision and teaching of *what it means to live life in the rule and reign of God, just as he lived it.* The word "disciple" is a Bible word that has all but lost its meaning in our day. Simply, it's to be an intentional follower of Jesus, his *disciplined learner,* his life-long student or apprentice. It means being in a committed relationship of disciplined learning, spiritual growth and formation – a "becoming" like a doctor, or engineer, or teacher, over many years of learning, training and practice.

Jesus put it like this: "If you hold to my teaching, you are really my disciples. Then you will know the truth, and the truth will set you free" (Jn 8:31–32). Notice the "if". You are *really* his under-study *if* you not only hear his teachings but "hold to" them, learning by obedient application in everyday life. *Then* you come to know the truth of who he is, you share life with him, and you are progressively set free. Free *from* what? From the dictates of evil within us and outside of us. Free *for* what? For God's governing love and leading from within and without. *This* is how you become godly, how you become formed and transformed into Christ's likeness. Your life is then built on the rock of *God's* kingdom "that cannot be shaken" while all else is being shaken and falls apart (Heb 12:28).

Contents and flow of thought

All authentic theology, spirituality included, is autobiographical as in personal and experiential. I begin with my story so that the reader can relate better to the book, and hopefully learn from my self-reflection as a fellow traveller on this spiritual path. It was the most difficult chapter to write, as self-disclosure with regard to relationship with God is most intimate. God can be more intimate to us than we are to ourselves. To tell one's story with integrity, being personal without being exhibitionist, glorifying God and not oneself, in order to genuinely help others, is a challenge. Storytelling is meaning-making and community-building as we seek to make sense of our lives. Each person's story is sacred, to be told and heard with deep respect. To reflect on and share our stories is significant for mutual spiritual growth.[6] The Bible is full of such stories – to a scandalously honest degree!

Followers of Jesus are not merely products of their own journey or self-learning. We are all "human becomings", the product of *key formative factors:*

- God's life, love and work in us by his Spirit;
- Our own corresponding choices and responses – or lack thereof;
- Our formation through our families and relationships, through the Christian scriptures and Christian community – learning from companions and mentors, historically and currently; and

---

[6] See my other autobiographical chapters in each of my *Doing* books. Frank Laubach (1884–1970), a missionary to the Philippines, wrote in a self-disclosing manner in his *Letters by a Modern Mystic*: "In defence of my opening my soul and laying it bear to the public gaze in this fashion, I may say that it seems to me that we really seldom do anybody much good excepting as we share the deepest experiences of our souls in this way." See *Man of Prayer*, 20–21.

- Their application in our day-to-day life context in the world.

Doing Spirituality is a distillation of my experience and knowledge gained through these God-given means of becoming. I first taught a series on spirituality and discipleship in the late 1980s. Then I formed it into a "Spirituality Course", which I taught in the 1990s at a Vineyard School of Ministry in Cape Town. The book you are holding is the expanded and updated version, with *two distinctive features*.

Firstly, it is from the kingdom theological framework mentioned earlier; a spirituality *of the kingdom* in contrast to other paradigms of spirituality in the history of the church, such as liturgical, ascetic, mystical, charismatic, social activist, or missional. They all find their proper place *within* the biblical theology of the kingdom. All spiritualities, without exception, are determined by a particular underlying paradigm, whether acknowledged or not. The vision of God's future rule and reign on a renewed earth, already begun in Jesus of Nazareth, determines (ought to) how we live – called *biblical kingdom spirituality*.

Secondly, this kingdom worldview is set against the glorious horizon of the Trinity – The Eternal Community – one God in three Persons: Father, Son and Spirit. Though the New Testament (NT) reveals God as one yet three, the word "Trinity" is absent. It was first used by Theophilus of Antioch near the end of the 2nd century. Articulation of Trinitarian theology was a post-NT development in the Christian church. It has recently come back into focus in academic theology, called "The New Trinitarianism". The mystery of the Trinitarian God is the fullness of spirituality. We are the canvas on which the Holy Spirit paints Christian spirituality in all its rich beauty: the image of Messiah Jesus. This portrait is framed in the kingdom of God, set against the infinite horizon of the Trinity.[7] Sadly, this Trinitarian reality is lost to many Christians as they are practical monotheists: they do not experience God *as* relationship – of the Father, *and* the Son, *and* the Spirit – in a shared life of love.

---

[7] Jurgen Moltmann brought these together in his study, *The Trinity and the Kingdom*. See also Fischer, *Towards a Kingdom Theology of The Trinity*.

My inadequate attempt to unveil this magnificent painting is in three parts: Introduction, Theology, and Praxis. I introduce each part with a concise overview of what is dealt with, summarizing the flow of thought and argument: from my personal story; to definitions and expressions of spirituality; to the main four Christian spiritualities in church history; to the theology of the kingdom and Jesus' spirituality and teachings; to John's perspective of Jesus and spirituality; to Paul's letters that explain Christian living in kingdom tension; to its praxis (practice) in the classic Christian spiritual tradition; to how the Spirit transforms us via spiritual practices; to how we live the *spiritual* life, and how the local church can do spiritual formation.

To be aware of…

Each chapter ends with a set of questions for personal reflection and group discussion. *Small groups can use this book as a program for spiritual growth:* each person reads the chapter during the week and works through the questions for personal reflection. Then, when the group meets, each person shares what they have learnt, and what they believe God has said to them. This can lead to a time of prayer for one another. It can be a mutual accountability process for spiritual growth in terms of the daily and weekly application and practice of what is being learnt.

Spirituality is a vast subject with tens of thousands of books on *Christian* spirituality alone. Thus, this text can attract myriads of footnotes like moths to a light. I have had to be selective not only in my content, but also in my use of footnotes. I cite sources – author and title, with details in the Bibliography – for an argument, if needed; or to give an important qualification or explanation; or to cite further helpful reading so as to broaden the reader's awareness of other traditions and resources. Do not be put off by references and quotes from people in other denominations and traditions. To read widely *without prejudice*, is to learn from all writers, eating the meat and spitting out the bones. Read this book in the same spirit.

I try to write simply and clearly, while stretching the reader in terms of biblical knowledge and theological thinking. As with all human disciplines, the field of spirituality has its own technical jargon that can be bypassed with lay language. I have chosen, however, to use technical terms when needed, giving explanations of their meaning so that the language of Christian spirituality and biblical theology can be heard and understood. Therefore, work with me in the more theological and philosophical sections because, knowing the *who and why* (assumptions and beliefs) behind the *what and how* (practices and application), will save you from mindless imitation of spiritual practices that tend to meaningless ritual and moral legalism.

I use gender-inclusive language as far as grammar permits. I use abbreviations for the books of the Bible due to my frequent reference to biblical texts – see the contents page in your Bible. I also abbreviate commonly used words or phrases like: for example (e.g.), and, in other words (i.e.). Or I indicate an abbreviation in brackets after I first use a word that is appropriate to abbreviate – as in the following paragraph. Such abbreviations are then used throughout the book.

I decided to go back to Before Christ (BC) and *Anno Domini*, "in the year of our Lord" (AD), for timelines, rather than the current usage of Before Common Era (BCE) and Common Era (CE). And I *italicize* non-English words, indicating whether they are Hebrew (Heb.), Latin (Lat.), or French. I do not indicate Greek words due to their frequent use in this primarily NT study. I also use *italics* to emphasize certain words or sentences. In terms of scripture, I use the New International Version (NIV), and secondly, the New Revised Standard Version (NRSV). My biblical quotes are from the NIV unless otherwise indicated. This includes my own "RAP" on some texts – the Revised Alexander Paraphrase.[8]

---

8   Familiarity with the wording of biblical texts can lead to a loss of meaning; the mind labels it as "known" and cannot see it in a new light. Over the years, I have taken to comparing various versions of a text to write my own RAP, to capture the intent and meaning in a fresh way, like Eugene Peterson's *The Message*. Note that I am not a formally trained Hebrew and/or Greek scholar, and a paraphrase is *not* a translation, therefore read my RAP comparatively with other *translations*.

Preface

Finally, my question to you, the reader, is: what one thing, above all else, do you want to do with your life? What is your life-goal? "Only one thing is needed", to be conformed to the likeness of God's Son. To will this one thing above all else is to become pure of heart. My book is an invitation to that end, to help you wrestle down everything in your life to an intentional, integrated and cohesive "one pursuit" of following Jesus in his kingdom. May he indeed meet you in these pages. May his Spirit use them to form and transform you a little more into his likeness. As in the Jesuit tradition, I pray that you may receive the grace to know Jesus more intimately, so that you love him more dearly, and follow him more closely.[9]

Alexander F. Venter

---

9   Ignatius' prayer for the second week of his exercises, in Ganss, *The Spiritual Exercises of Saint Ignatius*, paragraph 104, 56.

PART ONE

INTRODUCTION

My aim in this section is to introduce "spirituality" – both general and (specific) Christian spirituality. I do this by way of sharing my own spiritual journey in the hope that it will stimulate and challenge you, the reader, not only to reflect on your own journey, but also to take your spiritual life seriously. Then I discuss what spirituality has come to mean in our contemporary world and compare it with the original meaning in the NT, mainly from Paul's understanding. I conclude Part One with an overview of *Christian* spirituality in the form of four kinds of prayer and the historical spiritual traditions that they have produced.

CHAPTER 1

STORY: TRAVEL NOTES FROM MY SPIRITUAL JOURNEY

"I know your deeds, your hard work and perseverance...
yet I hold this against you: You have forsaken your first love.
Remember the height from which you have fallen!
Repent and do the things you did at first."
Jesus – Rev 2:2, 4–5

"This is love: not that we loved God, but that he (first) loved us.
We love (him) because he first loved us."
John – 1 Jn 4:10, 19

"You are my Son, my Beloved, in whom I am so pleased."
God – Mk 1:11 (RAP)

Summarizing my spiritual journey

A long time ago, I was asked to summarize my spiritual journey in a few sentences. I understood it in terms of the working definition of spirituality as my relationship with God and the person I have become. It went something like this.

Since I became a follower of Jesus, I have found that God comes again and again to draw me to himself in his unfailing love – largely because of my repeated failings. It's as if God seduces me time and again, despite myself. He draws me back to my first love, back to the arms of the Father, wooing me into ever-deeper communion. Each time this happens, my heart is softened, and my passion is renewed to serve God in his love for his pain-filled world. In all my ups and downs, joys and victories, insecurities and wanderings, and times of deep darkness, *God has been faithful*. He is *so* patient and persevering. Always forgiving. His intensely personal love conquers me. And it is more beautiful each day – but certainly not easier!

To illustrate the point, I remember, as a young pastor, studying the life of Paul in the NT. I put his letters into chronological order as per NT studies – despite the debates on dating and authorship. What struck me was the development in Paul's spiritual consciousness over the years of ministry. In one of his earliest letters (53/54 AD) he says: "I am *the least of the apostles* and do not even deserve to be called an apostle because I persecuted the church of God" (1 Cor 15:9, my italics, also in the texts below). He thought humbly of himself in reference to other church leaders. He knew God's mercy in light of his sinful past, making him feel unworthy of his calling and ministry as an apostle of Christ, especially in comparison to the other apostles.

About six years later, when Paul wrote from prison in Rome (60/61 AD), he pulls himself down a few pegs, thinking of himself as the least of all Christians: "Although I am *less than the least of all God's people*, this grace was given to me to preach to the Gentiles" (Eph 3:8). Paul's further journey with Jesus made him more keenly aware of both God's grace and his unworthiness to be God's servant to the Gentiles. The comparison is now with all the saints, not church leaders.

Four years later (64/65 AD, about three years before he was executed), Paul writes to Timothy. His journey with Jesus had brought him simultaneously to the heights of grace and the lowest rung on the ladder: "Christ Jesus came into the world to save sinners – of whom *I am the worst*. But for that very reason I was shown mercy so that in me, *the worst of sinners*, Christ Jesus might display his unlimited patience as an example..." (1 Tim 1:15–16). Referring to his past blasphemy and violence (v.13), Paul did not say "I *was* the worst of sinners", but "I *am...*" Note the significance of the present tense, indicating he still saw himself as the foremost of sinners. Is this not negative confession against his identity in Christ? Spurning "the finished work of the cross", as some would say? Or is it the morose introspection of an imprisoned old man? No, it's true humility, a refining of spiritual consciousness that sees oneself ever more clearly for who you are in reality – *both* God's Reality *and* this age reality. The longer Paul served Jesus, the more clearly he saw the embarrassing goodness of God's grace, and in light of that, his unworthiness as the worst of sinners. He knew he was saved by sheer mercy, a saint set apart as God's servant, to be an example of Christ's unlimited patience and infinite love.

True spirituality is paradoxical: the closer we are to the Holy One, the clearer we see the magnitude of our unworthiness and need for God. *And* we experience and appreciate the even greater magnitude of his love and grace, which inspires us to be its servant in proclaiming it to others. It gets better and worse and better at the same time. We are justified saints, declared righteous, yet we are repenting sinners, we still sin in this age. The truth is we are *both* saintly sinners *and* sinning saints! Truth, in refined spiritual consciousness, is the bifocal of both/and tension, not the binary of either/or dualism. The former produces true humility in full surrender to God's love.

My experience concurs with Paul. Because my heart is so deceitful, true self-knowledge and radical self-honesty has been a battle. The more I have learnt to embrace, believe and live who I am in Christ – not in super-spirituality or unhealthy denial of reality – the more I have become aware of my brokenness and vulnerability in light of God's unbelievable patience and prodigal love for me. My need for God's grace, and my need to draw on such grace, grows greater every day. I find myself having to literally "use up" more and more grace. Hopefully one day I will live entirely by grace and grace alone. *This* realization overwhelms me, causing me to surrender to God's love and service, again and again, at ever-deeper levels of joyous sacrifice and worship. The spiritual life is indeed one of ecstasy, agony and more ecstasy!

Salvation and first instruction

I was thirteen years old when I became a follower of Jesus on 7 June 1968, at the First Baptist Church in East London, South Africa. The minister was Rex Matthie, a down-to-earth, godly man, a great expository preacher. He became somewhat of an "uncle" to many of the young people. We called him Uncle Rex. God used him to set me on my way with Jesus, laying a good foundation for my spiritual life.

My conversion began when a Baptist friend in my grade told me about Jesus. Because I did not know much about God and Jesus, it took me six months to understand his explanation of who Jesus was and why I should give my life to him. Eventually, he invited me to a youth service. Afterward he looked me in the eye, "If you died tonight, would you be ready to meet God?" I realized… "No!" As I said it, I began to cry, much to my embarrassment, as some of the young people were watching.

It troubled me deeply, penetrating my subconscious. That night I dreamt I *had* died. In my dream my dad laid me in a coffin. I looked out a window watching my dad hold the rope. He lowered the coffin into the grave. When it hit the bottom, I had a most strange and awful sensation of falling off the earth. I knew I was being "thrown away" into outer space. I saw the earth receding. The stars flew past. I screamed and twisted and stretched and groped, trying to grab onto something – anything that would stop my acceleration into utter darkness. I woke up with my brother shaking me – my shouts had woken him! As I sat up, questions flooded my mind. Who are you? Who made you? Why are you on the earth? What are you living for? What's going to happen to you when you die? Is there life after death?

Part One: Introduction

In asking my dad, he said I was not to worry about such questions, I was too young to understand. They would explain all these things to me at university, he said! But I knew that my Baptist friend would help. When I told him the dream, he simply pointed his finger in my face and said, "God is calling you! Come to the youth meeting and give your life to Christ." At the next meeting, after the preaching, I went forward for prayer. Uncle Rex led me in a prayer to surrender my life to Jesus Christ. It was profoundly meaningful. A great weight lifted off me and I was free and at peace. I felt like I had come home to the arms of my heavenly Father.

Then he said, "You are now born again with eternal life, a new baby in Christ! As with all new babies, you need to do four things: 1) Breathe… exercise your lungs! This is prayer, breathing the air of heaven. If you stop praying you will die, so talk to God throughout the day. 2) Babies feed, drink milk, in order to grow. This is reading your Bible. It's your daily food. Read three chapters every day, two from the Old Testament (OT), and one from the NT. Then in one year you will have read through the whole Bible. 3) Babies cry, exercise their voice, learn to talk. This is witnessing. Tell people what Jesus has done for you – at least one new person every day. And 4) babies are born in families. You need to belong to a family to be cared for, so join the church and make it your spiritual home."

Being young and innocent, I simply believed and did these four things, rather religiously! So much so that some nights I would get out of bed remembering I had not told someone about Jesus that day. Getting on my bicycle, I would roam the streets looking for a person to "witness to"! I later came to terms with the (wrong) drive of guilt and legalism, but the single-minded pursuit to obey these four instructions laid a good foundation for my spiritual growth.

In what follows, I briefly share some *other key factors in my spiritual formation and development.*

"O God of second chances and new beginnings, here I am again!"

I remember coming to Uncle Rex in my mid-teens struggling with the onset of puberty. I felt guilty because of the strong urges in my body. I wondered if all other young guys struggled as much as I did. He answered, "Ninety per cent of young men your age masturbate and the other 10% lie". Phew! I was relieved! But I still felt guilty and needed to understand my developing sexuality; how to come to terms with it, to live well with it. Besides giving me practical advice, he gave me a prayer to pray: "O God of second chances and new beginnings, here I am again."

Every morning, I prayed these words. Each morning was a new beginning in God's presence, a new creation. At dark moments, I have wept those words to my Father, finding love and peace in his forgiving embrace. Over the years, it has slowly shifted my consciousness from my failings – my guilt and shame – to a greater awareness and vision of God as pure goodness and merciful love.

However, in all honesty, it's *not* always been easy to pray these words. At times I avoided them in my attempt to avoid God. You know what it's like trying to avoid God? Too guilty to pray. Trying to take a holiday from God. It's difficult to avoid God because he's everywhere! The scary thing is that he does not get insecure when we avoid him. He allows us to do so. And does not even seem to mind! Well, at least not immediately! My experience has been that somehow, in some way, without fail God *does* come to soften my heart, to draw me back to my knees to pray those wonderful words, "O God of second chances and new beginnings, here I am again."

Having said that, I am conscious of the fact that I can harden my heart toward God. If I do not respond when he comes, if I keep rejecting his loving advances, he does eventually back off and allows us to do our own thing. We can even reach a point when God hands us over to our willfulness, to our corrupted appetites, to our demons. However, we do not have to go there; Father is waiting with open arms.

Empowering of the Holy Spirit

As my relationship with God developed, I became aware of a lack of effective power in my "witnessing" and prayer life. Again, God sent another school friend to be his messenger. He told me, "If you want joy and power in your relationship with God, if you want to pray with fire and have anointing to witness for Jesus, you must be baptized with the Holy Spirit." I had no clue about the rights or wrongs of Pentecostal theology, but I wanted whatever God was offering. So my friend laid hands on me and I was filled with the Spirit and began to "speak in tongues", as the Bible calls it.

This was a major turning point. It revolutionized my prayer-life, opening a fountain of joy, praise, prayer and intercession, directly to God. A hot-line to heaven! No wonder Paul said: "I speak in tongues more than all of you" (1 Cor 14:18). I have found the freedom of speaking praise and prayer in unknown languages, given and known by God, profoundly therapeutic and powerfully mysterious. Paul says in Rom 8:26–27 that we do not know how to pray, or what to pray for, as we ought. The indwelling Holy Spirit helps us by praying directly through us to the Father and the Son with words that express our deepest inarticulate longings. I learnt to rely on the Spirit in my prayer-times by praying in tongues. At times I entered a groaning – even a wailing as if in labour – in which I felt strong surges of compassion and intercession for people, for mysteries I knew nothing about. Yet I knew that somehow it was a participation in birthing God's purposes. I noticed that it led to conviction and power in "witnessing" and in laying hands on people to impart power and healing.

I echo what Paul says: I do not understand the "tongues" and its related experiences. It transcends the mind. But I *do know* that the Spirit prays mysteries in me. Praising, praying and groaning in the Spirit releases my inner stuff to God. More importantly, it also represents and expresses *both* creation's groaning for its own liberation from the curse of sin *and* God's groaning for creation – and connects the two *within* me! As with Isaiah, we sense the sighs of the Trinity (Is 6:8), we enter into the conversation of the Father and Son by the Spirit – *and* into the redemptive activity that flows from it. I also *know* that as I "pray in the Spirit on all occasions" (Eph 6:18) I not only "build myself up" (Jude 20), but I experience union with the Trinity – I literally "participate in the divine nature" (2 Pet 1:4).

There were times, as a teenager, when I walked up and down in my room with my hands raised, praising God, singing with the most creative words – like "tongues of angels" (1 Cor 13:1). I would feel so exhilarated that I made strange sounds and laughed with joy! This led to an incident a year or so after my baptism in the Spirit when my father overheard me praising God in this manner. When I eventually came out of my room, I saw my father's troubled and angry face.

Opposition in the home

He had spoken to my mother (they were unchurched) and asked me: "What is going on in your room? What are those noises you make? Who are you talking to? Have you gone mad?" They were concerned and wanted to take me to a psychologist or psychiatrist. I did not respond well. I laughed, saying *they* were the crazy ones to think of me in those terms. My dad lost it. He stood up and punched me in a rage. I was humiliated beyond measure. Grabbing my Bible, I ran out of the house shouting, "This is a sinful house! I'm leaving!" I went to a public phone booth up the road, not to change into superman (I wish!), but to phone Uncle Rex. I explained what had happened and asked if I could come to stay at his house. "No ways! Go back to your parents, and apologize, and be a good son to them." So I went home, apologized, and tried to be a good son!

This was part of the growing hostility in our home to my having become "a born-again Christian". Although they meant well, my parents, as well as my older sister and brother, did not understand. They perceived I had become a fanatic "because you pray and read the Bible all the time!"

I loved going to church and was frequently on the streets handing out "gospel tracts" (Christian pamphlets) to people. My dad was so concerned that he forbade me to attend church for about eight months. It drove me to more prayer and Bible meditation to survive. I would wake early to be alone with God, often taking a piece of bread and a cup of water to have the most intimate communion with Jesus. I was so desperate that, for a couple of months, I prayed through the night on Fridays for my family's salvation. These were truly remarkable times in terms of my growing relationship with Jesus.

Time and again, after yet another hurtful comment or incident of rejection regarding my faith in Jesus, I would go to my room, kneel next to my bed, open my Bible to a psalm and begin to pray the words. Within a few sentences, tears would flow freely as I cried out my pain to God, seeking his arms of comfort. "Though my father and mother forsake me, the LORD will receive me" (Ps 27:10). I *so* identified with David in his prayers and struggles in the psalms that I began to memorize scripture as a means of praying it through the day. What encouragement, strength and perspective I found in this daily discipline of prayerful memorizing of psalms!

I learnt that God was my *real* Father – he fathered and mothered me when I needed it most. I learnt that Jesus was *really* my elder brother, showing me the way. I learnt that the Holy Spirit was my most intimate indwelling friend. I was not wise or godly in many of my responses to my family and others, but Jesus helped me. I identified with his rejection and the way he handled it: "During the days of Jesus' life on earth, he offered up prayers and petitions *with loud cries and tears* to the one who could save him from death, and he was heard because of his reverent submission. Although he was a son, he learned obedience from what he suffered" (Heb 5:7–8). My home situation was God's plan to teach me obedience by what I suffered, by prayer and submission to God's will. There is no doubt that God allows and uses hardship, opposition, persecution, weakness and suffering, as means of spiritual formation.

"For Thy pleasure..." and "One thing is needful..."

During this time, I came across two amazing biblical texts. Soon after I became a follower of Jesus, an elderly lady, Mrs M. Green, gave me a King James Bible (KJV). It was the old English: "For Thou hast created all things, and for Thy pleasure they are and were created" (Rev 4:11). This text struck deep into my consciousness: God made all things for *his pleasure* – that includes *me*! The context of the verse is that of the heavenly beings worshipping God around his throne and doing his bidding. I concluded that I can bring God great pleasure by worshipping him, not only in my times of prayer, but also serving him in all my thoughts, words and deeds.

It made me reflect: *why* did God make us *in his image*? I thought: for life *with* God. God came searching for Adam and Eve with a most haunting and lonely cry, "Adam, Eve, where are you?" God searches for *us*! He *really* wants us! He is a real Person with feelings and desires for love. We are created for friendship with God – he seeks our intimate companionship.[10] In some mysterious sense, we meet or fulfil something deep in God. I "theologized" as follows: just as Eve was created out of Adam and was bone of his bone, flesh of his flesh, and the two became one, so we are created out of God and are breath of his breath, spirit of his spirit, and the two become one. It was not good for Adam to be alone. Eve was created as a uniquely suitable companion to complete him and, by implication, for Adam to complete Eve. So, by analogy, we were uniquely created to companion God, to complete him – for his eternal pleasure – and God completes us for our eternal pleasure. Astonishing![11]

The second text that arrested me – with which I began my preface

---

10 A great help to me has been William Barry's, *A Friendship Like No Other*.
11 Although God is eternally complete and unchanging, the Godhead has, in some sense, been forever "changed" or "completed" in the Son coming to "seek and save what was lost" (Lk 19:10). In the Son becoming human and dying and rising again, there is *now* a resurrected human *body* (a God-human being) in the Trinity forever. *In Christ*, we (resurrected) human beings follow him into the Trinity – a shared life of oneness with God, just as God is one – which *is* eternal life.

– was the words Jesus spoke to Martha: "But one thing is needful; and Mary has chosen that good part, which shall not be taken away from her" (Lk 10:42 KJV). *The* "one thing" of undistracted devotion to Jesus, sitting at his feet, hearing his word, is what I wanted. The simple story of Martha and Mary, *and especially what Jesus said,* confirmed my life's priority: undivided devotion to Jesus and his word (teachings). This does not mean escape from hard work or from involvement in God's good but broken world! It expresses the priority of what we were created for in this life and the life to come. It also connected me with another favourite text in which David expressed his life's desire: "*One thing* have I desired of the Lord, that will I seek after; that I may dwell in the house of the Lord all the days of my life, *to behold the beauty of the Lord,* and to enquire in his temple" (Ps 27:4 KJV, my italics).

At that time, a friend shared a story that deeply impacted me,[12] because it strongly reinforced the message of these two texts. A nun began a process of learning to be with God in daily prayer for *God's* sake, not her own. She would kneel next to her bed and begin with a prayer to this effect: "Lord Jesus, I am *not* here to ask you for anything, but just to be with you. I want to love you in worship, love you in waiting and weeping at your feet. I want to be present and attentive to you. I want to give you joy and pleasure in this time together." Then she waited in silence, eyes closed, focused on God's presence, holding and loving him in her heart. She began with five minutes of adoring silence. After a few weeks of daily practice, becoming more fully present to Jesus' presence, she gradually extended her times of worship-filled silence to ten, fifteen, twenty and many more minutes.

One day, after years of this practice, she heard someone coming to her door, gently knocking and turning the handle. Not wanting to stop her concentration on Christ's presence, she thought her sister-nun would see her kneeling in prayer and would quietly withdraw, as had occasionally

---

12   From a Catholic magazine he gave me. Unable to source and cite it, I choose to believe it is true.

happened. But the person entered the room. A little distracted and annoyed, the nun kept to her discipline, deciding she would keep her eyes closed and not engage this rude sister. Then she became aware that the person was standing behind her – a warm authoritative presence filled the room. She felt drops of water falling on her head. One or two fell on her forehead and ran down her face, touching her lips. They were salty. A voice spoke, "My beloved daughter! I've come to thank you for your love, for washing my feet with your tears of worship." She whispered, "Jesus!" As quickly and quietly as he came, so he left.

This little story, describing a profound mystical experience of God's loving presence, conveyed what I longed for so deeply: "for Thy pleasure" and "this one thing is needful". I decided to "choose that part". It taught me that spirituality is a life of love in worship of God – being attentive to him, giving him joy and pleasure – in acts of intimate adoration, sweet companionship, and works of sacrificial service. I have to add that Solomon's Song of Songs fed this experience and pursuit of God during my teenage years – the time of my "nuptials" or "honeymoon" with Jesus. Praying through the Song of Songs again and again, inspired by reading Hannah Hurnard's *Hinds' Feet on High Places,* drew out such longing and desire for Jesus, that often I found myself awash with tears, overwhelmed with his loving presence.

Discovering the theology of the kingdom of God

On graduating from high school in 1972, I did compulsory military duty and later worked for a computer company. Then I was ordained to the ministry in 1975. In the late 1970s, I discovered the theology of the kingdom of God as taught by G.E. Ladd. My professor at the University of South Africa (Unisa) had prescribed Ladd's two key books on the kingdom (God's rule/reign) as our primary texts.[13] It was nothing short of revolutionary! The Gospel stories came alive and I fell in love with Jesus as never before. Seeing God's future kingdom present and active in

---
13   *The Presence of the Future* and *A Theology of the New Testament.*

Jesus of Nazareth – "the powers of the coming age" (Heb 6:5) – was like being born again, again!

It gave me a vision *of* life, and *for* life, in God's kingdom. I wanted to become like Jesus in the way he lived in such intimacy with the Father, in union with his will, knowing his mind, feeling his emotions, speaking his words, doing his works, seeing his wonders. I wanted to live and love as Jesus lived and loved, healing and freeing others with kingdom authority and power. "The reason the Son of God appeared was to destroy the devil's works" (1 Jn 3:8b). My short experience as a pastor had shown me that people are radically bound by evil, desperately struggling with all sorts of brokenness. My heart burned within me, longing to live for "*the reason… to destroy the devil's works*" in the lives of people, to free them in Jesus' Name.

The theology of the rule and reign of God shifted the focus from "my spirituality" to God and people. The staggering reality was that, as a follower of Jesus, I could be an instrument of *his* kingdom. So the challenge was: how could I live the life of the kingdom? How could I become that kind of person – like Jesus – through whom God's reign comes with compassionate power?

Kingdom theology led to *three life-changing developments,* each involving a costly decision to respond to my unfolding understanding of God's kingdom in Jesus and the call to follow him. Their impact on my spiritual formation is immeasurable, largely determining the person I have become, and will become, by God's grace.

Firstly, kingdom theology led me to John Wimber, who both taught and practised it in the way he did church. I decided to leave my Pentecostal pastorate and joined the Vineyard in 1981. Then my first wife and I sold up and went to Anaheim to work with John for eight months. We returned in 1982 to help plant – with two colleagues – the first Vineyard church in South Africa (in Johannesburg). My time with Wimber and my years as a Vineyard pastor gave me *a spirituality* of kingdom worship – intimacy with the Father – and of kingdom ministry, power encounter and doing church; continuing the Son's kingdom work by the Spirit's power.[14]

Secondly, a year or so after we planted the church, I began to go into Soweto as a matter of conscience – a white South African reconciling with black South Africans.[15] I believed that God's kingdom could rewrite "The Tale of Two Cities": *Joh*annesburg (white wealth and power) and So*weto* (black poverty and oppression) divided by apartheid (structural racism). I believed God wept over these two cities as Jesus wept over Jerusalem. Jesus died to abolish the great divide. God saw one city, one people: *"Johweto"*, a place of justice, reconciliation and unity, which God's people ought to have embodied. The church in South Africa had dismally failed. We were a copy of our divided racist society, not a model of God's future kingdom come in Christ. Going into Soweto birthed a reconciliation group of blacks and whites, which we called Johweto – a sign of the kingdom, a prophetic challenge to our government and nation of equality and dignity for all. The Johweto journey (1984 to 1996) was an exercise in *a spirituality* of kingdom reconciliation and justice.

Thirdly, my understanding of the kingdom led my wife and I into intentional Christian community. Johweto raised challenges of geography (we travelled from Johannesburg to Soweto) and of shared life (we only met in meetings). We needed to share life *together* as a witness of integrity to God's kingdom. After extensive discussions, a few white and black couples made a commitment to explore geographic community on the edge of Soweto and Johannesburg. We all liquidated what we owned, pooled our finances and bought a small farm, relocating in 1991. This indeed was life-changing. I have yet to record the ups and downs of this journey in intentional common-purse community as a place of kingdom formation and witness. It's been a most remarkable journey in *a*

---
14 See my story regarding the Vineyard in chapter 1 of *Doing Church*.
15 Soweto, a city of three million black Africans, alongside Johannesburg, serving the white economy in apartheid South Africa. I record the story in the first few chapters of *Doing Reconciliation*.

spirituality of community, of personal and communal transformation in learning to love as Jesus loved us.

Divorce and journey toward healing and wholeness

I entered full-time ministry in 1975, as a paid youth pastor in Rhodesia (now Zimbabwe). There I met and married a young lady in 1977. We went through a very sad and painful divorce in 1984/5. In personal terms, those two years were the darkest I have ever been through, without exception. There is no need to elaborate, except to say that it was yet another significant turning point in my spiritual life and growth.[16]

The pain of the marriage break-up, the divorce and its aftermath, turned me to God in a deeper way, driven by my need for healing. It began with Morton Kelsey's book on journalling and the spiritual life.[17] That opened the door to spiritual writings in the Catholic and Orthodox traditions. I began an intentional practice of classic spiritual disciplines like solitude and silence, various forms of meditation, the practice of contemplation (called centring prayer), journalling, dream interpretation, going on both led retreats and personal retreats, seeking a spiritual director and cultivating a spiritual companion. These practices, motivated by my reading of spiritual masters, were like drinking from an age-old reservoir of crystal-clear water – life-giving and healing. My Evangelical-Pentecostal spirituality was not enough to satisfy the longing for mystery that had been awakened in my deepest consciousness by this new dimension of experiencing God in silence, liturgical symbols and spiritual ritual.

The point is: If we turn to God in our pain, making the right choices in dealing with our brokenness, God uses it as a means of spiritual transformation. Brokenness and healing cannot be separated from spirituality. Wimber used to say, "Many people grow old but never grow up. Grow up before you grow old, or you will grow old bitter and twisted."

---

[16] I summarize my story in this regard, with the various factors in my healing journey, in *Doing Healing*, 24–28. Those healing factors were also key to my spiritual growth.

[17] *Inward Adventure*.

Healing and wholeness is a journey of knowing God – which includes growth in accurate self-knowledge, which in turn depends on how *honest* we are with ourselves. Healing, personal growth and authentic spirituality cannot be separated, just like the Trinity cannot be separated. Any spirituality that is not a part of, or leads to, a process of growth towards wholeness, with real self-awareness, is false spirituality.[18] That is why this book is the logical and important follow-on from *Doing Healing*.

"A long obedience in the same direction" and "Who are you becoming?"

As mentioned earlier, the Psalms have been my constant companion in my spiritual journey. Along the way, I sought for books and commentaries on the Psalter that would help me enter deeper into David's spirituality, into the spirit of those ancient prayers of Israel. Soon after my divorce, I came across Eugene Peterson's book, *A Long Obedience in the Same Direction: Discipleship in an Instant Society*. The title is taken from a most insightful quote of Friedrich Nietzsche:[19]

> *The essential thing 'in heaven and earth' is… that there should be long obedience in the same direction; there thereby results, and has always resulted in the long run, something which has made life worth living.*

What grabbed my attention – so masterfully illustrated in Peterson's expositions of the Songs of Ascent – was the fact that each small obedience towards *the one goal of God's intimate ruling presence in our lives* accumulates over a lifetime into the person we become. It's toward the end of our lives that we look back and see who we have *really* become. Only in retrospect can we actually see what/who we have lived for and

---

18 On the union of healing, self-knowledge and spirituality, see David Benner, *Psychotherapy and the Spiritual Quest*, and Gerald May, *Care of Mind, Care of Spirit*.
19 *Beyond Good and Evil*, Section 188, 106–107. Nietzsche had some helpful insights, but he seeded the "God is dead" theology.

who/what has formed us. How tragic to *then* realize we lived for what was ultimately worthless.

The sober truth is that our small daily decisions accumulate in a hidden, but decisive manner, to form the person we become, for better or for worse. This is *character*, not personality, nor temperament. It is the formation of *moral* character: the freedom to routinely choose to do God's will from joy-filled obedience. Or the formation of *immoral* character: enslaved to do wrong. Good character is a life-long, whole-life project, to end up freely and lovingly doing what God would do in any given situation at any given time, if he were us. That is, *good character conditioned by obedience:* the ability to naturally and easily "obey *everything* I have commanded you" (Matt 28:19); the result of a long obedience in the same direction to become like Jesus.

At this time (1986) I met Dallas Willard at a retreat that he led. He has been a primary mentor in terms of my spiritual life and discipleship to Jesus. Dallas made this statement: "The only thing that you and I will get out of our lives one day when we die and stand before God – when everything is stripped away and who we *really are* is made known – *is the person we will have become. So, who are you becoming?*" Like one of David's five smooth stones, it hit the Goliath of my false self between the eyes, penetrating my denial, bringing down all my pretences and self-made masks. Who I will be, or have become, in the hour of my death is the person *God* ultimately knows me to be. *That* is the person I take into eternity. All will be revealed; all will be made known for all to see. This is the spiritual formation of who I am becoming through every decision I make every day, for better or for worse, for good or for bad, for God, for self, or for the devil. To repeat: who are you becoming?

My "first love" and being "the Beloved"

I remarried at the end of 1987 and went through the amazing grace of undeserved love and restoration. Gillian and our two children, Zander and Misha-Joy, have been the best thing that has happened to me, besides God's personal gift of himself in Jesus Christ – my salvation. Life and ministry became pure joy!

However, as things go, I was so busy in Johweto that by 1993, I found myself in a place of spiritual dryness, going through the motions of ministry. I came to our national pastors' conference in October of that year feeling disconnected. From the opening night, God mercifully came to me and began to deal with me. He spoke to me from Rev 2:1-7. I had persevered and done well in so many ways, but God had one thing against me: I had forsaken my "first love". "Remember the height from which you have fallen! Repent and do the things you did at first." I wept and wept, asking my colleagues to lay hands on me and pray for me. In meeting after meeting, streams of living water poured into my soul, refreshing my love for Jesus. I left the conference with a soft heart and moist eyes, with a spiritual renewal of love.

My colleague and I decided to drive home after the last evening meeting so we could be with our families early the next morning. We did not make it. He fell asleep at the steering wheel. The car left the road at high speed and hit a concrete culvert. It cartwheeled back over front, bouncing in a farmer's field. When I came around, I found myself lying on my back, looking up at the stars, with the car covering the lower half of my body. I felt a most intense pain in the core of my being. My right hip was shattered. My left leg was broken in two places. I had some broken ribs and lacerations over parts of my body. Instantly the verse came to me: "I will not die but live, and will proclaim what the LORD has done" (Ps 118:17). I knew God had put limits on the accident. Then I realized that during the accident, I smelt something awful. I knew it was death. Death came to me but was not allowed to take me – so I believed – as David said: "The LORD... has not given me over to death" (Ps 118:18).

I was in hospital for six weeks in traction, then six weeks at home in bed recovery before I could get up and begin to walk again. The period in hospital and at home was simply amazing in terms of my tangible experience of God's personal love and presence. At that time, I was given Henri Nouwen's book, *Life of the Beloved: Spiritual Living in a Secular World*. What a profound piece of spiritual writing!

Through that little book, I came to understand that the "first love" God was calling me back to, was *his* love for me. I love him *only* because he *first* loved me (1 Jn 4:19). His love makes my love possible. His love has always been there, waiting for me, pursuing me, enabling my returned love for him. God's love for me is his love for his Son, "The Beloved", as recorded in Mk 1:11. When Jesus was baptized in water, the Father baptized him in his Spirit, saying: "You are my Son, the Beloved; with you I am well pleased" (NRSV). Here is the Trinity of the loving Father, the be-loved Son, and the outpoured Spirit of love. Augustine of Hippo (354–430 AD) describes this as The Lover, The Beloved, and The Love, in his treatise *De Trinitate*, (see the Bibliography; see also footnote 26).

Before Jesus began his ministry, the Father affirmed him in his identity as fully and completely loved. *Therefore* Jesus could love. He did his ministry and gave his life, even to the point of death, for us, *because he knew the Father loved him*. The same is true of Jesus' followers, as we are "accepted in *the* Beloved" (Eph 1:6 KJV). We are eternally and uniquely loved in Jesus. We need to hear God's voice again and again at the centre of our being: "You are my beloved son/daughter, in whom I delight, upon whom my favour rests, in whom I am well pleased." We need to hear it above all the other voices that shout from within and without: "You're not good enough, not successful enough… you've failed… you're rejected." We are *not* the identity of the three I am's: I am what I do; I am what I have; I am what others think of me. No! I am what God does for me, has for me, and thinks about me in Christ!

This was the theme of my meditation during my entire recovery from the near-death experience. I was at home in the tender embrace of the Father, the essence and centre of all reality. Even before the world began, he knew me, planned me, loved me – not in a generalized way, but in profound personalized love. "God loves each one of us as if there was only one of us to love," Augustine said.[20] He saw my unique face, knew my name, delighted in my coming existence. "Love" (*agape*) leads to "beloved" (*agapetos*): the one truly or specially loved. *Agapetos* is an intense, warm, personal, emotional term of endearment. This reality is not easy to personalize – to be loved, to receive love. We crave love, yet resist and reject it. We feel unworthy, often due to the past pain of conditional love, or outright rejection. I realized that I had to *learn* how to receive love, how to allow myself to be loved. Nouwen says, "*Becoming the Beloved means letting the truth of our Belovedness become enfleshed in everything we think, say or do*. It entails a long and painful process of appropriation or, better, incarnation" (his italics).[21]

So, I decided that my new identity is being God's beloved child, in "greatly lavished love" (1 Jn 3:1–2). Many times a day I proclaimed; "Your banner over me is LOVE" (S of Sol 2:4b). My life journey is to live into that reality, actively receiving God's love. Over the years, I have learnt to do this as follows:

- First, I choose to *accept* and *believe*, by constant mental and verbal affirmation, the fact of God's unconditional love as my reason for existence, the reality of love as my personal identity.[22]

- Second, I *actively trust* his personalized love for me in every moment. No matter what happens I choose to trust he loves me. I try to treat each moment as a gift of love, a means of grace, consciously developing the habit of *recognizing and receiving* his love in the sacrament of the present moment.

---

20 In William Barclay, *And He Had Compassion*, 51.
21 *Life of the Beloved*, 39.
22 Thomas Merton says in *New Seeds of Contemplation*: "To say that I am made in the image of God is to say that love is the reason for my existence, for God is love. Love is my true identity… Love is my true character. Love is my name", 60. "The commandment to love… (has) a prior commandment to believe. The root of Christian love is not the will to love, but *the faith that one is loved by God*", 74–75 (his italics).

- Third, I *surrender* to that love, which has always been there for me and is all around me. Like a person learning to swim, I have had to learn to lean back in trust and effortlessly surrender to the water of God's love surrounding me, his everlasting arms embracing and floating me in every situation.[23]

- And fourth, this growing reality – the *actual experience* of God's love – is so meaningful that it motivates love, spontaneously overflowing with love to all others. God's love both *calls forth* and *enables* my returned love to him in joy-full obedience, to do his will on earth as it is in heaven.

Nouwen's book taught me that God is totally taken with me! He celebrates me. He not only loves me, he actually *likes* me! When I preach on this I explain – with my wife rolling her eyes in despair – that God even laughs at my corny jokes! God *enjoys* my company! Being God's *Agapetos* is my identity and meaning in life. *That* is who I am, no matter how I feel or what people say, because God says so and I know so! *That* is my being and becoming by God's grace. This growing knowledge of God's love for us enables us to increasingly love him – and others – in return, and it incrementally produces natural and easy obedience to him in all things.

The accident, with my life-threatening injuries and the protracted recovery, was a symbol of a parallel inner journey – from deeper levels of rejection and brokenness to the healing and wholeness that *only* God's love can give. The test of its authenticity will be the fruit of love and the joy of obedience. Therefore, it's *not* about me and *my* spirituality, but about God and others; about his love and our obedience to "everything I have commanded you" (Matt 28:18–20).

The Trinitarian dance of love – *perichoresis* and *philokalia*

The development in my spiritual life of God's centring love led to an intentional exploration of God as Trinity. I wanted to learn to live *into*

---

[23] David Benner, *Surrender to Love*, 56–62. Gerald O'Mahony, *Finding the Still Point*, 22.

the life and love of God as Father, Son and Spirit – to participate in those relationships. Early in 1994, I came across two Jesuit Catholic theologians, William Barry and George Maloney, through whom I "rediscovered" the Trinity. We are called, in Christ, to enter and share in the fullness of the Trinity. The Trinity is the central shining mystery of our Christian faith, and all other revealed mysteries derive from it.

William Barry introduced me to the term *perichoresis* – the word used by the Eastern Greek church fathers from the 5th and 6th cent., to describe God as an Eternal Community.[24] They start with the distinction of Persons and move to the unity of the divine nature. Western theology works the other way around. In a "perichoretic view", God is a *Communion of Persons* in such sublime relational love that they are one nature, One Being-in-Love. *Perichoresis* was the technical term used to describe the "interpenetration" or intra-relationships in the Trinitarian God. It derived from *choreo*, used to express how each Person of the Trinity "penetrates", "fills", "is contained in", or "indwells" the other. This did *not* mean being assimilated into the other with loss of personal distinction. Rather, *choreo* meant the mystery of mutual interpenetration that reveals each in the fullness of their unique personhood.

Perichoresis is the exquisite relationships of Father, Son and Spirit: their *co-indwelling or co-inherence* with each other in perfect love and unity – without loss or confusion of persons. By their relationships of love each distinctive personhood is revealed and known. In this sense, relationship/community defines persons/personhood and not the other way around. We only know God as Father *in relation to the Son* as he eternally pours himself into the Son in total selfless love by the Spirit. We know God as Son *in relation to the Father* as he eternally gives himself

---

24 In *Spiritual Direction and the Encounter with God*, 79–80. Paul Fiddes' research and discussion with regard to the origin and meaning of perichoresis is definitive, in *Participating in God*, 71–89. George Maloney is truly a Trinitarian theologian and Christian mystic (in the best sense), whose books are essentially an exposition of The Perichoresis. A good place to start is *God's Community of Love* and then *Abiding in the Indwelling Trinity*.

Part One: Introduction

to the Father in returned love by the Spirit. We know God as Spirit *in relation to the Father and the Son* in her[25] eternal self-giving as mutual outpoured indwelling love in the Father and the Son. Therefore, we know the Persons by their relationships – they *are* their relationships and more than the sum thereof.

Furthermore, the love between the Father and the Son, by the Spirit of Love, is not a closed completion of the Trinity. It is rather an ecstatic love that explodes outwards beyond "The Self" to create "the other" in love, for love, through love – and that "other" is creation. And to fill and enfold creation by the Spirit – God's outgoing missional love – into the very life of "the One Love of the Three Persons (that) is an infinitely rich giving of Itself, which never ends and is never taken, but is always perfectly given, only received in order to be perfectly shared."[26]

This beautiful mystery grows with the word *perichoresis* being later associated with the dance of God. A development in the Middle Ages joined the word *choreo* (interpenetration) to the word *choreia* (dance), which then led to *perichoresis* being used as a metaphor for "the dancing (*choresis*) around (*peri*) of God". This is how the Trinity became spoken of as an Eternal Dance of Love. The relational circle of the Father, Son and Spirit is an exquisite reciprocal dance of pure interpenetrating love

---

25 The Hebrew for Spirit (*Ruach*) is a feminine noun, while the Gr. *pneuma* is neuter.
26 Merton, *New Seeds of Contemplation*, 68–69. Augustine's idea of the Holy Spirit as the love of the Father and the Son is debated in Western and Eastern theology – see Coffey, *The Holy Spirit as the Mutual Love of Father and Son*. This theory *does not depersonalize the Spirit* into a (impersonal) force or thing, just as John's "God is love" (1 Jn 4:8) does not depersonalize God into a primary attribute called love. And to say that God's Spirit fills creation in love to enfold it into the Trinity is not pan*theism (God is everything, everything is God; a *monist* worldview, where all is one and one is all, see Appendix 1), nor panen*theism (God is *in* all, all is *in* God; popular in postmodern theology, see Cooper, *Panentheism*), but is pan*meta*theism (God is *with* – in and through – created things as self-revelation, while simultaneously beyond and distinct from creation, the correct Hebraic view of God and creation; see Ponsonby, *God Inside Out*, 85–100). The Eastern Orthodox equivalent of the latter is "the uncreated energies of God's love" (discussed in chapter 9), see Losky, *The Mystical Theology of the Eastern Church*, 67–90, and Maloney, *Inscape*, 26–48.

and joy. So much so that they are One: we lose sight of *the dancers* for the sheer beauty of *the dance,* as Yeats says in his poem "Among School Children":

> *O body swayed to music, O brightening glance*
> *How can we know the dancer from the dance?*[27]

The dance draws in all who respond to God's personalized – yet global, even cosmic – invitation: "Shall we dance?" Those "in Christ" are caught up into The Trinitarian Dance of Love by the Spirit through the Son. We enter the mystery of shared life and love with the Father and the Son by the Spirit. By the quality and mutuality of our relationship with God (the dance), we come to know the Father and the Son by the Spirit (the dancers). Though the Trinitarian dance is intensely personal, it's never private and exclusive. It's *God's* dance: his Trinitarian nature means that we dance with God in community *with each other as human persons in God.* This is not optional! As dancers in the dance, we too become fully known, seeing and knowing one another and ourselves for who we truly are in the Trinity.

The closest earthly reality analogous to this beautiful *perichoresis* is marriage between a man and a woman, as per God's creation design. When marriage works as God intended, the relational intimacy can be the closest experience of heaven this side of heaven. The two become one in a most intimate ecstasy of dancing love – a profound mystery of becoming a being-in-love. This powerful marriage potential is only a faint reflection of the full reality to which it points, our dance with the Trinity, in which we participate as God's ever-expanding embrace of ecstatic love in society, to all creation, for the renewal of all things.

Thus, my point is that from the early 1990s, I experienced a deepening spiritual formation via my growing experience of God as Trinity; and this opened the treasure of Orthodox spirituality through *The Philokalia* –

---
27 Cited by Barry in *Spiritual Direction and the Encounter of God,* 80.

the spiritual writings of the Eastern Orthodox – introduced to me by George Maloney.[28] Most of the writings are by monks, whom Maloney calls "God's athletes" in spiritual training for fitness in eternal life with God here and now, and in the age to come. *The Philokalia* is a remarkable vision of the beauty of God in his shared life, love and truth, with an incisive understanding of human nature. The writers knew how to dance with God and defeat evil – with aberrant excesses in some cases!

We are indeed experiencing a renewal of a theology of beauty in the "new Trinitarianism" of the *perichoresis,* and more tangibly in the (research of the) historical Jesus and his vision and mission of God's kingdom. The sheer beauty of God, in Jesus, by his Spirit, causes (draws) us to fall in love with him ever more deeply. All else flows from that. It is *this mystery* that has fueled my passion and fired up my spiritual journey since the 1990s.

To conclude, Greek Orthodox Bishop Kallistos Ware says: "The final end of the spiritual Way is that we humans should also become part of this Trinitarian co-inherence or *perichoresis,* being wholly taken up into the circle of love that exists within God."[29] Personally, I have decided to "make the rest of my life an experiment" (in Frank Laubach's words)[30] to experience this final end of the spiritual way, day by day. I have chosen, and constantly have to re-choose and re-arrange my life, to do the "only one thing" that is of ultimate necessity in life.

---

28 In *Pilgrimage of the Heart: A Treasury of Eastern Christian Spirituality. The Philokalia* (meaning "love of beauty/good") contains texts from the 4th to the 19th cent., originally in Greek, then translated into Serbian and Russian. Five volumes have been translated into English by Palmer, Sherrard and Ware (see the Bibliography). See also Orthodox theologian David B. Hart, *The Beauty of the Infinite,* 15–28. God is true beauty as self-revealing mystery. Good and truth find their supreme revelation in beauty. Good becomes a burden and truth becomes empty labour *without (God's) beauty.*
29 *The Orthodox Way,* 28
30 "Can I bring God back into my mind-flow every few seconds so that God shall always be in my mind as an after image, shall always be one of the elements in every concept and precept? I choose to make the rest of my life an experiment in answering this question", in Letters by a Modern Mystic, *Man of Prayer,* 26

However, I am equally deeply mindful of the fact that *this is all of little value if it is not tested and lived out, formed and transformed, in local Christian community and daily life in the real world – for the world's sake.* And so my spiritual journey continues...

QUESTIONS FOR REFLECTION AND DISCUSSION

1. Take time to be quiet and ask yourself: What has God said to me through this chapter? Write down a few key things that God has impressed upon you.

2. How can you respond to what God has said? Do you need to do anything specific about it, in order to action it?

3. If you were asked to summarize your own spiritual journey with God in two or three sentences, what would be your summary?

4. Reflect on *how* I have shared my story. What can you learn from it? (What has helped you? What aspects do you question... are you uncomfortable with?)

5. Plan to put enough time aside in order to reflect on your spiritual journey. You have a story to tell of your relationship with God over the years. Invite God to guide you, and then think of when it began, trace its development by recording the key turning points – both some highlights and lowlights! See God's hand in it all. (I recommend you write your story, it's a very helpful discipline.)

6. Plan to share your personal stories in your small group, and then take time to pray for each person after they have shared.

CHAPTER 2

DEFINITIONS: UNDERSTANDING SPIRITUALITY

*God's plan of saving the world by the crucified (and resurrected) Messiah Jesus is weak and stupid to those who do not have God's Spirit. As followers of Jesus we have not received the spirit of this age, but the Spirit of God, who reveals God's thoughts and plans to us. The **natural person** – who does not have God's Spirit – cannot make sense of these truths because they are spiritual realities made clear only by God's Spirit. The **spiritual person** – who has God's Spirit – knows these realities because God's Spirit makes clear to us what Jesus thought and did (although the world judges us, thinking us crazy, as it did with him!). But I could not talk to you as spiritual persons because of all the unspiritual things you are doing to each other, with your fighting and factions. So I taught you as **carnal persons** – dominated by your corrupted appetites and selfish desires – as infants who need breast-feeding in Messiah's salvation, incapable of the solid stuff that matures spiritual persons.*
Paul – 1 Cor 2:12–16, 3:1–3 (a summary RAP)

Once, while waiting in an airport departure lounge, I sat next to a young Israeli woman. We had a brief conversation. She was born and raised on a Kibbutz in northern Israel. I asked if she was Conservative, Reformed, or Liberal, with regard to Judaism. I could see by her jeans she was definitely not Orthodox or Hasidic. Her reply was classic: "No, I'm not religious, but I *am* spiritual."

I asked her to explain. She said, "I don't belong to a synagogue, so I'm considered a 'secular Jew'. We're by far the majority in Israel. But many of us are spiritual because we treat all people as equals, including Palestinians. I practise my spirituality with times of quiet when I talk to God in my thoughts and write in my journal. I also care for mother earth – I try to live simply and sustainably."

This represents the growing sentiment with regard to spirituality, certainly in the Western world. What is meant by "spirituality" is the subject of this chapter. In general terms, it mostly means self-fulfilment and happiness in the name of "love" – whatever that is made to mean. Thus "spirituality" is personal and private, not to be questioned. It supposedly transcends religious affiliation, which is seen as outdated, narrow and divisive – spirituality is "post-religious", "post-Christian". Positively, it's often characterized by a sense of responsibility for society and the earth.

However, these are only certain elements of postmodern "spirituality". The word has come to mean so many different things to different people, drowning in a sea of subjective interpretations and experiences. Anything goes! Since there are so many "spiritualities" and expressions of "being spiritual", I will drop the inverted commas as I list ten distinct meanings of spirituality in use today, as I see it.

Ten postmodern meanings and trends in spirituality

By *postmodern* I mean the present era. Broadly speaking (Western) history has moved from the ancient world (4000 to 450 BC) through the classical period (to 600 AD), to the pre-modern or "Middle Ages" (to 1300 AD), then the modern (to the 1900s) into the postmodern era. These eras overlap; the dates are mere markers of the shifts. Since the mid-1900s, we have lived through revolutionary change in all aspects of life. We have shifted from the modern world with its rational-analytic and material-scientific view of reality, called "modernism", to the beginnings of the postmodern era with a new emerging consciousness, called "postmodernism".[31]

---

31 See Charles Jencks (ed.), *The Post-Modern Reader*. Every era is marked by an "ism":

A significant feature of postmodernism is the explosion in spirituality: the search for meaning and purpose beyond the modernist worldview. It is an attempt to recover spirit and soul – *the sacred* – in a secular technological world. We see this explosive interest all around us, especially in bookstores and the Internet. There are literally thousands of books on spirituality. I typed "spirituality" in Google search and it produced "about 647 million results in 0.49 seconds", spirituality of every kind the mind can imagine – no exaggeration. This reflects the lost state of humanity without a centre or compass, desperate to find ultimate meaning and true salvation.

Hence, from a Christian viewpoint, it's probably the greatest opportunity in history for evangelism. And for that matter, for any belief system that competes for the souls of humanity. The latest offer is the new spirituality of postmodernity: stop competing, join "the conversation" and enter the emerging "universal consciousness of love". It proves to be an undiscerning acceptance of "all things good". What this means is not clear; it covers a multitude of meanings – sins included – depending on what interpretation or experience you give it. We are facing a massive tsunami of ideas and beliefs, rituals and practices, calling for careful discernment based on authoritative criteria of truth. But *critical discernment* has become problematic, because truth has been so deconstructed that it means whatever *the individual* wants it to mean. The individual is the new (subjective) authority, alongside *science* ("research"), which remains society's "objective authority" via its "scientific proofs" of what is true or not true – which happens to change every now and then!

I list ten general trends – meanings and definitions – in this explosion of spirituality. I do not discuss and explain them; they are more for awareness as a contrast to the biblical understanding of spirituality that follows.

---

a worldview consciousness or dominant ideology that leads to a clash of worldviews, ideas and beliefs, on many fronts, not least with the biblical Christian worldview. At its deepest level, it is spirit wars.

Religious spiritualities: People generally accept that traditional religions produce particular spiritualities in their adherents, the fruit or character of their beliefs seen in their ethos, values, morality and practices. We can even talk about sub-spiritualities formed by particular emphases and practices within various religions. For example, in chapter 3, I discuss four spiritualities (spiritual traditions) in Christianity.

Eastern mysticism: Beyond formal Eastern religions, there are the ancient beliefs, experiences and practices of Eastern mysticism – present in our day in various esoteric guises. It's about transcendence of the material and rational into mystical union with (G)god(s). Since the mid-1900s, the West has turned to the East for this kind of spirituality because of its own spiritual-mystical bankruptcy.

New Age spiritualities: Eastern mysticism birthed the New Age movement, an amalgam of all sorts of ideas, beliefs and practices – an eclectic spirituality with a smorgasbord of choice. Take what makes you feel good, whatever works for you, from crystals, to meditation, yoga, clairvoyance, astrology, and even the Bible! Its many expressions are seen in the list that follows. People are New Age without realizing it, not knowing that they take on, and are formed by, aspects of New Age spirituality. This is *the* "new spirituality", claiming a universal *spiritual* consciousness beyond structured beliefs and organized religion. Humanity is supposedly coming of age, entering *the* New Age of Utopia or Aquarius.[32]

Gnostic spiritualities:[33] The New Age has revived classic Gnosticism: the pursuit of "secret" knowledge and esoteric practices for spirituality as in "salvation". We awaken and become one with the divine *in us*. We are, and become, (G)god. Gnosticism is the hidden hand (iron fist?) in the custom-made velvet glove of New Age spirituality. Its goal is the end

---

32 For example, the Mayan calendar predicted *the* New Age of universal peace would be ushered in on 21 December 2012. The new spirituality is said to be the Second Coming of the Cosmic Christ – a post-critical, post-religious, post-war universal spiritual consciousness. Vishal Mangalwadi, *In Search of Self Beyond the New Age*, gives a responsible Christian perspective of New Age spiritualities.
33 Gnostic is from *gnosis*, "knowledge", a belief system claiming we are all of one substance

of the so-called destructive masculine age – the "patriarchal" God of monotheism – by the coming psychic feminine age, which will reinstate the mother goddess of pagan monism.[34] A library of Gnostic texts, many called "gospels", was found in 1945 at Nag Hammadi in Egypt. Elaine Pagels has used them as the representation of *true* Christianity, and Dan Brown has popularized this *mis*representation (fiction) in his best-selling novel, while Michael Green has carefully explained why the Early Church suppressed these Gnostic texts.[35]

Pagan and (oc)cultic spiritualities: New Age Gnosticism is also a return to pagan, cultic, tribal and animist spiritualities – the worship of the mythical gods of Greece, the Germanic tribes, the Celts, not to mention the Americas, Africa and Asia. J.K. Rawlings and her Harry Potter series (over 360 million books sold) has brought about a re-symbolization of the Western psyche in the younger generation, away from the Judeo-Christian worldview, back to the pagan symbolic world of druids, wizards, witches, Wicca, spells, spirit-mediums, and magic.[36] These have been normalized and are even desired for personal experience. From the biblical viewpoint, this is nothing less than the worship of demons, a revival of ancient occult spiritualities.

Care of soul spiritualities: This and the remaining spiritualities are

---

with the divine – see *Appendix 1 for a detailed explanation*. See Meier's discussion of Gnosticism from *The Gospel of Thomas* in *A Marginal Jew*, Vol. I, 125-7. Gnosticism infiltrated the Early Church via Eastern mystery religions, leading to a serious battle for truth. Christianity is currently engaged in the same life and death spiritual battle for truth – it is spirit wars.

34   Monism means "all is one and one is all". It collapses all distinctions into one (divine) reality – a pantheism of God *is* all things. Good and evil, light and shadow are reconciled opposites of the same reality. In pagan monism, the divine is not only *in* but *is* everything, and everything *is* divine. See Peter Jones, *Spirit Wars*, 23–29.
35   Pagels, *The Gnostic Gospels;* Brown, *The Da Vinci Code;* Green, *The Books the Church Suppressed*.
36   Magic and miracle are opposites. Miracle is the Christian category of being servants to God's power revealed in Messiah Jesus by his *Holy* Spirit. Magic is manipulating spiritual power – spirits that do not confess Jesus as Lord – for our own purposes. Thus there is no difference between white (supposedly good) and black (evil) magic. It all falls into the category of *evil* spirit.

closely aligned and interwoven, all promising an antidote to Western materialism, but reveal a growing cultural addiction. Thomas Moore's best-seller, *Care of the Soul* (published in 1992), embodies the spirituality of psycho-emotional wellbeing, personal growth and self-fulfilment. Pop psychologies deal with what is now called "the sacred soul" – how to take care of yourself and live well – as popularized by Oprah Winfrey.[37]

Business and motivational spiritualities: The world of motivational talks on successful living and working privatizes spirituality and religion. Business retreats and training seminars use the latest psycho-spiritual "in-thing", including Feng Shui, aromatherapy, yoga, walking on hot coals. The hyped spirituality of success and prosperity is franchized as a life philosophy. Spirituality has invaded business, and big business has turned spirituality into a billion-dollar commodity.[38]

Care of body spiritualities: These are the healing, wellness, holistic alternative medicines, self-help, twelve-step programs, physical fitness, organic food, and "body technology" (cosmetic surgery, body art, etc.) type spiritualities. Not only has the soul and spirit been made sacred, the human body itself is worshipped. The obsession with the body is a spirituality that goes beyond health, body image and personal wellbeing, to the search for the holy grail of eternal youth – to live forever in a perfect body as defined and perfected by human beings.[39]

Creation spiritualities: The earth is also seen as sacred. Sociopolitical and spiritual groups have formed to save the earth from (human) destruction. Many revere earth as a mystical living organism, the mother of us all: Goddess Gaia. The range of concerns for the earth, from scientific debates on global warming, to sustainable living, to the worship of Gaia earth, is producing various kinds of creation spiritualities. "New science" spirituality is part of this; from the esoteric side of quantum physics to

---

37 For a Christian response, see Gary Collins, *The Soul Search*
38 See Jeremy Carrette and Richard King, *Selling Spirituality*.
39 See an insightful study by sociologist Ivan Varga, The Body: The New Sacred? The Body in Hypermodernity, in *Current Sociology*, 209–235.

the study of the stars and "new cosmology" debates.[40] This includes the emerging spiritualities of belief in UFOs and extra-terrestrials, as well as the pursuit of personal relationship with angels of all kinds. Paul warns against such "worship of angels" in Col 2:18. Public bookstores overflow with new books on these and every other kind of natural and supernatural, esoteric and angelic spiritualities.

Feminist and masculine spiritualities: The feminist movement from the mid-1900s, and the men's movement from the late 1900s, have developed feminine and masculine spiritualties respectively: how to live, think and act in the world in our gender-selves as female or male. But gender has been radically redefined by "self-identifying" as per gender preference and sexual orientation. Distinctions blur in the many new identities on offer: hetero-, bi-, homo-, trans-, metro-, non-, a-sexual (the androgynous ideal). They lead to sexual spiritualities that celebrate self-identifying preferences and their various practices and way of life. Sex is also being "sacralized" into *spiritual* experiences of orgasmic ecstasy – moments of self-transcendence in union with "the divine" – a revival of ancient Kundalini, tantric sex and pagan temple prostitution. This is nothing short of the worship, once again, of pagan gods.

These ten postmodern spiritualities, among others, are a mixed bag of the good, the bad and the ugly. While some have some good we can draw on – for the discerning – others are pure evil. It's not the place to examine how these spiritualities have made deep inroads into the church as "mixed seed", as weeds growing with the wheat in the form of Gnostic thinking, multi-faith universalist "Christians", esoteric-(S)spirit churches, consumer-entertainment church, the health-wealth and success-motivation "gospels"

---

40 Matthew Fox is a key name in creation spirituality, expelled from the Catholic Dominican Order in 1993 for teaching heresy – he's a New Ager. On "new science" spirituality, see *unorthodox* Catholic priest Diarmuid O'Murchu, *Quantum Theology: Spiritual Implications of the New Physics*. In contrast, for a more biblical orthodox approach to science and biblical interpretation, see John Polkinghorne's writings (*Quarks, Chaos and Christianity*).

– to mention a few. However, they point to legitimate human "quests" that Christian spirituality urgently needs to address: the quest for identity, happiness, health, perfection, truth, justice, beauty, stimulation, and mystery.[41]

These spiritualities give us an idea of what "spirituality" has come to mean. They confirm our preliminary definition, broadly accepted in recent studies: *spirituality is the way we relate to what is of ultimate value in our lives and the kind of person and world that it produces – the interior ethos and character of a person, organization, community or culture.*

In this sense, spirituality is a fruit or result of our particular spiritual formation. Or as Downey defines spirituality: "the quest for the sacred in the actualization of the human spirit (personal integration and fulfilment) through self-transcending knowledge, freedom and love, in light of the highest values perceived and pursued."[42] See below my biblical definition and understanding.

Reasons for the explosive search for spirituality

The above list gives some idea of the causes for the current explosive search for spirituality. They all reflect a hunger for spirituality, for ultimate spiritual connection in the recovery of the sacred, caused by disillusionment with modernism in terms of the loss of meaning and life purpose. Not to repeat what I said in my preface and earlier in this chapter, I briefly summarize.

The pre-modern or pre-critical world ("Middle Ages") with its spiritual, almost magical view of the world, gave way to the Renaissance and Enlightenment ("Modernism"), with its material-rational-scientific worldview. It was symbolized in French philosopher René Descartes' (died in 1650): "I think, therefore I am." He doubted everything in order to find certainty, and found it in thought: because we *think*, we *certainly*

---

41 See David Benner, *Psychotherapy and the Spiritual Quest*, 134–148. Also, Peter van Ness (ed.), *Spirituality and the Secular Quest*.
42 Michael Downey, *Understanding Christian Spirituality*, 15.

exist. The *rational* human being was born! This led to a separation ("dualism") between material and spiritual reality. Reason and science were separated from God and spirituality, the "secular" versus the "sacred", among other dualisms. The sacred was consigned to "faith and religion" that cannot be "proved". Liberal theologians applied scientific reasoning to the Bible – the tools of higher criticism and hermeneutics of suspicion – "disproving" the Bible. They concluded: it's a collection of stories and moral myths, not Spirit-inspired scripture.

Our (Western) minds have been fed rationalism, our bodies lavished with materialism, and our souls starved of spiritual mystery. We are mental-technological giants, but psycho-emotional and spiritual dwarfs. Modernism did *not* deliver the promised utopia of progress to freedom and prosperity. On the contrary, it gave us two world wars with atomic bombs and the holocaust. Fifty-two million people were killed in World War II, sacrificed to the god of humanist-modernity. We can now not only destroy humanity but the earth itself. We rape the earth of its natural resources, causing industrial pollution and global warming, with disastrous consequences. Thus disillusionment with Modernity has led to the current craving for *spirituality*.

However, at a historical level, the search for spirituality goes back to *the basic life questions of meaning and purpose* regarding our view of the world. Worldview consists of the most basic assumptions, ideas and beliefs of what is real and good, of who and what can be trusted. Greek philosophers like Socrates (470–399 BC), Plato (427–347 BC) and Aristotle (384–322 BC), among others, asked four basic life questions – in the three standard topics of classic philosophic reflection: *physics* (what is the real nature of things), *logics* (how we know/understand how things really are), and *ethics* (how to live and behave in accordance with that – the good life):

- *What is reality?*
- *How can we know what the good life is?*

- *Who is actually good?*
- *How can we become good?*

All major religions and philosophies address these or related questions.[43] Since Hiroshima and the Holocaust, and current international terrorism, *these* questions have come back at us with great force. We are realizing that reality is more than matter; that the good life is more than material happiness; that few people are truly good; and fewer know how to become good. The human *need* is to know ultimate reality and life's meaning. We generally *want* to be good, to live the good life, to create a good society and save humanity, including planet earth.[44]

The problem is, though we are willing to do good, we are also ready to do evil. The philosophers asked the right questions, but they underestimated human depravity and the radical nature of evil – as we do today. Postmodern spiritualities amount to the worship of the "Divine" self, the "reality" that chases "the good life" of self-serving happiness and freedom – to live like the gods. The *moral knowledge* that gives right answers to these life questions has been delegitimized and rejected as guilt-inducing religion, as dangerous to psychological health, a social construct to serve those in power. Christ-followers are (ought to be) the faithful custodians and humble messengers of *the* moral and spiritual knowledge that can literally save people and the planet: the message and ministry of Messiah Jesus – the kingdom of God.

At the deepest level, the search for spirituality is *the innate human*

---

43 Willard, *Knowing Christ Today*, 37–62, and Wright, *Paul and The Faithfulness of God*, 23, 1371–83. See Wright, *The New Testament and The People of God*, on related worldview questions: Where do we come from (origins)? Why are we here (meaning)? What went wrong (problem of evil)? How is it made right (salvation)? What will become of us (end goal)?

44 The Bible (Jesus and the Judeo-Christian worldview) has both the *spiritual* (of ultimate reality) and *moral* (knowing good and evil) knowledge in answer to these questions, enabling us to choose good and become good persons. Modern rationalism rejects it as unscientific – not "real" knowledge. Hence the crisis in the secular immoral West: we "perish for lack of knowledge" (Hos 4:6).

Part One: Introduction

desire for God. God has "set eternity in the hearts of (people); yet they cannot fathom what God has done from beginning to end" (Eccl 3:11). Hence our search for eternity, for ultimate spiritual reality. For the Greek philosophers, mystery cults, and religions (including Judaism), *the core assumption and goal behind the life questions was attaining godliness – union with God, or the gods.* We instinctively long for spiritual connection, because God created us for himself.[45] God is love – we are made in love, by love, for love – so we yearn for completion in perfect love. Biblically speaking, in contrast to Descartes, human identity is, "I am loved, therefore I am, and I love." As St Augustine famously said: "You have made us for yourself, O Lord, and our hearts are restless until they rest in you." Even atheists experience yearning restlessness, the disease of desire, the longing for love that *ultimately only God can satisfy.* All substitute satisfactions are a delusion, a false intimacy, an idolatry that leads to addiction and slavery. Looking to someone or something other than God to meet our deepest desires and needs is idolatry. We give power to who or what we worship. We become who or what we worship. The point is: we all have this same yearning and burning in the core of our being that fuels our search for spirituality.

Historical origin and meaning of "spirituality"[46]

The English word "spirituality" comes from the French *spiritualite,* which is derived from the Latin, and ultimately the Greek. *Spiritualite* referred to things pertaining to the Christian clergy and the inner life, regarding spiritual attitudes controlling our relations with God and the world. In the late-1600s, it was, however, used in a critical sense of Madame Guyon's (1648–1717) *"La nouvelle spiritualite",* referring to her "novel spirituality"

---

45 The focus of James Houston, *The Heart's Desire,* and Ronald Rolheiser, *Seeking Spirituality.*
46 Alister McGrath (ed.), *The Blackwell Encyclopedia of Modern Christian Thought,* 626–633. Gordon Wakefield (ed.), *A Dictionary of Christian Spirituality,* 361–363. F. Anthonisamy, *An Introduction to Christian Spirituality,* 19–24.

of mystical prayer as super-spiritual experiences unrelated to material and human reality. It passed into English usage with both the positive sense of the theory and practice of Christian living under the guidance of the Holy Spirit, and with the negative connotation of questionable mysticism.

The Latin derivative, *spiritualitas,* meant "the state of being spiritual", taken from the nature of ultimate reality and our relationship to it. Used by Pseudo Jerome in the 5th cent., it referred primarily to the *Christian* relationship to ultimate reality, i.e. God revealed in Jesus Christ by his Holy Spirit. Behind it lay the influence of Greek thinking: *any form* of "being spiritual" (Lat. *spiritualis*) meant relating to unseen spiritual reality, whether God, angels, spirits, demons, dreams, revelations, ideas and beliefs. Thus the idea of (forms of) spiritual*ities* arose, the plural form now in common usage.

Paul's (biblical) letters began to be translated from Greek to Latin in the late 3rd cent., using *spiritualis* ("spiritual") for a key word Paul used, *pneumatikos* ("spiritual", explained below). It came from the Lat. *spirare* – "to breathe", to have spirit in the sense of life. It's similar to the Greek root, *pneuma* – "breath" or "spirit". In that sense, the essence of "spiritual" and "spirituality" is *life,* in both the Latin and the Greek. It is *spiritual* life because we have spirit, and yet it is *physical* life because we have breath. That is to say, humans are *spirit-body-living-beings.* We breathe and live because we have/are spirit, yet when our breath/spirit leaves us, we die (physically). However, we continue to live because spirit is immortal.[47]

To summarize:

- The English spiritual/spirituality can be traced to Paul (more below), meaning our relationship with God *by his Holy Spirit* as

---

47 The Bible recognizes the reality of immortality, i.e. life beyond death. However, the Greek idea of an *immortal* soul/spirit is different to the Hebrew idea of an *eternal* being/spirit. *Only* God is eternal and infinite: not created, always was, ever will be. All other spirit/angelic and human beings were *created,* are finite, having no existence before their creation. However, they *are* spirit/soul, and thus immortal, continuing forever. God gives *eternal life* to those who trust him, which is a *qualitatively different order of life in immortality.* That is: resurrected *embodied* eternal life for human beings.

revealed in Messiah Jesus.

- It assumes the nature of ultimate reality as spiritual or (S)spirit (see Jn 4:24), which is unseen transcendent (beyond), but also immanent (in creation).

- It assumes human nature as spiritual: we are embodied spirits, or en-spirited bodily beings; both mortal (body/matter) and immortal (spirit/soul).

- Spiritual/spirituality is about our experience of God and life in *all* its dimensions, both in this life and in the life to come.

- Our spiritual nature or non-material "part" is our main means of personal (spiritual) formation and, in turn, of societal formation.

These points summarize the core assumptions underlying this chapter, and the book. The key is that humans have a personal non-material spirit. That is the primary power that forms our will, thoughts, attitudes, actions and relationships, and thus forms society in our socio-economic-political structures, which profoundly affects the earth. And all these dimensions of reality in turn affect our spirit: *our experience of God, and/or other spirit, and our consequent spiritual formation.*[48] Therefore, we *all* have a spirituality, a spiritual formation in our consciousness and character, thoughts and behaviour, one way or another, for better or for worse, depending on who or what has formed our human spirit, to whom or what we have given ourselves. What we ultimately value and give ourselves to (i.e. worship), over time forms us into its own image and likeness. We have all been spiritually formed into the person we presently are, and are becoming, whether we know it or not, like it or not.

---

48 For a philosophic reflection and theology of our experience of God, see Dupré, *Relgious Mystery*, and Kelsey, *Encounter with God*. Human nature is a dynamic interrelated unity: one dimension or element affects the whole of who we are, and *vice versa* (the Hebraic view). We are not dualistic beings with an immortal spirit/soul that lives in an inferior body, awaiting escape into ultimate spiritual fulfilment (the Platonic-Greek view). My discussion in *Doing Healing* on both *biblical* worldview (chapter 2) and human personhood (chapter 3) is foundational here.

However, we *can* change and be spiritually *re*formed, with God's help! *In a distinctive Christian sense,* spiritual formation is "the Spirit-driven process of forming the inner world of the human self in such a way that it becomes like the inner being of Christ himself."[49] Jesus' spiritual formation embodied God's consciousness and character of pure goodness and love, with global consequences. In radical contrast, Adolf Hitler embodied a spirituality of evil incarnate, also with global consequences.

A biblical understanding of spirituality – from Paul

The closest word and understanding of spirituality that we have in the NT is *pneumatikos,* used almost exclusively by Paul. What did it mean? Or rather, *what particular meaning did he give to it?* He was a Jew, well educated not only in the Hebraic worldview – the OT – but also in Greek philosophic thinking. Paul's genius was to re-interpret the Jewish scriptures in light of the Messiah, Jesus of Nazareth. And to translate *that* Hebrew Messianic faith into Greek thought and language in order to reach the Mediterranean world with "the gospel", *the Messianic good news.*

From the 4th cent. BC, Greek philosophers understood *pneuma* as more than human breath. It was the innate power – spirit or spiritual substance – that enabled a person to relate to spiritual reality beyond our observation and control. *Pneuma* gave life and formation to the person as soul (*psyche*) and body (*soma*). This is where the idea of *spiritual* formation arose, spirit (*pneuma*) forming the whole person, who we become. From *pneuma* they derived the adjective *pneumatikos,* to describe things "of" or "pertaining to" spirit (from the suffix *-ikos;* hence "spirit-ual" or "of the spirit"). *Pneumatikos* conveys "the sense of belonging to the realm of spirit/Spirit, of the essence or nature of spirit/Spirit, embodying or manifesting spirit/Spirit".[50]

---

49 Willard, *Renovation of the Heart,* 22.
50 J. Dunn, *Spirit,* in Brown (ed.), *The New International Dictionary of New Testament Theology,* Vol. 3, 689–707. Paul used *pneumatikos* to mean "of God's Spirit", his adjective to describe *spiritual* persons, *spiritual* life… law, understandings, discernment, gifts,

Paul used *pneumatikos* for *God's* Spirit almost in exclusion of other spirit(s). In so doing, he did not deny the Greek idea of spiritual reality, but defined it in light of the Messianic fulfilment of his Jewish faith – what it meant to be spiritual as per God's revelation through Messiah Jesus by his Spirit.

Being spiritual – particularly as a means of salvation – was a big issue in Paul's day. Polytheist Greeks looked for "it" (salvation/spirituality) in wisdom (*sophia*) and knowledge (*gnosis*) from the philosophers, and/ or from the gods and mystery cults. Monotheist Jews looked to the one Creator-God (*YHWH*) coming in power to save them at the end of the age, when his Messiah-King reigns *by his Spirit* poured out on "all flesh" (Ezek 36:27; Joel 2:28).[51] Paul's good news was that the end had come; God's new age of salvation had begun in this present evil age, through Jesus of Nazareth, the crucified and resurrected Messiah.[52] Jesus imparts *God's* Spirit to all who follow him, thus making them spiritual (saved), "of God's Spirit". But for Greeks, this made no sense; it not only lacked wisdom, it was stupid! How can a crucified God save people and make them spiritual? For Jews it was weak: how can a crucified Messiah save us and make us into God's holy people (1 Cor 1:18–25)?

Paul gives a clear answer in 1 Cor 2:12–16, 3:1–3 (read my RAP at the head of this chapter). He identifies two kinds of people, with a "hybrid" third category:

The spiritual person (v.15, *pneumatikos*): Those who trust in Messiah Jesus for *God's* salvation receive *God's* eschatological Spirit. They

---

manifestations, and resurrection bodies (Rom 1:11, 7:14, 8:2; 1 Cor 2:13–15, 3:1, 12:1, 14:1, 37, 15:44–46).

51 Heb. *Meshiach* and Gr. *Christos* both mean "Messiah", literally "Anointed King". Jesus is the Messiah (Christ) because he is *YHWH's* King, anointed *by his Spirit* to rule and reign.

52 Hebrew thinking is future or goal oriented: the end comes in Messiah. *Eschatology* is "the study of the end" or "last things", from *eschaton*. Jesus is God's goal or *eschatos* (Rev 1:17–18, 22:13, "The Last") in creation and history: he is "The End" of this passing age and "The Beginning" of all things made new. When I use *eschatological*, I mean the realization of God's end-time goal *in history* – his future kingdom and Spirit *already* come in Jesus. Adrio König uses *eschaton* as his point of departure in his excellent study of the kingdom, *The Eclipse of Christ in Eschatology*.

experience and know salvation. God's Spirit unites with their human spirit and the two become one (1 Cor 6:17). Thus they know (*gnosis*) God by his Spirit. They are spiritual, *pneumatikos*, "of God's Spirit". As no one knows the thoughts of a person, except that person's spirit or consciousness, so no one knows God's thoughts, except God's Spirit, *who reveals them to those in whom he dwells* (v.10). Thus the *pneumatic* (spiritual) person knows "the mind of Christ" (v.16): they spiritually discern "all things" by what God thinks, says and does. They know and experience this by revelation of the Spirit, *to the extent* they yield governmental control of all their faculties to the indwelling Spirit, in the ongoing process of their spiritual formation to Christlikeness.

The unspiritual or natural person (v.14, *psychikos*, "of the soul"): Those who do not have *God's* Spirit, the *un*spiritual, cannot understand *God's* salvation. Though they claim to have *gnosis* – secret wisdom or special revelation – it is *not* the knowledge of God *because they do not have God's Spirit in them*. Hence, God's thoughts, words and deeds in Messiah Jesus seem foolish to them. The unspiritual are natural or soulish (*psychikos*) persons who think, speak and live by "the spirit of the world" (v.12) – governed by the prevailing ideas, values and norms of this age. As Paul says: "The god of this age has blinded the minds of unbelievers" (2 Cor 4:4). But such unspiritual people do receive God's Spirit by putting their trust in Jesus.

Carnal behaviour (*sarkikos*, "of the flesh", 3:1, 3 NRSV): Paul is not denoting a third type of person *per se;* he's rebuking the *unspiritual* behaviour of *spiritual* people. The Corinthian believers saw themselves as spiritual – saved, having God's Spirit – but were behaving as worldly people dominated by their "flesh" (*sarx*). This referred to their fallen nature and corrupted appetites, evidenced in their quarrels, jealousies and factions (v.3). If they have the eschatological Spirit, they must think and behave by that Spirit, not by another spirit, value system, or corrupted appetites. Paul equates their behaviour to squabbling infants who urgently need to grow up and mature *spiritually* (v.2): to be formed, and transformed, in their inner governing tendencies by God's indwelling Holy Spirit.

In short, *the biblical definition of spirituality, of being spiritual, is to have God's Holy Spirit* through the eschatological salvation received by faith in Messiah Jesus. Then we grow to maturity in that salvation, meaning: (trans)formed by God's Spirit in every governing thought, word and deed toward Christlikeness. The Corinthian Christians viewed spirituality as having supernatural gifts and revelation, knowledge and wisdom, oratory and ecstatic Spirit-experiences, with little reference to changed character and behaviour. Paul says "No! That's *un*spirituality! It's carnality, of the spirit of this age. It's not of God, not of the Spirit of the age to come."

Two qualifications: the big picture and other religions/spiritualities

Paul's *Messianic-Spirit* view of spirituality sounds exclusive. We need to qualify it by a deeper grasp of his assumptions of reality – the biblical story or big picture he works from; and then to qualify it by commenting on other religions and spiritualities.

Paul describes reality as it is. Reality is what we run into when we are wrong. Ultimate reality is God and life in his kingdom: an invitation to live and work with him as perfect love and abundant life. God will not force himself on anyone. We choose to trust God as reality or we trust ourselves and become (G)god, creating our own (false) reality. If we do the latter, we suffer the (eternal) consequences.

So, Paul's big picture is of the one true God who has revealed himself to humanity in *general* through creation and conscience, *specifically* through Israel, and *fully* in his Messiah-King Jesus. All other gods are human creations and/or deceiving spirits. Worship of other gods is idolatry. Ultimate faith in anyone or anything other than God is *unbelief* and *faithlessness* (or unfaithfulness): "belief" or "faith" is used for the worship of *God*, just as Paul uses *spiritual* to describe those *with* God's Spirit and *unspiritual* to describe those *without* God's Spirit.

This eternal Creator-God made all things beautiful, bathed in his love. Humans are made in his image and likeness, in-breathed by his Spirit to share his life and rule over creation. However, we chose to rebel, to make *ourselves* (G)god. We fell from the reign of God's paradise-reality to the tyranny of evil's living-death. This is how sin entered creation, and death through sin – thus death and mortality came upon all, because all have sinned (Rom 3:23, 5:12). Death means *separation* from both God (Is 59:2, *spiritual* death) and the physical body (*physical* death).

Our (fallen) reality is that we are dead in our sins, separated from God. We follow the ways of the world – the (evil) spirit that works in sinners – gratifying the cravings of our sinful nature. In our fallen state, we are objects of God's wrath and judgment. *But* God's love and mercy triumphs over wrath and judgment in that he sent his Son to save us by dying *our* death, taking *our* judgment for sin, reconciling *us* to God. By trusting (faith, belief) Jesus, we are literally made alive in him – given God's gift of eternal life – in Christ's resurrection (Rom 6:23; Eph 2:1–5; 1 Pet 1:3). Salvation is *God's* life in us, "born again" by his Spirit. Jesus said: "Whoever hears my word and trusts God who sent me, *already has eternal life*. They *have been* delivered out of judgment and *have* crossed over from death to life" (Jn 5:24 RAP).

Most people, tragically, do not know or experience this salvation, this ultimate reality. When physical death comes to those who are spiritually dead – the *un*spiritual – they are lost to God by their own choice in the tyranny of evil's living death. Hell is separation from God in *this* life and the life *to come*, an "everlasting death" (2 Thess 1:8–9). When physical death comes to those who are spiritually alive – the spiritual – they enter the fullness of God's eternal life, awaiting its consummation in the resurrection of their bodies when Messiah returns. Heaven is joyous union with God in *this* life and the life *to come*, an abundant everlasting life (Jn 10:10b, 17:3).

Salvation and heaven are *not* escape into God's presence beyond the clouds – a disembodied spiritual bliss! Yes, "born again" or *pneumatikos* people go to be with the Lord when they die. But it's to "rest" in anticipation of their bodily resurrection. Salvation is "reigning in life" with Messiah – now in our mortal bodies, *and* in the age to come in resurrected bodies on a renewed earth (Rom 5:17, 8:19–23). God did not create humanity to leave the earth and "go to heaven". He created us to be his image *on earth*, to rule over his creation. So, God's goal is for heaven to come to earth when we rule and reign with Christ in resurrection bodies over his new creation. *This* is our vision, our destiny. *Anticipating its fulfilment in the way we live now, by the power of God's Spirit, is what biblical (or kingdom) spirituality is all about.*

If this is true, what about people of other faiths, religions and spiritualities?

Paul's view should *not* make Christians presumptuous or arrogant toward atheists and people of other faiths, religions and spiritualities. Any hint of this shows they have not understood Paul and their spirituality is in doubt (as Paul said of the Corinthians). If anything, the above should lead to profound humility, causing us to weep, both in wonder at God's merciful salvation and with deep sorrow and love for those without Messiah and his eschatological Spirit. Paul is our example: "For three years I never stopped warning each of you (in Ephesus) night and day with tears… for the love of Christ compels us" (Acts 20:31; 2 Cor 5:14).

In Rom 2, Paul says God is so much kinder, fairer, wiser, more merciful than we realize (v.4). We do not have to play God; he will do right by each and every person, because he is God and can do no other. Whether we are Jews who have God's *written* truth/law (his special revelation), or Gentiles who have God's truth/law in *our conscience and creation* (his general revelation), God sees every heart and knows those who are acceptable to him: "To those who by persistence in doing good seek glory, honor and immortality, he will give eternal life. But for those who are self-seeking and *who reject the truth* and follow evil, there will be wrath and anger" (vv. 7–8). Similarly, when Peter came to Cornelius' house (a Gentile), he said: "I now realize how true it is that God does not show favouritism, but accepts people from every nation who fear him and do what is right" (Acts 10:34–35).

And yet Paul's overall point in Romans 1 to 3 is clear: *all* have sinned, both Jew and Gentile, and therefore *all* need, and can only attain God's salvation *by faith in Messiah Jesus*, and thus receive his Spirit. How God makes these decisions of who is acceptable – revealing his Son and giving his Spirit to those in this *inclusive* category – is his business.[53] We are not God's counsellors; he is well able to take care of such things (Rom 11:33–36). Let *God* be God, and let *us* act justly, show mercy, and walk humbly with God (Mic 6:8).

This implies having a view of truth and goodness that gives respect and dignity to all, that enters into open dialogue with other faiths and rejects closed-minded Christian fundamentalism. What is good in other traditions *is* good; we can learn from it. We do not have to fear truth, no matter where it comes from. As we have seen, there are many spiritualities and expressions of spiritual formation leading to different kinds of people and communities – not all bad, not all good. Spiritual discernment identifies and affirms what is good, respects what is benign, lovingly points out what is erroneous, and assertively resists what is deceptive and evil.

Therefore, Christian spirituality is paradoxically inclusive *and* exclusive. It's an illusion to think that only Christian spirituality is exclusive. *All* spiritualities have elements – beliefs and practices – that are exclusive of *all* others; otherwise the particular spirituality would not exist. None admit that anything goes, that all expressions of spiritual living are acceptable – even the most inclusive of them!

---

53 Willard calls this idea of inclusivity "Christian pluralism" in a provocative chapter in *Knowing Christ Today*, 169–190. For a good study on this issue see Alan Race, *Christians and Pluralism*.

The exclusiveness of Christian spirituality lies in the life that it is, that it brings and produces: *God's* life in us by his Holy Spirit (trans)forming us into Christ-likeness. Let it simply be what it is, and let all see and compare. While it is exclusive due to growing conformity to Jesus Christ, it leads to genuine inclusiveness – not the ethically or politically correct kind that is accepted or rejected at will – but that of extravagant grace that genuinely loves and cares for all without discrimination.[54] However, unconditional acceptance of *the person* does not mean undiscerning affirmation and implied endorsement of *beliefs and behaviour* that is contrary to God's will as revealed in Jesus of Nazareth.

Conclusion: spirituality as five implications

Spirit-Formation: *In general terms,* spirituality is the power of what forms us, and through us the world around us, in relation to spiritual reality and ultimate values. Every expression of spirituality is motivated and empowered either by God's Spirit or another spirit, to form us – and the world – in its own image.

Life-Experience: *In Pauline terms,* spirituality is about *God's* Spirit, which is God's eternal *life* breathed into us by the resurrected Christ. So, salvation is *life in the kingdom of God:* living under God's Rule and Reign, learning to rule and reign with him. This is theological truth realized in personal experience. Spirituality is the *experience of God* in daily life; what some have called the "with-God life" – or, more accurately, the "God-with-us life" (Immanuel, Matt 1:20–23).

Discipleship-Character: *In practical terms,* spirituality is following Jesus of Nazareth, learning to live the kingdom life as *he* lived and taught it, so as to become like him in *consciousness and character.* It is being Christ's apprentice, living with him to learn from him – by his Word, Spirit and Community – to become like him. Thus we grow in the character of Christ, the "fruit of the Spirit" in Gal 5:22.

---

54 See Willard, *Spiritual Formation,* 7.

Power-Transformation: *In evidential terms*, spirituality is about God's Spirit that not only forms, but also transforms us, evidenced by God's authority and power operating in us to change the world around us (Acts 1:8 cf. 10:38). Spirituality is being like Jesus not only in character, but also *in power* – to defeat evil in all its forms through moral authority and the natural exercise of supernatural "gifts of the Spirit" (1 Cor 12:7-11), bringing God's kingdom salvation to all living reality.

Union-Mystery: *In ultimate terms*, spirituality is about God's Spirit remaking us in our true, full humanity as God's glorious image-bearers, through self-integration and transcendence *in union with God*. Human integrity and personal wholeness in union with God is the ultimate beauty and mystery of "participating in the divine nature" (2 Pet 1:4). We experience growing oneness with God in real terms, participating in the *perichoretic* dance of love with the Father and Son by the Spirit.

QUESTIONS FOR REFLECTION AND DISCUSSION

1. What meanings or expressions of spirituality in general have you experienced or been exposed to? What have you learnt from it (or them)?

2. Do you agree with the reasons for the explosion in spirituality? Anything to add?

3. What is your definition of *Christian* spirituality? Has this chapter changed your understanding in any way? How?

4. How would you answer the four worldview or life questions from the classic period?

5. Do you agree with Paul's understanding of being spiritual, of spirituality? Do you consider yourself either spiritual, or natural (unspiritual), or carnal – in Paul's terms?

6. What do you think of the qualifying inclusivity as I briefly presented it?

7. Do you consider yourself a spiritual person? How do you pursue spirituality?

CHAPTER 3

OVERVIEW: FOUR CHRISTIAN SPIRITUAL TRADITIONS

Therefore we must learn first of all that we ought always to pray and not to faint. For the effect of prayer is union with God, and if someone is with God, he is separated from the enemy... Through prayer we obtain physical well-being, a happy home, and a strong, well-ordered society... Prayer is intimacy with God and contemplation of the invisible. It satisfies our yearnings and makes us equal to the angels... of all the things valued in life nothing is more precious than prayer.
– Gregory of Nyssa (330–395 AD)[55]

Prayer: native breath of the soul, eschatological breath of heaven

My wife gave birth to our two children at a progressive birth unit. If the husband went to all ten antenatal classes, he could help during the birth – that is, if he did not faint! I went to all the classes and was fortunate not to be affected by the gory stuff. The midwife even allowed me to participate in the final stages of delivery. I also cut my son and daughter's umbilical cords. I will never forget the wonder and amazement as they took their first gasp of fresh air and began to cry. Life!

The immediate natural response to our first breath is to cry out with

---
55 In *The Lord's Prayer,* Ancient Christian Writers, Vol. 18, 24–25.

Part One: Introduction

new life. On receiving God's breath of life, Adam and Eve talked and walked with God in the garden (Gen 2:7f). *Prayer* is our "returned breath" to God, the native breath of the soul. We instinctively cry out to God when in danger! God breathed his Spirit-Life into the first humans in the garden. Jesus, fresh from his resurrection in a new Eden, breathed his Spirit-Life into his followers – born-again new Adams and Eves in God's new eschatological creation (of the coming age, Jn 20:22 cf. 2 Cor 5:17).

We experience this when we become followers of Jesus. We are literally born from above, taking our first breath of heaven (Jn 3:3–8). We breathe in Christ's Spirit fresh from The Resurrection, receiving God's *eternal* life. We become spiritual – in Paul's language – and our instinctive and immediate response is to cry, "*Abba*" (Aramaic for Father, Rom 8:14–16; Gal 4:6). As *physical* life requires constant breathing, *spiritual* life and health is dependent on constant prayer. Paul says: "Pray continually" (1 Thess 5:17). Therefore, prayer is not only the native breath of the soul, it's also the eschatological breath of heaven whereby we live heaven's life on earth, "equal to the angels" as Gregory of Nyssa said! We are God's Amazon rain forest, replenishing the foul air of *this age* with *heavenly oxygen!* Our praying-presence sustains our planet. As "salt and light", we dispel darkness, we stop the spread of corruption, saving humanity from evil (Matt 5:13–16). This is spirituality.

Jesus teaches us how to live this kind of (heavenly prayer) life because *he* lived it – he *was* it – not in a super-spiritual or otherworldly escapist sense, but in concrete engagement with *this* world. Jesus received God's Spirit "without limit" (Jn 3:34), seen in his distinctive spirituality grounded in his relationship with God as *Abba*. His characteristic use and meaning of "(my) *Abba*" in prayer (Mk 14:36) was unique in Judaism. For Jews it was blasphemous, a claim of equality with God. Hence they wanted to kill him (Jn 5:17–18). *Abba* was not the sentimental usage of "Daddy". It indicated a deeper, more intimate relationship with God as "my own dear father".[56] It was *this* experience of God, *this* prayer-life, which the

---

56 J.P. Meier's phrase in *Marginal Jew*, Vol. II, 294. In footnote 20, 358–359, he quotes

disciples witnessed and so strongly desired (see Lk 11:1f). In response, Jesus taught them the same prayer-relationship, "When you pray, say '*Abba...*'" This usage was equally distinctive of Jesus' first followers as seen in Rom 8:14–16 and Gal 4:6. That is why Paul's regular reference to God is "the God and *Father of our Lord Jesus Christ*" (Eph 1:3).

Approaches to an overview of Christian spirituality

Having defined both the contemporary and biblical understandings of spirituality, this chapter focuses on an overview of *Christian* spirituality in its primary forms and expressions. The above introduction on *prayer* – as relationship with *Abba*-God – is my point of departure and paradigm in presenting such an overview. It is also why I quoted Gregory of Nyssa from his teaching on The Lord's Prayer. The church fathers and mothers used the language of "prayer" rather than "spirituality", as we do today. Indeed, the spiritual life without prayer is like the Gospel without Christ. For them *prayer – intimacy with Jesus – was the most precious value in all of life*. It was neither an escapist spirituality into personal esoteric experiences with God, nor an empty ritual of religious performance – rather a robust whole-life engagement with God in the real world (although there were some excesses on both ends of the spectrum). *Arguably, prayer is the essence of our faith in, and experience of, God*. Prayer is our daily inbreathing of our Father's Person and abiding Presence by his Spirit, our primary means of spiritual living with God in this world.

Before I present my (historical) overview of Christian spirituality in forms of prayer, let me alert the reader to other approaches to its study and teaching. The common approach has been to discuss *the historical periods or spiritual eras* of Christian spirituality. Others tell *the stories and*

Jeremias and Fitzmyer's research that "Jesus' use of *abba* in his prayer to God was 'exclusive to himself and otherwise unknown in pre-Christian Palestinian Jewish tradition.'" He knew God as a truly loving interactive Father. Albert Nolan says: "The experience of God as his *abba* was the source of Jesus' wisdom, his clarity, his confidence, and his radical freedom. *Without this it is impossible to understand why and how he did the things he did*" (his italics), in *Jesus Today*, 71.

biographies of key spiritual leaders from various church traditions, orders, movements and denominations stemming from them. Another approach has been to examine *spiritualities defined by culture or nationality, and geography,* as in Asian, African, or Russian spirituality.[57]

Richard Foster's approach helpfully identified and analyzed six movements or "streams of living water" in church history. These traditions are differentiated by the distinctive focus or means of their spiritual formation:[58]

- Contemplative tradition (the prayer-filled life)
- Holiness tradition (the virtuous life)
- Charismatic tradition (the Spirit-empowered life)
- Social Justice tradition (the compassionate life)
- Evangelical tradition (the word-centred life)
- Incarnational tradition (the sacramental life)

I mention Foster's approach for awareness' sake – I cannot dialogue with it here – and to highlight the need for us to drink from *all* the streams of Christian spirituality, especially those we have not been exposed to, in order to mature in Christ.

A timeline of church history

To get the overview, I begin with a timeline of the main developments and expressions of Christian spirituality over the centuries. The Hebrew view of time and eternity is linear: having a beginning (God's creation) and moving to an end or goal (*eschaton*), which is the age to come (God's new creation).

Many see Christian spirituality as beginning with Jesus, then developing through church history in its various forms. It goes back much earlier. Jesus stands in a long line of Jewish spiritual tradition that goes back to the Hebrew prophets, to Moses, and especially to Abraham,

---

[57] A good example that combines these three basic approaches is James Wiseman in his comprehensive historic and global introduction to Christian spirituality, *Spirituality and Mysticism.*

[58] In *Streams of Living Water.*

the father of *YHWH's* chosen nation. Israel was chosen to reconcile humanity (the scattered pagan/Gentile nations) to God, but failed to be "a light for the Gentiles, to bring salvation to the ends of the earth" (Is 49:6 RAP). Jesus, however, succeeded. As Israel's representative, he embodied and fulfilled her spirituality and destiny, doing for Israel what she could not do for herself.

And more so: what God intended for humanity – not only Israel – Jesus fulfils and completes. Where Adam and Eve failed in their spirituality as God's image-bearers, to walk with him and rule over his creation, Jesus succeeded. He embodied humanity as God's quintessential image-bearer, doing for us what we cannot do for ourselves. Therefore, Jesus' spirituality reaches back beyond Israel and Abraham to the garden, restoring to us Eden's pristine possibilities – and more – in God's *new* creation, which we already experience in Messiah.

All this to say that Christian spirituality did not originate in Jesus *per se*. It reaches back to the best of Hebrew, and human, spirituality, *as fulfilled and embodied in Jesus*. So the timeline below gives an overview of the key developments and turning points in Christian spirituality through human history. The line spacing in Figure 1 is merely symbolic of the time periods involved: the roots of Christian spirituality *before Christ* (BC) cover over 4 000 years, and the period *after Christ* (AD) covers 2 000 years. Also, for the sake of perspective: there are currently over 2.2 billion Christians, 32% of the world population, made up of:

- 1.1 billion Roman Catholics
- 233 million Eastern Orthodox
- 380 million Protestants (Reformed/Evangelical denominations)
- 81 million Anglicans (Church of England – technically not Protestant, while some classify them as Protestants)
- 433 million Independents (Pentecostals/Charismatics and other independent groups – by far the fastest growing sector in Christianity)[59]

---

59 See http://www.wholesomewords.org/missions/greatc.html. These mid-2007 statistics are updates from 2001, in Barrett, Kurian & Johnson (eds), *World Christian Encyclopedia*.

Figure 1. Church History Time Line

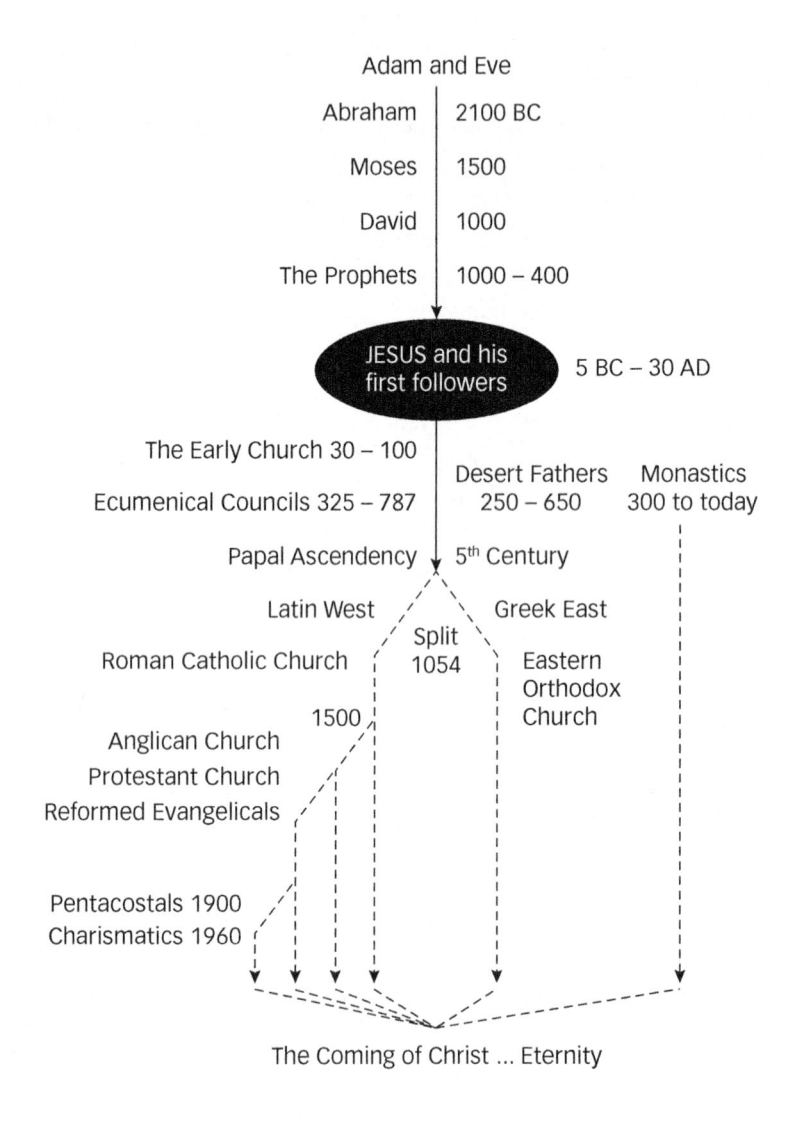

```
                        Adam and Eve
              Abraham  |  2100 BC
                Moses  |  1500
                David  |  1000
          The Prophets |  1000 – 400
                       ▼
              ( JESUS and his       5 BC – 30 AD
                first followers )
                       │
    The Early Church 30 – 100
                              Desert Fathers    Monastics
    Ecumenical Councils 325 – 787   250 – 650   300 to today
         Papal Ascendency  ▼  5ᵗʰ Century
              Latin West  ╱   ╲  Greek East
                         ╱ Split ╲
         Roman Catholic Church  1054   Eastern
                                       Orthodox
                         1500          Church
         Anglican Church
         Protestant Church
         Reformed Evangelicals

    Pentacostals 1900
    Charismatics 1960
                    ▼  ▼  ▼  ▼    ▼         ▼

              The Coming of Christ ... Eternity
```

A different view – four types of prayer

My approach to an overview of Christian spirituality was seeded by James Houston's four kinds of prayer: *verbal, meditative, contemplative and ecstatic*.[60] He discusses them in the context of praying with God's past and present people – "the communion of saints" – because each type of prayer points to a major spiritual tradition in the history of the church.

I have adjusted and added to Houston's basic diagram to create my own (see Figure 2 below), in order to not only illustrate the four prayer traditions, but also how they relate to four foci of formation – four ways of experiencing and knowing God. Diagrams are meant to give the big picture, capturing a field of knowledge with the key inter-relationships in one representation, yet without being reductionist (reducing complexities to simplicities that misrepresent the reality). This is my introduction to the four spiritual traditions – not neatly categorized as my diagram may suggest – some "overflow" into other quadrants.

The goal is balance and growth to maturity in all four dimensions of prayer and the spiritualities they produce – seen in Jesus in his relationship with *Abba*. He is, indeed, the centre, embodying the Father's presence in his *balanced practice* of these prayer dimensions. He woke early in the morning and would *often* withdraw from people, even from crowds who came for healing, to be alone with *Abba* (Mk 1:35, 6:46; Lk 4:42, 5:15–16). Why? Because he loved his Father, utterly depending on him: "Although I am God's son, I do nothing on my own initiative. Only what I see my Father doing, that's what I do. Only what I hear my Father saying, that's what I say" (Jn 5:19–20 RAP). Prayer was his primary means of *being with* his Father – experiencing, knowing, and being governed by God's presence, thoughts, words and deeds. Christian spirituality is centred in our daily experience of God, through which we are progressively conformed into the likeness of his Son (Rom 8:29).

---

60 In *The Transforming Friendship*, 248–274.

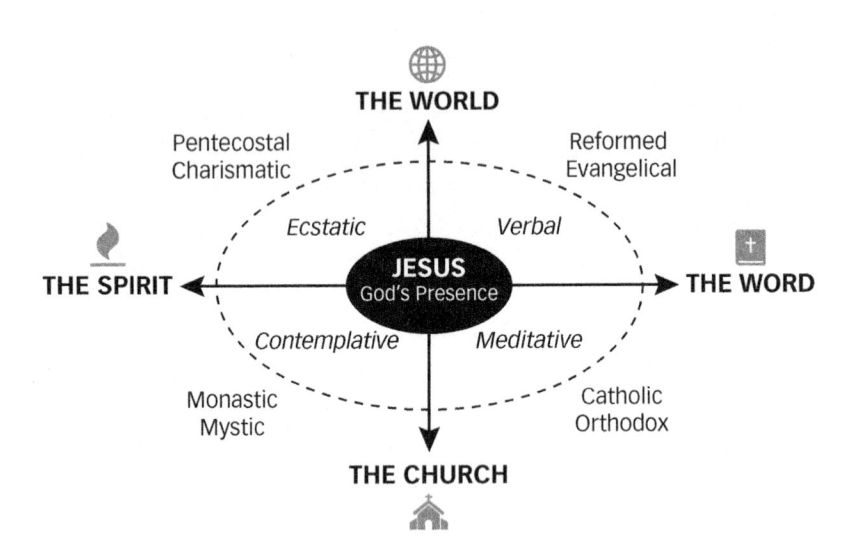

Figure 2. Overview of Christian Spirituality

```
                    THE WORLD
                        ↑
   Pentecostal          |          Reformed
   Charismatic          |          Evangelical
         ⸺ ⸺ ⸺ ⸺|⸺ ⸺ ⸺ ⸺
       ╱    Ecstatic    |   Verbal    ╲
      ╱              JESUS              ╲
THE SPIRIT ◀────── God's Presence ──────▶ THE WORD
      ╲                  |                ╱
       ╲  Contemplative  |  Meditative   ╱
         ⸺ ⸺ ⸺ ⸺|⸺ ⸺ ⸺ ⸺
   Monastic               |          Catholic
   Mystic                 |          Orthodox
                          ↓
                      THE CHURCH
```

Verbal prayer – Reformed/Evangelical spirituality

I begin with verbal prayer. It's the most common and easiest form of prayer, as in "The Lord's Prayer" (Matt 6:9–12; Lk 11:2–4). Jesus practised verbal prayer (see Jn 17; Heb 5:7), which he learnt from the Hebrew Psalter, Israel's book of praise and prayer. And likewise, the Early Church: "Let us continually offer a sacrifice of praise to God, that is, *the fruit of lips* that confess his name" (Heb 13:15). The psalms gave *words* for Israel to speak and sing to God; words that expressed their faith response to God and his *Word* to them, in the face of daily challenges in the real *world*. Jesus prayed the psalms continually. The historical and mainline churches also use the Psalter as their prayer-hymnal.

Although prayer is instinctive to all human beings, we learn to pray like babies learn to talk – from their parents and siblings. When the disciples asked Jesus, "Teach us to pray," he gave them *words* to pray. As we learn to pray, using prayers from scripture and spiritual leaders, we quickly go beyond written prayers to all kinds of *spontaneous* thanksgiving, praise and songs, to verbal confession, petition and intercession, freely and fully expressing ourselves to God. Verbal prayer is dialogue with God, our primary means of working with him in the world.

Protestants – Reformed and Evangelical traditions – epitomize verbal prayer. This spirituality, like the other three below, is bi-polar. In other words, it is bounded by two main means of formation: *The Word* of God (a high view of inspiration and infallibility) and God's heart for *The World* (a high view of evangelism, social justice and world mission). "Verbal spirituality" is not only about *praying* God's Word, it's about *proclaiming* the gospel and *teaching* God's Word. That is why the pulpit is the symbolic centre in most Protestant church sanctuaries, as opposed to the altar in Catholic and Orthodox churches.

But God's Word and World are also the spiritual roots of Evangelical social action: socio-political engagement on behalf of the poor and oppressed (17th to 19th centuries).[61] In this sense, it's a practical, rational and activist spirituality – but suspicious of the mystical and ecstatic. Some Reformed/Evangelicals reacted against liturgical institutionalism with its dead rituals, while others reacted to emerging liberal theology with its low view of scripture, lax personal morality, and worldly social ethics.

This led to reforming, and even revivalist, movements, e.g. the Anabaptists, Puritans, Pietists, Moravians, Wesleyan/Methodists. They emphasized personal salvation, prayer-experience of God, holiness and perfection, community and the centrality of scripture. In so doing, some – not all – turned from social action to a privatized gospel of *spiritual* salvation, *personal* morality, and overly literal interpretation of scripture (the "fundamentalist" label attached to some conservative Evangelicals). Others, however, upheld an integrated spirituality with responsible historical-critical methods of biblical interpretation, a balanced view and practice of sanctification, and a passion for prayer and evangelism, with

---

61 See Richard Lovelace, *Dynamics of Spiritual Life*, 355–400.

a *wholistic* social engagement motivated and grounded in the theology of the kingdom of God.[62]

Meditative prayer – Catholic/Orthodox spirituality

Verbal prayer naturally leads to meditative prayer. *Meditation is encountering God through reflection and response*. It is the conscious exercise of our mind and senses dwelling on scripture (Ps 1:2-3), and on symbols and images of God's presence in the liturgy, sacraments, icons[63] and creation. This leads to the Spirit's revelation and insight in our thoughts and senses – we *experience God speaking to us* and we respond accordingly, interacting with him. Meditative prayer is less verbal and spontaneous; more silent and reflective, guided and responsive.

Jesus was steeped in the practice of meditative prayer, seen in his profound insight into the Hebrew scriptures. In Hebrew, meditation is *memorization of God's Word*. Memorization of a sacred text is constant mental recall and repetition, mulling over its meaning to extract nourishment, to hear and respond to God. Jesus' extensive use of images from nature in his parables points to his encounters with God via meditation on creation as he grew up. In this sense, prayer is "answering God": God *first* speaks and reveals, we listen and respond.[64] Ignatius, founder of the Jesuits, designed his "Spiritual Exercises" to teach meditative prayer, using the five senses to imaginatively relive the text

---

62 Christian involvement in the world is *wholistic* (see next chapter): evangelism, church planting, care of the poor, development, justice advocacy, and ecological care. Christian spirituality is *not* selective; it is concerned with God's *entire* creation. I use *wholistic* to distinguish the biblical worldview of *Shalom* from the New Age usage of *holistic,* which represents radically different assumptions.

63 Many Christians reject the use of icons, believing the Orthodox "worship" them. Icons are symbols of God's shining presence like liturgical and creational symbols. We are the poorer for not exploring the riches they offer. See Henri Nouwen, *Behold the Beauty of the Lord: Praying with Icons,* and respected Reformed theologian, John de Gruchy, *Icons as a Means of Grace.*

64 Prayer is *dialogue,* "listening to God in the silence of our heart", Mother Teresa, *Words to Live By,* 40. For Eugene Peterson, prayer is "answering God", *Answering God,* taken from Hans Urs von Balthazar in his monumental book, *Prayer.*

(Gospel stories) – and liturgical and creation images – though he used the word "contemplation" for what is technically meditation.[65]

Meditative prayer produces a spirituality of incarnation and resurrection: "The Word becomes flesh (*our* very thoughts, emotions, words and deeds) and dwells among us, (we become) full of grace and truth" (Jn 1:14 RAP). *Christ's* incarnation and resurrection are evidenced *in us*. Roman Catholicism has a distinctive emphasis on the Incarnation, as the Eastern Orthodox has on the Resurrection. Catholic, Orthodox and Anglican spiritualities are representative of meditative prayer, characterized by the primary bi-polar formation of *The Word* and *The Church*. They have a high view of both, especially of The Church in its authority, symbols and traditions. In short, meditative prayer is the experience of God via the mind and senses in the word of God, and in the worship liturgy, sacraments, rituals and icons of The Church.

However, Catholic spirituality is diverse, flowing into all four quadrants of the diagram. It can be summarized in what became known as *Lectio Divina* in the Western (Catholic) Church.[66] *Lectio Divina* is Latin for "spiritual reading": praying the text, or reading the scriptures responsively. It is a four-step process widely practised today:

- *Lectio:* slow, thoughtful reading of the scripture;
- *Meditatio:* mental meditation on the text that "speaks" to you;
- *Oratio:* verbal response to God, praying through the meditation; and
- *Contemplatio:* silent contemplative rest and repose in God's presence.

The Eastern Orthodox also flows into the other quadrants, summarized in the "Hesychast" spirituality of The Jesus Prayer (from *hesychia*, meaning

---

65 George Ganss, S.J. *The Spiritual Exercises of Saint Ignatius*. See Kelsey, *The Other Side of Silence*.
66 First detailed as four steps by monk Guido II in the 12th cent. See Basil Pennington, *Lectio Divina*.

"quietness" or "stillness").[67] There is also a progressive process involved in praying The Jesus Prayer: "Lord Jesus Christ, Son of God, have mercy on me, a sinner."

- Prayer of *the lips*: the repeated *verbal* praying, phrase by phrase, in rhythm with our breathing throughout the day, which deepens into
- Prayer of *the mind*: we *meditate* on each phrase, each word, leading to
- Prayer of *the heart*: it goes beyond words and thoughts into our heart and spirit, called *contemplation* or *hesychia,* a sustained state of inner quiet in union with God beyond feelings and images.
- This, in turn, often results in *ecstatic* experiences of God.

Contemplative prayer – Monastic/Mystic spirituality

Technically, meditation and contemplation are two distinct types of prayer in Christian spirituality. Meditation is mental effort, using all our senses and faculties in our experience of God, both to reflect on and respond to God (the *cataphatic* method discussed below). Contemplation goes beyond our *conscious* senses – thoughts, words, feelings, images, sensations – to complete silence, experiencing God in the inner stillness of simple being. It is being united or "centred" in God by *negation* of the senses (the *apophatic* method discussed below) for direct, unmediated Spirit-to-spirit communion with God.[68] This altered state of consciousness facilitates intuitive experience of God's loving presence, a

---

67 See George Maloney, *Prayer of the Heart*, and Archimandrite Lev Gillet, *The Jesus Prayer*.
68 Commonly called Centering Prayer, also Prayer of the Heart, Silent Prayer, Mystical Prayer, Practising the Presence (see Maloney, *Journey into Contemplation,* and Keating, *Open Mind, Open Heart*). It is distinct from New Age, Hindu and Buddhist mysticism and transcendental meditation due to different assumptions, (G)gods, beliefs and practices, though they may share similar techniques.

knowing by unknowing – that is: not knowing by the "normal" means – via our senses – but a knowing by mystical Spirit-encounter beyond all (natural) knowing. With regular practice, meditative prayer can lead to *acquired* contemplation, as in *Lectio Divina*. However, there is also *infused* contemplation, an immediate gift of the Spirit that enlightens us with God's awareness of and in all things.[69]

References to Jesus' repeated withdrawal to quiet places allude to his contemplative practice, a continuation of his "hidden years" before his public life. His contemplative prayer was evidenced in his extraordinary intuitive union with *Abba*-Father – his state of being. It was the source of his life, identity, teachings, healings, and radical socio-political engagement in fulfilment of the Hebrew prophetic-mystic tradition as per Abraham Heschel's study, *The Prophets*. Beside Jesus, church fathers pointed to Abraham, Moses and the prophets as true contemplatives.

The Christian *monastic and mystic* traditions exemplify contemplative prayer. When Emperor Constantine recognized Christianity as the imperial religion in 313, secular political power and worldliness threatened to overrun the church. As a result, some Christians were driven into the desert by the same Spirit that drove Jesus into the desert, not to escape the world, but to face their demons and overcome evil – by becoming one with God in order *to change the worldly church* and the world itself.[70] First *individuals* lived alone in cells, called anchorites or hermits (e.g. St Anthony of the Egyptian desert, 251–356). Some began helping each other in communes – they were called *cenobites*. Then *monasteries* developed, with monks led by Abbots in a common

---

69 See *The Cloud of Unknowing*, by an anonymous mystic of the 14th cent. And Merton: "contemplation is a sudden gift of awareness, an awakening to the Real within all that is real. A vivid awareness of infinite Being at the roots of our own limited being." *New Seeds of Contemplation*, 3.
70 Maloney says: "They did not run away from the world in cowardliness or in self-centered spiritual egoism, but, rather, as conscious co-creators, fighters at the most advanced outposts… they were eschatological prophets, building community, a way of life with God that most closely would resemble the life to come in the *eschaton*", *Pilgrimage of The Heart*, 18.

life focused on *community* contemplation of God. Women also formed convents with nuns and Abbesses. Despite some excesses at times, monasticism has been the guardian of the mystical-contemplative tradition to this day.

Contemplative prayer has had a revival in recent decades. This is because prejudice against mysticism is being overcome in the Western Christian mind – where the perceptions of esoteric spirituality, "deeper life" elitism, legalistic asceticism, and the fear of New Age/Eastern mysticism were entrenched. *Mystery* popularly means that which baffles the mind and is beyond comprehension. In that sense God is (a) Mystery, unknowable in his *essence*. In fact, God is ultimately beyond all categories of being as we know it. We can, however, know God through his self-revelation in creation (general revelation) and his Word – Jesus and his Spirit (special revelation).

The English word comes from the noun *mysterion* (adjective *mystikos,* mystic). It's root *muein* means "to close the mouth", "to keep secret", derived from Gnostic mystery cults, both Greek and Eastern, from 2nd cent. BC. It referred to the *gnosis,* special knowledge, of the initiation rites revealed only to the initiates and the enlightened elite – they closed their mouths and kept it secret (see Appendix 1).

The NT uses *mysterion* in the opposite sense, taken from the Hebrew idea of "that which is hidden, *God reveals*". God's mysteries – thoughts and plans – are revealed to his people through his prophets (Dan 2:28; Amos 3:7–8). God's wisdom or plan of salvation, hidden in times past, is revealed to all nations in Jesus of Nazareth, the unlikely Messiah. *This mystery or secret* of God's love in Jesus' life, death and resurrection, is made known and is freely available *to all who trust in him* (1 Cor 2:7–10; Eph 3:2–11). The church fathers taught Christian mysticism, "mystical theology", as *the initiation into and ongoing experience of union with God in his love through Jesus Christ by the Holy Spirit* – received in the rites of baptism and continuous in the Lord's Supper, in contemplative prayer and other spiritual practices.[71]

Christians are again practising contemplative prayer due to its restful silence, mystical union and transforming grace – *so* greatly needed in our busy, fragmented and stressed lives. Leading 20th cent. Catholic theologian, Karl Rahner, predicted: "The Christian of the future will be a mystic or will not exist at all"[72] – not in the sense of having to be like John of the Cross or Teresa of Ávila, but in being a person *who actually experiences God and lives from that transforming reality*. Contemplative-mystic spirituality has been formed by the foci of *The Church* and *The Spirit*. Christians are returning to these means of contemplation, finding comfort and meaning in the liturgical rituals made alive by the Spirit.[73] We encounter the Spirit of Love in the beautiful mystery of Christ revealed in the sacraments and symbols of God's holy presence, often leading to ecstatic experiences of God.

Ecstatic prayer – Pentecostal/Charismatic spirituality

The church fathers called mystical encounters and spiritual gifts "ecstasies" and "consolations" of the Spirit. Contemplation leads to ecstatic prayer, or power-encounters with God.[74] The goal of the prayer journey is self-transcendence in joyous rapture with God – the *perichoresis* described at the end of chapter 1. As the Westminster Catechism says: "Man's chief end is to glorify God and enjoy him forever." Ecstasy is *the end-time foretaste* of the overwhelming joy of the Spirit in the new age of God's kingdom. It's being "drunk with the Spirit" (Acts 2:15–21; Eph 5:18f). Christian mystics saw such ecstasy in prayer as the climax of giving ourselves to

---

71 See David Regan's excellent study on *Christian* mysticism in *Experience the Mystery*. For a comprehensive study on Christian mystical theology and praxis in historical, global and inter-religious perspective, see William Johnston, *Mystical Theology*.
72 *The Practice of the Faith*, 22. Also Philip Endean, *Karl Rahner: Spiritual Writings*, 24.
73 See Christopher Jamison, *Finding Sanctuary*, on building a life of daily mystic contemplation.
74 Louis Dupré says *contemplation* is a unitive state of being entered into and cultivated, while *ecstasy* is transient experiences within that unitive state, which by no means constitute its essence; in *Religious Mystery and Rational Reflection*, 118–130.

God in mystical love-union with Christ by his Spirit – in anticipation of our eternal nuptials, our marriage to Christ.

Ekstasis means "to stand outside or go beyond oneself", as in giving oneself selflessly to the other. In so doing, one is "caught up in ecstasy" in momentary self-transcendence, altered state of consciousness. This reality applies to encounters with God (Holy Spirit) and gods (other spirits). It is similar to *entheos*, enthusiasm – to be "in (G)god" or "(G)god-possessed" – the excitement and energy that transcends the rational mind in encounter and union with (G)god ("enthusiastic prayer").

Taken from the religious cults, *ekstasis/entheos* meant *experiences of divine power* via temple priests/priestesses through divine oracles, sacred feasts and sex orgies. For the Hebrew prophets, it meant being moved upon by *YHWH's Ruach* (Spirit-breath). God's prophets were those on whom God poured his Spirit, *evidenced in ecstatic manifestations* like prophesying (Num 11:24–29, note Moses' prayer that *all* God's people would receive his Spirit and become prophets).[75]

However, the prophets were *not* evaluated and judged as true prophets by their ecstasies – Spirit-manifestations, shows of power – but by the effect and fruit of their ministry, and by the content and intent of their message (Deut 13:1f). *False* prophets had *the same* ecstasies; as did the mystics of the mystery cults who mediated encounters with the gods (or demons, as Paul says in 1 Cor 10:19–20). The ecstatic gift(s) of *God's* Spirit is not for self-indulgence, to feel or look good, to be powerful, or to make money. They are to fulfil God's salvation purposes in *the world*. Therefore, mystical/ecstatic experiences are not an end in themselves, but consolations from God for service. Though they are personal, they are not private – we account for them. But they are certainly not for public sensation. By its very nature, the supernatural is fascinating and can bewitch us. It can lead to idolatry – people want a quick-fix, a spiritual high.[76] Personal transformation, especially of character, takes much more

---

75 See Heschel's insightful discussion on ecstasy in *The Prophets*, 414–467.
76 The church fathers warned against giving undue attention to mystical-ecstatic

than ecstatic power-encounter – it takes a long obedience in the same direction toward Christlikeness.

Jesus was "The Anointed", filled with the *Ruach ha Kodesh* – Spirit of the Holy One. He had ecstatic experiences of prayer (Lk 10:21) and of power (Lk 4:18f). He came to anoint – baptize – with God's *Holy* Spirit, to fulfil the Hebrew prophets (Joel 2:28f; Mk 1:7-8; Acts 2:1-4, 14-21). Moses' prayer is answered in Messiah: *All* God's people now receive, and can be inundated with his Spirit, as seen at Pentecost. However one interprets the speaking in tongues at Pentecost and through the book of Acts, Paul makes it clear that "praying in the Spirit" is ecstatic prayer. Thus speaking in tongues – our "prayer-language" by the gift of the Spirit – is a large part of ecstatic prayer, because our spirit "utters mysteries" directly to God (1 Cor 14:2-3).

Contemplation leads to ecstasy, but ecstatic prayer is also a *direct* gift of the Spirit. Paul says we can choose to pray or sing "with my mind" – logically or discursively in our known language – *and/or* we can ecstatically pray or sing "with my spirit" in unknown languages by the Spirit (1 Cor 14:13-19). He evidently practised "praying in tongues" regularly and extensively when alone (v.18). Paradoxically, I have found this practice an effective means of "centring" in God, of contemplative spirit-to-Spirit communion beyond thoughts, words and images. The Early Church phrase "pray in the Spirit" referred to tongues *and other forms of Spirit-inspired prayers and experiences* (see Rom 8:26-27; Eph 6:18; Jude 20).

---

experiences and to images that appear in prayer. They taught discernment (*diakrisis*, to distinguish, discriminate) in accountability to respected leaders regarding such spiritual phenomena, due to *the dangers of deception* by spirits (1 Jn 4:1), by our own hearts, motivations, ego needs, brokenness (Jer 17:9-10). John Cassian (360-435) wrote how St Anthony of the desert said the greatest of all virtues was "the grace of discrimination", then gave sober stories of monks who were deceived – some died – by evil in the guise of ecstatic experiences ("angel of light", 2 Cor 11:14), in Palmer et al., *The Philokalia* Vol. One, 94-108. See my chapter on the "how to" of spiritual discernment in *Doing Healing*, 298-312. See Kelsey, *Discernment: A Study in Ecstacy and Evil*.

Pentecostal and Charismatic traditions exemplify "enthusiasm" formed by a focus on *The Spirit* and *The World* – not only enthusiasm for prayer and spiritual experiences, but also participation in God's mission in the world by the Spirit's power. Authentic ecstatic prayer with the Spirit's supernatural gifts produces a spirituality of world-mission, *not* one of withdrawal for personal fulfilment. On this point we must note: church growth research has shown that Pentecostal and Charismatic churches, since their birth in the early 1900s, have dramatically and exponentially outstripped the growth of Catholic and Orthodox, Protestant and Evangelical churches.[77] And we must add: the Spirit's formation is not only about power-gifts; it's about "the fruit of the Spirit" (Gal 5:22), Christ's character formed in us as a witness to the world. The best of Pentecostal/Charismatic spirituality upholds this crucial balance.[78]

Summarizing four ways of experiencing God – and their excesses

The four foci or means of spiritual formation lead to types of prayer and spiritual traditions. They also indicate four primary ways of experiencing and knowing God via our faculties *in the whole of who we are*. Each of the four ways is to be held in tension with each of the others, and not to be seen as clearly delineated experiences separate from one another. They dynamically overlap and interact. If one way or means of knowing God is pursued in isolation, or pushed to an extreme, it results in unhealthy excess – even heresy – seen in the diagram below (Figure 3). Also note that these four spiritualities and ways of knowing God feed into our personal "wiring", i.e. how different human temperaments "naturally take" to one or other spirituality – discussed in chapter 14.

---

[77] See Barrett, Kurian & Johnson, Philip Jenkins (eds), *World Christian Encyclopedia,* and Philip Jenkins, *The Next Christendom.*

[78] George Maloney says: "The truly charismatic Christian, baptized in the Spirit continuously in the circumstances of his daily life, is a mystic who has been transformed into a living incarnation of God's love for mankind." *Invaded by God,* 175.

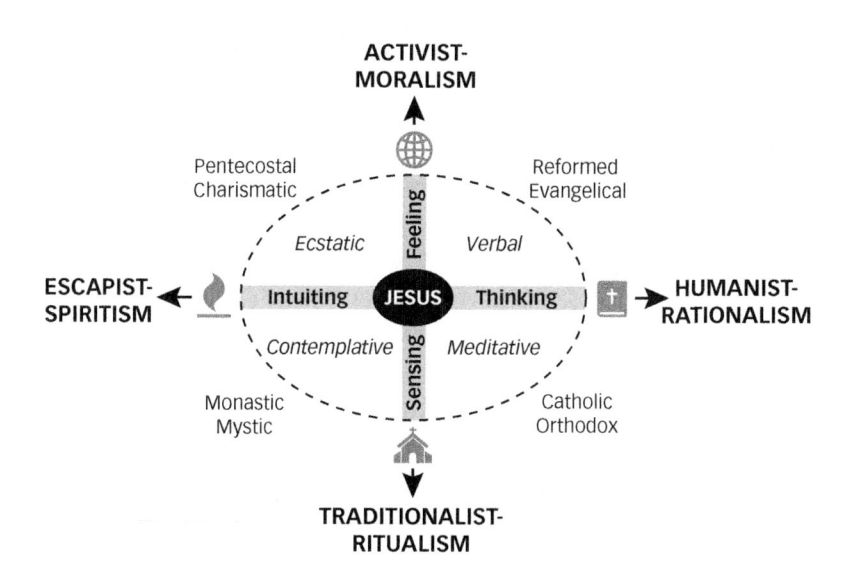

Figure 3. Our Experience of God (and Excess)

```
                    ACTIVIST-
                    MORALISM
                        ▲
   Pentecostal          │          Reformed
   Charismatic  ┌─ ─ ─ ─┼─ ─ ─ ─┐  Evangelical
              ╱       Feeling      ╲
             ╱  Ecstatic    Verbal   ╲
ESCAPIST-  ◄──  Intuiting JESUS Thinking  ──► HUMANIST-
SPIRITISM    ╲  Contemplative Meditative  ╱   RATIONALISM
              ╲      Sensing         ╱
   Monastic   └─ ─ ─ ─┼─ ─ ─ ─┘  Catholic
   Mystic              │          Orthodox
                        ▼
                 TRADITIONALIST-
                   RITUALISM
```

Thinking – The Word: A primary means of knowing God, of spiritual formation, has traditionally been the Word of God. We study and teach the Bible as God's authoritative self-revelation. Here our mind – the intellect, thinking, reasoning – is the faculty through which we experience and know God. We are called to love God *"with all your mind"* (Mk 12:30), i.e. using it *to the full* in knowing and experiencing God. Two extremes must be avoided: de-emphasizing the mind – suspicion of the rational as humanistic – produces a superficial proof-texting and anti-scholarly approach to the Bible (biblicist fundamentalism); or overestimating the mind's ability to know God by exalting it *over* scripture, leading to a presumptuous humanist approach to the Bible in a dry analytical rationalism (liberal scholarship).

We need a renewed and enlightened mind: the courageous use of our mind in all its faculties to know God by the diligent study of scripture

– humbly relying on the Spirit's revelation, and the church's dialogue of authoritative interpretation, and its daily application in the real world. This has been called the *cataphatic* approach to spiritual theology. *Cataphatic* refers to the *positive* way of engagement with God via *the active use* of the mind and senses, i.e. *meditation* via thoughts, words, images, feelings and sensations. Cataphatic spirituality is incarnational in the sense that God's indwelling presence becomes ever more real by an interactive knowledge of him through bathing our mind and senses daily in his Word, and by "finding him" in all things around us. In Appendix 2, I contrast *cataphatic* and *apophatic*.

Intuiting – The Spirit: The opposing tension on the horizontal axis of our diagram is the focus on the Spirit. We experience God's Spirit by intuition or faith, apart from – or transcending – the mind and senses. Intuition is immediate (S)spirit union with God, hence mystical; also known as *spiritual* or *revelation* knowledge of God. We must avoid a de-emphasis of the Spirit, a scepticism of the mystical/ecstatic, which leads to humanistic reliance in knowing God. On the other hand, we must avoid an excessive Spirit-focus that feeds our lust for the supernatural, for "ultimate" experiences. This leads to spiritual narcissism and pride (elitism), otherworldly escapism and undiscerning spiritism – where anything goes – not subject to corrective authority in scripture, church leadership and this-world engagement.[79]

Intuiting is the *apophatic* or *negative* way of knowing God by unknowing, trusting God entirely for his communication of himself apart from our senses – technically called *contemplation*.[80] Apophatic means the darkening, emptying and negation of our imagination and reasoning in approaching God. Moses entered the dark cloud of God's presence on Sinai. With his senses darkened, he met God "face to face."

---

79 For example, Quietism, late-1600s mystical movement of Madame Guyon and Fenelon: withdrawal from socio-political reality in unhealthy introversion to pursue ultimate spiritual union with God.
80 *The Cloud of Unknowing* is the classic exposition of *apophatic* contemplation.

This is symbolic of apophatic spirituality; also called kenotic spirituality (*kenosis,* to strip or empty, Phil 2:7): a self-emptying of the mind and senses, a stripping of all reliance on all our faculties to know God. This *indirect* way of *unknowing* leads to *direct unmediated knowing* by the purification of our "sixth sense": faith.

Sensing – The Church: In terms of the vertical axis, the focus on the Church for spiritual formation points to a sensual experience of God; *not* as in tainted sensuality, but as in our God-given *physical* senses. Besides the mind and intuition, we experience and know God through our five senses: *taste* the Lord's goodness, *feel* his touch, *hear* his voice, *see* his glory, *breathe* his fragrant presence. The tangible experience of God in the biblical tabernacle and later temple – via the blood, water, incense, bread, candles, images of angels – was fulfilled in Messiah Jesus and his people; God's ultimate embodied or tactile self-communication (see 1 Jn 1:1).

This has been called the *liturgical* way of knowing God. It refers not only to our sense-experience of Christ in the worship service, but to the Church itself as Christ's community in terms of its traditions, structures, authority, teaching, ministry, sacraments, liturgy, rituals, icons, candles, incense and stained-glass windows (wall banners in Charismatic churches). Some doubt and even deny such sense-experience of God. They de-emphasize church, despising the above liturgical elements. On the other hand, its excessive emphasis results in meaningless ritual and empty tradition, enslaved in institutionalism: "having *a form* of godliness but denying its power" (2 Tim 3:5). Many see the Church like this – old, irrelevant, powerless! The answer is *not* reactive withdrawal from "structured church", nor uncritical continuance, but ongoing renewal of the Church by creative new ways to facilitate experience of God.

Feeling – The World: The opposing tension to the Church is focus on the World as a means of spiritual formation. It points to experiencing and knowing God via our feelings – the affective or psycho-emotional part of us. Jesus and Paul are examples of full engagement in the world for *God's* sake, for the world that God created and loves. "For God *so loved* the world that he gave..." (Jn 3:16). If we love God, we love what he loves. Jesus experienced God's feelings (anger, compassion, joy, etc.) in God's kingdom work. Paul came to know God in the whole range of the emotions he experienced in his world mission – from the "fellowship of Christ's sufferings" (Phil 3:10) to "the love of God compels me" (2 Cor 5:14).

This *affective* approach to spirituality is difficult for some. They shy away from emotional or enthusiastic experience of God: "Feelings and passions are subjective, fickle and damaged, even sinful, not to be trusted. Love is altruism, a matter of the will, not of the emotions." Alternatively, if the affective-revivalist and world-engagement focus is pushed too far, we burn out on ministry and mission. We can be driven by socio-political causes, trying to put the world right in our own power. Such excessive spiritual-revivalism and socio-political activism results in a judgmental moralism, not only of those we "do things to", but also of those who are not saving the world as we are! The balance is an openness to experience God psycho-emotionally in a way that heals and rehabilitates our feelings and passions. Such balance moves our feelings and passions away from sinful conditioning towards God-availability, whereby we serve *his* purposes in the world, energized by *his* passionate love.[81] The health and objectivity of affective spirituality will depend on the level of accountability to the church in terms of discernment and direction, both from scripture and spiritual leadership.

In conclusion: Jesus is the centre, the embodiment of God's presence, the goal of the spiritual quest. He models what it means to be truly human, the ultimate example of authentic spirituality. He grew into *Abba's* character and likeness by a full and balanced experience of God in all four ways of knowing, in all four types of prayer and means of spiritual

---

[81] See my chapter on psycho-emotional healing in *Doing Healing*, 227–240. Dietrich von Hildebrand, in his definitive work, *The Nature of Love*, has restored an understanding of the powerful *affective dimension of love* – a spirituality of love.

formation. We are called to follow him in *his* path of spiritual growth – to be like him – living in anticipation of God's kingdom come on earth (the focus of Part Two of the book).

Here is my cryptic conclusion:

- Too much exclusively of the Word and we *dry up*;
- Too much exclusively of the Spirit and we *blow up*;
- Too much exclusively of the Church and we get *tied up*;
- Too much exclusively of the World and we *burn up*; but
- Holding all four in creative tension, pursuing each of them, we *grow up* into Christ in all things (the "how to" is Part Three, Praxis).

QUESTIONS FOR REFLECTION AND DISCUSSION

1. What is your overall impression of this chapter? What has God said to you?

2. What has been your understanding of Christian spirituality in terms of its various expressions or traditions? Has this chapter broadened your view? How?

3. Why did I choose prayer – the different types of prayer – as a means of giving an overview of the traditions of Christian spirituality? Why is prayer key?

4. How do the four types of prayer meet the four ways in which we experience God?

5. Which of the four spiritual traditions in the quadrants of the diagram has been your common experience? How has that experience been for you?

6. Which one(s) do you know least about, have the least experience of? What plan can you come up with to intentionally expose

yourself to other expressions of spirituality for the sake of balanced growth in Christ?

7. In terms of your own spiritual formation, the way you experience and come to know God (thinking – the Word; sensing – the Church; intuiting – the Spirit; feeling – the World), which one, or more, works for you? How can you explore the one or more that you are least practised in?

PART TWO

THEOLOGY

Part Two lays the foundation for a biblical theology of spirituality. The primary issues in life are the Who? and the Why? questions, not the What? and the How? Theology addresses the Who? and the Why? of spirituality, which is the basis for the Praxis (practice) of the What? and the How? (Part Three). When spiritual formation is not grounded in sound biblical theology, including a proper biblical anthropology and psychology, it degenerates into technique or "how to". Then the technology of spiritual formation becomes the primary pursuit, leading to its professionalization and marketing. *That* is the outward form and empty shell of godliness that denies its authenticating Spirit and power.

Who is spirituality all about? Who do we follow? Who forms us – and why? Why *Christian* (Messianic or kingdom) spirituality? Part Two is doing the hard work of digging up the ground of our worldview, ideas and beliefs about reality, about (Christian) spirituality in the theological paradigm of Jesus and God's kingdom. Doing spirituality is following Jesus in his kingdom, to become like him.

So we examine how Jesus received and gave God's Spirit in his proclamation and teaching, inauguration and enactment of the kingdom of God. And how it was modelled in Jesus' own (human) spirituality, in his ministry and teachings; first in the Synoptic Gospels (Matthew, Mark and Luke), then in John's Gospel as eternal life, and then in Paul's letters as Spirit and sanctification.

CHAPTER 4

THEOLOGY: GOD'S KINGDOM AND JESUS' SPIRITUALITY

"If you are a theologian, you will pray truly.
And if you pray truly, you are a theologian."
Evagrios the Solitary (345–399)[82]

"The knowledge of the secrets of the kingdom of heaven
has been given to you."
Jesus – Matt 13:11

In Part One we saw how spirituality means different things to different people. We also discussed the biblical meaning in Paul's teaching: spirituality is having God's Spirit as the eschatological gift by faith in Messiah Jesus. More so, it's to be *under the kingdom (ruling control) of God's indwelling Spirit in every thought, word and deed, as was Jesus.* Jesus brought God's kingdom and gave the Spirit, to fulfil Israel's end-time salvation as the Hebrew prophets promised. Hence, *the Spirit (spirituality and theology) of the kingdom.* This chapter is to summarize the biblical understanding of the kingdom of God and its key implications,[83] as the lens through which we see Jesus and the Spirit, i.e. Jesus' spirituality. Let me first bridge the divides between spirituality, theology and ethics/morality.

---

82 In *On Prayer*, in Palmer *et al.*, *The Philokalia*, Vol. One, 62.
83 For a good introductory theology of the kingdom see Derek Morphew, *Breakthrough*.

Spirituality, theology and ethics

These concepts and practices were originally one and the same, as seen in the quote from Evagrios, a hermit of the Egyptian desert. Theology is "the study of God" (from *theos*, God). Anselm famously defined it as "faith seeking understanding". Theology is not knowledge *about* God, studying him as an object of rational analysis or correct propositional truths about God. Theology is knowing him as subject, as one experientially knows a friend – God *is* a real Person! This did not exclude reflection on and study of God. To be a theologian meant *interactive knowledge* of God through relationship – to "pray truly" – as lived and taught by Jesus and his apostles.

To "pray truly" meant knowing God not only by the Spirit, but also included the study of God's word, submission to the church's authority, and engagement in God's world, as in the previous chapter. We also saw, in chapter 2, how worldview – our ideas about reality, beliefs about (G)god and life – determine our ethics. I use ethics and morality synonymously, referring to life choices and character, right and wrong behaviour (some see morality as personal and ethics as social rights and wrongs). Thus, the Church has always said that orthodoxy (right faith/belief) leads to, and is seen in, orthopraxy (right moral practices); and heterodoxy (wrong belief) leads to heteropraxy (wrong moral practices). Therefore, theology + ethics = spirituality, and *vice versa*.

As the Early Church spread into the Greco-Roman world, it interpreted Christianity in the prevailing ideas of Greek-Hellenist philosophy. In so doing, dualistic thinking entered the Church and subverted her wholistic-integrated and historical-experiential Hebraic worldview. Spirit/soul was seen as superior, separate from the inferior body; concept/theory was separated from experience/practice, and spirituality from theology – all with serious consequences. For example, as the ascetic-mystic side of Christian spirituality developed, especially in the monastic movement, it tended to drift from its biblical base and theological accountability. And as theology became more apologetic and philosophic, especially in centres of learning, spirituality became sidelined as suspect mysticism.[84]

As a result of this dualism, universities and seminaries have not taught Christian spirituality for the past millennium. The closest they have come to has been Moral Theology (ethics) taught in Systematic Theology. However, since Vatican II (1960s), after 1 000 years of separation, Catholic theology has worked to reintegrate spirituality. Protestant theology, groomed in Enlightenment rationalism, is also facing its prejudice with regard to spirituality and mysticism (seen as legalism and subjectivism). Interestingly, the Eastern Orthodox has always kept theology, ethics and spirituality as one reality. Some Western universities and seminaries have begun to offer degrees in Christian spirituality in an attempt to reintegrate theology, ethics and spirituality.

However, contemporary *popular* spirituality in the secular West is separating itself from faith and religious convictions. When this happens, when transcendent convictions or absolutes are overthrown, everything becomes relative. Self becomes the frame of reference and the final arbiter. I decide what is real, leading to *a private spirituality* of "what feels right for me", "my authentic self", "giving love", having little to do with truth, right and wrong, character and accountability. The dualisms (e.g. sacred and secular – too many to discuss here) produce inauthentic, fragmented people, leading to disintegrated schizoid society.[85] This is reflected in the serious crisis in leadership today. It's a failure, in essence, of character, of moral formation and public accountability, the result of dire socio-spiritual bankruptcy.

My point is that Christian spirituality, which is Hebrew Messianic faith, must be grounded in biblical theology, in the wholistic-integrated vision and personal knowledge of God given in Jesus of Nazareth by his Spirit. *This* is the power that changes behaviour by (re)creating people into

---

84 Seen in some scholastic circles, 11th to 14th centuries (not Thomas Aquinas, 1224–1274, who embraced the mystical tradition) and especially in Enlightenment rationalism, 17th to 19th centuries.

85 See Louise Kretzschmar on bridging these divides, *The Importance of Moral and Spiritual Formation for 21st Century Africa*, 86–110.

good persons, who in turn create good society. The vision and spiritual knowledge of God imparts true ethical knowledge of right and wrong. It forms moral character, which the Greek philosophers like Aristotle, called *arête:* the "habitual strength" to do what is right. Later Latin writers translated *arête* as *virtus,* giving us the English "virtue". It was an important word in the Early Church, meaning the strengths or virtues, character traits or spiritual habits, that both enable us to *know* right from wrong, and routinely to *do* right by resisting the wrong. That is, to become truly and fully human as God's image-bearer as per his original intention.

Therefore, *what is the biblical theology of Christian spirituality? Jesus and the kingdom of God.* David Bosch did a seminal study of the underlying shifting paradigms that formed missiology – the theology of missions – at various stages through church history.[86] The same study is needed for Christian spirituality. Such a study would begin and end with Jesus' biblical worldview of the kingdom of God.

The kingdom of God

Some biblical scholars in Europe began "the quest for the historical Jesus" in the 19th cent.: who was Jesus in his 1st cent. Jewish context? This led to what is known as the second and third quests by scholars in Europe, Britain and the United States in the 20th cent. It's now called Jesus Research into Second Temple Judaism, from the Roman occupation of Palestine in 63 BC to the fall of Jerusalem in 70 AD. Key factors that have led to Jesus research in the last sixty to seventy years have been, a) the discovery of the Dead Sea scrolls in 1947 – manuscripts from the Qumran-Essene community at the time of Christ – plus the availability of Jewish and other key inter- and post-testamental writings; b) the post-Holocaust Jewish-Christian dialogue; and c) the shift from modernism to postmodernism and its implications in terms of worldview and methodology regarding historical knowledge.[87] For the first time in

---

86 In his major work, *Transforming Mission: Paradigm Shifts in Theology of Mission.*
87 I cannot elaborate on these factors here. See Morphew, *Jesus Research and Kingdom*

Part Two: Theology

literally 1 900 years, we are rediscovering and reconstructing Jesus in his context with reasonable probability. This is unprecedented. It's nothing less than a new departure in theology, as was The Reformation, if not more so! And it is leading to a change in the way we follow Jesus and do church, based on his kingdom message and mission.

Most scholars agree: Jesus' central message and mission was the kingdom of God. In broad terms, it meant the fulfilment of Israel's destiny – her salvation – in the coming of God's Messiah-King to rule and reign. This has led to a recovery of apocalyptic-eschatology within theology: the study of "the end" (*eschaton*) as the "revelation" (*apocalypse*) of God's final cosmic triumph over evil – seen as the apocalypse. Hence, the eschatological theology of the kingdom of God in Jesus and the NT.[88] The phrase "the kingdom of God", *he basileia tou theou*, essentially means the reign of God: "God coming in power to rule."[89] It's synonymous with Matthew's "kingdom of heaven" – Jews used "heaven" in respect of "God".

Jesus intentionally and strategically used this phrase *to connote Israel's story* in fulfilment of the Jewish aspirations of his day: their prophetic hope of *YHWH*'s return to Zion to become king. J.P. Meier shows (footnote 89) that Jesus' particular interpretation and use of this phrase was unique in Judaism, and key to his self-understanding and mission – his life aims. He saw himself like King David, *YHWH*'s anointed restorer of Israel and bringer of the kingdom; like Moses, fulfilling Torah as a wisdom teacher; and like Elijah, an end-time prophet and miracle worker.

Theology, for a comprehensive exposition of these and other factors in the rise of Jesus research.

88 What follows are conclusions of the Jesus research scholars, see my Bibliography: Borg, Chilton, Dunn, Johnson, Keener, Meier, Morphew, Nolan, O'Collins, Ratzinger, Young, and Wright.

89 Meier's phrase (also Is 40:10a NIV) in *A Marginal Jew*, Vol. II, 237–288. Jesus used the Aramaic *mulkuta di elaha*, "kingdom of God" or "God's kingly rule", from "targums" (the Aramaic paraphrases of Hebrew texts by translators in synagogues, learnt by oral repetition, then recorded from late 1st to 5th centuries AD). See Stassen and Gushee, *Kingdom Ethics*, 23–25; and Chilton's *A Galilean Rabbi and His Bible* and *The Isaiah Targum*. Meier criticizes (264, 287) Chilton's tendency to strip Jesus of his apocalyptic-eschatology.

The idea of *YHWH's* kingship as the Creator and thus Ruler is everywhere in the Hebrew Testament. But there are three salient windows or pictures of God's kingdom that formed the Jewish mind and summarized Israel's story.

The Exodus: The *first* biblical reference to God's kingship is from the Exodus and Sinai covenant. *YHWH* delivered Israel with great power, defeating Egypt's gods and destroying Pharaoh's army. He was Israel's Warrior-King and she became his vassal nation in a covenant of love: *YHWH* will "tabernacle" and rule among them (Ex 15, 25:22 cf. 1 Sam 4:4). It was kingship *with a purpose,* not only to save Israel, but to form her into "a kingdom of priests and a holy nation". It was a threefold calling as his "treasured possession" (Ex 19:4–6, read this key text):

- to be *kings* sharing in his rule and reign – his kingdom – to "all nations" and the "whole earth";

- to be *priests* ministering to *YHWH*, offering sacrifices, prayers and praise on behalf of "all nations" and "the whole earth"; and

- to be *prophets* to all the scattered Babel nations, bringing them back to God – "a holy nation" set apart to embody and speak *YHWH's* word by the power of his Spirit to all people (see Num 11:29 cf. Joel 2:28f).

Where Adam and Eve failed as God's image-bearers, Israel's vocation was to be *YHWH's* (new) image-bearer among the nations, to reconcile fallen humanity to God. Thus, *YHWH's* kingship over Israel was *purposeful… his saving and ruling presence…* represented in his personal name (Ex 3:12–15 cf. 15:3, 18).[90]

---

90 God revealed *his name* in coming to deliver Israel. *YHWH* ("I Am"; LORD in NIV and NRSV) means "I am who I am… I was, I am, I will be here for you". It's a verb – an event – the Semitic idea of *name as (intervening) presence* (Deut 12:5). When we call *"YHWH",* he answers *"Hineni",* "Here am I" (Is 58:9). Having only consonants, the pronunciation of the tetragramaton, *YHWH,* is unknown. Later, considered too holy to (even attempt to) verbalise, it was replaced by *Adonai* (Lord in NIV, NRSV).

The Davidic Monarchy: The *second* window of God's kingdom. *YHWH* called David "my son", promising to rule Israel through David's future son: the Son of God or Messiah-King who will defeat her enemies and bring peace (2 Sam 7:11–16 cf. Ps 2). Solomon's reign of *Shalom* – of *wholistic* peace, wisdom and prosperity – was a preview picture of this promised kingdom (see 1 Kgs 4). But Israel's repeated sin of breaking the covenant eventually led to exile from *YHWH's* saving and ruling presence – given over to the rule of other powers/gods. The prophets had warned them, calling them to repent, predicting both their exile *and* their restoration when *YHWH* will again come in power to save Israel in a new exodus, with a new covenant as a renewed people (Jer 31:31–34), to save the nations and renew creation.

The Prophets: This *third* picture of God's kingdom was most detailed in Isaiah's expanding end-time, apocalyptic, cosmic vision. His key word for *YHWH's* coming reign in "the day of the LORD" is *yeshua* (salvation): "In that day you will say, 'Surely God is my salvation… the LORD, the LORD, is my strength and my song; he has become my salvation'" (Is 12:1–2, quoting Moses in Ex 15:2).[91] That future day will bring salvation *and* judgment: when *YHWH* becomes king in Messiah, he will judge and destroy evil, and will bring forgiveness, healing, freedom and justice for all. He will gather the exiles, make a new covenant, pour out God's Spirit, reconcile the nations, raise the dead, and renew creation. It will culminate in the kingdom banquet of the marriage of God and his people, of heaven and earth. A breath-taking vision![92] Paradoxically, all this will take place when God becomes king in his *Suffering Servant,* who atones for Israel's sin (Is 42, 49, 50, 53).

---

91 Isaiah's *yeshua* (salvation) is the Hebrew Joshua, or Greek Jesus ("*YHWH* Saves"). "You are to give him the name *Yeshua,* because he will save his people from their sins" (Matt 1:21). As with *YHWH,* when we call "Jesus", we invoke his intervening/saving presence, his kingdom come.
92 Is 2:2–4, 9:2–7, 11:1–9, 24:1–13, 17–23, 25:6–8, 26:19, 32:1–4, 15–18, 33:24, 35:1–7, 40:1–11, 42:1–9, 44:1–5, 49:6–13, 51:4–6, 11, 61:1–3, 65:17, 20–25, 66:10–16, 22–23.

The prophetic Book of Daniel was a primary apocalyptic reference or revealer of God's secret plans for Jews in Second Temple Judaism. Dan 2 predicts four empires, one following another. God's kingdom will come as "a rock" (v.34) to destroy the fourth kingdom (the Roman Empire), then will grow into a huge mountain filling the earth. In Dan 7, the four pagan empires are four beasts, with the fourth, most terrifying, oppressing God's people. God will judge and destroy it by "one like a *son of man*, coming with the clouds of heaven (to) the Ancient of Days. He was given authority, glory and sovereign power; all nations and peoples of every language worshiped him. His dominion is an everlasting dominion that will not pass away..." (vv.13-14). This *heavenly* (divine) and yet *human* figure (thus "son of man") represents and embodies "the holy people of the Most High (who) will receive the kingdom and will possess it forever" (v.18).

The question was: how long until this actually happens? Until the exile really ends? Daniel was told 490 years (Dan 9:2, 24) – not the 70 years of Jeremiah (Jer 25:12-14, 29:10-14), but 70 times 7 years, a Jubilee of Jubilees: The End! However one interprets the cryptic times and events that follow (Dan 9:25f), the 490 years bring us to Second Temple Judaism under repressive Roman rule. Pious Jews at that time had seen four kingdoms (Babylon, Persia, Greece, finally Rome) and were doing their calculations from Daniel in great anticipation. "Son of Man" had become a messianic title. Messianic expectation was at fever pitch. Many false messiahs arose before and after Jesus, e.g. the would-be messiah Menahem led the 66-70 AD Jewish revolt that resulted in the Romans destroying Jerusalem and the Temple in 70 AD.

Jesus and the fulfilment of the kingdom

The time had come! Enter two young men, John the baptizer in 24/25 AD and Jesus of Nazareth in 26/27 AD. Reading "the signs of the times", they preached God's kingdom come: imminent judgment *and* salvation

(Matt 3:1f, 4:17, 16:1-4). Jesus' apocalyptic paradigm[93] came from his mentor John, together with his own interpretation of Torah, the Psalms, and especially the Prophets (Isaiah and Daniel). Through spiritual formation and supernatural confirmation at his baptism, when God's Spirit came on him (Mk 1:9-11), Jesus believed God's new age began in him. As God's Anointed, he saw himself fulfilling the prophetic era that ended in John, his forerunner. Mark brackets Jesus' ministry, from his baptism to his death, with the veil between heaven and earth, the future age and the present age, being "torn" open (Mk 1:10 cf. 15:38). In other words, the heavens were open with kingdom break-through and availability in Jesus' life and ministry. He also believed he was Daniel's Son of Man, publicly calling himself by that title, while others said he was David's son, the promised Son of God or Messiah (Matt 16:13-17; Mk 14:61-62).

This explains Jesus' generic message: "*The time has come, the kingdom of God is near (at hand)*" (Mk 1:15) – probably taken from Is 56:1: "My salvation (*yeshua*) is close at hand..." *Yeshua* would fulfil Israel's destiny, but not as per public expectation and other would-be messiahs, e.g. he rejected the holy war theology of violence. His was a revolution of love, the holy war of Isaiah's Suffering Servant of *YHWH*, who ultimately defeats evil in atoning for Israel's sin by dying for the nation. *Yeshua* really believed that God's kingdom, the future age, had come in his ministry and in his death – in hope of vindication by resurrection.

The kingdom was *not a static realm or place*, a political structure as in the "United Kingdom" (Britain). Rather, it was *the dynamic action of God's rule* confronting and defeating evil powers opposed to God – the kingdom of Satan (Lk 11:17-22). Jesus experienced the kingdom as God's authority in a "field of force"[94] or power-zone – open heavens – of God's Spirit present

---

[93] "The kingdom of God" invading "the kingdoms of this world" (Dan 2:44-45, 7:13-14 cf. Jn 18:36-37); "the age to come" interrupting "the present age" (Mk 10:30 cf. Heb 6:5).

[94] Meier's phrase in *Marginal Jew,* Vol. II, 161, 402. This is different to a pan*en*theistic view of the Spirit as a field of force, which Cooper critiques in *Panentheism,* 259-281,

and active in him, at war with evil in all its forms. Luke clearly shows in Luke-Acts that the era of the kingdom is the era of the Spirit: the kingdom comes in the power of the Spirit. John says: "the reason the Son of God appeared was to destroy the devil's work" (1 Jn 3:8b).

Jesus' experience of the kingdom and understanding of scripture led to his message and practice of the kingdom. He said: "Torah and the Prophets prophesied until John the baptizer. Since John, till now, the kingdom of heaven is coming with power, breaking out and forcefully advancing[95] with miracles, fulfilling Is 35:4-6 and 61:1. People are breaking into 'it'! The least person *in* the kingdom is greater than John, because 'it' has now come and is available!" (my RAP on Matt 11:2-4, 10-13).

Thus we can "seize" the kingdom; we can be "in" or "out" of it; we must "seek" it (Matt 6:33); we can "see" and "enter" it (Jn 3:3-5; Acts 14:22). God's kingdom "comes upon" us by God's Spirit – his "finger" – delivering us from Satan's rule (Matt 12:28 cf. Lk 11:20).[96] By the Spirit's empowering of Jesus, as a human being, he intentionally fulfilled the Hebrew prophets, especially Isaiah's vision of wholistic kingdom salvation for all who "repent and believe" (Mk 1:15).

He preached to the poor, forgave sins, healed the sick, delivered the demonized, freed the oppressed, restored dignity and justice, confronted the powers (spiritual *and* socio-religious-political), fed the hungry, calmed the storms, raised the dead, and feasted with sinners, prostitutes and drunkards. In this way, he re-gathered the exiles, joyously celebrating

---

regarding Pannenburg's usage in *Systematic Theology,* Vol. 2, 79-102.
95 The kingdom "forcefully advancing" (Matt 11:12 NIV) or "has suffered violence" (NRSV) is from Mic 2:12-13: the kingdom breaks out in Jesus, the "One who breaks open the way... before them (Israel's remnant)... their king... the LORD" as they forcefully "break through" after him. See Brad Young, *Jesus the Jewish Theologian,* 49-74.
96 "Finger" recalls Moses' miracles that defeated Pharaoh and the Egyptian gods (Ex 8:19), i.e. Jesus' miraculous ministry was *the* new Exodus defeating Satan and his kingdom – he was *the* prophet that Moses promised would be "like unto him" (Deut 18:15-19 cf. Acts 3:22-23).

and sharing salvation with them in kingdom banquets, fulfilling the prophets in anticipation of God's end-time feast.[97]

Yeshua called *these* people into an all-inclusive *kingdom community* of disciplined learners. He saw them as the renewed Israel in which God reconciles the nations and transforms humanity, where he reigns and his will is done as it is in heaven (Matt 6:10). He symbolized the restored Israel by choosing twelve apostles, who will sit on thrones judging Israel "at the renewal of all things" (Matt 19:28).

His teaching was the new Torah prophesied by Moses (Deut 18:18), the new covenant of Jer 31:31–34, mediated in his own blood (Lk 22:20). Jesus' presence was the new Temple where people encountered *YHWH*, receiving forgiveness of sins and healing (Mk 2:5–11; Jn 2:18–22). He gave his "little flock" *this* kingdom (Lk 12:31–32, 22:29–30), to proclaim and demonstrate to all Israel (Lk 9:1f, 10:1f), and thus "bring salvation to the ends of the earth" (Mk 16:15 cf. Gen 12:2–3; Is 49:6). Joshua (Jesus) was leading the new Israel into the real Promised Land, God's kingdom – to "inherit the earth", not just a piece of real estate in the Middle East (Ps 37:11 cf. Matt 5:5).

In short, Jesus inaugurated and enacted God's kingdom in his words, works and wonders. Thus the kingdom came in his person – Christ is the kingdom itself, the *autobasileia* (Origen's word). He represented and embodied (the true) Israel, doing *for* Israel and *to* Israel what she failed to do, fulfilling her calling as Prophet, Priest and King. His popularity, and especially his authority, resulted in conflict with the religious-political authorities and spiritual powers. His triumphal messianic entry into Jerusalem and his enactment of judgment on the Temple in his last week, led to the authorities uniting to kill him. In so doing, ironically, they helped – or were used – to fulfil his kingdom mission (Mk 11:15–18 cf. 10:45).

Thus, the coming of the kingdom, the inauguration of the future

---

[97] See 1 Kgs 4:20–27 cf. Is 25:6–9; Matt 8:11–12, 9:9–13, 11:18–19, 21:31–32. As Bruce Chilton says: "he ate and drank his way around Galilee", *Rabbi Jesus*, 83.

age, climaxed in Jesus' dark vocation: his suffering and death. Dramatic cosmic signs took place: the eclipse of the sun, an earthquake, the temple curtain torn from top to bottom, bodies came out of graves, angels appeared in brilliant light (Matt 27:45-54, 28:2-4). These were apocalyptic references to the end of the world, to Judgment Day – The Day of *YHWH* – the final defeat of evil. *The future judgment happened in history, on Christ's cross* at Passover in 30/31 AD. He defeated evil by absorbing the full violence of evil, drinking God's cup of judgment for love of us. This was utterly revolutionary! He was God's King (*Meshiach*), the Suffering Servant "marred beyond human form (to) sprinkle many nations… pierced for *our* transgressions, crushed for *our* iniquities; the punishment that brought *us* peace (*shalom*) was upon *him*, and by *his* wounds *we* are healed" (Is 52:13-15, 53:5). By the blood of the sacrificial Lamb of God, judgment passed over Jesus' community in a new Exodus from death to eternal life (Jn 1:29, 5:24). Those not in his community faced, and will face, God's (final) judgment.

Jesus' bodily resurrection was the ultimate triumph over death and the devil, signalling the end of this age (Dan 12:1-2), i.e. the future resurrection took place *in history* as a "first fruit". Luke and John's accounts of Christ's resurrection connote a new gardener, a new human, in a new Garden-Paradise, with new heavens and a new *shalom-filled* earth.[98] Jesus' bodily resurrection is God's new creation *already* begun in the midst of – transforming – this old broken creation. The new humanity that the Son of Man represented and embodied was literally "born again", in-breathed by Jesus' resurrection Spirit (Jn 20:21-22). Indeed, his ascension was Daniel's "son of man coming with the clouds of heaven" to "the Ancient of Days", vindicated out of suffering by resurrection, given "sovereign

---

98 *Shalom* is the Hebrew Testament's idea/vision of God's wholistic-integrated reality: perfect peace, justice, prosperity and abundance, *the fruit of right relationship with God, each other and creation*; see Walter Brueggemann, *Living Toward a Vision: Biblical Reflection on Shalom*. On Jesus' resurrection and the implications for Christian living and Church mission, see N.T. Wright's scholarly tome, *The Resurrection of the Son of God*, or his popular version, *Surprised by Hope*.

power" and "all authority" to rule at God's right hand till his enemies are made his footstool. Ten days after his ascension, Christ poured out *this* sovereign power, the Holy Spirit, on his new humanity (the church), to advance his kingdom through them to the ends of the earth.[99]

In summary, the cross was the end-time judgment, the chaotic deep darkness of fallen creation over which the Spirit hovered – waiting for the word. The resurrection was the "big bang" of God's new creation, "let there be light". The ascension and Pentecost were the enthronement – the exploding power of the new creation's exponential expansion to the ends of the earth. Jesus' community is that new creation. He is the Head in heaven and we are his Body on earth, filled with his Spirit, doing his will as it is in heaven. The powers of the coming age in the gifts of the Spirit enable us to continue Jesus' kingdom ministry and mission. We defeat evil by bringing wholistic salvation to all, in anticipation of the consummation of the kingdom at Christ's return.

Figure 4 shows the paradigm or framework of God's kingdom as OT *promise*, NT *fulfilment,* and Second Coming *consummation*:

Figure 4. The Framework of the Kingdom of God

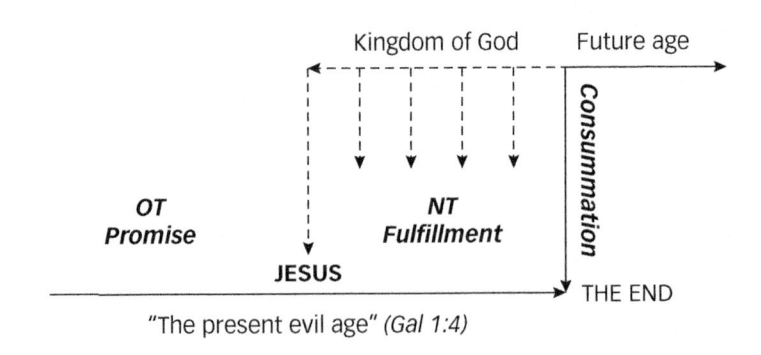

```
                        Kingdom of God      Future age
                    ┌──┬──┬──┬──┐
                    │  │  │  │  │     C
                    │  │  │  │  │     o
                    │  │  │  │  │     n
                    ▼  ▼  ▼  ▼      s
                                      u
        OT                NT          m
      Promise          Fulfillment    m
                                      a
                                      t
                                      i
                                      o
                 JESUS                n
        ────────────────────────────▶ THE END
        "The present evil age" (Gal 1:4)
```

---

99 See Dan 7:9–27; Matt 28:18–20; Mk 16:15–20; Lk 24:45–53; Acts 1:7–11, 2:29–36.

The key issue: the mystery of the kingdom

We live in the period of fulfilment, between Christ's first and second coming. This entire period is called the end times or "the last days" (Acts 2:17; Heb 1:1-2 cf. Deut 4:30). The OT prophets saw a one-off coming of Messiah in the Day of the Lord. They did not see an in-between period – a secret (*mysterion*) kept hidden in times past – now revealed in Messiah, by his holy apostles and prophets in the new covenant. That is, contrary to Jewish expectation, God's kingdom has burst into this world *without putting an end to this age*, and Gentiles enter the kingdom as full members of God's people *before the kingdom is consummated on earth*.[100] This was mind-blowing for the Jews.

Jews in Jesus' day expected one event, a decisive end and new beginning: *Meshiach* would save Israel by military defeat of her enemies (the Romans), gather the exiles, renew the covenant, rebuild the Temple, establish his rule from Jerusalem, reconcile the Gentile nations, and renew the earth under his Reign of Shalom. All these elements (a "package deal") made up the Jewish messianic expectation.

Jesus had a more nuanced and far-reaching vision of what God was doing through him. God's kingdom was coming in an unexpected and mysterious way: the future age was breaking into this age with power, but without ending it; the real enemy, Satan and *his* kingdom, was being defeated; the covenant was renewed in his blood; Torah was fulfilled in his life and teachings; the Temple was rebuilt in his resurrected body and in his body of believers indwelt by his Spirit; he has ascended to the Father's right hand and will rule from the heavens, reconciling all nations into his kingdom in anticipation of the new earth.

This was an unforeseen interim stage between prophetic fulfilment and final consummation. Jesus taught this mystery or "the secret" (*mysterion*, Matt 13:11) via parables: just as wheat and weeds grow side by side, so the kingdom of heaven and the kingdoms of this world, the future

---

[100] For this paragraph, see Matt 13:11-17; Rom 11:25, 16:25-26; Eph 3:3-6; Col 1:25-27.

age and the present age, exist side by side in a warfare of "eschatological tension". The mystery is that we live between the times, in the overlapping or co-existence of two ages – a unique ontological and existential reality. Theologians call it the "already" and "not yet" of God's kingdom.[101]

Understanding this *revealed* mystery is crucial. It explains much of our daily reality as Christians. *In fact, the remainder of this book is an exposition of this basic reality, the "eschatological tension" or warfare we find ourselves in.* We try to resolve the tension one way or another. No one likes to live in tension, in war! The bad news is: it will *not* be resolved till Jesus comes or till we die. The good news is: it is *the very means* by which God grows and transforms us. It's the stuff of our spiritual formation, the means of our training for reigning with Christ in this age *and* the age to come.

A common way of escaping the tension is to choose *either* the already *or* the not yet. Overemphasis either way leads to kingdom now or kingdom not yet theologies. They result in understandings and practices of Christian spirituality that become unreal, causing serious problems for their followers. Pushed too far either way, they become heretical. I will point out the implications and examples of these either/or theologies at relevant points as the chapters unfold.

Some scholars still argue for the kingdom being *either* present ("realized eschatology") *or* still future ("future eschatology"). There is a growing consensus, however, that Jesus and his apostles taught the kingdom as *both* present *and* future at the same time ("enacted inaugurated eschatology"). This Hebraic bi-polar thinking holds opposite truths in tension without logically reconciling or explaining their apparent contradiction.[102] The binary Western mind defaults to either/or, therefore we struggle with both/and, needing to harmonize paradoxical or contradictory opposites.

---

101 Dunn says this "one central feature" has been "the trigger", the key idea, in the re-emergence of kingdom theology in Jesus, in recent decades, *Jesus Remembered*, 405.
102 Technically called Semitic "dialectical negation"; see Meier, *A Marginal Jew*, Vol. 2, 142–143.

Morphew goes further by identifying four (not just two) paradoxical nuances in the Gospels that convey this Hebraic mystery of the kingdom:[103]

- The kingdom has come, is present: "is among you" (Lk 11:20, 17:20–21).

- The kingdom is coming immediately, is imminent: "is near" (Mk 1:15).

- The kingdom is yet to come: "is delayed" (e.g. Matt 25:1–30 teaches the delay of the bridegroom, and the master's coming – be ready and waiting!).

- The kingdom will come: is future at the end of the age (Matt 26:29, 64).

The kingdom has come, is about to come, is delayed, and will come. More accurately: the kingdom is present, yet delayed; future, yet imminent. All are true at the same time. Confusing! Jesus says in Matt 13 that it requires eyes of faith – spiritual insight – to see God's mysterious work… it's like seeds growing in soil; yeast mixed in dough; treasure hidden in a field; wheat and weeds growing side by side; good and bad fish caught in the same net of the kingdom only to be separated at the end of the age. Not even the rabbi-sage Nicodemus understood that we must be "born again" to see, let alone enter, God's kingdom (Jn 3:1–10). And those in the kingdom are truly peculiar: we are God's present-imminent-delayed-future people!

The four missional implications of the kingdom

What are the *essential missional implications* of the vision of the kingdom, in its fulfilment in Jesus and his community? In answer, I reduce the wholistic-integrated vision and nature of kingdom-salvation to four

---
103 In *Breakthrough*, 67–81.

irreducible purposes or implications. These confirm the four basic roles or functions of the Hebrew understanding of the Spirit,[104] whose coming is associated with Messiah's kingdom. They are *all* salvation, *all* kingdom-breakthrough – a package deal. We cannot separate them or selectively obey, at best championing some and devaluing others, at worst choosing some and rejecting others as "not the gospel of Christ". Followers of Jesus learn to see and do all four in a wholistic-integrated way of receiving the Spirit in his/her full work, as a seamless garment, in living the kingdom.

Power Encounter: The kingdom always comes in power; in dramatic ways like Lazarus coming out of the tomb, and in hidden progressive ways like the tiny mustard seed growing into a big tree. *Both* are miracles! The kingdom is power-encounter. The Spirit's power defeats Satan's power, bringing the new Exodus of salvation, healing, deliverance, and new creation. The Spirit comes with prophetic *charismata* (gifts), supernatural signs and wonders (Is 11:1–3, 61:1–3), empowering the church to do its ministry and mission. The church is the community of the kingdom: its instrument and witness on earth. My book *Doing Healing* articulates the theology and praxis of kingdom power-encounter for the church of Jesus Christ.

Personal Transformation: The kingdom comes in power, transforming us as individuals and communities of faith. Salvation is being born again with *God's* Spirit, who purifies and changes us from inside out. Spiritual life and growth, in progressive sanctification to Christlikeness, is the heart of the gospel of the kingdom – the new covenant work of the Spirit of Holiness (Ezek 36:25–27). The missional purpose of the Church is to be God's community of kingdom formation and spirituality, preparing Christians with the character needed to rule

---

104 I include creation-transformation and mission-fulfilment, in addition to the Spirit's two primary functions of power-anointing and purity-sanctification in the Hebrew Testament (see Keener, *The Spirit in the Gospels and Acts*). While Luke clearly emphasizes the Spirit's power and world mission, Paul's theology focuses more on the Spirit's sanctification and transformation.

and reign with Christ in this age and the age to come. This book, *Doing Spirituality,* is my study of this dimension of mission.

Social Transformation: The kingdom comes with power to transform individuals and, through them, societies and nations, even creation. The kingdom works through Christ-followers as salt and light (Matt 5:13–16) *in society*. People are reconciled to God, and one another – as in racial, cultural, political, economic, gender, and generational reconciliation. And, ultimately, with creation, as in ecological care in anticipation of the earth's renewal. The kingdom engages society at the levels of symptomatic relief (mercy ministry), root causes (justice advocacy) and social care (community development). It's all part of the Spirit's work of creation renewal (Gen 1:2 cf. Ps 104:30). This is the church's social-missional dimension. My book *Doing Reconciliation* is a kingdom theology and praxis for social transformation.

World Mission: The kingdom comes with power, transforming individuals and societies with a view to reaching *all* nations *so that the end may come* (Matt 24:14). The ultimate mission is kingdom advancement through evangelism and church planting, and Christian missions of all kinds, to all nations, till Christ returns. It's the missional function of the Spirit bringing God's end-time salvation to "all flesh" across all barriers, that "everyone who calls on the name of the LORD shall be saved" (Joel 2:28–32 NRSV). It's *doing* church as Jesus intended, as he commissioned his disciples in Matt 28:18–20. Used as a guide for church planting, my book *Doing Church* is an exposition of how to be and do church from a theology and praxis of the kingdom.

The fourth missional implication loops back to the first, the power encounter of the kingdom advancing to the ends of the earth. The circular movement of these four, like a wheel, rolls from Jesus and his first followers through church history, gaining momentum – with progressive kingdom breakthrough in the tension and warfare of the already and not yet – till Jesus returns. See Figure 5:

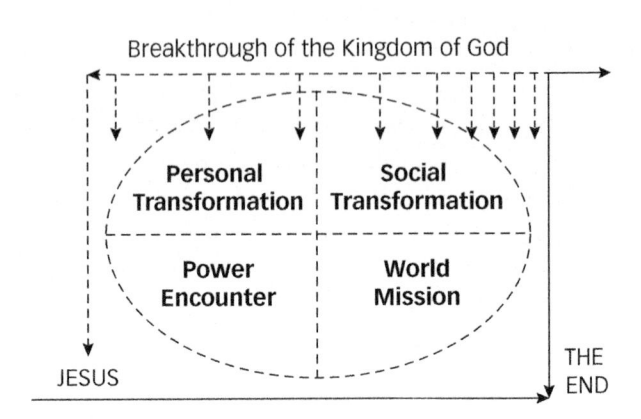

Figure 5. Missional Implications of the Kingdom

```
         Breakthrough of the Kingdom of God
    ┌─────────────────────────────────────────→
    │         ╱─────────┬─────────╲
    ▼       ╱  ▼        │    ▼     ╲  ▼ ▼ ▼ ▼
          │   Personal      │   Social      │
          │ Transformation  │ Transformation │
          ├─────────────────┼────────────────┤
          │   Power         │   World        │
          │   Encounter     │   Mission      │
           ╲                                ╱
    ▼        ╲──────────────┬─────────────╱
   JESUS                                        THE
                                             ↓  END
```

Personal transformation into Christlikeness – kingdom discipleship – is not just one of four missional implications, of *what* we do in the name of the kingdom. It gives the *why* and determines *how* we do each dimension. Spirituality is about identity and character, meaning and values, ethos and style, praxis and behaviour. It's about how, and on what basis, we do power encounter (style and practice of healing), spiritual formation (ethos of community and spirituality), leadership, social transformation, ecological care, evangelism, church planting, and world missions.

Therefore, beside "a theology of spirituality", we can speak of *"a spiritual theology"* as in Peterson's *Christ Plays in Ten Thousand Places* (see my Bibliography). We can speak in the plural, of *spiritual theologies*, as in a spirituality of healing, a spirituality of community, of leadership, of social action, and so on. These spiritualities – theologies and praxes of *why* and *how* we do things – are formed by our experience and understanding of *God's* kingdom as opposed to other understandings, kingdoms and spiritualities on offer. More so, they are formed by *our discipleship* to the historical Jesus and his Spirit in the kingdom he inaugurated. Here I agree with Luke Timothy Johnson, that the canonical Gospels "are remarkably consistent on one essential aspect of the identity and mission of Jesus", i.e. on the *character* or spirituality of his life and death as *the* pattern for all followers.[105]

In conclusion: introducing Jesus' personal spirituality

This brings us back to the historical Jesus, to *who* he was, *what* he did, and *how* he did it; and, more importantly, the person he became. I conclude by introducing Jesus' spirituality, formed mainly in his "hidden years" by his personal experience of *Abba*'s kingdom of love. My cameo portrait of *Yeshua*[106] will prepare us for what following Jesus in his kingdom means in the remaining chapters.

Pope Benedict XVI says that, in trying to see Jesus for who he was, *in his context*, we are unravelling "the Mystery of Jesus", which is "seeking the face of God", because he came to reveal God to humanity.[107] Normally, we start with our notion of "God", then fill Jesus with *that* meaning, seeing him as divine. It's the other way around. We must start with *the person* Jesus, seeing him *in his humanity*. *He* fills our notion, meaning and experience of "God". By studying the historical Jesus, we seek God, we see *Abba*'s face. YHWH said to Moses: "you cannot see my face, for no one may see me and live", so God showed Moses his "back" (Ex 33:20–23).

---

105 Johnson says: "Their (the Gospels) fundamental focus is not on Jesus' wondrous deeds nor on his wise words. Their shared focus is on the *character* of his life and death. They all reveal the same *patterns* of radical obedience to God and selfless love toward other people. All four Gospels also agree that discipleship is to follow the same *messianic pattern*. They do not emphasise the performance of certain deeds or the learning of certain doctrines. They insist on living according to the same pattern of life and death shown by Jesus", (his italics), *The Real Jesus,* 157.
106 Scholars notoriously create (the historical) Jesus in their own image: Jesus the Moral Teacher, or the Miracle Worker, or the Socio-Political Liberator, or the Spiritual Mystic. Meier says (*A Marginal Jew,* Vol. I, 21–40), we *cannot know* the "Real Jesus", who he actually was; we *can know* the "Historical Jesus" from historical evidence (up to a point; while some things are certain, most are *probabilities*); and we *should know* the "Christ of Faith", the Risen Jesus of Christian faith. All portraits of Jesus in truth are a mix of the latter two – mine included!
107 Ratzinger, *Jesus of Nazareth,* 1–8.

Jesus came to reveal God as *Abba*-Father – only he can do that (Jn 1:18). We see the Father's face in Jesus. And it's beautiful. Jesus reveals the mystery of God as ultimate beauty: The Beauty that irresistibly attracts and draws us to admire and fall in love with God *in* Jesus of Nazareth. Isaiah said: "Your eyes will see the king in his beauty" (33:17 cf. Jn 12:41). This is why Jesuit scholar Gerald O'Collins begins with, and then bases his entire biographical portrait of his historical Jesus on his beauty.[108]

My point is, that with regard to Jesus' spirituality, we need to see him as human more than divine. Jesus is one person with two inseparable natures: human and divine. The Nestorian heresy separated the natures, saying Jesus was two beings, God and a man united to God. They wrongly equated the *nature* with the *person*. We tend to do the same, thinking of Jesus as divine: The Son of God. The Jewish phrase "son of God", for Messiah, referred to *a human being* anointed by God's Spirit to be King. If Jesus' spirituality, in his earthly life, stemmed from his divine nature, he would be superman, unable to be emulated by any of us. However, if we take him seriously as a human person, like you and me, filled with God's Spirit, we would have to imitate him. And that is impossible, or so we think! So we avoid it!

Therefore, who was Jesus as a person? What was he like? What constituted his sense of identity and (extraordinary) spirituality?[109]

Leading Jewish scholar Jacob Neusner says the essential difference between Judaism (what he calls "eternal Israel") and Christianity, is

---

108 He takes it from Augustine of Hippo (354–430) who, in a homily on Psalm 45, taught that Christ, our Bridegroom-King, is "beautiful in heaven; beautiful on earth; beautiful in the womb; beautiful in his parents' arms; beautiful in his miracles; beautiful under the scourge; beautiful when inviting to life... beautiful when laying down his life; beautiful in taking it up again; beautiful on the cross; beautiful in the sepulcher; beautiful in heaven." Cited by O'Collins in *Jesus: A Portrait*, 2.
109 We have to qualify Jesus' spirituality as unique in some sense precisely because of his divine nature. Ratzinger argues in *Jesus of Nazareth,* 110–111, that we cannot make real sense of the evidence of "the true 'historical' Jesus of the Gospels" *unless we assume his divine Sonship,* or else we have to conclude he was a blasphemer, or imposter, or joker, or insane.

that rabbi *Yeshua* did not make followers of Torah *per se*, but of himself. Jews are people of The Book and Christians are people of The Person.[110] The Bible *is* important to Christians, but it's not the correct theology or obedient life (Jewish *halakha*) that saves us. *Yeshua* said: "You diligently study the Scriptures because you think that by them you possess eternal life. These are the Scriptures that testify about me, yet you refuse to come to me to have life" (Jn 5:39–40). By following and entrusting ourselves to *Yeshua*, in his life and teaching, we are saved and progressively transformed into his likeness.

Jesus' birth, upbringing and formation

Yeshua was born in 6 or 5 BC; was discipled by John in 26 or 27 AD; began his ministry in 27 or 28 AD; and died in 30 or 31 AD. Roughly, his thirty years of hidden preparation for three years of public ministry is a ratio of ten to one – the crucial years of formation of the profound spirituality evidenced in his ministry.

His conception and birth were controversial. The virgin birth is a matter of creedal faith for Christians, but many today dismiss it as having no historical basis. The tradition of the virgin birth – as an end-time event, one of many in his life – was the way Jesus was "remembered and retold" by his first followers.[111] His mother and father would certainly have told *Yeshua* and others about God's visitations when he was conceived and born – all signs of prophetic fulfilment of God's kingdom.

However, his conception *before* Mary and Joseph's wedding was scandalous in Nazareth, raising suspicion of suspect paternity and illegitimacy – called a *mamzer* in the Talmud (250–400 AD).[112] The *Mamzer* ("bastard") from Nazareth would have suffered social and religious rejection (see Deut 23:2 cf. Jn 8:19, 41, 48), raising questions

---

110 Neusner, *A Rabbi Talks with Jesus*.
111 See James Dunn, *Jesus Remembered*. On Jesus' nativity in particular see Raymond Brown's seminal study, *The Birth of the Messiah*.
112 Bruce Chilton, *Rabbi Jesus*, 12–13.

in *Yeshua's* psycho-emotional development of belonging and identity. His acceptance and love by *his Father* was a defining issue from a very early age. He evidently believed his parents' astonishing stories of what happened around his conception and birth, *finding identity and purpose in God as his heavenly Father* – whom he came to know as his real *Abba* – from whom he received and experienced perfect unconditional love. *This* enabled him to suffer rejection and opposition in his public ministry, culminating in betrayal by one of his closest friends in his violent God-forsaken death on a Roman cross.

Yeshua grew up in the small rural town of Nazareth in the Galilee, the hotbed of Jewish nationalism and resistance against Roman oppression. He had four brothers named after the patriarchs and unnamed sisters (Mk 6:3). Besides this, his family's annual visits to Jerusalem for the Passover (Lk 2:41), show his parents' devotion to Torah and hope for Israel's deliverance. They would have taught Israel's story to Jesus and his siblings via the scriptures by daily oral repetition and memorization, as in the *Sh'ma Israel*: "Hear, O Israel: the LORD our God, the LORD is one. Love the LORD your God..." (Deut 6:4–9).

Thus Jesus grew up in the Jewish worldview of his day: *YHWH*, the Creator God, chose Israel to redeem the nations. Israel's intended means of mission – the Land, Temple, Torah, and Jewish Identity – had become boundary markers for spiritual and ethnic purity. She was still in exile, given that the Romans occupied the land and oppressed the nation. The expectation of God's imminent coming – his saving presence in his Messiah-King – was at fever pitch. They believed God's kingdom would come, Israel would be saved, then the nations – and creation itself – would be reconciled to God. Jesus found his identity and destiny in *that* story.

Alongside his parental formation, Jesus went to synagogue school for training in the scriptures, and in reading and writing. He spoke Aramaic with a Galilean accent, a Semitic dialect close to Hebrew. He also spoke biblical Hebrew, and possibly some Greek, the language of business and trade. His father was a *tekton,* a tradesman skilled in carpentry and building. From an early age, Jesus worked with Joseph and learnt his trade as an apprentice. He was not poor as in a landless farm labourer or peasant. In modern terms, he was a lower class (blue-collar worker), working hard in a small family business, helping the family to make ends meet.

This was the context of his spiritual formation. Luke is the only Gospel writer who gives insight into Jesus' thirty "hidden years" in Nazareth:[113] a summary statement on years two to twelve (2:40), repeated almost word for word for years twelve to thirty (2:52), interrupted by a brief lifting of the veil – a visit to Jerusalem at the age of twelve (2:41-51). Luke shows that Jesus had come of age *before* his Bar Mitzvah at age thirteen – if in practice by then – when he accepted adult responsibility to be a "son of the commandment", i.e. to take on the yoke of Torah obedience. However, he had already done this, evident from his debating Torah in the Temple with the rabbis, who were astonished at his insight and wisdom.

More so, Luke reveals Jesus' profound consciousness of *God* being his Father when his parents find him in the Temple after three days of searching. Luke clearly contrasts Mary's words, "your father" (2:48, Joseph), with Jesus' reply, "my Father" (2:49, God): "Your father and I have been anxiously looking for you… didn't you know I had to be in my Father's house?" That is, at the age of twelve, *Yeshua* already had a profound awareness of his identity and destiny: to be in his Father's house (presence), working with him in his business (kingdom)… to be the one to bring salvation to Israel. Thus, while Luke refers to his normal physical and social development, he emphasizes Jesus' significant psycho-spiritual formation in the wisdom, grace and the favour of God (vv.40, 52).

We need to go down to Nazareth with *Yeshua* to learn from his thirty years of spiritual formation. Our task is to discover, prepare for,

---

113 This is in contrast to the fanciful stories of Jesus' childhood in the Apocryphal/Gnostic gospels (rejected by the Early Church as false), "the Gospel of Thomas portrays Jesus as a self-willed little brat who, throwing a tantrum, makes a child who runs up against him drop dead", says Meier, *A Marginal Jew,* Vol. 1, 115 (see 112-141).

and grow into our *life mission* in the kingdom as Jesus did. He came to know God personally and intimately as *Abba* in a growing relationship of love. In so doing, he gradually understood his identity and calling in his Father's purpose for Israel and the world. Jesus did not wake one day with a sudden revelation, "I am the Messiah!" It was a growing consciousness of realizing his unique sonship, supernaturally confirmed at his baptism, a living into his name *Yeshua*: "*YHWH* saves". He formed his consciousness and entire being, developing all his human faculties – his will, intellect, imagination, emotions, sexuality, relationships, and money – to serve *Abba's* purpose in returned love for the unconditional love he experienced in each moment, to save Israel.

Four key factors in Jesus' spiritual formation:[114]

A simple life: Jesus led a simple and unhurried life, far from our busy, complex, possession-pursuing and technologically driven lives. He was uncluttered, with an interior detachment from material things, needing only the bare necessities to live. That led to a psychic and spiritual poverty, a true humility and trust, depending on his Father for his daily bread as sheer gift. This attitude enabled him to receive God's riches as pure love in each moment. No *thing* possessed him. He was possessed only by his Father. He used *things* to love people as an expression of his human empty-ness and his total dependence upon the all-ness of his Father.

A hard-working life: Jesus worked hard with his hands – not long stressful hours as in our modern world of work – learning his father's trade from an early age. They had to labour diligently for the simple things their large family needed to live. Not having our modern devices for amusement and recreation after a hard day's work, they enjoyed family time and Torah talk in the glow of candlelight till they fell asleep. Jesus used his apprenticeship to his earthly father, whom he called *Abba*, as a spiritual discipline to apprentice himself to his heavenly Father. He knew

---

[114] See George Maloney on Jesus' hidden years, *Alone with the Alone*, 74–84.

his Father was always working and he sought to work with him (Jn 5:17). Daily work became his discipline of discipleship, his worship of yielding his will to *Abba* (Joseph *and YHWH*) in each moment, discovering the joy of obedience. The monotony of daily work was transformed into a life of infinite value and beauty in his Father's presence as he learnt to do only what pleased *Abba* (Jn 5:19, 8:29, 38).

An obedient life: Luke says (2:51) Jesus was obedient to his parents during his years of formation – including the apprenticeship just mentioned. Obedience was not automatic; he had to learn it, often in what he suffered (Heb 5:8). By obeying his parents' wishes, he discovered his Father's wishes and learnt the joy of obedience. Jesus knew that the material world, especially of human interaction, was the "place" where his Father spoke to him and loved him, training him in the returned love of submission to legitimate authority. To love was to obey, and to obey was to return love. Jesus grew in the joy and freedom of a long obedience in the same direction, continually learning to say, "not my will, but yours be done".

A life of prayer and Torah meditation: Jesus' unhurried life was soaked in prayer and daily meditation on God's word. Morning by morning, he awoke early to listen and learn from his Father (Mk 1:35 cf. Is 50:4–5). He also received regular teaching from his parents and Torah school. He learnt how to pray, which above all meant a union of wills, of heart and mind, in love of his Father's presence of love. Jesus' Aramaic for prayer (*zla* and *zlotha*) meant tuning into God's wavelength, as it were. It meant literally walking in the communicating presence of *Abba*, to discover his love in every facet of his humanity, in the scriptures, in people and creation all around him. Prayer and meditation moved beyond an activity to a state of being inwardly turned and attuned to his Father at every moment in loving adoration and self-surrender. This is how he grew into an abiding consciousness of *Abba's* intimate presence dwelling in him, enfolding him, leading him. This practice nurtured his identity as God's son and birthed his destiny to save Israel and the nations as *YHWH*'s Suffering Servant, enabling him to die on a cruel cross as the Lamb of God, in hope of resurrection.

To conclude: In his simple life in Nazareth, Jesus patiently and persistently developed the habits of heart, mind and body – the character and godliness – needed for his life mission. The implications of this profound spiritual formation will unfold in the next chapter, and the remainder of the book. To follow Jesus in his kingdom is to follow him in his spiritual formation, making our lives a life-long Nazareth, a long obedience in the same direction. Thus our consciousness and all our human faculties become attuned to the Father's presence in each moment as personalized love. *That* defines us in our identity and particular life mission in God's kingdom, continuing what Jesus inaugurated, doing God's will on earth as it is in heaven.

QUESTIONS FOR REFLECTION AND DISCUSSION

1. Define what theology, and ethics, mean to you. What relationship does it have to spirituality? Why is it so important to keep them together?

2. Prior to reading this chapter, what was your understanding of the kingdom of God (or kingdom of heaven)? Has it changed in any way? How?

3. Is it important to understand Jesus in his humanity, in his historical context, as a Jewish rabbi and prophet under Roman oppression? Why?

4. How do *you* see Jesus – his self-understanding, life goals and aims? Was he *really* God's Messiah? If so, how did he "fulfil" the OT promise and picture of the kingdom of God?

5. What do you make of the secret or mystery of the kingdom of God that Jesus taught? How would you explain it in your

own words? Why is it important – especially with regard to its implications for Christian spirituality?

6. If the kingdom really came in Jesus, what are the implications in your mind? What do you think of my reducing all the elements of the kingdom's mission to four basic implications? Do you agree with them?

7. Why were Jesus' hidden years – long years of preparation for his public ministry – so crucial? What can you learn from him in Nazareth? How can you wrestle down your modern lifestyle into applying the four key factors of Jesus' spiritual formation in your daily life?

CHAPTER 5

SYNOPTIC TRADITION I: KINGDOM DISCIPLESHIP

> *"The time has come: God's rule and reign is near – within your reach. Turn around! Change your thinking! God is doing a new thing – trust him! Come, follow me, and I will form you into fishers of people for God's kingdom."*
> Jesus – Mk 1:15, 17 (RAP)

The City of God

The Greek philosopher Socrates once described with great eloquence the ideal way human beings should live and the ideal society in which they would be able to live as perfectly as possible. His disciple, Glaucon, objected. He did not believe such a "City of God" existed anywhere on earth. Socrates answered: "Whether such a city exists in heaven or ever will exist on earth, *the wise man will live after the manner of that city, having nothing to do with any other, and in so looking upon it, will set his own house in order*" (my italics).[115]

We have painted the picture, the outline theology, of God's kingdom, the "City of God" in Socrates' words. The Bible begins in the *Garden* of God in Genesis and ends in the Garden-*City* of God in Revelation, the heavenly New Jerusalem on the new earth. But this is only after a

---
115 Cited in Rollo May, *Man's Search for Himself*, 276–277, and Maloney, *Prayer of the Heart*, 1.

long, painful detour in the desert of human rebellion and sin: a long *disobedience* in the *opposite* direction. The turn-around to the City of God began in 2100 BC when God called Abram into a journey of trust. He lived in tents, "looking forward to the city with foundations, whose architect and builder is God" (Heb 11:10). His vision of that city defined his life, living in anticipation of its experienced reality. But he lived and died for it in faith, without seeing or entering it. The Hebrew prophets further envisioned and journeyed towards that promised city (e.g. Is 26:1–2 cf. 60:14), without experiencing its fulfilment.

John the baptizer signalled *the end* of the beginning, of what began in Abraham and Moses and gained focus and momentum in the prophets. Jesus signalled *the beginning* of the end, of what began in him – the fulfilment of God's City – and will end in him, consummated on earth when he returns. Jesus saw God's kingdom *so* clearly. It totally captivated him. He lived and died for it, fashioning his life to achieve its mission. He believed "the time has come" (Mk 1:15); *Abba* would make it happen if he faith-fully lived for it. During his hidden years in Nazareth, he formed his consciousness and spirituality, the whole of his being, to anticipate and work with God's kingdom come. Then he announced, inaugurated and enacted it in his ministry and death, and was vindicated by God raising him from the dead.

The City of God began to come on earth as it is in heaven, and people "stampeded" into it. But it was partial and in principle, not full and final, which is the strange mystery of tension and warfare we live in. It's *this* vision of the kingdom and its present reality that we now examine *with specific reference to the kind of person that life and discipleship in the kingdom produces*. In the words of Socrates: how to become wise and live after the manner of the City of God, setting our house in order.

Matthew, Mark and Luke are called the Synoptic Gospels because they are very similar, compared with John's Gospel. Biblical scholars work from Mark, the earliest Gospel. Here I work from Matthew and integrate material from Mark and Luke, due to my preferred approach by Matthew on this subject. While each Gospel needs a chapter of its own to explain its particular approach to kingdom discipleship and spirituality – following Jesus in his kingdom – space does not allow for that.

Matthew presents Jesus as the Messianic King inaugurating The Kingdom of Heaven[116] in fulfilment of the prophets – *experienced in discipleship to him*. Jesus saw his followers as the returning exiles that "exodus" into God's kingdom; the renewed Israel of the new covenant, a holy people living God's commands by his indwelling eschatological Spirit. I examine kingdom discipleship (and thus spirituality) in "The Greats" of Matthew: The Great Commission, The Great Confirmation, The Great Confrontation, The Great Calling, culminating in The Great Commandment.

Introducing discipleship[117]

The NT word for disciple, *mathetes*, means learner, student, apprentice – from the verb *manthanein*, to learn. It derived from the Greek philosophic schools: one who learnt from, became a follower of, a particular *diadaskalos* (teacher) like Socrates, or Plato, or Aristotle. The Hebrew equivalent is *talmid*, from the root *lamad*, to learn: a person who learnt from and followed a particular *rabbi* (teacher). The master-disciple relationship was one of learning through devoted servitude, companionship and imitation – almost bordering on veneration.

The OT has very few references to *talmid* and *limmud*, "one who is taught" (Is 8:16, 50:4). It's because of Israel's consciousness as an elect people, that they are discipled as a community to *YHWH's* will by obeying his *mitzvot* (commandments). God's authority was his word (Torah), not a teacher or prophet *per se*. This anticipated the new covenant: "All will know me by my word and Spirit in them, from the least to the greatest"

---

116 *Basileia ton ouranon* and the underlying Aramaic that Jesus used, *mulkuta di semayya*, are both plural: technically "kingdom of *heavens*" or "of *the heavens*" (see 2 Cor 12:2–4).
117 Brown (ed.), *The New International Dictionary of New Testament Theology*, Vol. 1, 480–493, and Longenecker (ed.), *Patterns of Discipleship in the New Testament*, 1–5. See also Peterson on following Jesus in discipleship, *The Jesus Way*.

(Jer 31:33-34 RAP). Mentorships from Moses to Joshua, Elijah to Elisha, were different – only later seen in terms of discipleship.[118] The idea and practice of disciples (*talmidim*) to a rabbi (rabbinical school) and/or religious party arose in the inter-testamental and Second Temple periods – before and during Jesus' time – the beginnings of Rabbinical Judaism.[119]

"Disciple(s)" is the common designation in the Gospels and Acts for those identifying with *Yeshua*. Matthew uses "disciple(s)" 72 times, Mark 46 times, Luke 37 times, Acts 31 times, and John 78 times. The verb "to follow" (*akolouthein*) and participle "those who follow" (*hoi akolouthountes*) are also repeatedly used of both the crowds who thronged to Jesus, and of his committed apprentices and close companions. The Hebrew equivalent of "follow" is the verb *halak,* "to walk", and *halakhare*, "to go behind in a way of life" (e.g. Jer 26:4). Thus disciples/followers were more than students or pupils gaining knowledge of Torah; rather, they gained a living knowledge of God by watching and imitating their rabbi, patterning themselves after his teaching and example – *his way of life*. Greeks used the word *peripatein,* their "walk about" or "conduct of life". Jews used *halakha*: the behaviour or conduct of the rabbi's "way of holy living", as per their interpretation of Torah obedience.[120]

The earliest self-designation of Jesus' disciples was The Way (*he hodos*, Acts 9:2, 19:9, 23 cf. Jn 14:6): The Way of Messiah Jesus – his *halakha* of kingdom salvation. Others later called them *Christianoi*: Christians (Messianics), literally "those of the household of Christ/Messiah" (Acts 11:26). "Christian" has all but lost its meaning in our day; similarly,

---

118 In the NT, Josephus and later rabbinic writings. Luke (in Luke-Acts) sees Jesus' relationship to his disciples (Early Church) as modelled on Elijah and Elisha; see Craig Keener, *Gift Giver,* 59–68; Meier, *A Marginal Jew,* Vol. II, 1041–47 and Vol. III, 41–49.
119 Technically, Rabbinical Judaism started after the destruction of the Temple in 70 AD. In Jesus' day, there were disciples of John the Baptist (Matt 9:14), Moses (Jn 9:28), religious groups (the Essenes, Saducees, or Pharisees, Matt 22:16) and other rabbis (Hillel and Shammai).
120 This more general usage of *halakhah,* probably used in Jesus' day, must be distinguished from its later technical usage (in the Mishna, 200 AD): legal rabbinic opinions and specific rulings that were binding on human conduct. See Meier, *Marginal Jew,* Vol. IV, 39–40, 65.

"disciple". Both are religious and outdated. Many now use Christ-followers, even apprentices, to emphasize the committed relationship of following Jesus in his kingdom, to live with, and learn from, and become like Jesus Christ. We cannot re-live our lives with Jesus two thousand years ago. We can, however, be discipled by him today because he's risen, and lives in his followers, apprenticing us by his Holy Spirit. *To be a disciple of Jesus is to live in relational interaction with him daily, learning moment by moment from him how to live your life as he would if he were you.* It is learning from him how to live life *in the kingdom of the heavens*, in "the already" – *and* the "not yet" – of God's Rule and Reign. "The Greats" in Matthew spell out what this means and how it works.

The Great Commission: go make disciples of Jesus

I start at the end of Matthew, The Great Commission (28:16–20), as it introduces the key elements of kingdom discipleship. Kingdom spirituality is mission and goal-oriented, to bring God's salvation to earth. Matthew makes these the last words Jesus spoke to his apprentices before ascending into the heavens – arguably his most important words. It's a vision of co-mission with Jesus to go to the ends of the earth, making disciples in order to usher in the new age (24:14). This episode opens with the eleven apprentice-apostles seeing the risen Jesus and falling down to worship him – "but some doubted" (28:17b, Matthew's realism of the "not yet"!). Then Jesus said:

> *"I've been given all the say in the heavens and the earth. Therefore, go in my authority to the ends of the earth and make apprentices of me from people of all types: Plunge them into the reality of the Trinitarian God – the life and love of the Father, Son and Spirit – and teach them to obey all I have taught you. Be assured, I'll be with you always, at your side – inside you – by the empowering presence of my Spirit, till the job is done and this age ends."*[121]

---

[121] My RAP is inspired by a paraphrase from Dallas Willard. Compare it with the NIV or NRSV.

The Risen Jesus sends his disciples to make disciples, *not* of themselves, but *of him*. How? By a) initiating all kinds of people into the Trinitarian God through faith in Jesus, immersing them into the reality of the Father, Son and Spirit. And b) forming them into the kind of people who routinely and naturally do all Jesus did and taught. We tend to make converts, Christians, "born-agains", and we baptize them; but do we make disciplined life-long learners of Jesus, committed to do whatever it takes to become like Christ? Willard calls this "The Great Omission": we omit to make *disciples* as in *not* teaching and training believers "*to obey everything I have commanded you*". *What sustainable plan does your church have to train and enable its members to do all that Jesus commanded?*[122] Think about it. Seriously. *Do you personally have such a plan?* The following key elements of the Great Co-mission can motivate you to develop such a plan:

A vision of Jesus: They saw Jesus, bowed down and worshipped him. The more clearly we *see* Jesus in his kingdom for who he really is – the Jewish Messiah as the Risen Lord – the more we will worship him in surrendered obedience. As we *repent* and *believe* (Mk 1:15), we *see* God's kingdom come in Jesus, in his life, death and resurrection. We *see* death and the devil defeated. We *see* Jesus given all authority in heaven and on earth, now ruling from the heavens by his Spirit. Such a vision takes us beyond our doubts to truly trust him. The only adequate response to God's self-revelation in his Son is to bow down in returned love of service to him: *our worship*. Seeing Jesus in worship is the source of true spirituality and mission.

Sharing in his authority: As we see Jesus having *all* authority, we yield to *that* loving authority in worship. We turn from our authority, our kingdom, from doing our will. We surrender to his rule in our lives, doing his will on earth as it is in heaven. We become his *disciplined* followers. I can only make followers to the extent that I follow. Only disciples have authority to call and make disciples of Jesus, of his kingdom – not of us,

---
122 Willard's question in *The Spirit of the Disciplines*, 258–265, and *The Great Omission*.

not of our kingdom! To the extent we come *under* his authority, we *have* authority. Then we share in his authority in real terms: he backs us up!

Living in the Trinitarian reality: The first act of obedience of a Christ-follower is baptism, a ritual initiation into God's kingdom and community. It symbolizes our cleansing in the death and burial of our past sinful life and celebrates our spiritual resurrection to a new shared-life with God. This is made possible by Jesus' death and resurrection, in which we participate by baptism. To be baptized "in the name of" means "in the authority of, into the nature and character of". Through following Jesus, we are immersed into the relational life and love of the Father and Son and Spirit – we literally "participate in the divine nature" (2 Pet 1:4). We live in this world from the reality of God's Rule and Reign of Love. Jesus' apprentices learn to do just that, living the meaning of their baptism day by day, moment by moment.

Training in Christ's character: Disciplined learners who live in the reality of the indwelling Trinity initiate others into that same living reality. How? By "teaching them to obey everything I have commanded you" – Jesus' *mitzvot* (commands) and *halakha* (way of kingdom living). This raises two questions. Firstly, what is *everything* he commanded? It is summarized in "The Great Commandment" to love God and neighbour as we love ourselves (Matt 22:35–40, the focus of the next chapter). Secondly, how then do we obey? How do we live this life of love? Is it by *trying* to obey, to love, when we need to do so, in the particular moment when it's required of us? No! By *trying* we quickly find that we regularly fail. Rather, by *training* we will be able, with the help of God's Spirit, to become the kind of person who ends up obeying. Training over time enables us to choose naturally to do, by our transformed nature, what Jesus would do in any and every situation. That is, we *grow* into the moral character of Christ. (I explain trying versus training in chapter 10.)

Experiencing the Spirit's power: Then Jesus promised: "surely I am with you always, to the very end of the age". The risen and ascended

Messiah companions us by his outpoured Spirit – not only with us, but in us – God's empowering presence.[123] In being students of Jesus, and making students of Jesus, we learn to rely fully on the enabling presence of his Spirit. We simply have to! We learn from experience. All our *trying* quickly shows us that we cannot do it on our own. The more we cultivate, rely and act on the Spirit's abiding presence moment by moment, the more we experience and exercise his power in real terms. The end result of obeying the Great Commission is *actual power* to do his will, to bring his kingdom, on earth as it is in heaven.

The Great Confirmation: the Father's baptism of love

We go from the end back to the beginning of Jesus' ministry, to his baptism, the prototype of Christian baptism. Jesus went to the prophet John in the Judean desert for mentoring, believing he was the promised messianic forerunner (Matt 11:7–15). He received John's end-time message of God's coming kingdom and his baptism of repentance. It resonated deeply with Jesus, confirming his understanding of his own identity and vocation – and that of his nation. John baptized *with water* to reveal the *Meshiach* to Israel (Jn 1:29–34). The Anointed Spirit-bringer baptizes *with God's Spirit* (Matt 3:11) to inaugurate a new Exodus of the Spirit, the kingdom of heaven.

Spirituality means having God's Spirit, being governed by him in every thought, word and deed. Jesus was empowered by the Spirit at baptism and became the model of Christian spirituality, of discipleship to *YHWH*. We follow in his footsteps: baptized in water *and* in the Spirit, to confront and overcome evil, to bring the kingdom by the Spirit's power. Jesus receives and gives the Spirit of purification, power, creation-renewal, and mission – all present in his baptism.[124]

---

123 Gordon Fee's phrase from his definitive work, *God's Empowering Presence*.
124 Jesus' baptism was an Early Church *midrash*: an interpretation of prophetic texts to reveal *Yeshua* as *Meshiach*; see Meier, *Marginal Jew*, Vol. 2, 106–107, and Keener, *The Spirit in the Gospels and Acts*, and my four missional implications of the kingdom in the previous chapter (footnote 104).

Jesus insisted John baptize him "to fulfil all righteousness" (Matt 3:15), i.e. to obey God's righteous requirement to identify with Israel's sin – and repentance – in view of God's imminent kingdom. He who had no sin went into the water confessing Israel's sin, symbolizing his death (and resurrection) for Israel: a new Exodus out of the exile of foreign rule – slavery to sin, sickness, demons, death. He saw himself as Israel's representative; Isaiah's chosen Servant who would suffer Israel's sin. As he came up out of the water, *three significant things took place*: heaven was opened, God's Spirit descended on him, and a voice spoke from the heavens (Matt 3:16-17).

"Heaven was opened" is God revealing himself in kingdom breakthrough.[125] Mark says "the heavens (were) *torn apart*" (1:10 NRSV), the same phrase he uses of the massive curtain in the Temple being torn in two, from top to bottom, when Jesus died (15:38). The veil between heaven and earth, between this age and the future age, is torn open at Jesus' baptism – as the separation between the Holy God and sinful humanity is removed in his body and blood on the cross.[126] Mark brackets Jesus' ministry with these events – his baptism and his death – linking the two. He is saying: Jesus' baptism is Israel's new Exodus out of sin through Jesus' death, burial and resurrection for sinners (Mk 10:38, 45). The heavens – closed by the sin of Adam, now opened by the obedience of the last Adam – literally underwent cosmic change. Cosmic-spiritual reality shifted, and things have never been the same!

Then the Spirit came and rested on Jesus "as a dove";[127] the power and

---

125 Echoing Ezek 1:1f, the vision of the heavens split open to reveal God's chariot (throne, kingdom); it also answers Is 64:1: "Oh that you would rend the heavens and come down."

126 Hebrews 9 and 10 says as much: the Temple veil separates humanity and God, this age and the future age. It is torn in Christ, opening the way into God's presence, opening this age to the in-breaking of God's ruling presence – "the powers of the coming age" (Heb 6:5).

127 Connoting Gen 1:2, God's hovering *Ruach* (Spirit) transforming and ordering creation from chaos; and Gen 8:11, the dove with the olive leaf indicates God making peace in new creation after the flood.

peace of God's new creation out of the judgment of sin and chaos. God the Father *baptized Jesus with the Spirit,* confirming him as the Prophet-King, Spirit-bringer. He was set apart (made holy) and baptized (empowered) by the Spirit to fulfil his mission, as in Is 11:2, 61:1 cf. Lk 4:16–21. Jesus ministered under open heavens, i.e. with kingdom breakthrough by the Spirit's power. People experienced and entered that power-zone.

The "voice from heaven" signified God speaking his will to Israel, confirming the gift of the Spirit and affirmation of the Son.[128] God said, "You are my Son, my Beloved; I'm so pleased with you" (Mk 1:11 RAP). These words unite the roles of *YHWH's* Davidic Son (Ps 2:6–7) and Suffering Servant (Is 42:1): "You are my Son, my Anointed, today I present you… my servant, my chosen one in whom I delight. I put my Spirit on you" (RAP). Thus God affirmed Jesus as his Messianic Son, calling him "the Beloved" (*Agapetos*) – an affectionate term of endearment.[129]

This meant the world to Jesus. These words from heaven supernaturally *conferred and confirmed* his election, identity and life destiny. It confirmed all that he dared to believe about his conception and birth (as told by his parents); about who he was in God (his growing consciousness and calling while working all the years with his father Joseph); about his vision and experience of God as his *Abba* (healing any remaining rejection as the *Mamzer* from Nazareth, now *knowing* he was truly God's son). Jesus heard *Abba's* tender voice, felt his warm Spirit-embrace – his delight and favour. He knew he was uniquely and perfectly loved *before* he did anything for God in public ministry! Hence he did not need to do anything (like ministry) to prove himself; to earn Father's

---

[128] "A voice from heaven" was known as Heb. *bat kol,* "daughter of a voice". It was God's echo, not his clear voice as heard in the prophets by his *Ruach* (the Spirit had lifted from Israel with the last prophet Malachi). See Brad Young, *Jesus the Jewish Theologian,* 19–22. The voice was heard *after* the Spirit descended on Jesus, confirming him as the Anointed Beloved Son.

[129] The underlying Heb. *yachid* means "one and only" or "uniquely beloved". The Septuagint (LXX) translates it *agapetos,* used of Isaac when God spoke to Abraham to sacrifice him (Gen 22:2, 12, 16), and of the mysterious "pierced one" whom Israel will see (Zech 12:10).

love. *Because* he knew he was loved, he was free to love, giving himself in returned love by laying down his life for others. It was a baptism of power *and* love, the power of *Abba's* love, to fulfil his God-given mission.

The Early Church saw Christ's baptism as the prototype for all disciples – the Christian baptism of the Great Commission. In water baptism, they laid hands on new disciples to be baptized with the Holy Spirit, to be set apart and empowered to do Christ's ministry and mission in love. This is how new followers were affirmed and confirmed in their new identity as God's *agapetos* children, the Spirit in them calling out *"Abba"* (Rom 8:15–16). Paul refers to this baptismal experience in Rom 5:5: "God has *poured out* his love into our hearts by the Holy Spirit, whom he has given to us." See my summary comparison of Jesus' baptism with that of all Christ-followers:

Jesus' baptism:	Disciple's baptism:
Mark of discipleship – obeying his Father's call	Mark of discipleship – obeying Christ's call to follow him
Identifying with sinners – being without sin, he confessed our sin (Mk 1:5)	Identifying with Christ – being sinners, we confess him who forgives our sin
Symbolizing his death, burial and resurrection for us	Symbolizing our death, burial and resurrection with Christ
His baptism/empowering with the Spirit – to accomplish his Father's mission	Our baptism/empowering with the Spirit – to continue the Son's ministry and mission
Confirmed identity – uniquely The Beloved of the Father	Given new identity – Abba's beloved child (Gal 3:26–28, 4:6; Eph 1:6, 5:1–2)
Live and minister in open heavens	Live and minister in open heavens

The Great Confrontation: the Son's defeat of evil

Evil confronted and contested The Great Confirmation of the Father's love for Jesus. Immediately after his baptism, Jesus withdrew into the desert to be alone with Father in forty days of prayer and fasting (echoing the traditions of Moses and Elijah after their ecstatic revelations of God, Deut 9:9, 18; 1 Kgs 19:8). This was an "opportune time" (Lk 4:13) for evil to test Jesus. Satan is never more present than after an ecstatic power-encounter; even more so when we pray and fast – if he cannot keep us from it in the first place!

However, the Synoptic emphasis is on *the confirming Spirit*, who actually *drove* Jesus into the desert *to be tempted by the devil*. The confrontation was brutal and lonely, seen in Mark's stark statement, "being tempted by Satan, he was with the wild animals, and angels attended him" (1:13). The three temptations attacked Jesus' identity and mission: "*If* (or since) you are the Son of God, then..." Reading the text carefully, the deeper dynamic was Satan's challenge to God's nature and character, as evil always seeks to do. Jesus defeated each temptation by using and obeying God's word (Matt 4:3–10 cf. Deut 8:3, 6:13, 16). In quoting Deuteronomy, Jesus recalls, and representatively identifies with, Israel's forty years of desert testing.

"My son" was first used by God *of Israel* in the Exodus from Egypt (Ex 4:22–23). Israel was humbled and tested in the desert to reveal their hearts. If they trusted the one true God, keeping the *Sh'ma*,[130] they would inherit the Promised Land. Where Israel failed, *Yeshua* obeyed, embodying and fulfilling Israel's calling as *YHWH's* Beloved Son. His baptism was the new Exodus. God's Fire and Cloud came on him, driving him into the desert to be tested on behalf of Israel for forty days (symbolizing the forty years). *Yeshua* overcame evil, proving to be Israel's

---
130 Deut 8:1–3 cf. 6:4–5: "Hear (*Sh'ma*), O Israel: The LORD our God, the LORD is one. Love the LORD your God with all your heart and with all your soul and with all your strength." The desert temptations challenged *this* – God's nature and Israel's (Jesus') trust and obedience to him in the *Sh'ma*.

true representative, God's faithful and loving Son, worthy to inherit the kingdom: the Promised Land.

After forty days of fasting, with pangs of starvation, the devil tempted Jesus to prove – or use – his Sonship to meet his own needs: "If you are God's Beloved Son, tell these stones to become bread. Use your Spirit-power to make manna as Moses did" (RAP). But Jesus did not allow his material needs and appetites to dictate – as Israel did in the desert. He refused to doubt God's love and fulfil his mission by taking it into his own hands. He would rather depend on *Abba* for the good life that comes through obeying "every word that comes from the mouth of God" – that was his food, his very life (Jn 4:34). It ultimately meant he would love God by giving his body as bread for the world (Matt 26:26).

Satan then tempted Jesus to do something spectacular and heroic to demonstrate his Sonship: "throw yourself down" from the pinnacle of the Temple – promising from scripture that God would save him. People would see the miracle and believe he was the Messiah![131] This pitted his Sonship against God's Fatherhood, demanding miraculous intervention to prove Father's love for him (cf. Matt 27:40–43). But Jesus refused to wow the people. Rather trust God than "put the LORD your God to the test", as Israel did in the desert. He would *not* provoke or presume on God as his Father to achieve his kingdom mission, let alone do his own heroics to impress or prove himself to others. God *was* totally trustworthy; he *was* secure in *Abba's* love.

Finally, Satan took Jesus to a high mountain and showed him all the kingdoms of the world: "I will give you *all* their authority and splendor, for it has been given to me, and I can give it to anyone I want. So if you worship me it will *all* be yours" (Lk 4:6–7). A shortcut to ultimate power; the easy way to rule as David's Son *without* being the Suffering Servant (also echoed in Peter in Matt 16:22–23 cf. 4:10); but Jesus said: "Get

---

[131] A later rabbinic *midrash* (teaching), probably from an oral tradition in Jesus' day, said Messiah would appear on the pinnacle of the Temple; see Young, *Jesus the Jewish Theologian*, 30–33.

behind me, Satan." Jesus refused this idolatry – which Israel had indulged in – having no need to find identity and worth in position, possessions, privilege, power or prestige. Why? Because he knew he was truly loved by God his Father. He would "worship the LORD your God and serve him *only*"; choosing a long obedience in the same direction, even to death, trusting *Abba* for the kingdom. God was indeed faithful, vindicating Jesus in resurrection, giving him all the authority (*exousia*) – thus the power (*dynamis*) – in the heavens and the earth, stripping Satan of his authority.

Satan left him only to return at another opportune time (Lk 4:13), implying spiritual warfare of varying intensity till Jesus' death. The Book of Hebrews says Jesus *learnt (the nature of) obedience* through what he suffered (his temptations, 5:8). Being God's Son did not guarantee obedience. It does not mean he disobeyed and then became obedient. Rather, from his earliest years in Nazareth, to the cross, he learnt obedience by praying in each test – at times with loud cries and tears, asking God to save him, and was heard because of his "reverent submission" (5:7). This made him "perfect" (5:9, *teleios* – mature, complete). His long obedience built the moral muscle that enabled him to say "not my will, but yours be done" when his biggest tests came – Gethsemane and Golgotha – at the end of his life. (It does not get easier the older we grow; the biggest tests are toward the end. We must develop the moral muscle for the long haul, to achieve God's full purpose and finish well.) So, Jesus was tempted in every way as we are, yet was without sin (4:15). He overcame Satan for us, modelling how we can defeat evil. He empathizes and helps us when we are tempted, as we confidently come to his throne to receive mercy and find grace to help us – because he ever lives to intercede for us at the Father's side (4:16, 7:25).

As with baptism, the Early Church saw Jesus' Great Confrontation as a *midrashic* (interpretative instruction) prototype for *all* Christ-followers. The devil tests *our* identity as Beloved in Christ; he tests *our* character and calling, by tempting us to question and doubt *God's* character. Satan uses daily life situations to tempt us with what is common to all human beings, summarized in the three temptations to…

- *be independent of God*: depending on *our* powers to meet basic needs; or
- *presume on God*: do things to test God, to prove his love for us; or
- *be God*: seeking identity, love and control in glory, power and possessions.

I must add how the monks, from the desert fathers and mothers, taught Jesus' three temptations through hard-won experience. The first is the *economic* temptation, our relationship to material need, countered by the *vow of poverty*: to truly trust God for all things. The second is the *social* temptation, our relationship to people, addressed by the vow of celibacy (*discipline of chastity*, see chapter 12): treat people purely as God's image, not to be used or abused for our purposes. The third is the *political* temptation, our relationship to power, defeated by the *vow of obedience*: worship God only, by obeying him, in bending our will to the spiritual leaders he sets over us. Re-read The Great Confrontation in light of this hermeneutic and it will instruct you.

The Great Calling: discipleship of the kingdom community

Jesus "returned *in the power of the Spirit*" (Lk 4:14) to lead Israel into the Promised Land, God's kingdom. His generic message, proclaimed wherever he went, was: "The time has come, the kingdom of God is near, repent and believe the good news" (Mk 1:15). It meant, in that context: "The end has come! Judgment *and* salvation are upon us. Israel's history has reached its climax. Turn to God. Change your mindset. Open yourself to what God is doing in his rule and reign – it's literally within your reach." This was Jesus' call to enter the kingdom, to be part of God's action by the Spirit's power, defeating evil and liberating people with healings and miracles into a new way of living (*halakha*) under his Rule and Reign of Love.

Jesus called people to enter this reality – to live in and from God's kingdom – by becoming his *talmudim* (disciples) in his *yeshiva* (learning community). This was truly radical, coming from such a young thirty-year-old rabbi. No self-respecting rabbi went around calling people to follow him; people chose their own teacher. *Because the kingdom had come,* Jesus boldly took the initiative with unique authority, calling people to apprenticeship in his kingdom community. Some left all to follow him in his mobile family – some for short periods, and some till his death. Others joined his movement, remaining in their homes and occupations, forming little local cells of followers (as did the disciples of the Pharisees and other groups in various towns and villages). It is clear that there were varying levels or circles of discipleship, relationship, commitment, learning and following:[132]

- the twelve, chosen "to be with him" as apostles to symbolize the re-gathered tribes of Israel – exemplars of discipleship (Mk 3:13–19);

- his mobile mixed-gender community (Lk 8:1–3), that grew and shrunk as he travelled around Israel;

- the seventy-two that he sent out after the twelve (Lk 10:1);

- many other supporters and sympathizers in towns and villages (Mk 2:15); and

- the large crowds that flocked after him.

Jesus' first call to discipleship was among fishermen on the shores of Galilee: "Follow me, and I will make you fish for people."[133] Beside the physical following of Jesus then, *this is the generic call to apprenticeship*

---

[132] See Meier's analysis of the nature and levels of discipleship in *A Marginal Jew,* Vol. III.
[133] Matt 4:19; Mk 1:17 NRSV. See Luke's version, 5:1–11.

for all people at all times. If he were calling builders to follow him, he would say, "I will make you build people for the kingdom." Or mothers of people for the kingdom, or business people for the kingdom, and so on. In whatever life occupation Jesus finds us, he calls us to follow him in and through that occupation *for the kingdom.* He seldom calls us to leave it, unless the occupation is a sinful practice. As Christ-followers, we live our kingdom *vocation* (calling and mission) through our daily *occupation* (work). We cannot physically follow Jesus today, but he still effectively disciples us in our daily life context. After his resurrection, he spent forty days weaning his disciples from dependence on his physical presence, preparing them for discipleship by his invisible presence by his Spirit, through his word, in his community and in his world.

My point is that the basic call to discipleship involves three essential elements:

- following – "Come, follow me";
- forming – "and I will make you" (to make is to form, see Is 43:7); and
- fishing – "fishers of people".

Discipleship to Jesus in his kingdom means *following* God in Messiah, being *formed* in his community, to *fish* his world for the kingdom. Let me introduce these three non-negotiable kingdom values. I discuss their outworking in the next chapter.

Follow me

Jesus echoed *YHWH*'s call to Israel to "follow",[134] when he led her out of Egypt through the wilderness to Canaan. Jesus meant: "Follow me as *I* follow *YHWH*, as Israel's representative, as *YHWH*'s obedient Son."

---

[134] Deut 5:1, 31, 7:4, 8:19, 10:12, follow *YHWH* – not other gods – by following his commands, i.e. "walk in all his ways". The Exodus generation died in the desert; only Joshua and Caleb entered the Promised Land, as "they followed the LORD wholeheartedly" (Num 32:11–13).

By following rabbi Jesus' way of holy living, his particular *halakha* or interpretation of Torah, people entered the kingdom and learnt to live in it as he lived in it – they were "born again".

Only in retrospect did Jesus' first followers understand they were following God. Jesus' resurrection vindicated him as Messiah, the eternal Son who came to reveal God to humanity – God incarnate. The point is, they followed Jesus *as a human being who followed God*, being deeply impacted by who he was, by his spirituality. They experienced the presence of *YHWH* in his presence, often astounded at what he did (his compassion and miracles) and taught.[135] Who was this man? They wanted to follow *YHWH* as he did – to be true Israelites, consummate human beings. His highest value was to follow *YHWH*, to truly know him, to live intimately with *Abba*.[136] Thus he initiated his apprentices into the same intimate relationship with *Abba* that he experienced.

We see this in Luke's emphasis on Jesus as a person of prayer, and thus of the Spirit: *"As he was praying"* at his baptism, the heavens opened and the Spirit came on Jesus (3:21); he *often* withdrew from ministry for prayer (5:15–16); he prayed all night before choosing the twelve (6:12); he prayed before disclosing his identity to his disciples (9:18); *"As he was praying"* on a mountain he was transfigured (9:28–29); his disciples observed Jesus praying and asked to be taught how to pray (11:1f); he prayed for Simon-Peter's faith not to fail (22:32); he agonized in prayer before his crucifixion (22:41f); and he prayed while hanging on the cross (23:34, 46). The result of this "intimate following", as Luke shows in his Acts of the Apostles, was a church born, empowered, sustained and exploding in and through constant Spirit-prayer.

"Follow me" pre-eminently means knowing God intimately: to

---

135 William Barry says that Jesus "provoked the same kind of awe in his first disciples and in Christians for centuries that the presence of God provokes." *A Friendship like No Other*, 156.
136 Spirit-intimacy is of higher value than obedience because, by nature, it leads to obedience. Caleb and Joshua obeyed *because* they had "a different spirit" (*YHWH*'s, Num14:24).

love the LORD your God with all your heart, mind, soul and strength. This first and highest value of discipleship is *the worship dimension* of apprenticeship to Jesus in his kingdom.

I will form you

This echoes *YHWH*'s formation of Israel as his holy nation, in preparation for the Promised Land. Imagine following *YHWH* through a fallible man, Moses, and being spiritually formed by him in a mobile community of over two million "stiff-necked" people, for forty years, in a desert? To follow Jesus is to join his kingdom community, to be formed in and through community. We follow *as church*. We learn to pray *in community*: Jesus taught us "*Our* Father", not "My Father". We follow his way, receive his word, and do his will, in the concrete expression of his local family of formation. Jesus saw his disciples, those who do God's will, as his *real* family – before his biological family (Mk 3:31–34). *Because the kingdom had come*, Jesus' call was radical: leave home or blood family, or any life-attachment that keeps you from "joining up", and follow in order to be formed (Mk 10:21, 29–30).

From a kingdom view, Jesus' family of disciples – his Messianic *yeshiva* or "church" – was (is) mysteriously divine and human at the same time. The church is a divine organism birthed by the already of the kingdom as its witness and instrument on earth, a sign and phenomenon of the coming age. It is God's Temple in which he now dwells by his Spirit, just as he dwelt in Jesus' flesh body. Jesus is present by his Spirit whenever his followers gather (Matt 18:20), i.e. church is an event of kingdom come. *But* the church is also a this-age phenomenon, a human organization living and struggling in the not yet of the kingdom, made up of sinning saints, institutional structures, fallible followers of Jesus. To opt out of (local) church due to the pain-filled not yet aspects of God's community is truly tragic. The mystery is that God uses *this* contradiction, *this* eschatological tension, as the primary means of (trans)formation of his family, The Church of Messiah Jesus.

For example, Jesus first called uneducated, smelly fishermen to follow him. Then he called Matthew the tax collector, a financial cheat who enabled the Roman occupation. How did he cope with the smelly guys? Then Jesus called Simon the Zealot, who was part of the "religious right wing", zealous for Torah purity and Israel's liberation – prepared to achieve it by violence. Simon had to face Matthew, a sellout to the Roman system and the most despised of Jews. They were ideological and religious opposites. How did he cope with Matthew's raucous party for Jesus, with serious sinners like drunkards and prostitutes in attendance? How could *Jesus* call *such* people to follow him, *and party with them?* Yet Simon and Matthew followed and were formed. Jesus was the reconciler who reconciled opposites in his community of reconciliation.[137] He was the glue that held together people who would not otherwise stay together. He spiritually (trans)formed them through "the opposite other" in his diverse community. It was radically inclusive, even of women; unheard of in his day (Lk 8:1–3).

We can choose our friends, but we cannot choose our brothers and sisters; they just arrive on the scene by God's sovereign design for our growth and maturity. We love God by *learning* to "love one another as I have loved you" (Jn 13:34–35) – those different and even opposite to us. God uses others to "press our buttons" so that we face our "stuff" in order to grow up! In short, God's ordained means of growth to maturity is being in family, with all the sibling rivalry, under God's fathering headship.

This second value of forming – and being formed in – local faith community is *the equipping dimension* of apprenticeship to Jesus in his kingdom.

Into fishers of people
God called and formed Israel to be "a kingdom of priests and a holy nation" (Ex 19:6) – not for her own status or enjoyment, but to enter the land and be God's witness; a model of his Rule and Reign of Love,

---
137 See my book *Doing Reconciliation*, chapter 5, for more on this.

bringing his kingdom to the nations. It was following and forming for a purpose. But Israel failed, and was exiled. By "fishers of people" Jesus meant – besides calling actual fishermen – the prophetic work of God's end-time messengers sent to announce the end of the exile. They "fish" Israel (Jer 16:14–16) out of the exile of sin, sickness, demons and death, into God's kingdom. Jesus inaugurated the kingdom, calling disciples – the returning remnant – to be *those* end-time messengers fishing Israel and the nations for God before the coming judgment. *All* disciples are called to follow and be formed *for the fulfilment of God's eschatological mission and purposes:* to bring the kingdom by fishing people for God, saving them from coming judgment.[138]

As already noted, Jesus not only called fishermen, but tax collectors and people in other occupations. Likewise, *all* disciples throughout history are called to follow and advance the kingdom in and through their daily occupation and life context. This is the ultimate fulfilment of the basic requirement or commandment of Torah, to "love your neighbor as yourself" (Lev 19:18) – which includes loving your enemy, as Jesus taught (Matt 5:44).

This third value of fishing the world is *the missional dimension* of apprenticeship, bringing us full circle back to our beginning, the Great Commission: go to the ends of the earth and make apprentices of Jesus from people of all types.

In summary: the kingdom framework of discipleship

We have examined the Great Commission, the Great Confirmation, the Great Confrontation and the Great Calling. Their common message is: *the kingdom of God has come in Jesus, therefore enter the kingdom by becoming his disciple.* Each "Great" adds particular content to what it

---

138 Jesus saw himself and his followers fulfilling *YHWH's* well-known role in the OT as The "fisher of people", both for salvation *and* judgment (Jer 16:14–16; Ezek 29:4–5, 38:4; Amos 4:2; Hab 1:14–17). See Lane, *The Gospel of Mark*, 67–69. These texts were probably the basis of Jesus' parable of the kingdom as fishing both good and bad fish (Matt 13:47–50).

means to follow Jesus in his kingdom – a growing vision of Jesus and his spirituality, and our walking in it.

This brought us to the basic framework of kingdom apprenticeship: Follow, Form, and Fish. As with the three-legged African pot, if one of these irreducible elements is removed, it collapses; it ceases to be Christian spirituality or discipleship. Our problem is selective obedience. We choose following in personal relationship and refuse to belong and commit to his community, the local church. We have been hurt and/or given up on "organized church". Alternatively, we pursue intimacy with God by withdrawing from the world, despising "worldly involvement". Or, some Christians and churches are so preoccupied with God and themselves, with little or no outside exposure, that they become cultish and incestuous. Other churches pursue social service to the extent it becomes their identity – they are social-care centres, no longer centres of worship and prayer. Others are so into church growth they become a business franchise, with little or no community and discipleship. We can go on with these permutations, but I have made my point: following Jesus is a package deal of God, community and the world; of worship, apprenticeship and mission. It's *this whole* "package" that leads to transformation.

Two concluding explanations and added values: we see from Jesus and his disciples that follow, form, and fish takes place as *fits the context* of their lives, with a view to establishing their identity in the kingdom as God's Beloved – *free to love*.

Fitting context: We do discipleship as fits our life context because it involves the whole of our lives, not just our spiritual lives. Discipleship is whole-life and life-long. So, we do it in a way that is relevant to our place, occupation and season in life, which shifts and changes as time passes. *We arrange and keep re-arranging our lives, learning from Jesus how to live our lives as he would if he were us*. We cannot be David in Saul's armour and expect to defeat Goliath. We must do what fits, what works for us in harnessing the whole of our lives into following, forming, and fishing.

Part Two: Theology

Freeing love: The heart of it all is transformation into Christlikeness. The great centre of follow, form and fish is being God's Beloved, in Jesus, The Beloved. To be-loved by the Father in his Son through his outpoured Spirit is to be free to live and love as the Trinity lives and loves. *To the extent we know we are truly loved by God, we are free to love truly – as Jesus did.* Few believe they are loved, or are worthy of love, due to conditional and manipulative love, and/or abuse and rejection. Few of us know how to be-loved, how to receive love, and therefore how to love. This brings us to the Great Commandment – *freeing love* – able to love God (following), one another (forming) and our neighbour in the world (fishing).

This is all so that *others* may also follow and be formed with us in community, to fish their family and friends to follow Jesus… an ever outwardly expanding (perforated) circle of inclusive love, the dance of the *perichoresis*. The outworking of this discipleship framework is discussed in the next chapter. See my diagram (Figure 6) of the five core elements and values in the framework of following Jesus in his kingdom:

Figure 6. The Framework of Discipleship

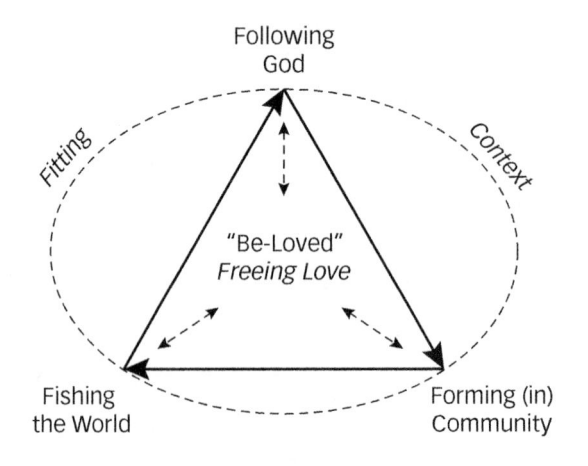

QUESTIONS FOR REFLECTION AND DISCUSSION

1. Has this chapter sharpened your vision of Jesus and the kingdom – the City of God, in Socrates' words? If so, in what way? How do *you* apply Socrates' advice?

2. What is your understanding of discipleship? How would you define it?

3. What did you learn from our discussion of The Great Commission? What of the Great Omission? Do you have a plan to end up obeying *all* Jesus commanded? Is it really possible to end up obeying everything…?

4. Why was Jesus baptized? Why was it so important for him, and for subsequent Christ-followers? Have you been baptized as a disciple of Jesus? How does his baptism give meaning to *your* baptism?

5. Do you relate to Jesus' testing in the desert in your life of discipleship? How? What are the most frequent or common temptations that you struggle with?

6. What is your response to the Great Calling to discipleship? What can you agree to and/or disagree with in my explanation of the call to discipleship?

7. Is the discipleship framework a reality in your life? How can you make it work for you? For your church? Which of the three core values – and/or the two added values – is weakest in your life of discipleship? What can you do to turn it into a strength?

CHAPTER 6

SYNOPTIC TRADITION II: THE GREAT COMMANDMENT

> *"Teacher, which is the greatest commandment in the Law?"*
> *Jesus replied: "'Love the LORD your God with all your heart and with all your soul and with all your mind.' This is the first and greatest commandment. And the second is like it: 'Love your neighbour as yourself.' All the Law and the Prophets hang on these two commandments."*
> Matt 22:36–40

The task of this chapter is to unpack the Great Calling, the Framework of Discipleship, introduced in the last chapter. We will do this specifically *in regard to Jesus' teachings* – his kingdom way or *halakha* – how to live and behave as the renewed Israel of the new covenant. In my terms, it's focusing on the centre of the triangle of Follow, Form and Fish: our spiritual formation to "freeing love", the dance of the *perichoresis*. It's living out our identity as God's Beloved, modeled in Jesus' spirituality – all with a view to fulfilling God's kingdom mission on earth.

By way of introduction, and in summary of all we have being saying thus far, I begin with the four life questions referred to in chapter 2, and compare the answers that the Greek philosophers gave with those of Jesus, as I understand it.

Answering life's basic questions

What is reality? For the philosophers it was the ultimate (superior) spiritual world of ideas, knowledge and wisdom, of gods and spirits. This exists hand-in-glove with (inferior) material reality and explains it. For Jesus, reality was the one Creator God and his kingdom – who and what we can count on in immediate and ultimate terms – breaking into the "reality" human beings have created for themselves.

Who lives – or what is – the good life? The "who" is related to the "what" in how we define the good life. Aristotle said life's goal (*telos*) was the good life of a flourishing human being with a fully formed character. He called this *eudiamonia*, "happiness".[139] People pursue the goal of happiness, meaning the good life of the rich and powerful, of amoral material prosperity, to live like the gods! For Jesus the *telos* goes beyond human happiness to his vision of God's in-breaking kingdom: the *Shalom* or blessedness of life lived in God's kingdom, open to all who follow him.

Who is good? Aristotle said those who are "perfect" (*teleios*, complete or mature – derived from *telos*, to complete the goal). For Aristotle, *teleios* was mastery over our temperament, appetites and behaviour, being able to do what is right by force of training to habitual perfection. For Jesus, as we shall see, the good or *teleios* person is the one who truly loves God and neighbour. Love completes or fulfils God's law – all that God requires of us – because love overflows with *his* goodness as the natural fruit of a heart made new by God's Spirit, rooted and growing in his kingdom of love.

How can we become good? Greeks had various answers: from *gnosis* and *sophia* (knowledge and wisdom), to mystical experiences, to strenuous self-discipline, to creating the ideal society that forms people into good persons. Aristotle taught three steps to become good: 1) get the end vision or *telos* clear in one's mind; 2) develop the *arete* or moral strengths – later called virtues – needed to get to that goal of being a truly good

---

[139] For this and further references to Aristotle, see Wright, *Virtue Reborn*, 30–33.

person; and then 3) moral training: practice those strengths or virtues till they become the habitual second nature of *teleios*. Jesus would have both agreed and disagreed. Discipline alone can never change and perfect us as God's good image-bearer. We need a new heart and spirit. Aristotle underestimated human sinful nature. However, when born again with a new heart in God's kingdom (Jn 3:5), Aristotle's three steps apply. We enter Jesus' kingdom with new life *and take on his yoke of disciplines and practices* – moral training. Why? To learn from him how to live the life of the kingdom as he lived it, because it's already in us by his Spirit. Taking on Jesus' yoke trains us in the habits of life suited to the future age, till it becomes our second nature in this age, because it's already our true nature in Christ.

Jesus was not in dialogue with Greek philosophers and he did not philosophize in these terms. As a Jew he theologized the essence of these questions in terms of Torah obedience. Our language of "morality and ethics" was Jesus' language of "doing the will of God" in his framework of Israel's covenant and eschatology – because he believed the end had come, was coming, and would certainly come. National salvation and Jewish spirituality was *the* debate in Jesus' context: how can Israel *obey Torah* and be the holy nation God intended *so that YHWH's* Messiah-King will come and save her from her enemies? Jesus' answer to this key question, on everyone's lips in his day, is well summarized in his invitation to eschatological rest.

Jesus' invitation to the good life: the yoke of the kingdom

Besides personally *calling* disciples, Jesus *invited* people into the kingdom, to follow him and receive God's end-time rest and lightness of being. "Come to me, all you who are weary and burdened, and I will give you rest. Take my yoke upon you and learn from me, for I am gentle and humble in heart, and you will find rest for your souls. For my yoke is easy and my burden is light" (Matt 11:28–30).

In typical rabbinic fashion Jesus quotes just a portion of sacred text to interpret and apply its context. He quotes Jeremiah 31:25 with its context of the new covenant (read vv.31–34) by which *YHWH* will "refresh the weary and satisfy the faint". Jesus invites the "weary and burdened", the returning remnant tired of exile under pagan rule, worn out by trying to be good by measuring up to the (old) covenant. Like beasts of burden overloaded by what others put on them, they carry "heavy loads" of legalistic expectation to be acceptable and pleasing to God (Matt 12:1–14, 23:4).

In quoting Jeremiah, Jesus speaks as *YHWH* calling people to *him: he* lifts their burden and gives *the promised kingdom rest*. Jesus is the end of the exile, the beginning of the new covenant, the gift of the new heart. He also echoes Ex 33:14, where *YHWH* says to Moses, "My Presence will go with you, and *I will give you rest.*" Jesus believed he was/is *YHWH* with us, Immanuel, God's personal presence alongside of us, giving us rest. When we come to Jesus we come home to the arms of the Father, we come to *know* him experientially (Matt 11:27 cf. Jer 31:33–34) in his end-time salvation of unconditional love, acceptance and forgiveness.

Then Jesus says, "Take my yoke upon you and learn from me." This is clearly apprenticeship as in following, being formed, to fish. Keeping to Jesus' metaphor: we are yoked with him to plough up "your fallow ground; for it is time to seek the LORD, that he may come and rain righteousness on you" (Hos 10:11–12 NRSV). We come into harness with Jesus to plow up our hard hearts, and that of Israel and the nations, in anticipation of the end-time rain of kingdom righteousness.

Jews in Jesus' day knew the phrase: "the yoke of the kingdom of heaven." They "put it on" by reciting their core creedal confession, the *Sh'ma* of Deut 6:4–5, three times a day. In practice this "yoke of the kingdom" (reciting the *Sh'ma*) meant gaining God's acceptance and rest by taking on "the yoke of studying Torah."[140] The "rest" that the Scribes and

---

140 Taught by Ben Sirach between 190–175 BC, in Sirach (Ecclesiasticus) 51:23–27. See D.A. Carson, *Matthew,* 277–278; and Jacob Neusner, *Judaism when Christianity Began,* 24.

Pharisees offered Israel was the heavy yoke of legalistic interpretation and literal obedience of Torah (see Matt 12:1-14). The rest that Jesus offered was God's eschatological Sabbath in the gift of *his* yoke of the kingdom: *the new covenant of Jeremiah 31*. This was Jesus' radical reinterpretation of Torah *because the kingdom had come in him*. The "wise and learned" Scribes and Pharisees just did not get it. But it was the Father's "good pleasure" to reveal it to the "little children", those returning to *YHWH* by coming to Jesus. They humble themselves in child-like faith in rabbi Jesus and his kingdom-Torah teaching (Matt 11:25-26).

Jesus' *gift* of end-time rest ("come to me and I will give you rest") was entrance into a life of discipleship ("take my yoke upon you and learn from me"), resulting in *sustained* rest in God's kingdom ("you will find rest for your souls").

Jesus' yoke is *the discipline* of discipleship: "Learn from me." How do we do this? By taking on his life practices, his spiritual disciplines, learning from him to live the life of the kingdom as he lived it in the "unforced rhythms of grace."[141] This grows his gentle and humble heart in us: the new heart and mind of the new covenant, on which the Spirit writes God's Messianic Torah. That changes us from the inside out. Yoked with him we learn from him, side by side, Spirit to spirit, step by step, as the One who knows God's way of holy living (*halakha*). Jesus took God's yoke in his years of apprenticeship in Nazareth, walking and working with *Abba* day by day, imbibing his heart, wisdom, words and works. We follow suit and "find rest for your souls".[142] The gift of rest becomes an abiding reality in the whole of our being. We live in and from rest, by relationship with Jesus. This fulfils the rules of Torah.

So we discover his "yoke is easy and (his) burden is light". The carpenter from Nazareth was apprenticed by his (F)father to make easy yokes. It only chafes when we pull in the wrong direction or go ahead

---

141 Petersen's phrase in *The Message*, in his great rendering of Matt 11:28-29.
142 Jesus is quoting Jer 6:16, i.e. "the ancient paths" and "the good way" lie in taking his yoke, in which we find (live in and from) eschatological rest. See also Heb 4:1-11.

of him. When we lag behind, he stops to gently encourage and humbly strengthen us. When he moves on, we either decide to continue with him or slip out of his yoke to live our own lives. He knows us well, better than we know ourselves, patiently pacing us without laying "heavies" on us. Our rest is in pacing ourselves with Jesus as he paced himself with *Abba*. He is not in a hurry. We must learn to live the unhurried life. He does not drive us, but gently leads us, having all the time and stamina in the world (literally) to do God's will furrow by furrow, field by field, as it is in heaven. Our long obedience beside him in the same direction forms and transforms us into his image, into the kind of person who naturally does his will, easily and joyfully obeying all he commanded. That is, if we remain long enough under his yoke, doing his kingdom practices, we discover that "his commands are not burdensome" (1 Jn 5:3). In fact, they are light (not heavy) and pure joy! They free and empower us to live and love as God lives and loves.[143]

Commonly, people try to be good and do right, to obey God's commands, *without coming under Jesus' yoke; without having the new heart of the new covenant*. It simply does not work. We cannot do it in our own power.[144] Then we conclude that God's commands are guilt-inducing ideals that cannot be obeyed, or that the yoke is simply too difficult, the cost of discipleship is too high. So we avoid it. Yes, it does cost us. It costs us our life;[145] only to receive *God's* life, love, rest, gentleness, humility, ease and incredible lightness of being. The cost of *not* taking his yoke, of

---

[143] Dallas Willard calls it "the secret of the easy yoke", *Spirit of the Disciplines*, 1-10. The Psalmist calls it freedom: "I run in the path of your commands, for you have set my heart free." (119:32)

[144] Aristotle's idea of disciplining ourselves into goodness by sheer habitual practice of the strengths or virtues leads to the problem of repeated failure and guilt, and/or the pride of self-made character (he was naïve about fallen human nature). Only God can save and change human beings. Jesus taught and modelled the humility of grace-formed character in those God saves – with their co-operative effort.

[145] As Dietrich Bonhoeffer said in *The Cost of Discipleship*, 99, "When Christ calls a man, he bids him come and die" – the costly grace of Christlike character, not the cheap grace of pseudo spirituality.

non-discipleship, is far, far higher. We pay the terrible price of weariness, heaviness, homelessness, guilt, condemnation, and exile from God, in the whole of our being. Life is far more difficult and "hard" outside of Jesus' yoke (Prov 13:15b).

The Great Commandment: the Kingdom-Spirit of Love

The context of law, holiness and love

Coming back to Jewish spirituality and national salvation in the face of fierce Roman occupation. Judaism was fragmented into various groups, each offering their answer to the crisis, their particular *halakha* of Torah obedience.[146] But there was an overarching hope that if Israel just obeyed – to be a kingdom of priests and a holy nation (Ex 19:6), keep the *Sh'ma Israel* and imitate God ("Be holy because I, the LORD your God, am holy", Lev 19:2) – *then* they will be saved as a nation. This was the dominant consciousness pervading Israel as the politics of holiness: be the holy nation that God intended *so that* he will send Messiah to restore the kingdom to Israel.

Politics is "ordering the life of the *polis*" (the city). Jewish life was ordered by The Holiness Code of Leviticus 17 to 26, centred in 19:2. To be "holy" meant "to be set apart" for God and his purpose. To be set apart from the "unholy", in Jesus' day, meant upholding the boundary markers that separated Jews from Gentiles: keeping circumcision and Shabbat, eating kosher food, dress codes, and all the purity laws governing every detail of daily life. These were like identity badges worn by true (holy) Jews. Righteousness was seen by outward conformity to prevailing holiness expectations, ordering life by shame (if you disobey) and honor (if you obey). The Scribes and Pharisees policed it, putting "heavy loads" on people. This conveyed and nurtured a view of ultimate reality as judgmental, needing appeasement – a legalistic and hostile image of God,

---

146 The Pharisees and Scribes, Sadducees, Essenes/Qumranites, Zealots, Herodians, Chief Priests and Elders; see Meier's study of each group's particular response to the times, in *A Marginal Jew*, Vol. III.

rather than that of a loving and merciful Father.[147] This represented a perversion of the intended purpose of the Mosiac Law, which was meant to make Israely holy, but failed due to the hardness of their hearts.

Jesus' end-time teaching (Messianic Torah) and lifestyle radically subverted and challenged this view of God. He enacted and inaugurated the kingdom as God's merciful intervention to save Israel and the nations – not because Israel was becoming righteous or holy – quite the opposite! Jesus understood from both the scriptures and personal experience that YHWH chose Israel for no reason other than *love*,[148] that YHWH is pure mercy and grace, faithful to his promises to the Patriarchs, seen in the self-revelation of his glory to Moses in Ex 33:18–23. This historical and experiential theology of God led Jesus to portray God as a prodigal father, scandalously excessive in his love for Israel (*read Lk 15:11–32*): a watching father (waiting for Israel's return from exile); a running father (welcoming her home); an embracing and kissing father (forgiving her rebellion, sin and degradation); a celebrating and dancing father (feasting with his people); and a pleading father (appealing to the self-righteous establishment to join the party, to enter the kingdom of Father's love and joy).

Jesus purposefully enacted *that* reality of YHWH's prodigal love in his life and ministry. He had kingdom banquets with sinners, tax collectors, prostitutes and drunkards (Lk 7:34 cf. Matt 21:31–32; one reason why the religious leaders rejected him). In this way Jesus, the Spirit-bringer, offered Israel the new covenant: "I will sprinkle you… you will be clean… I will give you a new heart and put… my Spirit in you, and move you to follow my decrees" (Ezek 36:24–28 cf. 11:19–20, 18:31). Moses prophesied Israel would be exiled due to her continued disobedience, but when restored, YHWH "will circumcise your hearts… *so that* you may love him with all your heart and with all your soul… you *will* again obey

---

[147] See Richard Niebuhr's four views of reality ("the total environment") as indifferent, or hostile, or judge, or friend, in *The Responsible Self*. Also Marcus Borg, *Jesus A New Vision*, 99–103.

[148] "Simply because YHWH loved you, he chose you and set his affection on you…" RAP on Deut 4:37, 7:7–9, 10:15; Ps 18:19; Is 42:1 cf. Jesus' baptism of love, Mk 1:11.

the LORD and follow all his commands" (Deut 30:6-8 cf. 4:30). Jesus saw the new or circumcised heart as the sign of the new covenant, made and sealed in his own blood (Lk 22:20).[149] Indeed, *he* was the enfleshed fulfilment of the new covenant, indwelt by the *Ruach ha Kodesh* (Spirit of the Holy). *YHWH*'s Torah was inscribed in *his* heart, governing his every thought, word and deed: the Living Word doing God's will on earth as it is in heaven.

Thus, obedience and holiness in *Yeshua's halakha* was the result of, not a requirement for, God's love, acceptance and salvation. Jesus embodied and offered *that* salvation by eating with people – among other practices of kingdom ministry. His followers were made and became holy – because God is holy – through sharing life with him in his costly gift of transforming love and grace, by the indwelling Holy Spirit. Thus Jesus decisively subverted and confronted the dominant consciousness, the oppressive politics of holiness, by his politics of mercy and compassion (Lk 6:36) – more accurately, his *halakha* of the Kingdom-Spirit of love.

The great love commandment(s)

In light of this, we need a closer look at Jesus' *halakha*, his *Messianic* Torah of the new covenant of love. What was his view and interpretation of Torah? Meier shows[150] that Jesus operated fully within Torah, in some ways more so than the Pharisees. Jesus clearly intensified the *moral* requirements of The Law (anger, forgiveness, sexual ethics, divorce and remarriage, truth telling, love of neighbour and even enemy), while relaxing other requirements; particularly ritual and ceremonial observance (Sabbath law, sacrifice, food laws, purity requirements). The latter is *the* point of

---

149 Clearly, Jesus taught and inaugurated the particular *prophetic stream* in Moses, Isaiah, Jeremiah and Ezekiel that predicted Israel's (exile and) restoration in a new covenant with a circumcised *heart* that by nature obeys *YHWH*'s will *in love*, enabled by his eschatological Spirit *in* them, writing his word on their hearts and minds: see Deut 4:25–31, 6:4–7, 10:14–16, 30:1–10 (v.6) cf. Gen 17:10–11; Lev 26:41–42; Is 43:6, 49:8, 54:10, 59:21; Jer 4:4, 9:25–26, 31:23–34, 32:37–40; Ezek 11:19–20, 18:31, 36:24–30; Rom 2:28–29; 1 Cor 7:19; Gal 6:15; Col 2:11.
150 In *Law and Love* (Vol. IV of *Marginal Jew*).

difference and departure for rabbinical Judaism as Jacob Neusner argues in *A Rabbi Talks with Jesus*. Jesus' nuanced approach and interpretation was to actually fulfil Torah's intent, not to undermine, negate or abolish it (Matt 5:17-20).

Furthermore, did Jesus have an overarching approach – a kind of interpretative key – to Torah? From the Mishna (200 AD) and Talmud (500 AD) we see the rabbinic tendency to reduce the whole of Torah to its "main point", to find and obey its "fundamental principle", so as to obey all commandments (*mitzvot*). There are various differing proposals in this regard.[151] In total there were 613 *mizvot*, with "The 10 Commandments" already seen as a kind of summary. Mark's Gospel (early 60s AD) has the earliest evidence of this tendency.

Mk 12:28-34: One of the teachers of the law asked Jesus, "of all the (613) commandments, which is the most important?" Matthew has "which is the greatest commandment?" (Quoted at the head of this chapter, see also Matt 23:23). Jesus answers by using a known rabbinic technique called *gezera sawa* (in the Tosepta, Mishna): joining two texts from different books for mutual interpretation if both share a common key word or phrase. Jesus, as Mark records, 1) cites word for word Deut 6:4-5 (the *Sh'ma*: "Hear, O Israel... *love* the LORD your God with all your heart...) and Lev 19:18b ("*love* your neighbour as yourself"); 2) joins them back to back; 3) prioritizes them first and second; and 4) concludes by affirming their absolute superiority, "There is no other commandment greater than these."[152]

According to Matthew, Jesus takes the conclusion further. *Love is not only primary in the whole of Torah, but actually fulfils it*: "All the Law

---

151 I am quoting Neusner in *Judaism when Christianity Began*, 25-27, where he lists many such rabbinical reductions in direct quotes from the Mishna and Talmud.

152 Meier's excellent chapter on Jesus' love commands shows how his answer, and its manner (these four points), is unprecedented and unparalleled in all of Jewish literature: OT, Apocrypha, inter-testamental writings, Philo, Qumran (Dead Sea scrolls), Josephus, the NT, Mishna and Talmud, in *Marginal Jew*, Vol. IV, 478-646. On *gezera sawa*, see 493-494.

and the Prophets hang on these two commandments" (22:40). "Hang on" means "depend on", "summed up in", "fulfilled in". Matthew's theme is that *Yeshua* actually *fulfils* the Law and the Prophets (5:17). He structures his Gospel with five narrative and teaching sections (Matt 3-7, 8-10, 11-13, 14-18, 19-25), connoting Moses' five books; thus presenting Jesus as the new Moses bringing the Messianic Torah in fulfilment of Deut 18:18-19. So, by implication, Jesus' great love commandment(s) sums up and expounds Torah in his life and teachings.

Hence my discipleship framework in the previous chapter is built around loving God (Following), loving our neighbour in the disciple community (Forming), and loving our neighbour in the world (Fishing) – which includes loving our enemy (5:44).[153] And we practice this, as fits our particular life context, in order to be "centred" in God's love, to be free to love as he loves – as embodied in *Yeshua ha Notzri* (Jesus the Nazarene) by the indwelling *Ruach ha Kodesh* (Spirit the Holy).

Jesus gives his double love command – triple love command if we include love of enemy – in the context of his eschatology. As angels love God wholly and completely in the kingdom of heaven, doing his will in pure love "as it is in heaven"; so likewise in the resurrection all human love, including sexual, will be transcended and perfected in God's love (Matt 22:30). *Because* of the kingdom already come, Jesus' followers are to love like those in the resurrection, like the angels, enabled by "the powers of coming age" (Heb 6:5) in the battle of the kingdom not yet come.

Therefore, the love that Jesus commands is more than a feeling; it's an action. It's not the Hollywood idea of love. For the Jews, love was intensely practical and tangible. It is covenant caring. Though love includes feelings – even passionate emotions – it's essentially *willing* the good of the other, as seen in the *positive* form of the Golden Rule: "In everything, do to

---

153 Meier shows, in the same chapter, Jesus' command "love your enemies" was equally unparalleled in all of Jewish and Greek (pagan-philosophic) literature, 528-551. Luke places Jesus' double love command in a different context (10:25-37), where love of neighbor clearly implies love of enemy in the parable of the Good Samaritan (Samaritans saw Jews as enemies).

others what you would have them do to you, for this sums up the Law and the Prophets" (7:12). Love is a *command,* a decision, to go around "doing good" as Jesus did, freeing people from evil (see Acts 10:38).[154]

In summary, the love that Jesus commands

- fulfils all that God requires of us in the Law and the Prophets
- is grounded in, and stems from, God's first love for us
- is a response to his "affection set on us" – our returned love
- flows from the "circumcised heart" of the new covenant
- is enabled by God's indwelling Kingdom-Spirit of Love
- is practised as intentional consistent (even sacrificial) doing of good, not as occasional random good feelings.

What follows is an overview of Jesus' teaching on discipleship from this interpretative key – God's Kingdom-Spirit of Love – based on Jesus' "Sermon on the Mount". This is a body of kingdom teaching Jesus repeatedly taught in parts or in whole, in various ways and places; remembered and reproduced by his first followers.

The Sermon on the Mount (Matt 5 to 7)

Like Moses, Jesus ascended a mountain (hillside) and gave his students his Messianic Torah. He began with beatitudes, the "Blessed be's" (5:3–12). Luke has some "Woe be's" (6:24–26; also in Matt 23). Jesus drew from Hebrew proverbs and wisdom sayings with their eschatological reversal of society: when the kingdom comes those whom we least expect will be blessed, rather than those we now consider blessed – the rich, the well

---

154 Meier says Jesus "articulates his teaching not in terms of philosophical virtues but in terms of concrete commandments cited from the Mosaic Torah – the obligations being expressed not by abstract nouns but rather by verbs with imperative force." (574). For an insightful study on *the practice* of loving, see Kelsey, *Caring.* The Golden Rule was/is widely known in Greek, Roman, Rabbinic, Hindu, Buddhist and Confucian ethical teachings, *but all appear in its negative form:* "Do not do to others as you would not want them to do to you." Only the NT presents the positive imperative.

fed, the happy – those we think live "the good life." The end-time reversal of fortunes is the key to interpreting Jesus' beatitudes.

They have been (wrongly) taught as *prescriptive* conditions – kingdom characteristics – to which we must all aspire: "Blessed are the poor, the meek, the hungry, etc". However, we are *not* blessed because of our condition. To become poor, mournful, meek, hungry for justice, merciful, pure of heart, peacemakers, and persecuted *in order to be blessed*, in order to receive the kingdom, is a works-gospel of performance spirituality. Correctly interpreted, they are *descriptive* of the true Israel on whom the kingdom comes – the returning exiles in Jesus' new Exodus. They are blessed not because of who they are, but because they turn to God in their condition. The blessing is not in the condition, but in the kingdom.[155] We are "blessed" (*makarios* means "so happy, to be envied", like Aristotle's *eudiamonia*) as the future kingdom comes upon us and *reconditions* us in the present – as we follow Jesus.

"The poor in spirit", in contrast to the spiritually proud and materially self-sufficient, receive the kingdom now as they (re)turn to God by following Jesus – thus they are blessed with God's rich resources. The same applies for the other descriptive beatitudes: those who mourn are blessed because they receive kingdom comfort in Messiah (citing Is 61:1–3); the meek inherit God's promises (Jesus quotes Ps 37:11); and those who seek justice, who show mercy, who pursue a pure heart, who make peace, who are persecuted for doing what is right… all find their particular fulfilment – blessing and happiness – in the kingdom that comes on them as they follow Jesus.

The kingdom re-conditions us from the inside out by its end-time blessings, producing true spirituality: the Israel and humanity God intended as his image-bearers. It is these kind of ordinary people – made extraordinary by the coming of the kingdom – that are the salt of the earth and the light of the world. *They* fulfil Israel's vocation by bringing

---

[155] Willard's phrase. See his incisive discussion on the beatitudes in *Divine Conspiracy*, 111–143.

salvation to the ends of the earth (5:13-16 cf. Is 49:6).

Like their Master, these followers fulfil Torah (5:17); having a *righteousness* to which Torah truly points.[156] It surpasses the righteousness of the Scribes and Pharisees (5:20) because, a) the kingdom's coming intensifies the ethical demands of Torah in fulfilment of their original intention, and b) the righteousness of the Scribes and Pharisees was about behavioural conformity to Torah obedience ("to get eternal life... to enter the kingdom", 19:16-24),[157] but without the new heart and Spirit that makes it possible. Hence it mostly produced judgmental hypocrites who said one thing and did another, misleading and even destroying others – seriously arousing Jesus' anger (23:1-39). Jesus' *halakha* of kingdom righteousness was the way of the new covenant, the gift of the new heart and Spirit of Holiness, producing "oaks of righteousness... for the display of (*YHWH*'s) splendor" (Is 61:3). Its focus is the inner transformation of the governing inclinations, intentions and motivations of the heart. *As we come under the rule and reign of the Kingdom-Spirit of Love, we are progressively transformed from inside out, enabling behavioural obedience.*

This becomes clear in Jesus' six contrasts or antitheses (5:21-48). He quotes selected commands of the old covenant saying, "you have heard it said", then gives *his intensified ethic* as the eschatological (new covenant) authority, "but I say". His interpretation fulfils what God originally intended in giving the Mosaic Torah.

Firstly, "You've heard Moses: 'Don't murder!' But I say don't harbor anger in your heart. Unresolved anger and hatred leads to murder" (5:21-26 RAP). Therefore, be quick to reconcile any disturbance in relationships *because* the kingdom has come.

---

156 Righteousness is from the Heb. *tzedak*, meaning faithful justice (God's covenant faithfulness that makes us faithful), in right standing with God, right way of living, doing God's will as it is in heaven.

157 Jesus endorsed the common view of "obey the commandments and you will enter (eternal) life – the kingdom" (vv.17, 23), but clearly implied *that* is fulfilled in *"follow me"* (v.21).

Secondly, "You've heard Moses: 'Don't commit adultery!' But I say don't even lust. The intention of adultery is as good as the act" (5:27–30 RAP). Adultery of the body stems from idolatry of the heart, which the new covenant remedies: "I will cleanse you from all your impurities *and from all your idols*. I will give you a new heart" (Ezek 36:25–26). Cut off adultery *at its roots* – lust-filled thoughts – as radically as cutting off your right hand if it causes you to sin. Jesus was *not* teaching self-mutilation; he was rather dealing with temptation at its source: thoughts and intentions.

Thirdly, Jesus rebukes divorce (5:31–32) and its abusive practice "for any and every reason" (19:3–9). Though he acknowledges Moses' concession of divorce – *only* for adultery, due to hardness of the heart – he affirms God's original intention in creation: the two become one, so what God joins let no one separate. The kingdom makes this possible because marrieds (learn to) love truly as God truly loves.

Fourthly, Jesus repudiates oaths, swearing by God or sacred things to establish one's truthfulness (5:33–36). In the kingdom there is no manipulation, deceit or lying, only transparent truthfulness! Be that now: mean what you say, say what you mean.

Fifthly, the kingdom moves us beyond retaliation, an "eye for eye, tooth for tooth", when insulted or injured. The kingdom moves us to conciliation: "Do not resist an evil person", rather overcome their evil deeds by sacrificial love (5:38–42, radical in the face of Roman oppression).[158] Kingdom justice is revolutionary forgiveness and generosity as seen in Jesus (Lk 23:34).

It goes further, lastly, to "love your enemies" (5:43–47). Here Jesus reverses the known interpretation of Lev 19:18 in the schools of Shammai, Essenes and Zealots: after "love your neighbour" they added "and hate your enemy".[159] The context in Lev 19 shows that the neighbour to be

---

158 Wright says the word "resist" (*antistenai*) in 5:39 is "almost a technical term for revolutionary resistance of a specifically military variety", in *Jesus and the Victory of God,* 291.

159 For example, the Essenes at Qumran in their Community Rule commanded love for

loved is the fellow Israelite, therefore (they said), it implied hatred of those outside God's community, the enemies of God. Jesus rejected this holy war theology – that sanctioned violence in God's name – asserting a strand of scripture that commands doing good to our enemies (e.g. Ex 23:4–5; Prov 25:21–22; Paul quotes the latter in Rom 12:17–21). Jesus' justification and motivation for this radical command is to imitate the Father in heaven who sends rain on the righteous *and* the unrighteous. The kingdom makes us children of the Father, living heaven on earth by imitating the generous and prodigal love of our Father – otherwise we are no different to others who only love their own.

Jesus' conclusion is: "Be perfect, therefore, as your heavenly Father is perfect" (5:48). This does *not* mean sinless perfection. As we have seen, *teleios* ("perfect") is the mature person who has arrived at the *telos* (goal) of becoming truly good. For Jesus, the goal is to be perfect – complete, whole – in loving God, neighbour and enemy. *That* is true goodness, being fully human in God's image, being the Israel God intended. Luke's version is, "Be merciful (compassionate), just as your Father is merciful" (6:36), powerfully illustrated in the parables of the Good Samaritan (10:25–37) and the Prodigal Son (15:11–32). Jesus' "be perfect" and "be merciful" restated what it meant to imitate God as per Lev 19:2, "Be holy because I, the LORD your God, am holy." Jesus interpreted and fulfilled the Holiness Code in the politics of love, not in legalistic conformity to holiness expectations.[160] Mercy heals, renews and grows wholeness (holiness) in the Kingdom-Spirit of Love. The end-time goal of Torah and the Prophets is the perfection of the Father's love and mercy, to which Jesus' apprentices are called. *How do we become like this?* Through kingdom practices.

"the Children of Light" in their community and hatred of "the Children of Darkness" outside their community (1QS 1:3–4, 9–10, 2:4–9), in Wise, Abegg and Cook, *The Dead Sea Scrolls*, 117–118.

160 This does not mean Jesus was soft on the *moral* sins (sexual and other) listed in the Holiness Code (Leviticus 17 to 26). In fact, he intensified their ethical demands because the kingdom has come.

Kingdom practices (Matt 6:1-18)
To become like our Father, to "be perfect" (mature in mercy, Lk 6:36), Jesus teaches certain "acts of righteousness" (6:1 NIV) or "practicing your piety" (NRSV). The OT language is "to do righteousness" (Ps 106:3; Is 58:2). The manner in which Jesus teaches is to expose the underlying assumptions that motivate the outward form or practice of piety (spirituality), by contrasting false hypocritical spirituality with genuine kingdom spirituality. He addresses three chief acts of Jewish piety: *alms giving, prayer,* and *fasting.* They are similar to Aristotle's practice of virtues for moral training until *teleios* becomes our habitual second nature.

Jesus introduces each practice with "*when* you…" not "*if* you…" (vv. 2, 5, 16), i.e. he assumes regular practice of these disciplines for his disciples. He teaches on *why* and *how* we do them, addressing each with the same structure of argument. Examine for yourself how he applies the following to giving, prayer, and fasting:

- The motivation in doing them is *not* to be seen and praised by people.

- The result or reward of such motivation is just that: people notice you and praise you.

- The right motivation is to do it for God – in secret, not in public, because in reality we all live before the audience of One – it's our gift to God. Only God sees and knows our hearts. We will all account to God.

- The result is that God sees, responds and acts in co-operation with us. God's kingdom power beyond us works in and through us, mostly unconsciously; and others see its outworking, and then they praise God.

It is sad to see how some spiritual practices have become public fanfare. Some church leaders draw such manipulative attention to monetary and other giving that it's like blowing trumpets before those who give, or who give the most (v.2, see Js 2:1-7). Gullible and desperate people follow such leaders in the tens of thousands. This is light years away from Jesus' teaching to not let our left hand know what our right hand is doing (v.3), to guard against the deceitfulness of our hearts (Jer 17:9). The point is that our beliefs and values are seen in our particular practices; how we do them. Mindless conformity to outward forms and rituals is religious legalism, whereas the transformation of beliefs and motivations of the heart leads to meaning-full rituals.

When it comes to prayer Jesus goes further than the other two. He emphasizes the absolute importance of personal uninterrupted private prayer: "go into your room, close the door, and pray in secret" (v.6 RAP). Prayer is talking to God *as your father*; not the superstitious repetition of empty phrases – as pagans do before their gods – believing the more intensely we babble away with words, emotions and raised voice, the more likely God will hear us. Having heard some pastors and people pray, I have felt sorry for God, hoping he has earplugs! Seriously, if we listen to *how* we pray, and observe *how* we do spiritual practices, it will reveal much about our concept of God – sometimes more pagan religiosity than personal relationship.

The Lord's Prayer (Matt 6:9-13)

Jesus teaches his disciples how to pray by giving them a model prayer. The so-called Lord's Prayer derives from the Jewish longing for *the* kingdom seen in the *Qaddish* ("Sanctification") prayed at the close of every Synagogue service.[161] Jesus' prayer interprets what *that* kingdom meant.

"Our Father in heaven" does not mean God far away up there in heaven. It addresses God as the Fatherly Ruler of heaven and earth who

---
161 The *Qaddish* is: "Exalted and hallowed be his great name in the world which he created according to his will. May he let his kingdom rule in your lifetime and in your days and in the lifetime of the whole house of Israel, speedily and soon. And to this, say, amen!" Carson, *Matthew*, 170.

is close and available to us, intervening in our reality (see Gen 21:17, 22:11, 15). And more so since the heavens were "open" at Jesus' baptism (Matt 3:16). Luke simply has *Abba* ("Father", 11:2), Jesus' typical address signifying his profound relational intimacy with God, which he taught his disciples.

The first three petitions are for *God's* glory: "Your... your... your..." May your name be hallowed asks God to fulfil his new covenant promise to sanctify (*qaddish*) his name in Israel and the nations (Ezek 36:23f). May your kingdom come asks God to manifest his rule here and now, and at the end of the age, in fulfilment of Is 52:7: "Your God reigns!" The third petition defines what that means: the kingdom is your will be done on earth as it is in heaven. Wherever, whenever the kingdom comes, manifests, breaks through, God's will is done as it is in the heavens. Thus Willard defines the kingdom as the range of God's effective will, where *in effect* his will *is* done.[162] I have my kingdom where my will is done. You have yours. So, praying for *God's* kingdom to come confronts my will, my kingdom. I am the first constituent of earth where God's will is to be done: "not my will, but yours be done" (Matt 26:39, 42 RAP). Are we *willing* to surrender to Love in all of who we are and have?

As we pray this, God's kingdom comes in us, and through us to the piece of earth around us: our closest relationships, our homes, workplace, community, and Israel and the nations. Rightly understood and practiced, these three petitions are subversive of, and revolutionary to, earthly and spiritual powers. God's rule relentlessly advances by "coming into play" in personal, socio-political and cosmic confrontation and transformation, till his will is done in all dimensions of created reality.

The last three petitions are for *our* needs, "us... us... us..." Give us today our daily bread is asking for tomorrow's bread today: the eschatological manna, or bread of heaven (in-breaking kingdom), that sustains the new Israel between the times on its way to the promised kingdom. Forgive us our debts as we also forgive our debtors, echoes

---

162 In *Divine Conspiracy*, 29–30.

the Jubilee of Leviticus 25, in which all debts were to be cancelled and all slaves set free every fiftieth year. Jesus' mobile community and his groups of followers in every town and village were to pray for God's end-time forgiveness now, *and* to model it in fulfilment of the Jubilee by forgiving others (v.12, 14–15). In other words, his disciples embody the revolutionary "year of the LORD's favor" (see Lk 4:16–21).[163]

And lastly, lead us not into temptation but deliver us from the evil one climaxes *the realism* of the mystery and warfare of the already and not yet of the kingdom. We ask God to not only keep us from daily temptation and sin, but also from the great testing that will befall humanity – which Jesus endured for us in the desert, in Gethsemane and on Golgotha. That is, we pray for (Jesus') victory over evil in all its forms, here and now, and at the end of the age, *because* the kingdom and the power and the glory belong *to God*, both now and forever more! Amen!

Kingdom treasures – absolute priority (Matt 6:19-34)

Regular practice of these and other spiritual disciplines, from a heart renewed with kingdom motivation, stores up "treasures in heaven" (v.20). This phrase does not mean being so heavenly minded we are of no earthly use. "Heaven" is not "up there in the sweet by and by"; it's a synonym for God and his rule actively present. Storing up treasures in heaven is developing a secret life, a hidden history with God, through giving, prayer, fasting and other such good works and spiritual practices. *That* is of eternal value, a growing "weight of glory"[164] that profoundly affects how we live our present lives. It becomes our very heart: "for where your treasure is, there your heart will be also" (v.21). Treasuring the kingdom above all else – to "seek first the kingdom" (v.33) – has a way of uniting our divided and fragmented heart into one life pursuit (see Ps 86:11–12). It purifies our eyes so that our "whole body (is) full

---

163 Jesus took Is 61:1–2 as his kingdom mandate in *actual* fulfillment of God's end-time Jubilee; see Yoder, *The Politics of Jesus,* and Trocme, *Jesus and the Non-Violent Revolution.*
164 As C.S. Lewis calls it in *Weight of Glory.*

Part Two: Theology

of light" (vv.22-23); i.e. we become generous, free from enslavement to money and materialism (the idolatry of Mammon), to worship the one true God (v.24).

Therefore, kingdom people simply "do not worry" about life's necessities such as food, drink, clothing, care and security – let alone life's comforts. "Pagans run after all these things" (vv.25-32).[165] Rather, our life-priority is to *"seek first his kingdom and his righteousness"* (v.33a). How? By regular spiritual exercises and practices in pursuit of the mission of the kingdom. Then, Jesus assures us, "all these things will be given to you as well" (v.33b) – life's necessities, with some comforts! We learn to trust God in his caring provision as our loving Father fully in charge of his universe – including ours! In the truest sense of what Jesus meant, and in Ignatian "indifference" to material needs, we can sing Bobby McFerrin's song: "don't worry, be happy!"

Jesus saw the kingdom, the Father's Rule and Reign of Love, as treasure hidden in a field, as a pearl of great price (13:44-46). For Jews, the coming of the kingdom was *everything*: it would literally save them and the world. Humanity also instinctively searches for this ultimate holy grail of salvation. When found, it's of such inestimable value that we are willing to joyfully "sell" everything we have to "get" (enter) the kingdom. Furthermore, if anything hinders us from entering the life of the kingdom we must "cut it off" (18:8-9) – even leaving our blood family if necessary (10:37-39, 12:46-50). This is precisely why Jesus taught his followers that the kingdom was to be *their absolute life priority*: pray "your kingdom come, your will be done" and "seek first the kingdom of God and his righteousness."[166]

---

165 Ignatius says, "It is necessary to make ourselves *indifferent* to all created things", using them to the extent they help us pursue the kingdom, and freeing ourselves from them to the extent they hinder us from it – in the Principle and Foundation of his exercises; Ganss, *The Spiritual Exercises*, 32.

166 Contrast this with *the priority Jesus set himself*: "*I* will build *my* church" (Matt 16:18-19). As a pastor I have found that when I seek *God's* kingdom Jesus builds *his* church. When I focus on building the church, I stop seeking the kingdom – then it becomes *my* church, *my* kingdom, *my* ministry – and Jesus finds himself outside *his* church,

The roots and fruit, heart and mouth reality (Matt 7)

Jesus' apprentices are not to judge others self-righteously as hypocrites do (7:1–5). Rather, we are to evaluate character by its fruit – how people habitually think, speak and behave, and what it produces in their lives and those around them. This is especially true of leaders whose fruit "comes out" in their people. Jesus emphatically says fruit is *not* seen in *charisma* – doing miracles in his name; but in *character* – doing "the will of my Father" (7:21–23).[167] We can do "signs and wonders" in Jesus' name without him knowing us. Once again, it's not a matter of being known, even admired by others, but *being known by God*. Fruit does not lie! "Do people pick grapes from thorn bushes, or figs from thistles? Likewise, every good tree bears good fruit, but a bad tree bears bad fruit... by their fruit you will recognize them" (7:16–17, 20).

Jesus repeatedly used this image to teach the source of character formation, whether good or bad, true or false spirituality. "Make a tree good and its fruit will be good, or make a tree bad and its fruit will be bad" (12:33). This brings us full circle to the beginning of the chapter: how does one make a tree – *a person* – good (or bad)? The answer is: by changing our nature, what we are rooted in, what our hearts treasure. "The good person brings good things out of a good treasure, and the evil person brings evil things out of an evil treasure" (12:35 NRSV). What is in us comes out of us, in our talk and walk, showing who we really are: "for out of the abundance of the heart the mouth speaks" (12:34 KJV). What is stored up in us, what we imbibe and dwell on, choose to believe and value, spiritually forms our being and becoming – revealing its character in our thoughts, words and deeds, for good or for evil.

Jesus explicitly says: "The things that come out of a person's mouth come from the heart, and these defile them. For out of the heart come evil thoughts—murder, adultery, sexual immorality, theft, false testimony, slander" (15:18–19). This is a repeat of his list of inner governing

---

knocking at the door, wanting *his* church back (Rev 3:20).
167 I discuss this in more detail in *Doing Healing*, 174–176, 305–308.

tendencies in his six antitheses in 5:21–48. Our fallen nature trains us from childhood to habitually practice its sinful inclinations in these and many other ways, forming us into its own image and likeness. Jesus was *not* naïve about fallen human nature, about its capacity for evil and its need for transformation. Neither was he naïve about the nature of evil itself.

We may be able to control our talk and behaviour by sheer willpower and discipline for a time, but eventually our true (sinful) nature breaks through. We can pretend or play-act ("hypo-crite") and thereby fool others, even ourselves, but we cannot fool God. It's what Jesus said of the Scribes and Pharisees, "You clean the outside of the cup and dish, but inside they are full of greed and self-indulgence. First clean the inside of the cup and dish, and then the outside also will be clean" (23:25–26). Our character slips out when we least expect it; when we are caught off-guard.

In short, we can only "make a person good" – change their *fruit* – by changing their *root*. We can only change our nature – who we have become by what we are rooted in – by entering and rooting ourselves in God's kingdom. We receive the new heart of the new covenant that progressively transforms us into God's image and likeness as we seek first his kingdom through its practices. *Then* God's thoughts, words and deeds, his nature and character, naturally and routinely begin to flow from the kingdom treasure stored up in our renewed hearts. *This* is what Jesus called being "wise" as opposed to "foolish" in his conclusion to "life in the kingdom"; his Sermon on the Mount (7:24–27). If we build our lives on the rock of the already of his kingdom, obeying his Messianic Torah by intentional spiritual formation of the gift of the renewed heart, we will withstand all the storms of life and whatever evil may throw at us in the not yet of the kingdom.

Lastly, the cost and reward of kingdom discipleship
Space does not allow me to touch on the other four teaching passages

in Matthew: the kingdom's mission (chapter 10), its mysterious nature (chapter 13), its forgiving community (chapter 18), and its judgment and consummation (chapters 23–25). However, I must conclude with a strong theme in Matthew (and Luke, and stronger in Mark): *the cost of following Jesus* in his Kingdom-Spirit of Love. Jesus' own personal following of YHWH in his kingdom mission cost him his life, only to receive it all back, and much more, in his bodily resurrection.

The story of Jesus in the Synoptic Gospels is also the story of his students. In following him they too – and you and me – journey to suffering and death in hope of resurrection. As quoted in footnote 145, Bonhoeffer's profound saying: "When Christ calls a man (a person!), he bids him come and die." Life in the kingdom unavoidably involves suffering. And more so the more we yield to God's rule and reign of love, increasingly obeying his commands in pursuit of the kingdom's mission.

Why is this so? Because we live the already of the kingdom in the war of the not yet – an all-out cosmic battle within us, and outside of us. Jesus said, "If you want to come after me you must deny yourself, take up your cross, and follow me. If you want to save your life you will lose it, but if you lose your life to me you will find it" (16:24–25 RAP). To deny oneself is to say no to your sinful inclinations and selfish interests; no to your own agenda in life; and yes to God – yes to what he wants. God's agenda is truly in your best interests, for your highest good. To take up your cross means being prepared to suffer and die for Christ's sake. The cross was a not a silver or gold jewelry piece to adorn the neck; it was a means of execution, a rugged wooden stake on which people were crucified – a symbol of cruel death. So, what Jesus said was extremely serious. Following him had the real possibility of martyrdom – as he was martyred for the kingdom he proclaimed and inaugurated.

Whenever our will and God's will cross, *that* is the cross we carry. At *that* point we choose to save our lives or lose them by dying to self: "not my will but yours be done." Jesus was able to pray this at the end of his life, in his final test in Gethsemane, triumphing over evil, *because he had prayed and practiced it daily*. As already mentioned, he *learnt obedience* through what suffered, by daily yielding his will to his Father (Heb 5:7–8). His long obedience in the same direction – to death and resurrection – led to his suffering in a world fundamentally disobedient to God, a world set against God. For Jesus, obedience was the ultimate freedom and joy of love of God and neighbour. In this age one cannot truly love without suffering. In the age to come love will be perfected, free from all pain.

In loving God by loving others, we go against the tide. If we truly live the kingdom, we are difficult persons to have around. People have to either join us, or remove themselves from us, or get rid of us – as happened with Jesus. We are in a life and death battle not of our own making. Jesus warned of suffering and persecution because evil opposes us at every turn, as the prophets experienced (5:10–12). We are like sheep among wolves; so be "innocent as doves, but shrewd as snakes" (10:16–31). Paul says, "Everyone who wants to live a godly life in Christ Jesus *will* suffer persecution" (2 Tim 3:12 RAP). In short, the great paradox is that if we live for ourselves – for "the good life" of self-preservation, security and prosperity – we lose our lives. But if we lose our lives in following Jesus, we find the good life – God's eternal life – an experience of resurrection power in this present age.

Summarizing the Synoptic tradition

Authentic spirituality is found in following Jesus, being his "disciplined learner" in his kingdom community, for the sake of the world. Jesus' life journey and spiritual formation is our model, our becoming. We embark on his same journey as:

- We respond to *The Great Calling* of "Follow, Form and Fish", coming under Jesus' kingship in his yoke of kingdom discipleship.

- We submit to *The Great Confirmation* of his water baptism, receiving the Father's confirming-love in Spirit-impartation.

- We are led into *The Great Confrontation* in the desert of this evil age, being tested by spiritual warfare as we die to our sinful tendencies – enforcing Satan's defeat already suffered at the nail-pierced hands of Jesus.

- We obey *The Great Commandment* of love – loving God, fellow believers and neighbours, including our enemies. It's the essence and whole of Jesus' kingdom ethics (end-time morality), the *halakha* or way of life that conforms to – enabled by – the coming of God's end-time kingdom.

- All in pursuit of *The Great Co-Mission* of the kingdom: making disciples of all nations, immersing them into the Trinitarian Reality, training them to live in and from that reality – obeying God's Rule and Reign of Love in all God says and does – through Jesus' empowering presence, till the end of the age.

QUESTIONS FOR REFLECTION AND DISCUSSION

1. What is your overall impression of this chapter? What has God said to you?

2. Without looking back at the answers, what are *your* answers to the four basic life questions the Greek philosophers debated? Do you agree with what I said Jesus would have answered?

3. What did the Scribes and Pharisees present as their answer (*halakha*) to *the* issue or crisis in Jesus' day – Jewish salvation from her enemies? What was Jesus' answer to this issue? (Do you agree with my explanation?)

4. How would you summarize Jesus' understanding and practice of authentic spirituality?

5. Why is love – of God and neighbour – so central for Jesus?

How does he define and practice God's double (or triple) love command?

6. How have *you* understood and defined love? After reading this chapter, has anything changed in this regard? How are *you* practicing (God's) love?

7. What is the role of kingdom practices or disciplines in spiritual formation toward Christlikeness? Have you *really* come under Jesus' yoke?

CHAPTER 7

JOHANNINE TRADITION: LIFE IN UNION WITH THE FATHER

"As the Father has sent me, so I send you"
When he had said this, he breathed on them and said,
"Receive the Holy Spirit"
Jesus – Jn 20:21–22 (NRSV)

This chapter examines spirituality from John's perspective in his biography of Jesus, written late 1st cent.[168] John does not use Paul's word for "spiritual", *pneumatikos*, discussed in chapter 2. However, he communicates the same idea via God's Spirit dwelling in Jesus and in Jesus' teaching on "the Promise of the Father" in John 14 to 16 – the eschatological Spirit indwelling his disciples. Like the Synoptic Gospels, John grounds spirituality in *Jesus and discipleship to him,* set within the inauguration of the future age in the historical Jesus.

After his prologue (1:1–18), John frames his Gospel, from beginning to end, with stories of the Spirit's coming and calling/following Jesus. In 1:29–34 the Spirit comes *from heaven* without limit *on Jesus* at his baptism, to "remain" on him,[169] revealing him to Israel as Messiah. This

---
168 I cite John's letters and Revelation when needed, assuming common authorship. For authorship, date, sources, context and historical value of John's Gospel, see Keener's comprehensive introduction in *The Gospel of John, Vol. One.*
169 Not lifting off again as in the OT. John uses "remain" (1:32–33, NIV, from aorist *meno*, meaning home-dwelling, abode-abiding), to refer to the Father and Son *dwelling* in

Anointed King will baptize all who follow him with the same end-time Spirit. This then leads into personal accounts of calling and following Jesus (1:35-51). Discipleship to *this* teacher is relational, experiential and transformational – he supernaturally reveals hearts and changes names (symbolic of identity and character transformation). Thus they believe he's the Messiah (1:41).

The Gospel ends with the Spirit coming, this time, *from the Risen Jesus into his disciples*, remaining in them (20:21-22). Jesus breathed on them, sending them into the world just as his Father sent him. This leads into post-resurrection stories of (renewed) calling and following, with even greater transformational effects (20:24-31, 21:1-22). Thomas' confession, "My Lord and my God" (20:28), in response to the full revelation of Jesus as *Messiah and God,* is the affirmation of faith of all disciples of all time – we who believe without physically seeing him (20:29).

It's all about Jesus and discipleship to him from beginning to end. *As* the Father sent Jesus with his indwelling Spirit, *so* Jesus sends his followers into the world with his inbreathed Spirit. *We are to be Jesus to this world just as he was the Father to his world,* bringing heaven to earth, nothing more and nothing less.[170]

Like the Synoptics, John's underlying framework is the Jewish eschatological hope of Messiah Jesus fulfilling the future age in this present age. Instead of using "kingdom of God" for this reality (used in 3:3, 5; also 18:33-37), John prefers *zoe aionios,* "life of the ages", translated "eternal/everlasting life" in our English Bibles. He uses it seventeen times. It has the same meaning as the simple *zoe* ("life") that occurs thirty-six times. John writes *so that* we may believe Jesus is the Messiah, and that by believing we may have *zoe* through him (20:31).

---

each other and in the disciples by the Spirit (14:20, 23). I use *indwelling* to indicate this mystical theology, not as a rational idea, but as an experiential reality of transformation into Trinitarian consciousness.

170 John's theme is: "As" the Father-Son relationship, "so" the Jesus-disciple relationship (we emulate Jesus except for his deity and redemption). John uses "as" (*kathos*) to mean both the standard (model) and the source (means) of the applied "so…"; see 13:34-35, 20:21, and footnote 195.

He also uses "heaven", "above", "not of this world", for the coming age; and he uses "earth", "below", "this world" for the present age (3:12–13, 8:23).[171] Thus Jesus comes from heaven to earth to drive out the "prince of this world" (12:31, 16:11; 1 Jn 3:8, 5:18–20). Though John clearly upholds the tension of the already and not yet (5:24–29; 1 Jn 3:2), he tends toward a realized eschatology: the future events – expected at the end when the Son of Man comes in glory – already happen in Messiah Jesus. For example, to believe in Jesus is to have resurrection now (11:25).

All this shows John's different use of language, source material and mystical theology. If the Synoptics are like climbing Mont Blanc in the Alps, John's Gospel is like climbing Mount Everest in the Himalayas, with many more challenges regarding the overlap of historical narrative, theological interpretation and layers of meaning. His distinctives are most apparent at the theological level, seen in Jesus' discourses; akin to Jewish *merkabah* mysticism (e.g. "eating" and "drinking" Jesus in John 6 is like consuming Divine Wisdom in some Jewish texts, inviting mystical contemplation of God). Clement of Alexandria in the late 2nd cent. said John differs from the Synoptics as a "more spiritual Gospel".[172] More so as we see how John sets Jesus and discipleship, Jewish eschatology and mysticism, *against the broadest possible horizons of the (eternal) relationships of Father, Son and Spirit* (though the formal theology and language of the Trinity only developed in late 2nd cent.).

Therefore, I examine discipleship and spirituality – spiritual formation toward Christlikeness – in light of John's eschatology and mystical theology of oneness with God. I use John's key words – Logos,

---

171 John's dualism is *eschatological* (also his light/darkness, spirit/flesh), not to be confused with Greek and Gnostic dualism, which is *cosmological*: the body/material world is mortal/dark versus the spirit/soul that is immortal life/light (the divine spark); see footnote 33 and Appendix 1.

172 On the reference to Clement and *merkabah* mysticism, see Keener, *The Gospel of John, Vol. One*, 49–50, 167–68. To minimize footnotes, my sources also include commentaries by Beasley-Murray, Calvin, Carson, Morris, Tenny and Wright (see Bibliography for details).

Life, Light, and Love – to guide us; concluding with comments on the mystical experience of oneness.

Logos

John opens his biography of Jesus in his prologue (1:1) with the words of Gen 1:1, "In the beginning..." In other words, the creation of the heavens and the earth, and John's implied *new* creation, began in the heart and mind of God as Eternal Community. His use of *Logos* – "the *Word* was with God... and was God" – establishes Jesus' eternal pre-existence (deity) and intimacy with God. He is the *extrinsic* disclosure or visible revelation of the *intrinsic* mind and nature of God as relational life, light and love.

John's brilliant choice of *Logos* communicates to both the Greco-Roman world and his Jewish readers. For Greeks it meant the word in God's *mind* that is also *spoken*. Applied to the universe, it's the thought and reason – the Divine Rationale – behind and in all creation. Jews used *logos* in the Septuagint (Greek translation of the Hebrew Testament) as "the Word" of God that creates and governs all things. It is *YHWH's* spoken word (Ps 33:6), his Torah revealed to Israel through Moses (Deut 32:46–47). But it's also God's wisdom – his mind, plan and will – behind his word. Both Wisdom and Word are personified as divine, existing eternally with God at his side, active in creating and governing the universe (see Prov 8:1f).

Creation's climax was God making human beings in his image and likeness to rule over creation – this was "very good" (Gen 1:26–31). John similarly climaxes his prologue with: "The *Logos* became flesh and made his dwelling among us" (1:14). This is God's *new* humanity created in Jesus of Nazareth, the last Adam (the new gardener, 20:15), exuding God's glory, governing creation with grace and truth. It's more than very good! Jesus restores God's image on earth as the *visible* source and sustainer of God's new creation in the midst of the old, making all things new.

The reality that the eternal God entered the human race, dwelling in "flesh" (*sarx*), is mind-blowing! John does not use *soma*, the dignified word for the body. He uses *sarx,* our meat and skin, mortal smelly stuff – frail physical temporality in contrast to God's glory and word that lasts forever (Is 40:5–8). God's glory shone through Jesus' lowly humanity (*sarx*), especially as he suffered our sin and death. His frail flesh was the lightning conductor connecting heaven and earth; energizing us with God's life, light and love – in livable proportions so that we are not vaporized! Contrary to Greek and Gnostic thinking that despised human flesh, God dignifies our bodies by incarnating himself in the historical Jesus – in anticipation of our physical resurrection, secured and assured in Jesus' own bodily resurrection.

John not only connotes the new humanity in the new creation in 1:14, but also echoes Exodus 33 and 34 – the new Moses on a new Sinai (Deut 18:15). God's Word (Torah) came from heaven through Moses in stone tablets. It dwelt ("tabernacled") in Israel in the Ark of the Covenant, glowing with God's glory-light (*Sh'kinah*). The ark was God's throne, the mercy seat, from which he ruled his covenant people by his Law. For John, God's full and final Word/Torah spoken from eternity came in Jesus, the new Moses. This *Logos* came not in stone, but in Jesus' flesh, "tenting" among us with the *Sh'kinah* of the One and Only God. Jesus is the embodied Torah of living obedience to God's commands. He is the new and living Temple, the Holy of Holies that makes us holy. He is God's mercy seat, ruling between (the cherubim of) grace and truth. He is the new covenant; replacing hearts of stone with hearts of flesh, on which he writes his Messianic Torah by the indwelling *Ruach ha kodesh*. The Spirit of Holiness enables us to do what God intends and requires: "the Law was given through Moses; (the fullness of) grace and truth came through Jesus Christ." (1:17)

John concludes his prologue by saying we cannot see or know God except through "the one and only Son, who is God himself" (1:18) – he has revealed him. In so doing, John differentiates the Father and the Son (the *Logos* made flesh). And he highlights the most intimate of relationships: the Son, "who is at the Father's side" (1:18),[173] makes him known to us. *The same phrase* is used in 13:23 and 21:20: the beloved disciple reclines beside Jesus with his head on Jesus' bosom, hearing his heartbeat, asking for a most intimate disclosure. Jesus is uniquely qualified to reveal God as Father due to his relational intimacy *"with God"* – repeated in 1:1 and 1:18. This *inclusio* opens and closes John's prologue, showing intimacy's absolute priority.

Therefore, if we see Jesus, we see the Father. He is God's "face", allowing us to truly see and know God without dying (Ex 33:20, Moses saw God's "back", v.23). Jesus' disciples continue his revelation of God's face to the world through entering *that* relational intimacy with the Father and the Son: just as the Father sent Jesus so he sends us into the world with the same intimate eschatological Spirit.

To summarize John's prologue, and his biography of Jesus: the *Logos*, who created and governs all things in eternal intimacy with God (and was God), became flesh in Jesus of Nazareth. This incarnate Wisdom and Word of God had *zoe aionios*, the Life of the eternal ages, in him. The Life was God's Light shining in the chaotic darkness of this world's sin and death. This Life and Light was the ultimate act of self-giving Love; God's personalized Love in Jesus – enfleshed in its fullest revelation on the cross. *To follow Jesus* is not only to be saved from sin and death, but to be given God's Life, Light and Love by entrance and participation in the relational intimacy of the Father and Son by the end-time Spirit. This is the clear message that emerges from John's progressive chronological use of Life, Light and Love.[174]

---

173 "Who is in the bosom of the Father" (KJV) or "who is close to the Father's heart" (NRSV): a most intimate image in ancient Israel of a son cuddled in the lap of his father, embraced to his chest.

174 I capitalize Life, Light and Love in this paragraph to highlight John's personification of these God-attributes: God/Jesus is Life… Light… Love (8:12, 11:25, 14:6; 1 Jn 1:2, 4, 4:8).

Life

The incarnate *Logos* has life in him (1:4), the life of (the new) creation. John has a Hebraic view of life,[175] deriving *zoe aionios* from Dan 12:2, "the life of the age(s)." The Heb. *hayye olam* is the eternal resurrection life of the coming age. This life is *God's* kind of life, more a quality of life "to the full" (Jn 10:10) than a length of life. God is life. He gives life as a gift, intended for complete wellbeing here on earth. This is Heb. *shalom,* meaning wholistic *embodied* life: spiritual, psycho-emotional, physical, relational, political, economic, ecological wellbeing, based on right relationship with God, each other and creation. As David said (Ps 16:9-11, 49:15), life is full fellowship with *YHWH* that overcomes mortality and the grave, with joy and pleasure now and forever in the future resurrection.[176] *This* eternal life has now come and is available in Jesus of Nazareth, the Messianic Lamb of God who takes away the sin of the world (1:29, 41). All who receive him are forgiven of their sins, put in right relationship with God (*shalom*) and thus receive *zoe aionios*.[177]

Those who reject Jesus (1:10-12), who refuse to believe in him, reject *God's* salvation. They will not see life, but will "remain" in death, separated from God. Their choice condemns them to perish under God's judgment on sin – God's wrath "remains" (abides) on them in this age and the age to come (3:16-18, 36).

Zoe is John's spirituality as in *salvation, growth, knowing* and *the Spirit.*

Salvation: Eternal life is salvation, and that life is Jesus: "I am the way, the truth and *the life*" (14:16). The "I am's" of Jesus imply that he comes

---

175 See Ladd, *A Theology of the New Testament,* 255-259.
176 Not a *disembodied* spiritual bliss in the "ever now" – the Greek idea of immortality as *timelessness.* Hebraic time is *linear:* this age and the age(s) to come, without end. See Cullmann, *Christ and Time.*
177 To receive Jesus is to be *born of God* with his Spirit-life (1:12-13, 3:3-6); to follow him in *relational discipleship* (1:35-39, 43); to *believe* him (1:50, 2:11, 3:15-16); and to receive *salvation* (fulfilling God's purpose for the Jews, 4:22). All four are synonymous and inseparable in John. *Discipleship* is seen in receiving and obeying Jesus' teachings (8:31); in loving as he loves (13:34-35); and in bearing much fruit in his life and moral character (15:8, 16).

as *YHWH* – the "I am" of Exodus 3:14 (cf. Jn 8:58) – to save Israel and the world. In story and teaching we see Jesus as the "I am…" the water of life (John 4), bread of life (6), light of life (8:12, and 9), good shepherd and door (10), resurrection life (11), Spirit life (14 to 16, 20:22), and true vine (15). They are all realities of the future age of salvation present and available in Jesus.

Going back to Dan 12:2, Jesus sees *zoe aionios* as *spiritual* resurrection in anticipation of our bodily resurrection at the end of the age (5:21, 25–29). This means "born again", born "from above" (1:12–13, 3:3–6). He echoes Ezek 36:25–27: the new covenant Spirit of Holiness cleanses (water) and indwells (Spirit) God's people, motivating and enabling them from within to do his will. This spiritual rebirth with moral empowerment is realized in following Jesus. It also recalls God *breathing* his Spirit into humanity in Gen 2:7 (creation), and into Israel in Ezek 37:4–10, 14 (new creation, resurrection). It's the same phrase John uses of Jesus *breathing* his Spirit into his disciples after his resurrection in 20:22: the creation of a new species of being human – spiritually resurrected or reborn children of the Father who live out his nature and grow into his image – as embodied and modeled in the Son.

Those *not* born of God are children of the devil who live out *his* nature by continuing in sin (8:42–44). Thus John's test of salvation-spirituality is character and behaviour, either godly or ungodly (1 Jn 3:9–10). In short, this impartation of life (not a gnostic quickening of innate powers or divine spark) makes us *spiritual* in the true sense, "of God's Spirit", seen in empowered moral change. Followers of Messiah literally "passover" (5:24) from death to life in a new Exodus, and live by the Fiery Cloud (the Spirit) in a new covenant, training for the Promised Land (our inheritance). In eschatological terms, we receive and learn to live the Spirit-Life of the future resurrection in the present, being progressively transformed in the whole of our being, training for life and rule in resurrected bodies on the new earth (Rev 21:1f).

Growth: Jesus models the relational and developmental nature of *zoe aionios*. The Father has life in himself, eternally pouring it into his Son (5:26), and experienced by Jesus in his humanity as a growing consciousness of his indwelling Father by his Spirit. Jesus was apprenticed to his Father in a shared life of love: "The Son can do nothing on his own initiative; he only does what he sees his Father doing – whatever the Father does the Son imitates. The Father loves the Son and shows him all he does" (5:19-20 RAP). *Likewise*, Jesus pours his life into his apprentices (5:21, 17:2); transforming our consciousness to his indwelling presence by his Spirit, teaching us to live by *his* initiative, doing *his* will in all things. Eternal life is growth with God to maturity.

Life, *by definition*, by its very nature, is the power to relate and assimilate. That is, life reaches out and relates to what is beyond and takes it in, to enhance its own life-properties. The organic life in a seed remains dormant until it's buried in the soil, then it draws moisture and nutrients from the soil to sprout and grow. As humans, we drink water, eat food, and breathe the air that is beyond us in order to live. Those who are inbreathed by God's Spirit-Life not only come alive with God's life, but ongoingly depend on *that* breath – Jesus' resurrection life, heaven's oxygen, God's Spirit – to live and grow into the fullness of *God's* life and character.

If we drink *the water of life* from Jesus, then a *spring* of eternal life starts in us (4:14). The thirstier we are, the more we drink from him, the spring becomes *streams* and *rivers* of "living water" flowing from within us (7:37-39). Others can then drink and live. Eating *the bread of life* becomes a feast of eternal life, of "real food and real drink" whereby we "remain" (abide/dwell) in him and he in us (6:53–56).[178] Jesus concludes: "Just as the living Father sent me and I live *because of* my Father –

---
178 "Eat" (*esthio*) in vv.51, 53 is "to bite, consume", a decisive action at the outset; while the present tense "eat" (*trogo*) in vv.54, 56, 57, 58 is "gnawing, chewing, feasting", referring to a progressive action to maintain a growing state. See commentaries of Tenny, 78, and Morris, 379.

constantly imbibing his life by feasting on him, to remain in him – so, in the same way, if you continually feast on me you will live *because of* me" (6:57 RAP).[179]

Knowing: No wonder Jesus defined *zoe aionios* as relational *knowing*: "This is eternal life: that they may know you, the only true God, and Jesus Christ, whom you have sent" (17:3). Real life is to know the only true God who is revealed in Jesus. No other god, spirit or belief can give eternal life. We experience the end-time blessings of eternal life to the degree we know the Father and the Son – specifically, the indwelling community of the Father and Son in the Spirit of love (14:23). This knowing is personal and experiential – acquired relationally, rather than rational knowledge acquired by study. *Ginosko* in 17:3 ("know") is used of sexual union in Matt 1:25. It's the Heb. *yadah*, "knowing" by interactive relationship, both as in sexual intimacy (Gen 4:1, 17) and in spiritual intimacy (Deut 34:10). Jesus fulfils the new covenant by enabling us to know God (*yadah*, Jer 31:34) in unmediated personal relationship by his indwelling Spirit – just as Jesus knew his Father intimately.

Jesus, the Good Shepherd, says, "I *know* my sheep and my sheep *know* me – just as the Father *knows* me and I *know* the Father" (10:14–15). The mutual knowing of the Father and Son was experienced by Jesus in his humanity as a relational shared life of growing oneness of thought, word and deed (10:30, 38). *That* is the model and means of the mutual knowing between Jesus and his followers. *Just as* his Father calls Jesus by name, "my Beloved" (Mk 1:11), leading him as he listens to his Father,[180] so Jesus calls his sheep by name, leading them as they hear his voice and follow him (10:3–4, 9). *Just as* the Father lays down his life, eternally pouring it into his Son, "begetting" him in love (1:14, 3:16); *so* Jesus lays down his

---
179 This eating and drinking in Jewish mysticism (fulfilled in Messiah Jesus) refers to spiritual practices like contemplating Wisdom (Sirach 15:3, 24:21), meditating on God's word (Deut 8:3 cf. Matt 4:4), and doing God's will (Jn 4:34). It's also seen in church history as referring to the Eucharist, the sacrament (means of grace) of receiving the body and blood of our Lord.

180 Jesus says he *only* speaks and does what his Father tells him (8:28, 12:49–50).

life for love of his sheep that they may live (10:11). We too, in following Jesus, become truly fruitful as we freely lay down our lives in love of others (12:24–26), generating life in them.

This shared life of knowing is a growing oneness of heart and mind, *evidenced in us doing God's will and works* (10:27, 30; 1 Jn 2:3–4); *just as* Jesus always did what pleased his Father in returned love of his intimate presence (8:29, 38). Jesus teaches this "life to the full" (10:10) from his own lived experience of *full* life with his Father, not from conceptual theology or ecstatic revelation. We will never reach the end of this fullness, of knowing God in the beauty of his shared life and love as Father, Son and Spirit. Even in our resurrected finiteness throughout eternity, we will never exhaust the infinity of knowing the Trinitarian mystery.

The Spirit: *The gift of the eschatological Spirit makes all this possible:* "the Spirit gives life" (6:63). Before Jesus died, he prepared his disciples to receive "The Promise of the Father" (John 14 to 16). The Spirit was given when Jesus was glorified in his death and resurrection (7:39, 20:22). He would not leave them as orphans: he came to them in his resurrection as "another Advocate" (NIV, *Parakletos,* 14:16, 18), whom he would ask the Father to send. "Another" means Jesus was their *Parakletos* living *"with"* them, while the Spirit will be "another Jesus" living *"in"* them (14:17), in order to make them "another Jesus" – continuing his ministry – "in" the world, but not "of" the world (17:15–18). *Parakleo* is "to come alongside" as an interceding advocate who counsels, encourages, helps and strengthens (us).[181]

The daily interactive life that Jesus' apprentices enjoyed with him as their enfleshed *parakleo* teacher-friend, is *the same life* that we now enjoy with him and the Father, enfleshed in us *by his Spirit,* as witness to the world. Therefore, the Spirit will teach us, remind and convict us, reveal truth to us, speak what the Father and Son say to us, and will glorify

---

[181] It's used elsewhere *only* in 1 Jn 2:1: Jesus is our intercessor advocating our defense at the Father's side (see Heb 7:25), while the Spirit is our indwelling intercessor/advocate on earth.

Messiah by making known to us all that belongs to the Father and Son – among other things (see 14:16–20, 26, 15:26, 16:7–15).

Light

Life and Light are universal religious symbols. Jews saw them as Wisdom and Torah; the means of God's salvation. The life described in the incarnate *Logos* is the light of humanity (1:4, 3:19), the light of the world (8:12, 9:5). John's allusion to (new) creation develops in 1:1–5: God *spoke* light into darkness at creation, bringing order out of chaos by the hovering Holy Spirit (Gen 1:2–4). Jesus is God's (spoken) word come as light (1:4) into the darkness of broken creation, bringing order out of chaos by the resting Spirit, and beginning God's new creation (1 Jn 2:8). The darkness could not comprehend or overcome the light (1:5): the revelation of God's salvation. This sets up John's eschatological dualism of light and darkness – symbolizing salvation and judgment (death), ethical purity and sin, truth and falsehood, belief and unbelief.

Let us look at John's spirituality of light as *salvation, truth,* and *glory.*

Salvation: Jesus fulfils the Jewish hope of end-time salvation as "the light of life" (8:12).[182] He is the "true light" (1:9) that eclipses the witness of John's "lamp" (1:6–9, 5:35), as well as all other would-be messiahs and false hopes. He shines into darkness, defeating sin and death, offering salvation to Israel and the Gentiles. The light (Jesus) shines on everyone, forcing a distinction between those who reject him (1:10–11) and those who receive him (1:12–13) – seen in the story of the healing of the blind man in 9:1–41. He received not only physical, but also spiritual and ethical sight. Jesus wholistically enlightens all who believe, while confirming sighted people in their spiritual blindness (pride) and guilt (unbelief). "For judgement I have come into the world, so that the blind will see and those who see will become blind... you claim you can see, (but) your guilt remains" (9:39–41).

---

182 See Ps 27:1, 36:9, 49:19, 56:13; Job 33:28, 30; Is 9:2, 42:6–7, 49:6, 53:11, 60:1–2.

Jesus was the Son of Man (9:35-38 cf. Dan 7:13-14) bringing the end Day of Judgment: "*now* is the time for judgement on this world" (12:31). All who accept him are saved; all who reject him are damned. The verdict is that most people love darkness and reject the light because their hearts are sinful, and their deeds are evil (3:19). They hate the light and refuse to come to it, fearing it will expose their true (sinful) nature (3:20). Darkness is not only the absence of light; it's the rule of evil in this age[183] that keeps people slaves to sin (8:34), children of the devil (8:44).

Those who see the light and believe (1:7), putting their trust in The Light, become children of light (12:36). No longer lost – walking and stumbling in darkness (12:35, 46; 1 Jn 2:11) – they have "the light of life" (8:12). Jesus shows them how to live life the way he lived it, as he is "the way, the truth and the life" (14:6). Therefore, "whoever claims to live in him must walk as Jesus did" (1 Jn 2:6). "The way" and "walk" are typical Hebrew words for choice of behaviour and lifestyle; either sinful or righteous (see Ps 1); either in darkness or in light; in lies or in truth (1 Jn 1:6-7). Jesus fulfilled God's righteous way of living as revealed and required in Torah – God's light for our path (Ps 119:105) – enabling us to do the same.

Truth: The light of life is not only "the way" but also "the truth" of salvation. John uses truth (*aletheia*) and true (*alethinos*) in its Hebraic sense: *emeth* is being true/truthful in relationship, reliable and trustworthy, applied to God and people. However, John does *not* exclude the Greek meaning of truth as genuine reality: what is true is real and reliable, not false or unreal. That's more a rational category while Hebrew truth is moral (relational, incarnational), though they overlap. As "the truth", Jesus is the incarnational reality of God's covenant faithfulness: he is the promised eschatological salvation as "the *true* light" (1:9), "the *true* bread" (6:23), "the *true* vine" (15:1). To follow Jesus and his teachings

---

[183] See 3:19-20, 12:35,46; 1 Jn 1:5-6, 2:8-9, 11.

is to "know the truth" that "sets you free" from slavery to sin, lies and falsehood – from the very nature of the devil, who "did not hold to the truth, for there is no truth in him" (8:31–32, 34, 36, 44).

To trust God is to trust Jesus (14:1), thereby entering a true trustworthy relationship with God. And this happens by "the Spirit of Truth", who indwells and enables us to live truthfully in a new covenant (14:17, 16:13; 1 Jn 4:6). That is why those who "live by the truth come to the light", revealing their true nature as God's people with God-enabled character (3:20–21). These are the "true worshippers" the Father seeks (4:23).

John's test of truth/reality is simple: if we claim to be in the light of God and yet walk in darkness, we lie and do not live by the truth. But if we walk in the light as he is in the light, we have *koinonia* (shared transparent life) with God and other light-walkers, confessing and receiving forgiveness whenever we sin (1 Jn 1:6–7). Again, true spirituality is seen in how we live, in conduct and character.

Glory: John relates light to God's glory (1:14, *doxa*), revealed and restored to Israel and humanity in Jesus. God first dwelt in the temple of creation, the Garden, filled with his glory – including Adam and Eve's radiant bodies.[184] But their rebellion put the lights out! Then God came in acts of power and deliverance, manifesting his glory (Heb. *kabod*). His glory was also seen as his nearness or personal presence manifested as fire and cloud (divine light, *Sh'kinah*); seen in the Exodus, at Sinai, in Moses' tabernacle and Solomon's Temple. God was "glorified" (enthroned, exalted) when *Kabod YHWH* ("The Glory of the LORD") dwelt in the Holy of Holies on the mercy seat, between two cherubim, ruling Israel. However, Israel's repeated sin led to *Kabod YHWH* departing (*ichabod*) from the Temple, followed by Israel's exile. God promised to restore his luminous glory in a new Temple in "the Day of the LORD." *Then* knowledge of the glory of the LORD will fill the earth as the waters cover the sea. The end-time glory of *that* latter Temple would be far greater than the former.[185]

---

184 For this section on glory see Beale, *The Temple and the Church's Mission*.
185 For this paragraph, see Ex 24:15–17, 25:22, 33:9–23, 34:29–35; 1 Sam 4:4, 21;

There is no record of *Kabod YHWH* returning to Israel after her restoration from exile, or after King Herod rebuilt the Temple from 20 BC to 26 AD. While Herod was building his Temple the true Jewish King was born. Jesus' birth was the Day of the LORD: the eternal *Logos* became flesh, filled with *Kabod YHWH* (1:14). He was the new Adam and new Temple. God's nearness, his manifest presence, had returned to Israel. Eyes of faith saw God's *Sh'kinah* in Jesus' body, the end-time Temple (2:18–22). This "latter Temple" glowed with far greater glory as the place of God's dwelling, of forgiveness of sins (1:29), of healing and miracles (2:11, 5:1–15, 11:4, 40). Jesus is the Temple where God is worshipped in spirit and truth (4:23–24). It spelt judgment on Herod's magnificent man-made, world-renowned, but empty-corrupt Temple. Jesus prophetically enacted *that* judgment in the Temple (2:13–17), then took it into his body on the cross – delivering all who turn to him – vindicated by bodily resurrection (2:18–23). The Romans destroyed Herod's Temple in 70AD.

The Synoptics show the glory returning to Israel in Jesus' transfiguration on Mount Tabor, prefiguring his glorification in resurrection and ascension to his throne on Mount Zion (heavenly Jerusalem). John, in stark contrast, sees the *Kabod YHWH* returning in Jesus' lowly humanity; shining through his frail flesh in his incarnation, life and ministry; climaxing in his greatest reveal: "*lifted up*" – exalted and glorified – in his crucifixion (3:14–15, 12:32–33). His entire life was a transfiguration of ever-brighter *Sh'kinah* culminating in glorification: his betrayal and death (13:30–32).

This is dramatically portrayed when Pilate presented Jesus to the crowds, flogged and beaten, with a crown of thorns thrust on his head: "*Behold* the man… *Behold* your King" (19:5, 14 KJV). John is saying, *this* literally fulfils Isaiah's prophecy, "Your eyes will see the king in his beauty" (33:17), which turns out to be the suffering Servant-King in 52:13f: "*See* my servant… raised and *lifted up* and *highly exalted*… his appearance was so disfigured… his form marred beyond human likeness." *This* is the One

---

2 Chron 7:1–3; Ezek 9 and 10, 43:1–9; Is 60:1–3, 66:18; Hab 2:14; Hag 2:6–9.

who is (reveals) the luminous beauty of the *Kabod YHWH* in Is 6:1-4: "I saw the LORD seated on a throne, *high and exalted*", his glory filled the Temple. John concludes, "Isaiah... *saw* Jesus' glory and spoke about him" (12:38-41) – after he quotes Is 53:1f. *This* is it! We are full circle back to 1:14: *this bloody man* is The King in all his glory. Presented on Good Friday, the sixth day of creation, he is humanity made in God's likeness, *the true image of the true God, the crucified God*.[186] *This* Jesus is the climax of creation, God's redeemed humanity, ruling his new creation from the cross – revealing how "very good" God is (Gen 1:26-31).

Jesus personalized Isaiah's prophetic theology by seeing and believing his own death as his glorious eschatological enthronement (12:20-33). The cross was his throne: God's mercy seat between two thieves where his blood of sacrifice was sprinkled, where he ruled in judgment of the world, driving out the prince of this world, drawing all nations to himself to drink deeply of the water and blood that flows from his pierced side – his Spirit poured out for all who are thirsty (19:33-37 cf. 7:37-39; 1 Jn 5:6-12). This is the end-time river of living water flowing from under the threshold of the new Temple (Jesus and his followers, Ezek 47:1-12 cf. Jn 7:38-39), bringing life, healing and fruitfulness wherever it goes to the ends of the earth. It is the renewal of the first river of Gen 2:10-14, now flowing from a new Garden of Eden, watering the new earth already begun in Messiah Jesus.

Jesus expressly came and lived for "this hour" of glorification by his Father (12:23, 27-28, 17:1). He gave glory to his Father by completing his work, returning to the glory he had with him before the world began (17:1, 4-5). Jesus gave his disciples *the glory* his Father gave him (17:22) *by revealing the Father in the Spirit of truth* (16:14-15, 17:6-8). In turn they will give him glory (17:10) by completing his work of witness to

---

[186] The title of Moltmann's acclaimed book on God's suffering love in Jesus. See Wright's insightful explanation of "Here's the Man!" in *John for Everyone*, Part Two, 116-120. See also Fiddes, *The Creative Suffering of God,* who dialogues with Barth, Moltmann, Tillich, and others on this theme.

the world (17:22-23). Jesus sanctified himself, setting himself apart to do his Father's mission, *so that* we too may be set apart (sanctified by the truth) to do his mission: "As you sent me into the world, I have sent them into the world" (17:17-19). And as with Jesus, this mission leads to *our* death: our daily dying to self and eventual physical death, by which God glorifies us and we glorify God in pure joy – with ever brighter numinous (12:24-25, 21:19).[187] *Then* we will be with Jesus where he is, seeing and sharing in his eternal glory with the Father in consummated love (17:24). Wright rightly concludes his chapter on *The Glory of God in John's Gospel* by saying, "This is John's ultimate vision of the nature of Christian discipleship."[188]

Love

Pause for a moment in the glorious light, the *Sh'kinah* of the inner sanctum. We stand on *the* most holy ground: The Love of God enfleshed in Christ on the cross.

John's eschatology fuses the horizons of eternity past and future in the historical Jesus. At a point in eternity, the infinite mystery beyond all grasp that we call God, silent and invisible, exploded outward in love, creating all things. Then stepped into finite creation *as love*. God, without becoming any less than God, entered the human race as a vulnerable baby, the eternal *Logos* (pre-incarnate Son) made flesh. In him was the life of the future ages, the light of the world, sacrificed on a cruel cross to save creation turned against God. *This* is Love – God's ultimate act of love from eternity – enfleshed and personalized in Jesus of Nazareth. This is *in deed* the revealed mystery of love, enabling us to know and love God. As Karl Rahner said, "We find God because

---

187 We fulfill Dan 12:3, "The wise will shine like the brightness of the heavens, and those who lead many to righteousness, like the stars forever and ever." And Prov 4:18, "The path of the righteous is like the first gleam of dawn, shining ever brighter till the full light of day." See 2 Cor 3:18.
188 In *Following Jesus*, 40.

God, by Himself with His own reality 'descending', has lost Himself as love into His creation, never again to leave it."[189] In other words, God chooses in love to "limit" himself to bring others into being in time and space, then enters creation that we may ascend, "lifted up" in the Son, into the limitless love of the Father and Son by the Spirit. And our "ascending" love to God is always a participation in God's descent to the world that it may ascend to God.

I discuss John's spirituality of love under the headings of *meaning, sacrifice, circles of love, Father-Son love,* and *Jesus-disciple love.*

Meaning: Love occurs fifty-seven times in John's Gospel, both *agape/agapeo* (forty-four times) and *philia/phileo* (thirteen times). He uses them interchangeably. Love occurs fifty-one times in his letters, all of them being *agape/agapeo*. The Early Church chose *agape*, the rarest of the four Greek words for love,[190] making it the supreme ethical virtue. Not that *agape* already had the meaning they wanted it to convey. Rather, they used it to cover all the meanings of love, *but within a new defining framework*: God's standard or kind of love incarnated and revealed in Jesus.

John's root meaning behind *agape* is Hebraic wholism, not Greek dualism. The Great Commandment says YHWH is one, thus love him wholistically with all your heart, soul, mind and strength, just as he *first* loved you (1 Jn 4:19). As noted in the previous chapter, *YHWH* loved Israel *not* for her attributes or achievements. He *chose* to love (*aheb*), placing his "affection" on her by entering a covenant of *hesed,* "unfailing love". This was the basis of their responding love for God and "the stranger", seen in their choice to obey his commands.[191] When John says, "God is love" (1 Jn 4:8, 16), he means by nature (essence) *and* character (choice,

---

189 This quote and what follows is in Endean (ed.), *Karl Rahner: Spiritual Writings,* 57.
190 See Lewis, *The Four Loves,* friendship affection (*phileo*), erotic passion (*eros*), family relations (*storge*), willing the good of others (*agape*). What follows is key – how the Christians used *agape* – see Wright, *Virtue Reborn,* 157–159, and Carson, *The Difficult Doctrine of the Love of God,* 25–30.
191 See Deut 4:37, 6:4–5, 10, 7:7–9, 12–13, 10:12–19, 11:1, 13, 23:5, 30:6, 16, 20.

behaviour) God loves.[192] Being God, he can be and do no other. Love implies one who loves (Father); the object of love (Son); and love itself (Spirit). So, God is love in relation to him/herself, in relation to creation, and especially in relation to humans. Love is a primary perfection of God, governing his every will, thought, emotion, word and deed, in harmony with all his other attributes – including his wrath/anger.[193]

John's point is that *because of Jesus* we see and know *this* love of God. He fulfils and embodies God's unfailing covenant love for *Israel*. More so, he *is* God's passionate love for *this world*: "For God so loved the world that he gave his one and only Son, that whoever believes in him shall not perish but have eternal life" (3:16). This popular text is tucked between vv.13–15 and v.17, fusing the crucifixion (the eschatological Son of Man's ascent, "lifting up") and the incarnation (the eternal Son of God's descent, "sending"). John is saying this is *how* God loved the world. Jesus is God's ultimate gift of Self – his mission of love to save the world. To believe and follow Jesus is to receive and experience God's love: the ultimate source of reality, eternal life itself. To reject Jesus is to reject love and perish.[194]

Sacrifice: Of the fifty-seven occurrences of love in John's Gospel, forty-five are in the passion narratives (John 13 to 21). In other words, (God's) love is defined as self-sacrifice, the gift of oneself (15:13; 1 Jn 3:16). John uses Jesus' washing of feet at the last supper ("having loved his own in the world, he now showed them the full extent of his love", 13:1), to demonstrate God's self-stripping, self-humbling and self-giving love in King Jesus, the Suffering Servant of Is 52:13f. The remainder of the Gospel – Jesus' passion, intimate dialogue with his disciples and his Father, his death and resurrection – is the full exposition of the outpoured love that

---

192 We dare not reverse it, "love is God"; then we make love (whatever we mean by it) divine and worship it as multitudes do today – many claiming "a spirituality of love."
193 See Carson's helpful study on this, *The Difficult Doctrine of the Love of God*.
194 "Perish" (*apollymi/apoleia*) means lost/destroyed, used for both physical and eternal destruction: Jn 3:15–16, 10:10, 28, 11:50, 12:25, 17:12; Matt 10:28, 18:14; Lk 13:3, 5; Rom 2:12, 14:15; 2 Cor 2:15, 4:3; 2 Pet 3:9. The key text is 2 Thess 2:10.

washes and enfolds us into Jesus and his Father by the Spirit, the Eternal Community of Love.

The message of the washing of the feet is: "I have set you an example that you should do as I have done for you" (13:15). What does this mean in practice? Jesus goes on to say, "A new commandment I give you: Love one another. *As I have loved you,* so you must love one another. By this all (people) will know that you are my disciples, if you love one another" (13:34–35). In computer terms this is a quantum upgrade of the old commandment's operating system in Lev 19:18, "love your neighbour *as* (you love) yourself." As fallen human beings "love of self" is flawed as a measure and means of loving others. We selfishly indulge ourselves, or struggle with self-rejection, even self-hatred. Jesus' operating system upgrade is a new *measurement* of love: to love our neighbour *as* Jesus loved us. *And* a new *means* of love: to love *as* Jesus loved is to be empowered by *his love* "to the full extent" of *its* source – his Father's love (see 17:26).[195] The "old" love of self is eschatologically fulfilled in the "new" love of Jesus, that of the future age which is "already shining" (1 Jn 2:8). By *this* love all will know we are his disciples, that we have passed from death to life (1 Jn 3:14), that we truly love the unseen God (1 Jn 4:20).

Circles of Love: Jesus' outpoured love is the model and means of the relational circles of love that emerge in John's Gospel – all grounded in the Father's love:

- The Father loves the Son (3:35, 5:20, 10:17, 15:9, 17:23–24, 26).
- The Son loves the Father (14:31).
- The Father loves believers (14:21, 23, 16:27, 17:23 cf. 3:16).
- The Son loves believers (11:3, 5, 36, 13:1, 23, 34, 14:21, 15:9, 12, 19:26, 20:2, 21:7, 20).

---

195 See Meier's exposition of "As (*kathos*) I have loved you…" – it's both "just as" (the standard or model) and "since" (the source or enabling). *A Marginal Jew,* Vol. IV, 564–565.

- Believers love Jesus (8:42, 14:15, 21, 23–24, 28, 16:27, 21:15–17).
- Believers love God (5:42, love of/for God is frequent in John's letters)
- Believers love one another (13:34–35, 15:12–13, 17, 17:26).
- People love "the world" (sinful things, 3:19, 12:25, 43) and "the world" loves its own (15:19), and hates God's own as it hates Jesus (15:18–19).
- But God loves "the world" (3:16) – the people – so as to save them.

The reader can add references from John's letters to these circles to complete his ethic of love. Let me unpack this beautiful mystery, *The Dance of Love*.

From eternity past and future, the intra-Trinitarian love of the Father and Son by the Spirit comes to earth in Jesus to redeem humanity. He becomes the pattern of love in the redeemed who are caught up in the Son by the Spirit into the Trinitarian relations of life, light and love. We see this in the four circular parallels of "just as… so is…": as the *Father-Son* love, so is the *Jesus-disciple* love, and so is the *disciple-disciple* love, and so the *disciple-world* love (to love the people, not the things of this world, 3:16; 1 Jn 2:15–17). The dance originates in the Father-Son-Spirit relationship – the ultimate *origin, model* and *means* of each reciprocal circle of love. Its *mission* is to save the world (descending theology), with *the goal* to enfold all who respond into the Father-Son life of love by the Spirit (ascending theology). Indeed, this is *only* possible by the third Person of the Trinity, the self-effacing Spirit of Love. S/he choreographs and leads the dance, both as a whole and in each overlapping circle, ever outwards to the ends of the earth. See Figure 7. All the circles are perforated to show *the invitational inclusivity of God's ever-expanding love*. Note that inclusivity is not undiscerning acceptance of other beliefs and practices. True love differentiates, distinguishes and confronts; even as it unconditionally invites, enfolds and unites.

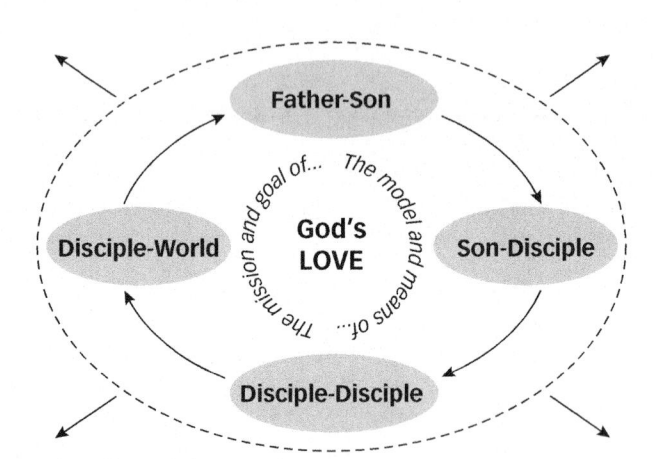

Figure 7. Cirles in the Dance of Love

Father-Son

Disciple-World — **God's LOVE** (The model and means of... / The mission and goal of...) — *Son-Disciple*

Disciple-Disciple

The diagram is my inadequate attempt to capture John's theology of love. Allow me to summarize, in more technical terms, its five characteristics. *Love is…*

- *Ontological:* grounded in God's being – the Father-Son-Spirit life of love.

- *Incarnational:* demonstrated in Jesus – the Father-Jesus love and Jesus-disciple love. Nowhere in John does God say, "I love you"; he demonstrates it in Jesus, in relational intimacy and acts of self-sacrifice.

- *Ethical:* practiced by moral obedience and deeds of service – the disciple-disciple love – reflecting Jesus' greatest deed of service, his sacrifical death.

- *Missional:* witnessed to/by the world – the disciple-disciple and disciple-world love – "that the world may believe that you have sent me" (17:21).

- *Mystical:* experienced as intimate union with God and fellow believers. John's mysticism is *not* flight from social responsibility or ethical purity. Union with God is seen in ethical and missional integrity, which if lacking, is indicative of union with a god or spirit other than the One revealed in Messiah Jesus.

Father-Son love: As the *model and means*, and the *mission and goal*, of God's Kingdom of Love on earth, the Father-Son love requires closer examination. Just as the Father eternally pours himself into the Son in self-emptying love by the Spirit, so the Son pours himself out in returned love for his Father by the same Spirit of Love.[196] We know this because we see it in the *historical* Jesus: "not my will but yours be done." At every turn we see how he intimately responded to his Father in love, how he selflessly loved his disciples and people in the world. How did Jesus experience, *in his humanity*, the Father's love that so defined him and his work?

His spiritual formation in the Father's love was via his parent's love and training, Torah study and memorization, prayer and contemplation. John highlights *Jesus' profound consciousness of the Father's abiding intimate presence* (see 8:16, 29, 16:32). He experienced it as love in each moment, each event, being apprenticed in his Father's daily work: "for the Father loves the Son and shows him all he does", telling him not only *what* to say but even *how* to say it (5:20 cf. 12:49–50, see my earlier comments on this). This revelatory relationship by the Spirit in the sacrament of the present moment was a tangible participation in his Father's love. He lived fully in the present moment, being fully present to his Father.

His awareness of his Father placing (entrusting) all things in his hands (under his authority) was affirming love (3:35). *Therefore* he could lay aside all privilege and power and pour out his life in love (13:3f). Because he knew the Father's love, he freely chose to lay down his life in love for

---

[196] See Coffey, *The Holy Spirit as the Mutual Love of the Father and the Son*, in the immanent Trinity (God's essence) and economic Trinity (Trinitarian relationships in creation), in descending theology (his incarnate mission in Jesus and the Spirit) and ascending theology (return to the Father).

his sheep to fulfil God's purpose (10:17). He faced death by praying the night before... and experienced *both* exquisite union, a completion in love with his Father and his followers (17:21–23), *and* secure comfort in knowing "you (Father) loved me from before the creation of the world" (17:24).[197]

No wonder such burning love kindled the passion to *always* please his Father (8:29). He learnt from personal experience to "remain" in and live from his Father's love every moment of every day. How? By obeying his commands (15:10). Obedience not only kept him in Father's love; it had become his human nature. To obey was a natural overflow of returned love from his very being... in love: "The world must learn that I love the Father and that I do exactly what my Father has commanded me to do" (14:31). As Ladd says, "Jesus' whole ethic in John is summed up in love."[198] And love is summed up in obedience – moral character. Gnostic mysticism sought revelation knowledge and spiritual experiences as the means of salvation and spirituality. Once again, John's test of authentic spirituality/mysticism was intensely practical: lived obedience to God. Our lived lives do not lie – at least not for long – sooner or later our true character comes out for all to see.

Jesus-disciple love: Jesus lived and loved from the Father's love: "*As the Father has loved me* – my measure and enablement of love – *so* have I loved you. Now remain in my love as I've remained in my Father's love" (15:9 RAP). In fact, the Father's love was *so very real* to Jesus that he lived to make his Father known to his disciples (17:6–8). He prayed that "*the love you (Father) have for me may be in them* and that I myself may be in them" (17:26). Jesus *in* us by his Spirit enables us to receive and

---

197 Jesus' profound consciousness of the Father's *eternal* love: the Father is the fountain (origin and source) of love, the only one, even within the Trinity, who does not need to be loved in order to love. "Only in the Father is this perfect equation realized: *to be is to love*. For the other divine persons, *to be is to be loved*. The Father is an eternal relationship of love and does not exist outside this relationship." Raniero Cantalamessa, http://www.zenit.org/en/articles/father-cantalamessa-s-2nd-lent-homily-2015/
198 *A Theology of the New Testament*, 279.

experience Father's love, and respond in love as he did. As we obey his commands (14:15) by loving one another as he loved us (13:34-35), we "remain" in his love as he remained in his Father's love (15:9-10). Love motivates obedience and obedience matures love, deepening the reality of the Father and Son's loving presence "homing" in our bodies (14:21, 23). The Incarnation continues in us. Thus, as we see with Peter, *honest love for Jesus*, no matter how weak or faltering, is the only real basis for life, ministry, leadership, and even death (21:15-19). Jesus simply asks, "Do you love me?" The answer (love) is seen more in deeds than in words or emotions.

Therefore, the clearer we see the Jesus of history *for who he was* in his humanity, the more we fall in love with him *for who he is* as the Christ of faith. We go beyond love for Jesus based on gratitude for what he's done for us – forgiveness, eternal life, healing – to loving him for himself, for his intrinsic beauty. He indeed was (is) a truly beautiful person; the incarnation of the ultimate Beauty we call God. It is *beauty* that attracts, draws and causes us to fall in love; embracing our entire existence. It is beauty – love of The Beautiful (*Philokalia*) – that is the right framework for goodness and truth; to our being good and truthful.[199]

Be ravished by a vision of this remarkable young rabbi from Nazareth! Be overcome with sheer admiration and fall into love with him – just as he evidently was in love with his Father. This love is supremely spiritual and intensely practical, deciding literally everything in our lives, as Pedro Arrupe S.J. says:[200]

> *Nothing is more practical than finding God, that is, than falling in love in a quite absolute, final way. What you are in love with, what seizes your imagination, will affect everything. It will decide what will get you out of bed in the morning, what you will do with your*

---
199 On *Philokalia* see footnote 28. Divo Barsotti says, "Without beauty, the good becomes a burden and truth becomes a useless and empty labour. It is in beauty that truth and the good find their supreme revelation." Cited in O'Collins SJ, *Jesus*, 1.
200 The Jesuit Superior General 1965-83. See ignatianspirituality.com/fall-in-love/

evenings, how you will spend your weekends, what you read, who you know, what breaks your heart, and what amazes you with joy and gratitude. Fall in love, stay in love, and it will decide everything.

Oneness

John's conclusion of love (and life and light) is mystical oneness – completion in union with God and unity with fellow Christ-followers. Jesus prayed, "that all of them may be one, Father, just as you are in me and I am in you. May they also be in us so that the world may believe that you have sent me" (17:21). Having pointed to this oneness – mutual indwelling – throughout this chapter, I draw it all together with some concluding comments.[201]

The medium of this sublime text (17:21), Jesus in prayer, *is its message*. Most scholars say John 17, Jesus' prayer, is the Holy of Holies of this Gospel. Prayer is the primary means of consummated love in union with God and fellow believers. For Jesus, prayer was adjusting his whole being to the Father's indwelling presence, to be receptive to his personalized love in every moment. Maloney says, "As we progress in deeper prayer, we grow more intimately in union with God as Trinity, the core of all reality, and we begin to live in the power of that burning love which surrounds us in all things and permeates the depths of our being. Prayer moves away from a *doing act*… to become a constant state of *being* in His love."[202]

John's oneness of love is *not* Greek or Gnostic mysticism: absorbed into the deity, so possessed by its spirit that we lose ourselves. Assimilation with loss of identity, even personality, is not what Jesus is praying for. "What makes Christianity a unique religion over all others is its accent on love that, as Teilhard de Chardin SJ writes, differentiates

---

[201] See chapter 1 where I introduced union with God as *perichoresis*: Eastern Greek Fathers used the texts of mutual indwelling in John 14 and 17 for their theology of the interpenetration or co-inherence of the Father, Son and Spirit, experienced *within the believer* (14:20, 23).
[202] *Entering Into the Heart of Jesus*, 117–118 (his italics).

as it unites."[203] God's love draws us into union with the Trinity and each other, making us one in heart, soul and mind, while differentiating God and each other. We are completed in our unique humanity and God in his divinity, though he is eternally complete. Though we participate in God's divine nature (2 Pet 1:4), we are not, and will never become, God – contrary to the promise of New Age/Gnostic monism where all is lost in one universal consciousness (see footnote 34).

John's union of oneness is Hebraic. Adam and Eve were created *for God* as his image, *and for each other* as differentiated image. The two "cleave" and "become one" in a psycho-spiritual-sexual bond, a marriage covenant (Gen 2:23–24). This was not assimilation of one by the other leading to a loss of difference and uniqueness. It was a growing oneness of shared life and love *at all levels of human personhood* – psychologists call it intimacy – by two different but complementary creations, male and female. Cited earlier, this oneness is the Hebrew *yadah*, "knowing" each other in love, resulting in fruitfulness (offspring, Gen 4:1, 17, 25). It is used of God and Israel "cleaving" and "knowing" each other in the (old) love covenant. In the promised new covenant God literally indwells his people by his Word and Spirit, whereby we *yadah* him and he us – without priestly intermediaries (Jer 31:31–34; Ezek 36:26–28).

Jesus inaugurated the new covenant in his blood of atonement that restores "at-one-ment" with God. The new covenant fulfilled in Jesus (God's *Logos*) and his Spirit (God's *Parakletos*), makes us one with God and his people, maturing us into our full humanity as his image-bearers. Jesus is our model and means of this oneness with God,[204] *not* as Fatherly robotic control of Jesus by the remote Spirit, but as relational union of persons. In Messiah, by his Spirit, we grow in *this* union with God,

---

[203] Maloney, *Entering Into the Heart of Jesus*, 143. Thomas Merton says, "When we all reach that perfection of love which is the contemplation of God in his glory, our inalienable personalities, while remaining eternally distinct, will nevertheless combine into One so that each one of us will find himself in all the others, and God will be the life and reality of all", *New Seeds of Contemplation*, 70.

[204] Though, as divine, Jesus' oneness with God was in some sense unique (see 10:30).

whereby our will, imagination, thoughts, emotions, words, actions and behaviour, become one with his, as indeed it was with Jesus.

Jesus taught his followers *that* reality: "on that day – after my death and resurrection when the *Parakletos* is in you – *you will realize* that I am in my Father, and you are in me, and I am in you" (14:15–20 RAP). By the Spirit's consciousness we become *conscious* of our mutual indwelling with God. Jesus illustrates what this means with the image of the Vine and its branches (15:1–16). Here John's key word, *meno,* comes to fullness – see footnote 169. He uses it eleven times in 15:1–16, giving both the theology behind the vine and the branches (vv.1–8), and the interpretation of its fruit (vv.9–16). The vine was a dominant image for Israel (Is 5, Ps 80). Jesus saw himself as the fulfilment of Israel's destiny: "I am the *true* vine". His disciples were "the branches", the renewed Israel of the new covenant, abiding in the life, light and love of the Messianic Son, producing Israel's God-intended fruit.

This image of organic union goes beyond the idea of relational intimacy. The vine is deeply grounded and rooted in the Gardener's (Father) loving care. As the branches *meno* in the vine, the vine *menos* in the branches, releasing all the moisture and nourishment (Father's life, light and love) the branches need to produce good fruit. Jesus makes the application clear: by imbibing and obeying his words (15:3, 7, 10 cf. 8:31) we abide in him and he abides in us. This is the discipline of Hebraic prayer-meditation and memorization of (Messianic) Torah as in Ps 1:2–3, 119:9–16. As we produce fruit *God* disciplines (prunes, 15:2) us so that we can be more fruit-full (see Heb 12:10–11). What then is the *"much fruit"* of such union that brings glory to the Father and proves that we are Jesus' apprentices (15:8)?

In a word: Christlikeness – moral character. John spells out this lasting fruit of loving union with Jesus, for which we are chosen and appointed. Most scholars agree that vv.9–16 interpret vv.1–8. The fruit is a natural and easy...

- *Meno*-ing in Jesus' *love* as he did in his Father's love, by obedience to Jesus' word just as he obeyed his Father's word (9–10).
- Jesus' *joy* in us making our joy complete (11).
- Jesus' *freedom* in us to lay down our lives for others in love (12–13).
- Jesus' *friendship* in revelational intimacy with him and the Father (14–15).
- Jesus' *authority* in prayer – the Father gives us whatever we ask in his name – because his and our will have become one (7, 16).

All of this, then, is what Jesus prays for when he asks the Father that "they may be one as we are one: I in them and you in me. May they be brought to complete unity" (17:22–23). The entire purpose is not a self-indulgent spirituality or an elitist mysticism, but *missional witness*: that "the world will know that you sent me and have loved them even as you have loved me" (17:23). Do we grasp what this means? God stakes his universal public credibility of Jesus and his love *on the unity or disunity of his church!*[205] This is staggering! God either has great faith in us, in our eventual obedience to his relentless love, or he knows something we do not know!

The present-day church in all its disunity mirrors our spiritual/mystical bankruptcy. We do not obey Jesus, we do not love one another as he loves us, making our union with God questionable and spurious, no matter what spirituality we claim. No wonder the world does not believe. However, Jesus *did* pray, and continues to pray to this day at the Father's right hand for our unity as *the* credible expression of the Trinitarian Com-Unity. Therefore, I choose to believe God is at work with us as Jesus was with Peter, despite our faltering faith and failing love (21:15–19). I have more faith in Jesus' faithful prayers and God's unfailing love, than in our continued disobedience. His relentless love will triumph – his integrity and honor are at stake!

---

205 John was addressing the disunity caused by some leaving the faith community due to persecution from Jewish authorities (the synagogue/church split), which is more overt in his letters.

In conclusion, to make all this practical and personal I offer the following prayer-confession that I wrote years ago. I continue to use it as a spiritual discipline to transform my consciousness to intimate partnership with God, praying it by heart daily, as often as I can. I pray each phrase with my breath, in and out, so it enters my subconscious, that my spirit continues to pray while I sleep. *The Partnering Prayer – The 10 Communications of God* is the ten basic ways God communicates himself to us, as I understand it, in our bodies and through all our faculties into the world. The first two are invocations of whole-body awareness. Then they move from the head down to the feet, doing God's will as it is in heaven.

Keep or remove or change the adjectives in brackets. Do what works for you. Learn this by heart and pray it as often as you can throughout the day every day for at least a month. You will then feel the effect it has on you in terms of heightened awareness of God's indwelling presence. You will become aware of how God communicates in all your bodily faculties, shifting your consciousness to living union with God in you, and through you, into the world around you.

Father and Son
My body is your temple
By your Holy Spirit
Let me…

> *Sense your (indwelling) presence*
> *Feel your (loving) emotions*
> *Think your (wise) thoughts*
> *Hear your (intimate) voice*
> *See your (creative) works*
> *Breathe your (sweet) fragrance*
> *Speak your (life-giving) words*
> *Touch your (broken) creation*
> *Walk your (righteous) ways*
> *Do your (perfect) will*

As it is in heaven

– Prayer by Alexander F. Venter

QUESTIONS FOR REFLECTION AND DISCUSSION

1. Step back and ask: what's my impression of this chapter? What are the two or three key things that struck me – what God is saying to me? Pray it through.

2. Another overall impression: has this chapter adjusted your understanding of what it means to follow Jesus, of spiritual formation to Christlikeness? In what specific ways has your view been adjusted or even changed?

3. How do you understand the significance and meaning of John's usage of *Logos* for the incarnation of the eternal Son of God? Describe it in your own words.

4. What is eternal life? What does it mean for you to have eternal life – do you have "it"? How does it determine your life of apprenticeship to Jesus and the Father?

5. How do you understand John's usage of "light" in his Gospel? Think of what it means practically for you in your life with Jesus.

6. How do you define love? Write it out. Why is love at the heart of it all – of God, of Jesus and his disciples, and of your life? How can you learn to love as God loves? List some practical things you can do in this regard.

7. Lastly, do you experience God as Father, and Son, and Spirit? How truly intimate – one in will, mind and emotions – are you with God?

8. And intimate with fellow Christ-followers? Do you need to reconcile with anyone? Or intentionally seek unity with other believers and churches?

CHAPTER 8

PAULINE TRADITION: SANCTIFICATION IN KINGDOM TENSION

"My dear children, for whom I am again in the pains of childbirth until Christ is formed in you."
Gal 4:19

"For those God foreknew he also predestined to be conformed to the image of his Son."
Rom 8:29

"And we... are being transformed into his image with ever-increasing glory, which comes from the Lord, who is the Spirit."
Cor 3:18

We have examined the Synoptic and Johannine traditions. Now we look at Paul. How does he, in his life, ministry and letters, conceive of spirituality as in discipleship to Jesus? How does he view it particularly from the perspective of Jewish eschatology fulfilled in Messiah Jesus, in the already and not yet of God's kingdom?

I discussed, in chapter 2, Paul's view of spirituality in his use of *pneumatikos*: being spiritual. He did *not* mean spiritual experiences, or ascetic gymnastics, or supernatural Spirit-gifts (*charisms*), or revelation knowledge (*gnosis*), or secret wisdom (*sophia*), or motivational oratory – all of which the Corinthian Christians believed to be true spirituality, or measures thereof. Their carnal behaviour as in divisions, arguments and immorality, revealed their world-likeness, or *un*spirituality. To be spiritual is simply to have God's Holy Spirit in us (John's *Paracletos*), progressively governing every thought, word and deed, transforming us into Christ-likeness. Thus we become truly human: radiating God's glory as God intended for his earthly image-bearers – we were not created or destined to be immortal disembodied spirits or divine gods. For Paul, this takes place – we *only* receive God's Spirit – as we entrust ourselves to Messiah Jesus in the end-time salvation he gives us through his atoning life and death, and victorious resurrection and ascension.

This chapter, then, explores Paul's view of the nature and growth of salvation, God's Spirit-Life in us, which saves and transforms us to Christ's likeness in this evil age and into eternity. It's an event *and* a process *and* a goal. Called transformation, or the broader term sanctification – to be set apart for God and made holy – this process is popularly known as spirituality or spiritual formation. In Paul's pneumatic word, we are spiritualised (*pneumatikoi*) by God's Spirit. Or, in Paul's words above: Christ is *formed* in us; God predetermined us to be *con*formed to his Son's image;[206] and we are being *trans*formed into his likeness from one degree of glory to another – all by the Spirit of the Lord.

First a comment on interpreting Paul. For centuries his letters and theology have been interpreted in light of the 16th to 17th cent. Reformation debate of law and grace ("justification by faith") in reaction to salvation by ritual obedience ("righteousness by works") in the Roman Catholic Church. This became the lens through which the Gospels were read: the free grace of salvation in Jesus by faith in his atoning death that clashed with legalistic Judaism represented in the Pharisees. And so

---

206 "Image" is *eikon* (1 Cor 15:49, 2 Cor 3:18, 4:4; Col 3:10). We become a living icon of King Jesus as he is *The* Icon of God, fulfilling our original created purpose to be God's human icons on earth.

Part Two: Theology

Paul's letters were seen as *real* theology for *real* teaching while the Gospels were *mere* stories for church homilies – moral lessons to encourage the faithful.

The quest for the historical Jesus, now called Jesus research, with its recovery of eschatology (kingdom theology), has turned the above on its head. Instead of seeing Jesus through the eyes of Paul the Protestant Reformer, we now correctly see Paul the converted Jewish rabbi through Jesus the rabbi-Messiah. Scholars now accept that the Gospels are a genre of historical biography, widely known in the Greco-Roman world, that teaches *real* theology via historical narrative – the lens through which Paul is now being read. This has led to a "new perspective" in Pauline studies:[207] reading Paul in his historical context as he lived and taught the fulfilment of the Jewish story in Jesus. He was a rabbi converted to faith in the Risen Jesus, which led to a re-vision of his Torah understanding and Israel's story. Paul became a leading interpreter of Messianic Judaism (The Gospel, Christianity) for Jews and Gentiles.[208] One can see how his thinking developed in his letters[209] – though he wrote to address local church issues of life and faith – culminating in a breath-taking cosmic vision of all things reconciled and made new under one head, King Jesus.[210]

---

207 See N.T. Wright, *Paul in Fresh Perspective* (the precursor of his later monumental work, *Paul and the Faithfulness of God,* in two volumes), and other books on Paul by Wright, Dunn, Fee, Hays, Maloney, Schnelle, and Thompson, in my Bibliography. E.P. Sanders, *Paul and Palestinian Judaism,* is the foundation text for the "new perspective". Specifically, from a Jewish apocalyptic-eschatological lens, see books on Paul by Beker, and Ladd's, *A Theology of the New Testament,* 359–568.
208 See two seminal books by Richard Hays, *Echoes of Scripture in the Letters of Paul* and *The Conversion of the Imagination: Paul as Interpreter of Israel's Scriptures.* Wright dedicates his Pauline benchmark two volumes to Hays, calling him "a prince among exegetes…"
209 For the dating and limits of the Pauline corpus (which letters are from Paul), read Dunn and Wright. I accept the traditional Pauline corpus held by most evangelical scholars, including the pastoral letters.
210 Wright says in *Paul in Fresh Perspective,* p.12, Paul's "particular view of salvation, (is) not as an *a*historical rescue *from* the world, but as the *trans*historical redemption *of* the world" (his italics).

We must read Paul, not as the founder of a new religion called Christianity (as some have argued), but in keeping with Jesus' messianic Judaism. What Paul taught and lived was in direct continuity with Jesus' kingdom message and mission.

Jewish background and conversion

Saul, or Heb. *Sha'ul*, was a Hellenized Jew from the cosmopolitan port city of Tarsus. Fluent in Greek and Hebrew, he was an ideal bridge person between the Jewish and Greco-Roman worlds. Trained as a rabbi, his worldview was based on Israel's story of *monotheism and creation, election and covenant,* and *eschatology*. The one Creator-God chose Abraham and his seed as his means of reversing humanity and creation's exile due to Adam and Eve's sin, and to reconcile the scattered Babel nations to God. He redeemed Israel out of Egypt in the Exodus and made a covenant to form Israel into a holy nation as his instrument of reconciliation. Though Israel entered the Promised Land, her continued disobedience resulted in her own exile. But God promised return and restoration when he becomes king in his Messiah, *who will fulfil Israel's destiny,* reconciling the Gentile nations, bringing this evil age to an end to usher in the new age of *YHWH's* kingdom of heaven on earth.

Saul's spiritual formation was in the strict school of the Pharisees – discipled by none other than the rabbi-sage Gamaliel in Jerusalem (Acts 5:34, 22:3). Rabbi *Sha'ul* was "faultless" in "legalistic righteousness" (Phil 3:4-6, see his impeccable credentials), believing Torah obedience would lead to personal and national salvation. He zealously persecuted the followers of The Way to death (Acts 22:4) because they subverted Israel from Torah observance, as their leader *Yeshua* had supposedly done. *Sha'ul* knew of *Yeshua ha Notzri,* that he proclaimed the kingdom of heaven, did many mighty miracles, taught his kingdom *halakha* as The Way – The Messianic fulfilment of Torah. And yes, he got what he deserved: nailed to a Roman stake, publicly crucified, the end of all such false messiahs.

However, on one of his authorized missions to arrest followers of The Way, *Sha'ul* had a supernatural encounter with none other than *Yeshua*. Appearing in a bright light, Jesus spoke to Saul, as attested by his travelling companions (Acts 9:3f). This mystical but tactile vision blinded him for three days, till Ananias, one of Jesus' followers, laid hands on him. His restored physical sight symbolized his spiritual illumination. He now knew *Yeshua* was actually alive, thus risen from the dead as his disciples (pro)claimed, imparting the promised end-time Spirit which Saul received when Ananias laid hands on him (Acts 9:17–18). Thus he became a fully devoted follower of the Risen Lord. My RAP, in short, is that Saul had a head-on collision with The Light that knocked his lights out, to enlighten him to follow The Light, and take The Light to the nations in the enlightening power of the Spirit!

For Saul, Jesus' bodily resurrection – not resuscitation, but the promised Resurrection at the end of this age that began the Messianic Age as per his Jewish eschatology – literally changed everything. He realized: THE Resurrection *has* happened! It has begun *in history*, a few years ago! *Yeshua's* kingdom of heaven is real. He inaugurated it – The Messiah-King! The future age has actually begun in this present evil age, yet without ending it! *How on earth does this work?* Saul's teaching and life-mission was an outworking of this amazing mystery.

He also realized that the Risen Jesus mysteriously lives in his followers by his Spirit, because Jesus said, "Saul, Saul, why are you persecuting *me?* Touch my people and you touch me!" (Acts 9:4–5 RAP). To follow Jesus is to be part of his Body. Thus he submitted to the touch (laying of hands) and baptism of Jesus' followers, joining The Way (Acts 9:17–20). Saul counted all the advantages he gained in Pharisaical Judaism as "loss", even "rubbish",[211] *in order to gain Messiah,* to truly know him and his salvation in his kingdom people. This was no leaving of Judaism as some say, rather a realignment and fulfilment of Judaism in light of Messiah

---

211 Paul's use of the crude *skybalon* ("rubbish", Phil 3:8), meaning refuse, even excrement, shows the strength of his feelings – read the context to appreciate it (3:2–11 cf. Gal 5:12).

Jesus and his Spirit. Saul's life became a stretching forward to reach *that* goal, the prize for which Jesus had arrested him (Phil 3:12-14) – fully aware that Jesus said he was "my chosen instrument to carry my name before the Gentiles and their kings and before the people of Israel. I will show him how much he must suffer for my name" (Acts 9:15-16).

Therefore, *Sha'ul* was profoundly conscious of God's shocking grace in the Risen Jesus appearing to *him* – God's enemy – now chosen "as one abnormally born" to an apostolic (missionary) calling to the nations in fulfilment of Israel's vocation.[212] God's grace, and Saul's realization thereof, motivated him to "work harder than all of them" (the other apostles, 1 Cor 15:9-10). With even *greater zeal* he proclaimed and taught the faith he had persecuted. He *re*interpreted the Jewish story in light of Messiah Jesus and his Spirit. He worked out what it meant for Jews and Gentiles and creation, by the Spirit's revelation *and* accountability to Jesus' apostles in Jerusalem (Gal 1:11-2:10). About eleven years after his conversion, on his first authorized mission to plant churches in the Mediterranean world with Barnabas, his name was changed to Paul (Greco-Roman name, Acts 13:9). And yes, he did suffer deeply, like his Lord, because of his fearless witness to *Yeshua's* name, message and mission.

Paul's Messianic Judaism and eschatological framework

Hays' research (footnote 208) reveals Paul's "storied structure of thinking", now called narrative theology; how he thought within the Jewish biblical narrative and taught his pagan converts to do the same (Gal 3-5, 1 Cor 10). Wright builds on this, probing Paul's mindset, his Messianic (Christian) worldview in its clash and crossover with the Jewish, Greek and Roman worldviews. He shows how Paul reworked Israel's story and scriptures *in light of Messiah Jesus and the gift of his eschatological Spirit,* focused in three core Jewish beliefs – the three key questions raised by the Risen Lord's encounter with him:

---

212 1 Cor 15:8 (read vv. 1-11) cf. 9:1; Acts 22:14-16; Gal 1:15-16, 2:6-10.

Part Two: Theology

- Who was/is this Jesus, now risen from the dead? Rethinking the one true God (*monotheism and creation*) freshly revealed in light of Jesus and the Spirit.

- Who are Jesus' followers? One with him? Rethinking the one true people of God (*election and covenant*) freshly reworked in Jesus and the Spirit.

- What is the salvation that Jesus realizes and promises? Rethinking the one true future of God (*eschatology*) freshly reimagined in Jesus and the Spirit.

- There was a fourth (radical implication) that Paul constantly asked and taught: how *then* do we live as *Christ*-followers, as God's renewed Israel of the new covenant? Rethinking the one true mission of God (*spirituality, ethics, mission*) freshly lived in Jesus and the Spirit.

Our focus is God's end-time salvation and it's outworking in spirituality and mission. Arguably, *Paul's starting point was his reimagined Jewish eschatology* and how it redefined God's true nature, and his one true people and their mission, in light of Jesus and the Spirit. It was not a patchwork exercise sewing doctrines into a quilt; rather a dynamic revision of a seamless garment. So I first summarize Paul's revised Jewish eschatology and its nature of salvation as event, process and goal. Then I discuss its outworking in terms of the (missional) spirituality that it produces.

His foundational Hebraic worldview of *ha'olam hazzeh* and *ha'olam habbah,* "the present age" and "the age to come", is cited in Eph 1:21 (*ho aion houtos* and *ho mellon aion*). This phrase came from Jewish apocalyptic writings, in use in Paul's day. It was Jesus' underlying framework for his kingdom message and mission (Mk 10:30). Paul preached "the kingdom of God" (Acts 20:25 cf. 28:31) as per Jesus, but used the term *in*frequently in his letters, [213] though the concept and its reality is assumed in every letter by his constant reference to Jesus as *Kristos*.

This age is a fallen world in rebellion against God – "the present evil age" (Gal 1:4) under Satan's rule. Heb. *ha satan*, "the oppose/accuser" of God and his ruling purposes, is "the god of this world (who) has blinded the minds of unbelievers" (2 Cor 4:4), "the ruler of the kingdom of the air, the spirit who is now at work in those who are disobedient" (Eph 2:2). This kingdom of darkness (Col 1:13) comprises real spirit-beings described as rulers, authorities, principalities, powers, spiritual forces of evil in the heavenly realms, demons, deceptive "angels of light".[214] They operate in this age via *Adam's disobedience*, by which sin and death entered creation and now reigns (Rom 5:12–14). Humanity "in Adam" – made in God's image to rule creation – is *not* a hapless victim of evil, but a ready participant in evil. Adam gave his God-given ruling-authority to evil. Creation is, rather, the hapless victim of human rebellion.

In Rom 1:18–32 to 3:9–19 Paul analyzes the radical evil that reigns in the ruined soul and broken creation, concluding: *all* are guilty before God, both Jew and Gentile. The downward spiral of human degradation to total depravity is from *God's self-revelation* in creation (conscience) and the law (Torah);

- *To human suppression* of "the truth of God": exchanging it for a lie by worshipping created things, not the Creator – *idolatry* and its consequences;

- *To spiritual death*: the consequent separation by sin – exile from God;

---

213 1 Thess 2:12; 2 Thess 1:5; Gal 5:21; 1 Cor 4:20, 6:9–10; Rom 14:17; Eph 5:5; Col 1:12–13; 2 Tim 4:1, 18. Paul's use of *Kristos* (Christ = Messiah-King) is kingdom language. To highlight this Wright translates Christ as King in his *The Kingdom New Testament*. Scholars have debated Paul's infrequent use of "kingdom of God" and his probable dynamic equivalent: "justification by faith", or "grace", or the mystical "in Christ", or other words/concepts. See Wright, *Paul and the Faithfulness of God*, 36–46, and Dunn, *The Theology of Paul*, 19–23.

214 See 1 Cor 15:24; 2 Cor 11:14; Rom 8:38–39; Eph 1:20–21, 6:12; Col 1:16, 2:8–10, 15.

- *To darkening of hearts and minds*: futile and depraved thinking – deception;

- *To corruption of desires and bodily appetites*: psycho-emotional disorder – enslavement to sinful desires;

- *To degrading the body*: shameful immorality and fatal mortality – exchanging God's natural created design for what is unnatural and degenerate;

- *To disintegration of society*: shameless lust-filled use and ruthless abuse of one another – exchanging the image (*eikon*) of God for the likeness (*eikon*) of the devil, where his will is done on earth as it is in hell;[215]

- *To creation's exile and ruin*: the cosmic curse of sin and death – earth's "bondage to decay... groaning... for liberation" (Rom 8:21–22).

Paul begins this description with, "For the wrath of God is being revealed from heaven against all (this) wickedness" (1:18), ending with quotes from the OT (3:10–18), concluding with "there is no fear of God before their eyes" (3:18, quoting Ps 36:1). It's a typical Jewish reference to the end-time judgment, the Day of *YHWH's* wrath, the final defeat of *ha satan* and all evil. Jews and Gentiles that do not turn from sin to God, from death to life, incur *this* judgment. As "objects of (God's) wrath" (Eph 2:3) they are punished along with the forces of evil, eternally exiled from God's presence (1 Thess 4:6; 2 Thess 1:5–9). Hell is God's total absence and evil's full presence and reign. Paul saw salvation as God's faithful mercy, and righteous judgment as God's loving justice – not the capricious wrath of the pagan gods.

---

[215] "Filled with every kind of wickedness... they invent (new) ways of doing evil... they not only continue to do these very things but also approve of those who practice them", Rom 1:29–32. "Every inclination of the thoughts of the human heart was only evil all the time" (Gen 6:5, 8:21).

The logical/binary mind stumbles at such bi-polar (not dualistic) thinking, unable to hold opposites in tension. Hebraic thinking has no such problem. God is perfectly good, compassionate and forgiving, "yet he does not leave the guilty unpunished; he punishes..." (Ex 34:6-7, both statements are side by side without contradiction). God can even use *ha satan* to fulfil his sovereign purpose; e.g. God sent an evil spirit to torment King Saul (1 Sam 16:14-16). We logically try to reconcile love and wrath, mercy and judgment. So, some say God's *essential* nature of love overcomes his *attributed* nature of wrath – a human projection. No! Precisely *because* God is love his anger is aroused at sin and injustice, judging the perpetrators sooner or later, unless they repent. One cannot think of all the horrendous atrocities perpetrated on innocent victims in our world and not think that God gets angry! If God indulges *those* sinners in sloppy sentimental love he would not be God.

So, more accurately, God's essential nature is spirit (Jn 4:24), and *all* his attributes and perfections of love, joy, mercy, holiness, justice, righteous anger, and so on, are *not* contradictory. They work wisely together, even mysteriously, in perfect expression of his love for humanity and creation's highest good (see footnote 193).

All sin has consequences, whether seen or unseen. Sin incurs judgment (Eph 5:5-7; Col 3:6, 4:25). That's how reality works. The West denies the reality of God, sin, judgment, death and evil, to its own peril. We believe in the myth of progress: just enough technological development ("we'll solve global issues"), psychological insight ("I'm okay, you're okay; we're all beautiful"), and personal liberation (from Christian/religious guilt) will save us. We will come of age in the utopia of self-actualization. Such deceptive humanism dismisses the massive counter evidence of the moral disasters in recent history. *We have no respect or fear of God before our eyes.* We domesticate (G)god into "universal love" – making it mean whatever we want; making (G)god in our own image; collapsing distinctions of right and wrong in an undiscerning spirituality or "oneness of love" (the monism cited in footnote 34). This is neither biblical love, nor the biblical God. Because we do not take God seriously, we take ourselves far too seriously – idolatrously so! And *therefore* we do not take evil seriously, while it takes us super seriously; bent on our destruction by separating us from God. Satan has deceived humanity into the denial of both God *and* evil through the worship of Self, by which he rules this present evil age.

So, if we do not face the reality of sin in its radical ruin of humanity and creation, and the consequent righteous judgment of the Creator-God, we will not be able to expose and defeat evil in *God's* name and power. We will see no reason to repent, to turn from sin and evil. Neither will we be able to appreciate God's amazing mercy in our undeserving salvation in King Jesus. Paul reverses this: the revelation of God's gracious salvation, seen in the cross of the King (Rom 5:6–8), unveils the reality of God's judgment, and thus the true nature of sin and evil (Rom 1:16–32).[216]

This judgment and defeat of evil is *the great hope of salvation*. For Paul, hope is the key word in Jewish eschatology (Rom 5:4–5 cf. 8:18–25). It's the hope of The End of this age of Satan's reign of sin and death when God becomes king in Messiah, putting all things right, making all things new. It's the hope of The Beginning of the new age when God's people (those who trust him) will be saved by his eternal Spirit-Life, vindicated in resurrection with trans-physical bodies to rule and reign with Messiah, doing his will on earth as it is in heaven. It's also the hope of creation liberated and made new with heaven literally on earth. *This* hope of God's one true future is both the prayer of the Jews and the deepest need and longing of humanity.

His encounter with the Risen Jesus made Paul realize God's end-time salvation *and* judgment had broken into the world, into Israel, into

---

[216] The NRSV makes it clear: verses 17, 18 and 19 begin with *gar* (for, therefore). 17 *For*, or therefore, the Gospel reveals God's righteousness (salvation through the King's cross). 18 *Therefore* God's wrath is revealed against all wickedness. 19–32 *Therefore* the true nature of evil is exposed for what it is (19–32). See Wright, *Paul and the Faithfulness of God*, 764–771; also Rutledge's seminal study, *The Crucifixion*, on the death of Christ that removes "the weight of sin and evil". See Willard's incisive analysis of radical evil in the ruined soul, in *Renovation of the Heart*, 45–60.

his own life. He experienced and expressed it as "the ends of the ages have come" upon us (1 Cor 10:11 NRSV), or "on whom the fulfilment (culmination) of the ages has come" (NIV). God's promised cosmic salvation *and* judgment interrupted this age in Jesus, dissecting history – see Figure 8 below. The kingdom has come: inaugurated (in principle) and actively present (in practice) in Jesus and God's Spirit. The Day of Judgment, the defeat of evil, and the Exodus out of the kingdom of darkness into the kingdom of light, took place in the victorious Messiah, *Christus Victor* (Gal 1:4; Col 1:12–13). *Especially so in his crucifixion* (Col 2:15; Rom 5:6–11), vindicated in his resurrection and ascension to God's "right hand in the heavenly realm" to rule over all authorities, powers and dominions in this age and the age to come (Eph 1:20–23).

This eschatological in-breaking led Paul to reimagine the future when The End would finally and fully come – summarized in 1 Cor 15:20–28. King Jesus' bodily resurrection was "the firstfruit" (first of all who follow) of The Resurrection at the end of this age. It reversed Adam's sin and death, defeating its reign. He ascended to God's right hand to "reign until he has put all his enemies under his feet", the last enemy being death itself. This will happen on his return when he resurrects the righteous dead to reign with him in his consummated kingdom on a renewed earth. *"Then* the end will come, when he hands over the kingdom to God the Father… so that God may be all in all." Paul taught Christ's Second Coming in keeping with the other apostolic NT witnesses (1 & 2 Thess). But he focused on the interruption of this age, "the *mysterion* (mystery, secret) of Messiah… for ages past kept hidden in God… now revealed by the Spirit" (Eph 3:2–9).[217] This was the Gospel, the good news of end-time salvation *now* available in Jesus and the Spirit – reconciling Jew *and* Gentile in Messiah's Body as one true people of God. *Therefore, how do these Messianics (Christians) experience and live the mystery of this salvation?*

---

217 As Jesus taught, via parables, that "the *mysterion* of the kingdom of heaven" was God's promised future age present in him, mysteriously working in this age without ending it (Matt 13:11–17).

Part Two: Theology

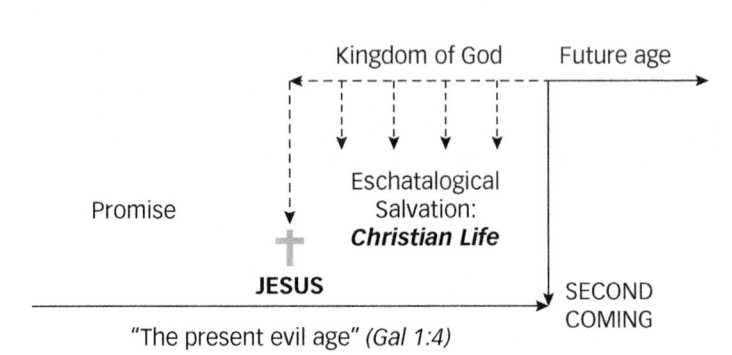

Figure 8. Paul's Eschatological Framework

```
                    Kingdom of God      Future age
              ┌─ ─ ┬ ─ ─ ┬ ─ ─ ┬ ─ ─ ┬ ─ ─
              │    │     │     │     │
              ▼    ▼     ▼     ▼     ▼
              │       Eschatalogical
  Promise     ▼        Salvation:
              ✝       Christian Life
                JESUS                    │  SECOND
  ──────────────────────────────────────▶▼  COMING
       "The present evil age" (Gal 1:4)
```

Nature of eschatological salvation and Christian living

Paul uses many words and metaphors to teach the rich nature of salvation. He uses a few key ones in an early text (my italics), "We... thank God for you... *loved* by the Lord, because God *chose* you as firstfruits to be *saved* through the *sanctifying* work of the Spirit and through belief in the truth. He *called* you to this through our Gospel, that you might share in the *glory* of our Lord Jesus Christ" (2 Thess 2:13-14).

Years later he wrote a similar expanded text, "We know that in all things God works for the good of those who *love* him, who have been *called* according to his purpose. For those God *foreknew* he also *predestined* to be *conformed* to the image of his Son, that he might be the firstborn among many... Those he predestined, he also *called*; those he called, he also *justified*; those he justified, he also *glorified*" (Rom 8:29-30). Some key words (italicized) overlap in these two texts – Paul's *ordo salutis*; the order of events in the process of salvation – as summarized in my diagram below. Let me explain this *ordo salutis* within the kingdom framework.

Before creation God planned, *loved* and *knew* all human beings (Eph 1:4). In *love* he *chose* (predestined, *proorisas*, means to choose or mark out beforehand) some to be saved: those he *foreknew* would believe in the truth of salvation.[218] This salvation *conforms* them to the image of God's Son by the *sanctifying* work of the Spirit. But, at a point in real time, God *calls* them through the Gospel to repentance and faith in Messiah Jesus. Obeying the *call* by faith, God *justifies* them, declaring them in the right (forgiven), now one with God's true people.[219] The Spirit is active in pre-salvation drawing them to faith. Justification is the moment of regeneration, being born again with their new nature in Christ. Now *justified*, the Spirit's *sanctifying* work comes into its own, setting them apart for God and his purpose: to make them holy as God is holy, *conforming them to the King's likeness*. So they are *glorified* – sharing in the King's *glory* of resurrection and ascension to his heavenly rule and reign over his enemies, till his last enemy (death) is finally destroyed. This is *all* salvation. The loved-foreknown-predestined-called-justified-sanctified-glorified people of God are saved and transfigured with ever-increasing glory till their bodily resurrection.

In short, God's one true future – eschatological salvation – reaches back to before creation, and to the beginning of our lives here on earth, to the event of our call and justification, and the Spirit's process of *forming* the Messiah in us, *con*forming and *trans*forming us into his image from one degree of glory to another, till the goal is realized: our full glorification in resurrection to rule and reign with the King.

This raises the first of two notable features in Paul.

---

218 Peter also says God chose us *according to his foreknowledge* by the sanctifying work of the Spirit (1 Pet 1:2). This is *not* deterministic, fatalistic; people still choose in real time to believe or reject God's truth and his salvation – suffering the consequences if they reject (Rom 1:18f, 2:8–9; 2 Thess 2:10–11). God's sovereign choice (based on foreknowledge) versus human freewill is a real paradox.

219 "Justify" is a judicial term: God's future Judgment Day declaration on who is "acquitted" – now realized in Messiah. For Paul, it redefines God's people (Gal 2:11–21): Jews *and* Gentiles are justified, declared righteous, *not* by the works of the law (Torah observance was the 'badge' that identified Jews), but by *faith* in Messiah Jesus (the 'badge' identifying God's one true people). Wright, *Paul in Fresh Perspective*, 120–122, and *Paul and The Faithfulness of God*, 925–1032.

First, he uses three tenses of salvation: past, present and future; or event, process and goal. He uses them *twice* in Rom 5:8–11: *having been* reconciled by Messiah's death we *are now* justified by his blood, how much more *shall we be* saved through his life. In 2 Cor 1:10 Paul says God *has* delivered us, *will* deliver us, and will *continue to* deliver us. Salvation is not a one-off event; "once saved always saved, done that, got the tee-shirt". The truth is: I have been saved (past event), I am being saved (present process), I will be saved (future goal). The end-goal (*eschaton*) of salvation is God's one true future, already inaugurated in history in King Jesus, dynamically active by his Spirit throughout this present age, till the King returns to physically consummate it on earth.

The second feature is his two ways of describing this "mystery of God, namely, Christ, in whom are hidden all the treasures of wisdom and knowledge" (Col 2:2–3). He says earlier (1:27–28), "this mystery, which is *Christ in you*, the hope of glory... (to) present everyone fully mature *in Christ*." Christ in you and you in Christ.

The latter "in Christ" was a common way of referring to a person who represents a group in life and destiny. For example, "For as *in Adam* all die, so *in Christ* all will be made alive" (1 Cor 15:22). Those *in Adam*, all humanity born of Adam, have fallen from God's glory and are under the reign of sin and death. Those *in Christ*, all believers born of Messiah, are justified through his death and made alive in his resurrection (Rom 5:12–20). By believing in Jesus we are (spiritually) immersed into his death and resurrection, symbolized in water baptism (Rom 6:1–10). In Jesus' death *for* our sin we die *to* our sin, no longer slaves under its rule. In his resurrection we rise *to* new life, born again *with* Messiah's eternal life, now under his Spirit's rule. Being raised with him, we ascend and are "seated with him in the heavenly realms *in Christ Jesus*" (Eph 2:4–7), "far above all rule and authority, power and dominion" (Eph 1:21). "*In Christ*, the new creation has come: The old has gone, the new is here" (2 Cor 5:17). This is Paul's *top-down view* of the already of the kingdom, our *position and status* in the King – God's heavenly Reality. We are *already* justified, sanctified and glorified in the King, reigning with him (Rom 5:17). See Figure 9 below.

Paul also describes the mystery as "Christ in you": "I have been crucified with Christ and I no longer live, but *Christ lives in me*" (Gal 2:20). How so? By his end-time Spirit. When we are united to Messiah we are one (S)spirit with him: our bodies are temples of the indwelling Holy Spirit (1 Cor 6:17–20). The King lives in us by his Spirit, who forms his person and power, character and *charisma* in us. To this end Paul laboured, travailing as in childbirth "until Christ is formed in you" (Gal 4:19). This is his *bottom-up view* of the "not yet" of the kingdom in the real world, our *life of faith* in the King by his Spirit in us – our earthly reality. As Paul says, "... it is Christ who lives in me. And *the life I now live in the flesh I live by faith in the Son of God*, who loved me and

Figure 9. Eschatological Salvation (Rom 8:29-30)

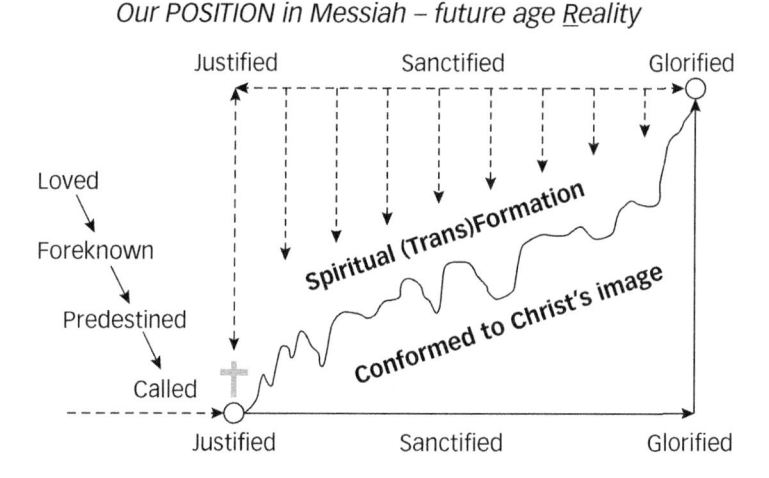

Our POSITION in Messiah – future age Reality

Justified — Sanctified — Glorified

Loved → Foreknown → Predestined → Called → Justified — Sanctified — Glorified

Spiritual (Trans)Formation
Conformed to Christ's image

Our SALVATION in this life – this age reality

gave himself for me" (Gal 2:20 NRSV). Faith is not one-off for a salvation event. Faith is persevering trust and dependence on Jesus in our daily tests and trials in the real world, sharing in the King's sufferings, being assured of his sacrificial love and resurrection power – *Christus Victor* in us by his Spirit!

In summary, as per Figure 9: while we are *already* saints, justified, sanctified and glorified *in Christ*, we are forgiven sinners *being* justified, sanctified and glorified in real terms, through *Christ in us* by his Spirit. Where God's future age Reality breaks into this present age reality – God's heavenly Reality encountering us in our personal earthly reality – it progressively transforms us into the King's iconic likeness. *That* encounter is our real up and down salvation journey as we follow Jesus from justification, through sanctification, to glorification – seeing him face to face.

Spiritual life in the already and not yet of God's kingdom

We are back to Paul's word *pneumatikos*, "spiritual" – to have (live by) God's Spirit. His climactic use of this word is on resurrection, in 1 Cor 15. Jesus reversed Adam's sin and death in his death and resurrection (v.22), becoming "the last Adam, a life-giving Spirit" (v.45). He breathes his Resurrection-Spirit-Life into all who believe, creating a new *pneumatikos* species – one new humanity, God's Church – to reign in life in a new creation already begun.[220] This *spiritual* resurrection to new life anticipates our future *physical* resurrection with a *spiritual* body (*soma pneumatikon* vv.44–46). Between the time of our already spiritual resurrection and our not yet physical resurrection, the Spirit "spiritualizes" us till our mortal flesh is literally "spiritualized", i.e. transfigured into a trans-physical body "so (that) we bear the image of the heavenly man" (vv.47–49). This is all the sanctifying work of the Spirit: spiritual formation and growth to

---

[220] See Gen 2:7 cf. Jn 20:22; 1 Cor 2:12–16, 10:32; Eph 2:15; Rom 5:17; 2 Cor 5:17. Paul uses "Spirit of God" and "Spirit of Christ" as one and the same Spirit (Rom 8:9–11).

maturity in the King's life and character, till we share in the full likeness of his glorious bodily resurrection.

In short, *salvation is a life: God's* life in us, a new creation. It's *spiritual* life because it is *of the Spirit* living in us, governing us to the extent we yield control. Paul uses another key word to describe this end-time work of the Spirit, namely *arrabon*, the "deposit, down-payment" of what is to come (2 Cor 1:22, 5:5; Rom 8:23; Eph 1:13-14). The Spirit is God's seal of ownership over us, the already deposit that guarantees the full reality in the not yet of what is still to come. The *Spirit's* life, work, and reign in and through us in this age, not only anticipates the fullness of *our* life, work, and reign in the age to come, but *guarantees* it will *actually happen*!

Paul takes this further in 2 Cor 3 in his discussion of the new covenant, sealed in Messiah's blood (1 Cor 11:25). The Mosaic covenant was the letter of the law chiseled onto tablets of stony hearts enslaved to sin, unable to keep the covenant. Thus it was a ministry of condemnation and death, though it came with such glory that Moses had to veil his face. The new covenant of King Jesus is the gift of the Spirit who writes God's Torah into renewed hearts, freed from sin, able to keep the covenant – fulfilling Ezek 11:19, 36:26-27. This is a ministry of life with moral empowerment to obey God. It came with so much more *un*veiled glory in Messiah, that we who behold him become like him with ever increasing glory; transfigured into his image by the Spirit of freedom (2 Cor 3:17-18). Paul's point is: *this* new covenant, lived out in God's *pneumatikos* people, is not only a sign of the new age inaugurated in this present evil age, but is the transforming power of that future age at work now.

From 2 Cor 4 to 13 Paul develops his view of new covenant life and ministry *in eschatological tension,* and concludes (12:8-10, 13:4) that it's the paradox of God's *power* (the already) working – even perfected – in our *weakness* (the not yet). It does not deny, despise or obliterate weakness (as in kingdom now theology); neither does it indulge weakness in faithless fatalist acceptance (as in not yet theology). We see it in Jesus:

his greatest triumph in inaugurating the kingdom, when God's power most manifestly defeated *ha satan*, was not in his healings, miracles and exorcisms *per se*. It was in his time of greatest human weakness and death, Gethsemane and Golgotha. It's a theology of power *and* weakness, of suffering *and* victory, of death *and* resurrection. The irony is we already have "this treasure" of the power and glory of the future age in us, in "jars of clay", in our not yet resurrected bodies that suffer mortality and death. The purpose is *to show* that the power is from God and not from us (4:7). *This is the nature of spiritual life lived in the mysterious tension of the overlap of two ages, and this is spiritual warfare.* If you do not grasp this reality you will fall into *either* kingdom now *or* kingdom not yet theologies.

Paul describes the end-time tension like this (4:8–12, my added brackets):

> "We are hard pressed on every side (the not yet), but not crushed (the already); perplexed (not yet), but not in despair (already); persecuted (not yet), but not abandoned (already); struck down (not yet), but not destroyed (already)... For we who are alive are always being given over to death for Jesus' sake (the not yet), so that his life may also be revealed in our mortal body (the already). So then, death is at work in us (the not yet), but life is at work in you (the already)."

New covenant life and ministry is (6:4–10) *"in great endurance; in troubles, hardships and distresses; in beatings, imprisonments and riots; in hard work, sleepless nights and hunger (all realities of the not yet); in purity, understanding, patience and kindness; in the Holy Spirit and in sincere love; in truthful speech and in the power of God; with weapons of righteousness in the right hand and in the left (all realities of the already); through glory and dishonor, bad report and good report; genuine, yet regarded as impostors; known, yet regarded as unknown; dying, and yet we live on; beaten, and yet not killed; sorrowful, yet always rejoicing; poor, yet making many rich; having nothing, and yet possessing everything (all overlapping realities of the already and not yet side by side)."*

If you identify with this, experience any of these strange contradictions, be reassured, you are not crazy! You are simply having a heavy dose of eschatological tension! Re-read the texts – I could cite more – they describe the norm of life and ministry on the dangerous fault-line; not of two overlapping continental plates, but of two colliding cosmic ages. The tremors of opposing pressures are felt in us and around us; teaching the antimony of fierce faith *and* honest realism, the paradox of resilient hope *and* radical honesty, the mystery of suffering *and* victory, of death *and* resurrection. As already people we learn how to live in the not yet, but not in spiritual escapism or utopian triumphalism. Equally, as not yet people we learn to live in the already, but not in denial of the harsh realities of this fallen age.

This does not come naturally or easily! Living in this tension of warfare is not normal to human nature – we want to avoid, neutralize, or escape it. Paul embraced both extremes equally without trying to reconcile them in "the radical middle".[221] Neither did he escape or transcend the tension into either/or theologies: *either* imposing forms of triumphalist perfectionism on present reality, on the basis of "the finished work of the cross" (kingdom now);[222] *or* accepting forms of defeatist resignation as

---

221 This phrase in Vineyard circles has had unintended consequences: it has neutralized healthy tension by integrating the good of opposites in a middle way. Kingdom life and truth is not in the middle, nor in either the already or the not yet, but in embracing "the radical opposites" (new Vineyard phrase?) equally, simultaneously living on the edges in *both* the already *and* not yet.
222 Paul defended his ministry and the Corinthians from "Super Apostles", "false apostles", who preached a "different Gospel" (forms of kingdom-now, 2 Cor 11:1–12:5). They had the same elements of the triumphalist dominion theologies prevalent in our day: The Man of God game of titles, position, power, privilege and prestige; the hyped up power-manifestations of heavenly signs and wonders; the divine health and wealth gospel; ever-new Spirit-revelation in motivational oratory; sinless perfection in the extreme grace of the finished work of the cross; or the second blessing of total sanctification in some holiness movements. Paul did not have much battle with kingdom not-yet

in "whatever will be will be" till some golden daybreak when the King comes (kingdom not yet). And note that in all the above scriptures, and others like Rom 8:18–39, Paul did *not* account hardships, sufferings, weakness, even sickness (e.g. Gal 4:13–14), to God punishing us, or to God's lack of goodness and care. Neither did he attribute it all to the devil *per se,* thus glorifying evil. *He understood it as the reality of life in a fallen world mysteriously interrupted by God's rule and reign.* That made him *push through in faith,* trusting God in suffering and hardship of all kinds, believing God will work in all these things for his good in this age, and ultimately for the age to come.

From Abraham's time Jews have known life between promise (past) and fulfilment (future). David's psalms wrestle with this tension (present): "how long, O LORD?" (6:3, 13:1). Israel prayed the psalms daily as *the* means of instruction and strength to live in the faith of *YHWH,* to trust perseveringly in his promises while facing unmet expectations with raw honesty, not denying the harsh realities of life. Some presumptuously took matters into their own hands to bring the "kingdom now", paying the price for it. Others succumbed to the realities of exile, of hope deferred, and gave in to idol worship, rationalizing it in various "kingdom not-yet" ways. Praying the psalms is a God-given means to live well in eschatological tension.[223]

Why eschatological tension? Mercy, mission and moral formation

Why did God in his wise providence plan eschatological tension, the overlap of two ages? Why did he not just send Messiah once in a kingdom complete in perfect holiness? Why an interim period in anticipation of future perfection?

Paul believed it is *God's grace and mercy* for humanity to hear the

---

theologies because the strong expectation of Christ's imminent return stunted their development in his day.
223 See my book *Praying the Psalms.*

Gospel of Messiah and be saved – hence the priority of preaching to all nations (Rom 10:9–17). If the kingdom had fully come, it would have been final judgment once and for all. The time between Christ's first and second coming ("these last days", Acts 2:17, Heb 1:2) is to show "the riches of (God's) kindness, forbearance and patience", because it is his "kindness (that) leads you to repentance" (Rom 2:4). God our Savior wants all people to be saved, to come to know the truth – for there is one mediator between God and humankind, King Jesus, who gave himself for all people (1 Tim 2:3–6).

Paul also believed it's for our sanctification: *moral growth and character formation* in Christlikeness. We are in training for reigning with the King *in this life* and *the life to come*. The already-not-yet tension in its consolations and desolations, joys and sufferings, is for our spiritual development and eternal witness. God uses it to grow fitness for shared kingdom life with Jesus by his Spirit. And our fitness to rule in conformity to the King's character and *charisma* is missional: to participate in the completion of the *Missio Dei* (God's mission) in this age. More so, it's to prepare us with the character needed to share the King's glory in eternity – to rule over his coming new creation, already begun and entrusted to us in Jesus and the Spirit.

Paul says that in being justified we stand in the King's grace and "boast in our hope of sharing the glory of God. Not only that, but we also boast in our sufferings, knowing that suffering produces endurance,[224] and endurance produces character, and character produces hope, and hope does not disappoint us, because God's love has been poured into our hearts through the Holy Spirit that has been given to us" (Rom 5:1–5 NRSV, see also Js 1:2–4). It's an upward spiral of growth: while we boast in our *hope* of future glory, we also boast in our present sufferings – the already-not-yet clash of realities – because it produces perseverance,

---

224 Paul's theme of the strange power of suffering of all kinds in the kingdom: 1 Thess 3:1–4; 1 Cor 4:9–13; 2 Cor 4:7–18, 6:3–13; Rom 5:3f, 8:17–27; Phil 1:29f, 2:17f, 3:10; Col 1:24f.

which grows godly character, which in turn strengthens our *hope* of shared glory in bodily resurrection to reign with Messiah. And *this resilient hope sustains us in our daily struggles*, because God's love, poured into us by his Spirit, reassures and secures us.

So, our present sufferings are not worth comparing with the glory that will be revealed in us. Because *we know* that God works in all things – every tension, test, suffering – for the good of those who love him, to achieve his purpose to conform us to the image of his Son (Rom 8:18, 28-29). "Therefore we do not lose heart. Though outwardly we are wasting away, yet inwardly we are being renewed day by day. For our light and momentary troubles are achieving for us an eternal glory that far outweighs them all. So we fix our eyes not on what is seen, but on what is unseen, since what is seen is temporary, but what is unseen is eternal" (2 Cor 4:16-18).

Clearly then, the already-not-yet is for our spirituality, our ethical training for moral character, "in order that the righteous requirement of the law might be fully met in us, who do not live according to the flesh but according to the Spirit" (Rom 8:4). That is, the Spirit of Holiness renews and sanctifies our hearts, enabling us to fulfil the moral requirements of Torah (the ceremonial and priestly-purity laws fall away in the new covenant – Messiah fulfilled them).[225] Our bodies, with all their faculties, literally come under the Spirit's governing impulse of love, to obey God in love.

Ethics is about morals, as in behaviour and actions, right and wrong choices, and what motivates and governs them – spirituality in the true sense. *Christian* spirituality is *Christ-like* choices motivated by God's governing Spirit in us. It is *eschatological* ethics: behaving and acting *in the present* as we certainly will when future perfection comes. Perhaps Paul's clearest nuanced statement about ethical life, Christian spirituality between the ages, is Rom 13:11-14 (with my insertions in brackets): "Understand the present time: The hour has already come

---

225 See Rom 10:2-3, 14:1-15:13; Gal 4:8-11, 5:1-6; Col 2:13-23.

(future age) for you to wake up from your slumber (this age), because our salvation is nearer now (future age) than when we first believed. The night is nearly over (this age); the day is almost here (future age). So let us put aside the deeds of darkness (this age) and put on the armour of light (future age). Let us behave decently, as in the daytime (future age), not in carousing and drunkenness, not in sexual immorality and debauchery, not in dissension and jealousy (this age). Rather, clothe yourselves with the Lord Jesus Christ (future age), and do not think about how to gratify the desires of the flesh (this age)." Daytime people behave in the light of the future age, no longer doing deeds of darkness. Thus, Christian ethics is based on God's future salvation already present in Messiah and the Spirit.

Paul's ethics is not about rules but about Rulership. It's not a matter of a new set of rules for those who become Christian. Rather, it is about a new Rulership of Love that has entered the world, enabling us to live up to its rule, and to grow in participation and exercise of that Rulership through practice and training.

This lifts ethics, in its Greek philosophic understanding, into a new paradigm. As per the three standard topics of classic reflection (see chapter 2), the philosophers said that once one understood and knew how the world was (*logics*, the nature of reality and human beings), and how things work (*physics*), it was the human task to live the good life (*ethics*), which was in accordance with, not against, that reality. Paul radically reframed this view: *God's* Ruling Reality has broken into and is renewing the world in Messiah. Those who are *in Messiah* have been renewed as God's good human image-bearers. Their task is to live the good life of the *new* world, in keeping with *its* Reality, not against *it*.[226] This messianic framework of a new world, a new identity, and a new end-time missional ethic, fulfils and transcends the true aspirations of the Greek moralists – as too it does Jewish covenantal ethics.

---

[226] See Wright, *Paul and the Faithfulness of God*, 1371–83. Also Wright, *Virtue Reborn*, and Thompson, *Moral Formation According to Paul*.

Israel's story and how moral transformation takes place

Though conversant with Greek philosophy, Paul was a Jewish thinker. So, we need to draw the above together by showing how he understood spirituality – moral formation – within the Jewish story, retold in light of King Jesus and the Spirit. Wright shows how Paul "theologized" from the *meta-narrative of Israel;* clearly seen to underly his letter to the Romans[227] – also evident in his Galatian and Corinthian letters.

Thinking and living Israel's story reveals Paul's typical Hebrew *community* mindset. Community defined personhood, not the other way around. Spirituality and moral formation was primarily a community pursuit, not an individualistic pursuit as in Greek philosophy. Some rabbis taught that if *all* Israel were to keep Torah for a single day, Messiah would come and save them. Ironically, God sent his King in Israel's continued disobedience, to save *and* enable God's true people to truly keep Torah. Hence Paul instructed faith *communities* in ethical living: "that Christ is formed in you" is the plural "you", the Galatian church. Most of his imperatives (instructions) are plural, placing moral formation in *the* context that makes it possible: the local church. Personal spiritual pursuit is not negated, but empowered by community commitment, support and accountability. There is no such thing as the lone-ranger mindset of individual heroic sainthood, either in Paul or in Jesus!

The meta-narrative in Romans follows the story of Israel:

Chapters 1–3, *all humanity, both Jew and Gentile,* is guilty before God and needs salvation – to be put right with God by Jesus' *redemption* (3:21–26).

Ch. 4, *Abraham* is the example of the *faith* that is "credited as righteousness", putting him right with God. Therefore, both Jews and Gentiles are justified – acquitted and declared righteous – by faith in Messiah.

---
[227] *Romans* in New Interpreters Bible, and *Paul for Everyone – Romans: Part One* and *Part Two*.

Ch. 5, *Adam's* sin with its reign of death enslaved both Jew and Gentile just as the Pharaohs enslaved Israel for 400 years. King Jesus is the ransom (price) that redeems (buys back) those slaves who trust in him, freeing them to reign in life.

Ch. 6, *The Exodus* out of slavery to sin and death is through the waters of baptism, i.e. actual participation and transformation in the King's death and resurrection. This frees us into *God's* rule, to become "slaves of righteousness."

Ch. 7, We do not come to Sinai to receive *The Law*, the old "marriage" covenant that failed to govern Israel's life and behaviour – not because Torah was unspiritual – Israel was! They had unrenewed hearts of stone: "I don't do the good I want to do, but I do the evil I don't want to do." Paul describes the person under The Law – or the inner law of conscience for Gentiles (2:14–15) – not a regenerate believer in conflicted guilt. The Law exposed their sinful nature and condemned them, thus failing to equip them in the wilderness to reign in the Promised Land.

Ch. 8, Rather, we receive *the Spirit* in the new covenant in Messiah's blood. The Spirit renews our hearts to govern our life and behaviour – the equivalent of entering the Promised Land. For those in Messiah there is no condemnation, because The Law *of the Spirit*, who gives eternal life, enables us to fulfil *the Spirit of* The Law, to live eternal life. Led by the Cloud and Fire in the wilderness of moral formation, the Spirit equips us through tests and temptations, sufferings and groaning prayer, for our inheritance (8:17–39): the Promised Kingdom of bodily resurrection, with creation's liberation, to reign with Messiah.

Ch. 9–11, *Ethnic Israel:* Paul then explains how and where Jews fit into this revised messianic story.

> Ch. 12–16, *Spiritual living*: Paul concludes with instruction on moral living in relation to the church, government and society, as witness to living the kingdom.

We need to zoom in to the time between Exodus and inheritance: the wilderness journey between Messiah's first and second coming, to focus on *how moral formation works in practice*. The answer? We live *the reality* of our Exodus, i.e. we daily live out *the meaning* of our one-off Christian baptism of death and resurrection (Rom 6), also enacted in regular partaking of the Lord's Supper.

How do we do this? Paul says: by mind (knowledge), by heart (believe), by attitude (reckoning), and by action (offering).

First, "*we know*" (6:3,6,9, emphasized three times, i.e. get it clear in your *mind*) we *have been* baptized into the King's death and resurrection. What happened to him, on our behalf, happened to us in our Exodus conversion. This *has* freed us from sin into new life, our new identity in the King. We *know* this *has happened* – our true reality.

Second, "*we believe*" (6:8) that this is true, that we will live with him, living resurrection now. It is a *heart-choice* to trust what we know to be true, as Paul later says, "it is with your heart that you believe" (10:9-10).

Third, we adopt *that attitude*. How? By *reckoning* and *resolving* (6:11-12). We *reckon* (count) ourselves *now* dead to sin and its enslaving rule, and *now* alive to God under his Spirit's grace-full rule. Thus, we *resolve* (decide) that we will no longer allow sin to reign in our mortal body via our corrupted appetites and desires.

And fourth, *we act* on our knowledge, faith and attitude to stop the practice of sin by practicing righteousness. How? By the *dual action* of offering ourselves proactively to God and *not* reactively to sin (6:13-23). This *dual practice* is a daily spiritual discipline of worship that draws on the indwelling presence and power of the Spirit. Positively, we practice our "yes" to God by *offering* our body and its members to him as instruments of righteousness. It means we do right by conscious prayerful choices daily in the moment of testing. Negatively, we practice our "no" to evil by *not offering* our body and its members to sin as instruments of wrongdoing. We consciously refuse to act on the inner habitual impulses of our previously sin in-habited members, when tempted to do so via our corrupted thoughts, desires and appetites. The more routinely we do this *dual action* by *daily practice* – a long obedience in the same direction – the more our body-members are rehabilitated into slaves of righteousness, leading to lived holiness. Then we naturally do right by our habituated new nature, free from sin's slavery *in real terms*, and living resurrection now.

Renewing the mind, re-inhabiting the body

A key summary is 12:1–2 (RAP): "Don't conform but transform! How? Offer your body to God as a living, holy, pleasing sacrifice – worship that brings your mind into line with God's mind. Don't allow this age to squeeze you into its shape of thinking; instead, be transformed by renewing your mind in God's thinking – to be in shape to work out and live his perfect will."[228] Besides the body, *Paul places great emphasis on the mind, prioritizing its renewal in the way we think* – and thus what we (choose to) believe, and consequently what we do. We are not given a set of rules. We must develop the mind of Christ by the Spirit to *think through* how to live godly lives. Clearly then, faith renews our thoughts, and our thoughts become our words, which become our actions, which become our habits, which become our character, which becomes our destiny both now and in eternity – incarnating God's perfect will.

The dual action/practice of offering our body and renewing our mind, which results in our moral formation, assumes a psychology or view of the human body as *in-habit-able*. God created and designed the body to be his earthly icon, his *habitation* by his Holy Spirit, radiating his glory.

---

[228] My RAP is inspired by Wright's exegesis in *Paul and the Faithfulness of God*, 1123. For an excellent study on Paul's emphasis on the mind and its renewal, see Keener, *The Mind of the Spirit*.

Our body is God's instrument of his will done on earth as the angels do in heaven. Through Adam's sin and separation from God, the body and its members have been *in-habited* by evil spirit, by virtue of – and leading to – the *habitual* practice of sin. This downward spiral of participation in evil forms our bodily members in its image to naturally do its will on earth as it is in hell. Sin *in-habits* the members of our body in such a way that they operate with a (sinful) mind of their own: "it is no longer I myself who do it, but it is sin living in me" (7:17).

Jesus and the Spirit redeem and reverse this process in our Exodus out of slavery to sin. The Spirit's life literally indwells our body, leading to – by our virtuous responses – the *re*-habiting (retraining) of its very members. They are *habituated* to God's presence and government by the Spirit's *in*-habited impulse to naturally do his will as it is in heaven. "The result is eternal life" (6:22): the spiritual conditioning and moral fitness for *full* life with God, able to share his glorious government and joy forever!

"Offering" – just like "sanctification", the above work of the Spirit – is the language of Temple and priesthood. The Spirit sets us apart and makes us holy for God's dwelling: we are the eschatological Temple filled with God's *Sh'kinah* (glory), both as church (Christ's Body, 1 Cor 3:16–17) and individual believers (our bodies, 1 Cor 6:19–20). The Spirit also sets us apart as the holy eschatological priesthood who *offer* sacrifices as daily worship *of God*.[229] So, to *offer* the members of our body *to sin,* as instruments of evil, *is idolatry*. Who or what we worship, whether God or idols, over time incarnates itself into our bodies and its members, forming us into its image. Paul's regular call to turn from idol worship was to *both* Gentile converts *and* Jews! He called for holy living: cleanse your heart, mind and body; keep yourself pure as *God's* temple, free from all sinful entanglements, especially sexual sins.[230]

Continuing in Rom 8:1–16: *the practice* of moral formation between Exodus and inheritance, between the already and not yet, is the battle

---

[229] Rom 6:13, 16, 19, 12:1; also 1 Pet 2:5; Phil 4:18; Heb 13:15–16.
[230] Rom 13:8–14; 1 Cor 1:2, 6:9–20; 2 Cor 7:1; Eph 5:1–18; 1 Thess 4:3–8, 5:23.

between "life according to the Spirit" (our new nature in Christ, the already) and "life according to the flesh" (our old sinful nature, the not yet). Do *not* confuse Paul's use of "the flesh" with the body itself as inherently sinful or inferior – the Gnostic view. That leads to "harsh treatment of the body" via spiritual disciplines, which "lack any value in restraining (let alone rehabilitating and transforming) sensual indulgence" (Col 2:23).[231] So life in the Cloud and Fire of the Spirit is again *a dual action*.

We *proactively* feed the new: consciously "set *our mind* on what the Spirit desires", *acting* on the governing motivations of "the mind of the Spirit", growing in Christ's character. This is how the Spirit *in us* – who raised Jesus from the dead – actually gives life to our *mortal* bodily members to do God's will, though our body is still subject to death (8:10–11). And we *reactively* starve and "put to death" the old (8:13): we resolve *not* to set *our mind* on corrupt desires, conscientiously turning from and killing off old sinful tendencies. "The mind of the flesh" leads us back to Egypt to be slaves again to sin and fear. But the Spirit leads us by the hand as God's children to the Promised Land, equipping us with fitness for full kingdom inheritance.

In 1 Cor 10 Paul asks if we are any different to Israel in the wilderness? He retells Israel's story via the lens of Messiah and the Spirit. The generation that came out of Egypt, except for Joshua and Caleb, died under God's displeasure *due to their repeated sinful choices in the daily tests they faced*. Twice Paul says: what happened to them are examples to *warn us* ("on whom the culmination of the ages has come", vv.6, 11) *not to set our minds on sinful desires*. Do not test God as they did. "Be careful", we too can die (v.12 cf. 11:30). So his instruction is (v.13) to *know* that whatever temptation we face is common to everyone; that God is faithful and will *not* let us be tested beyond what we can bear; that he *always*

---

231 See Dunn's spectrum of eight meanings in Paul's usage of "the flesh" in various contexts, in *The Theology of Paul*, 64–66. In Rom 6–8 "the flesh" is the sphere of sin's operation; i.e. the body and its parts, offered/used to sin, are enslaved (*in*-habited) to evil by regular practice. The body is equally, in Christ, the sphere of the Spirit's operation (*re*-inhabited) to be a slave of righteousness to holiness.

provides the way out by the Spirit and prayer so that we not only endure it, but overcome it, and mature through it.

Finally, we "understand the present time" and live accordingly as we "*clothe yourselves* with the Lord Jesus Christ, and do not *think* about how to gratify the desires of the flesh" (Rom 13:11–14). Notice, "do not think about…" – the renewal of the mind again. Clothes symbolized the old or new self (life, nature, identity, character): therefore, *put off* the old and *put on* the new. This was the language of Christian baptism (Gal 3:27). To clothe ourselves, to put off and put on, is living *the reality and meaning* of our baptism and regular breaking of bread.

It's the same dual action: you *have* died with Christ, so *put off* the old nature ("the flesh") with its sinful practices and death-fruit. You *have* risen with Christ, so *put on* your new character in Christ ("the Spirit") with its righteous practices and life-fruit. We follow Jesus by imitating him: *participating* in his death and resurrection every time we die to sin and live to righteousness. This *transforms* us into his image, our new nature, sharing in his ascension and rule *in real terms* in *this* life.[232]

Paul uses the same language of Romans in Eph 4:17–32 and Col 3:1–14. If anything, he is blunter in Col 3:5, 8, "put to death… rid yourselves of all" the sins he lists, *because if you do not kill them they will kill you* (v.6)! No compromise! To put to death the lists of sins – outward practices of inner corrupt desires, later called vices – we must *think through appropriate replacement practices* to live out our new nature in Christ. For example, Eph 4:23f, we put off falsehood by the regular practice of truthfulness; we put off anger by the regular practice of reconciling before going to sleep; we put off stealing by working with our hands, making things to give to others; we put off filthy language and demeaning talk by speaking words of grace, and so on. By these practices among many

---

[232] Rom 5:17 cf. Eph 1:18–23 (esp. 22–23). Schnelle, in *Apostle Paul*, 547f, shows Paul's paradigm is *participation and transformation* in Christ's death and resurrection. This underlies his *indicative and imperative* statements (what Christ has done/who we are in Christ, and his "therefore" commands to live accordingly), which is commonly seen – inadequately so – as Paul's real paradigm.

others – Paul's typical lists of spiritual imperatives and disciplines ("be kind to one another, forgive each other", and so on) – we put on, in real terms, Christ's character traits, later called virtues.

Therefore, while participation in Christ's death and resurrection is our daily dying to self, enabled by the Spirit, transformation is the fruit of the Spirit's work. We see retrospectively that the Spirit's power *was* indeed at work, even in our weaknesses, growing the King's character in us. Spirituality is *the fruit* of the Spirit's work in us, seen by others. In Gal 5:19–23 Paul contrasts "the *works* of the flesh" (plural – disintegration of sin) with "the *fruit* of the Spirit" (singular – integration of Christlikeness). In other words, the fruit of the Spirit's work is growth in Christ's character: love, joy, peace, patience, kindness, goodness, faithfulness, gentleness and self-control.

Summary and concluding points

First, Messiah and the Spirit *reverse* the downward spiral of degradation detailed earlier in Rom 1:18–32. That is, *the upward spiral of transformation* begins with God's self-revelation in Messiah and his new creation. Acknowledging and believing this revealed truth, we are reconciled to God and receive his Spirit-Life. Our hearts and minds are renewed and enlightened. This rehabilitates our desires and bodily appetites, renewing and reorienting them to godly passions. They in turn re-inhabit our body-members with practice(s) of godly obedience. Hence our mortal bodies are sanctified, *in real terms,* as God's Temple, restoring God's *eikon* on earth as witness to the world in anticipation of the resurrection. This leads to transformation of our relationships and society,[233] ending in the goal of creation's liberation and renewal.

Second, this spiritual (trans)formation *requires moral effort*. If we do not responsively co-operate with the sanctifying work of the Spirit, the

---

[233] The "household rules" fit here – common in the Greco-Roman world, but radically reframed by Paul in his messianic worldview (Eph 5:21–6:1–9; Col 3:18–25) – no elaboration for lack of space.

grace of God will be lost on us ("without effect", 1 Cor 15:10). Paul gives commands/imperatives to Christ-followers to obey God by a) appropriate thought-out disciplines that reverse specific sinful behaviours and, b) assumed standard practices of worship such as daily prayer. This *effort*, motivated by grace, must not be confused with *earning*, denied by grace. Grace (*charis*) is "gracious enabling gift": God's generous unmerited gift of end-time salvation through Jesus and the Spirit. Eph 2:8–10 says we are saved by grace through faith (itself a gift of grace), not by our own efforts or righteous works, so that no one can boast – because *we* are *God's* work of art in King Jesus *to do good works* prepared in advance for us. In other words, we are not saved *by* good works, we are saved *for* good works. Rather than making us passive, grace and faith motivate responsive effort and action. Phil 2:12–13 makes it clear (my RAP): Continue to conscientiously work out the salvation that God has and is working in you – with trembling awe – and discover that *God* is working *his* willing and acting in *your* working, to fulfil his good purpose. Grace means we cannot *merit or earn* salvation, but it certainly inspires *moral effort* to work it out in our daily lives till we die.

Third, spiritual practices are about *following, imitating, participating*. We are spiritually re-formed into the King's living icon on earth by *imitatio Christi:* we follow Christ by imitating him in *his* life practices, participating in *his* death and resurrection in *our* daily dying to sin and living to obey him. More so, we imitate God our Father, as his beloved children (Eph 5:1–2), by imitating Jesus. And to do that we follow, even imitate, his best followers, who are our spiritual leaders *in deed*. Paul says, "follow (imitate) my example, as I follow (imitate) the example of Christ" (1 Cor 11:1). His life and teaching, and that of the respected church elders, was a model of discipleship and spirituality; of practices that trained and coached, mentored and led followers in The Way of Jesus (1 Thess 1:6; 2 Tim 2:2–3, 3:10–17). The example of leaders and our discipline of submission to them are basic to spiritual formation.

Fourth, life between the times in the overlap of the ages is by definition *spiritual warfare*. Messiah *has* defeated evil, *is* defeating evil, and *will* defeat evil. We, who have the King's Spirit, experience this conflict precisely because we are his primary instruments in defeating evil in this age. Paul teaches that the Christian life is a daily wrestle, a daily fight against evil in all its forms. We win ground, as it were, "little by little" from the world, the flesh and the devil, just as Israel did in entering the Promised Land (Ex 23:30). Each battle grew their capacity and character that was needed to *fully* inherit and possess the kingdom.

This is basic to our spiritual formation because our immediate battle is in us – in our mortal body – and then in the world around us. That is Paul's point in Rom 8: just as *the body* in its groaning frailty and passions is the battlefield and training ground for our reigning, with a view to its resurrection; so likewise *the earth* in all its groaning frustration under the curse is our battlefield and training for reigning, in anticipation of its liberation and renewal. Learning to rule over our will, imagination, thoughts, passions, words and deeds – in our "still subject to death" bodies – enables us to demolish strongholds, arguments and pretensions set up against the knowledge of God in the world. These are our spiritual weapons to bring every thought captive to obey King Jesus (2 Cor 10:3–6). Therefore, in the war with Satan and his "spiritual forces of evil", we must "put on" (again!) the "full armor of God" (Eph 6:10–18). The armour and weapons are the spiritual practices (virtues, moral strengths) of essential truth, heart righteousness, bold witness, protective faith, a strong salvation mind, use-full knowledge of God's word, persistent prayer and prayerful vigilance.

Fifth, the goal (*telos*) of moral formation is not *eudaimonia*, the happiness of a fully flourishing human being, as the Greek philosophers taught. Paul's goal was fully *mature* human beings in the image of Messiah: to "present everyone fully mature in Christ" (Col 1:28). His next phrase is grace-enabled effort: *"For this* (goal) *I toil and struggle with all the energy that he powerfully inspires within me*" (v.29 NRSV). To become fully human and fully alive as God's shining icon on earth is to be formed, conformed, and transformed into *Christ's* character (authority) and *charisma* (power) as the New Adam, the quintessential human being. Self-fulfilment (*eudiamonia*) is part of it, but maturity (*teleios*) is the whole of it – because it is *missional*: that God's kingdom may come in and through us into the world, to the ends of the earth, for the renewal of all things. More so, maturity is for *eternity*: training for reigning throughout the age(s) to come. Therefore, to neglect our growth to maturity in the King, and the effort that it requires – or to deem it as simply unimportant – would be *the* greatest miscalculation not only in human history, but also for eternity!

Above all else: Love

Finally, for Paul, love is primary. Maturity in King Jesus is the Spirituality of Love. To know the breadth, length, height and depth of the ocean – of the ever-expanding universe – of God's love, is to be "filled with all the fullness of God" (his mind-blowing prayer in Eph 3:14–21). In practice, this is being "filled with the Spirit" (Eph 5:18f), which means everything in us comes fully under, and is exquisitely attuned to, the Spirit's Reign of Love. Saturated with God's love by the Spirit (Rom 5:5), we are able to do God's will whenever we need to do it, as it is in heaven. In keeping with Jesus, Paul taught love as *the* ethic that fulfils the entire law of God (Gal 5:14; Rom 13:8–10). Moral formation is not keeping the rules but being filled with the Spirit's rule of love, which enables us to obey in love of God, neighbour and enemy. It means thinking his thoughts, feeling his feelings, speaking his words, and doing his deeds – in love – as he would if he were you in any and every situation.

Greek moralists taught courage, prudence, temperance and justice, as the core or "cardinal" *arete;* the moral strengths of character (Latin writers used *virtus*, hence virtues).[234] To be a rounded flourishing person in the

---

234 See Wright, *Virtue Reborn*, 30–33. Beside others, the principle or "cardinal" virtues are

Greco-Roman one had to cultivate and live these virtues. In contrast, the early Christians settled on humility, patience, chastity and love – all of which were largely ignored, even despised as weakness in the Greco-Roman world. It shows the radical inversion of values, the revolution of the up-side-down kingdom of the crucified and risen King that turns the world right-side-up.

In possibly his earliest letter, Paul highlights "the fruit of the Spirit": the values and virtues, character traits of Christ, cultivated in those who live by the Spirit – *with love at the head of the list* (Gal 5:22–25). And also "faith, hope and love" (1 Cor 13:13; 1 Thess 1:3, 5:8) which, he insists, continue in the age to come, in contrast to the (temporal) gifts of the Spirit. *But the greatest is love.* Paul confirms this years later while imprisoned in Rome: "over all these virtues put on love, which binds them all together in perfect unity" (Col 3:14). Indeed, despite his emphasis on the mind, more important than all knowledge, even love of the truth, *is to know how to truly love.* This fulfils the *Sh'ma*: Hear, O Israel, love God and neighbour (Deut 6:4–5 cf. 1 Cor 8:1–6; Gal 5:14). For Paul "the only thing that counts is faith expressing itself through *love*... (therefore) serve one another humbly in love" (Gal 5:6, 13).

The point is: Paul taught the pursuit of various *arete* (virtues) to achieve the *telos* (goal) of *teleios* (maturity/perfection) in Christ. Space does not allow me to elaborate on each of these character virtues. However, as mentioned earlier, it is remarkable how the first Christians chose the most obscure Greek word for love, *agape*, and filled it with their messianic meaning to proclaim Jesus to the world. *Agape* is the gift of oneself – selfless love as seen in Jesus – the lens through which they saw all other kinds of love (see footnote 190).

Peter Carnley rightly points out that "love, as the gift of oneself, is particular and unique" due to the particularity and uniqueness of each person who loves – and is loved. Jesus was remembered by the very distinctive and intensely personal love he showed to others, culminating

---

"the hinges" (the literal meaning) that open the door to *eudaimonia*, human flourishing.

in his selfless sacrifice on a cruel cross to save humanity. "*Agape* did not mean generalized love"; it meant "the particularity of Jesus' love... *Agape* itself is the gracious activity of the Spirit, the medium of the presence of the raised Christ himself."[235] In other words, the early messianic communities *experienced this love as an active power present by the Spirit*, referred to in Rom 5:5. It is ultimately *God's* eternal love incarnate in Jesus and the Spirit, from which literally no one or no thing can separate us (Rom 8:35-39).

In summary: love became the foundational cornerstone and completing capstone of life and maturity in Christ. It's *the* ethic that determined church life and Christian living, *the* lens through which life itself was viewed, giving value and dignity, meaning and purpose, to all human beings. Love is the very nature of being itself. It's not so much what we do, it's who we are: being-in-love. Hence Paul's RAP: "Imitate God your Father as his dearly beloved children: *learn to live a life of love*, just as Jesus particularly and uniquely loved us, giving himself up for us as a fragrant sacrifice to God" (Eph 5:1-2). Simply lose yourself in a life of worship of God by humbly and practically serving others in love.

I end with Paul's poem (1 Cor 13:4-8) that defines *agape*-love. It describes the kind of person who is being-in-love, governed by *God's* love:

Love is patient, love is kind.
It does not envy, it does not boast, it is not proud.
It does not dishonor others, it is not self-seeking.
It is not easily angered, it keeps no record of wrongs.
Love does not delight in evil but rejoices with the truth.
It always protects, always trusts, always hopes, always perseveres.
Love never fails.

---

235 Carnely, *The Structure of Resurrection Belief,* 332, 336.

QUESTIONS FOR REFLECTION AND DISCUSSION

1. What is your overall impression of what this chapter (or God) is saying to you?
2. What is new or different for you in this chapter? What do you disagree with?
3. How did Saul's coming to faith in Jesus as Messiah impact his understandings and subsequent living of life? How did you come to know Jesus and what change did it have on your understandings and living of life?
4. What's your view of Paul's analysis of humanity's fall and degradation in Rom 1–3? Do you agree with it? And with his teaching of God's judgment?
5. How do you relate to Paul's eschatological view of human history, as the already and not yet of God's salvation and rule in Messiah? Why this strange reality of spiritual tension and warfare? What is it for? How do you cope with it?
6. How do *you* define salvation? How would you articulate Paul's understanding of salvation? What role does it play in Christian spiritual formation?
7. Practically, how does spiritual-moral formation actually take place, as per Paul's teaching? Does it work in *your* daily life?
8. Which of the cardinal virtues (moral strengths) do you identify with most: the Greek moralists or those of the Early Church… and Paul's fruit of the Spirit? Do you intentionally cultivate the character traits of Jesus in your life? If so, how?

PART THREE

PRAXIS

Praxis means practice: the practical application of biblical theology to Churchlife and Christian living. It answers the what? and the how? of spirituality, as opposed to the who? and why? of theology. Initially there was no such distinction between theology, spirituality and practice, as in the famous dictum by Evagrios The Solitary: "If you are a theologian, you will pray truly. And if you pray truly, you are a theologian" (footnote 82).

Theology is now subdivided into various branches. Practical Theology starts with Church and Christian practice and reflects on it within its particular context in light of Systematic and Biblical Theology, including Theological Ethics – so as to adjust the praxis accordingly. It is *a circular reflective movement*: from the current praxis to the context, to theology and ethics, then back to redefining the praxis.

Part three is therefore an exercise in both practical theology and the application of biblical theology to spiritual praxis. I examine the traditional (historical) paradigm and practice of the Christian spiritual path; how transformation takes place; the menu of the classic spiritual disciplines, and other related aids or tools; ending with a chapter on daily spiritual life in creative tension.

CHAPTER 9

CHURCH TRADITION: THE TRINITARIAN SPIRITUAL PATH

*"First pray for the gift of tears,
so that through sorrowing you may tame what is savage in your soul"*
Evagrios The Solitary[236]

*"His divine power has given us everything needed for life and godliness,
through the knowledge of him who called us by his own glory
and goodness. Thus he has given us his very great and precious promises,
so that through them you may **participate in the divine nature**,
having escaped the corruption in the world caused by evil desires"*
Peter – 2 Pet 1:4

The classic spiritual path in Christian tradition is known as the three stages of *purification* of the body/soul, *illumination* of the mind/intellect, and *union* of heart/spirit with God. In the Latin West (Catholic and Protestants) it is *Via Purgativa, Via Illuminativa, Via Unitiva* (*via* is "the way of"). The Greek East (Orthodox) have the same stages, but as prayer of the lips – purification; prayer of the mind – illumination; and prayer of the heart – perfection or divinization (from *theosis*, union with God

---

236 *On Prayer*, in Palmer et al., *The Philokalia*, Vol. One, 58.

by participating in the divine nature, without confusion of persons).[237]

Early monasticism was key to the emergence, practice and articulation of this spiritual path. Its goal was perfection as in "how to obey the commandments of Jesus Christ by living as consciously as possible in the loving presence of the indwelling Trinity so as to pray always."[238] It was also known as the Trinitarian way, because it is through the Son (purgation) by the Spirit (illumination) to the Father (union), in keeping with Trinitarian theology from the 4th cent. onwards.

Historical development and background factors[239]

The Early Church shifted from strong expectation of the immanent return of Messiah (e.g. 1 & 2 Thess) to facing its delay; even facing their probable death before Jesus' return (e.g. 1 & 2 Tim). In their kingdom worldview inherited from Jesus, the first Christ-followers, if anything, leaned to a realized eschatology. Paul had to correct kingdom-now excesses. As Christianity spread through the Roman Empire, vicious persecution arose, leading to a theology of martyrdom in the post apostolic Church. Expectation of Christ's (delayed) return was projected onto a heavenly hope of rewards when they die. Hence they prioritized living faithfully for Messiah in the life and death battle *of this continuing evil age*. Post NT writings shift from an end-time emphasis to a not yet consciousness – with a heavenly focus – in an emerging *liturgical* and *ascetic* paradigm that defined spiritual practices as faithful living.

Liturgical, from *leitourgia*, is the service of worship offered in the church through Messiah by the Spirit. Christian community was the

---

237 This is *not* the New Age/Gnostic idea that humans are, and become, the divine in us via spiritual knowledge and practices. *Christian* divinization (discussed below) is also called deification, inGoding, transfiguration, Christification, divine-humanity, sophianization (*sophia*, wisdom) – all understood as Paul's idea of sanctification and glorification – see Christensen & Wittung (eds.), *Partakers of the Divine Nature,* and Stavropoulos, *Partakers of Divine Nature.*

238 Maloney, *Prayer of The Heart*, 5.

239 The usage of Greek in the church fathers preceded the Latin, so I use Greek terms to explain the spiritual path, drawing more on Eastern texts, while integrating the Latin.

place of safety and strength, so the structure and nurture of church in its worship and ministry became the locus of spiritual formation for witness. Ascetic, from *askesis*, means exercise and training. It refers to the practice of accepted disciplines for spiritual fitness in worship and ministry, mission and martyrdom, in the changing context of the day. Indeed, *praxis* meant the regime of ascetical practices that exposed and put to death the false self, the old sin nature, to uncover and nurture our new nature in Christ, our true self.

In short, Jesus and the Early Church's kingdom worldview that defined discipleship and spirituality, shifted to an emerging liturgical and ascetic paradigm with a mission and martyr focus. The ascetic paradigm, however, already present in Paul (1 Cor 9:24–27), became dominant when Emperor Constantine decreed tolerance for Christianity in 313. Social acceptance and political power resulted in the Church becoming worldly and wealthy. In reaction, Palladius records in his *Lausaic History*, thousands of men and women fled the cities to build communities of Paul's new creation in the deserts of Egypt, Syria and Mesopotamia. Their separation from the world was not *ontological* ("the world is evil") but *Eschatological* (God's kingdom has come), and thus *missional* (as witness to the world). They "declined to be ruled by men, but had no desire to rule over others" except to rule over their own thoughts and bodies, sins and demons.[240] So, it can be said, monasticism was born under the motto: *Fuge, tace, quiesce*, "Flee, be silent, be still", attributed to monk Arsenius (350–445).

Desert fathers arose, like Anthony of Egypt (251–356), the first iconic hermit who began seeding the three-fold spiritual path.[241] Many came to learn from him, including Evagrios, who's above quote on prayer is typical of the way of purification. Then Syrian monk Pseudo Dionysius (early

---

240 Thomas Merton, *The Wisdom of the Desert*, 5.
241 Maloney says in *Pilgrimage of the Heart*, 18, "For these early athletes of Christ (ascetics), the desert was the twilight zone between the profane world that groaned under the bondage of sin and the heavenly Jerusalem of the transfigured world to come… men intoxicated with God."

6th cent.) first used the phrase "mystical theology", framing the threefold path into an ascetic-*mystic* paradigm.[242] He taught the negative way to know God by unknowing, by mystical love and faith beyond the natural senses – first introduced by the Cappadocian fathers (see footnote 243).

This points to other background factors to the spiritual path as in the two ways of knowing God, explained in chapter 3. The common positive (*cataphatic*) way of knowing God via thoughts and senses: *meditation*. And the uncommon negative (*apophatic*) way of unknowing by negation of the senses: *contemplation*. Both ways are needed as each feed into the other. It is not either/or; see Appendix 2.[243]

There was the shift from NT kingdom theology to the post-apostolic debate on Christology: Christ's human and divine nature. This then led to Trinitarian theology, summarized in carefully worded statements in the Apostolic, Nicene and Athanasian Creeds – partly in answer to the various heresies that attacked the Church, which I will refer to when needed. The Trinity undergirded the spiritual paradigm.

And there was the wholistic Hebraic spirituality of *the heart* passed on by the NT apostles: total existential encounter with God – the heart being *both* the core essence *and* whole person, from which life flows (Prov 4:23).[244] Then an *intellectual* spirituality arose, influenced by Hellenist philosophies (Platonic, Stoic), with Gnostic traits.[245] *Some* adopted

---

242 These part-paradigms (*missional, martyrdom, liturgical, ascetic, mystical*) find their place and meaning *within* the NT *kingdom-in-tension* whole-worldview. If the whole is neglected, or shifted into kingdom now or not yet part-paradigms, then the part becomes the (false) whole – the new lens through which spirituality is seen, interpreted and practiced – leading to imbalance, then excess, then heresy.

243 Johnston says that the 4th cent. Cappadocian fathers (Basil the Great, Gregory of Nazianzus and Gregory of Nyssa) "blend apophatic and cataphatic into a single paradoxical experience" in "the mystical tradition that flows from them." *This is the ideal*. In *Mystical Theology*, 16.

244 Seen in the Antiochean school of Ignatius (martyred in 108), in Polycarp (martyred in 155), Irenaeus of Lyon (130–202), Anthony of Egypt, and Maximus the Confessor (580–662).

245 Seen in the Alexandrian school of Clement (150–215), Origen (185–254), Evagrios and others.

the dichotomy between spirit and matter: we are souls with spiritual intellect trapped in a burdensome body, due to sin. And so "humanity's full realization would come in suppressing the material of the body and releasing the spiritual of the intellect to contemplate a reality that existed beyond this present world."[246] This calls for correct interpretation of the writings of the post-apostolic Church, the desert fathers and monastic movement, by demythologizing their cultural context and discerning neo-platonic "mixed seed". Failure to do so will lead into wrong thinking and naïve imitation of their (sometimes extreme) practices.

On the other hand we must not "throw the baby out with the bathwater" in our Protestant prejudice against Monasticism, Christian mysticism,[247] Catholic and Orthodox spiritualities. We will miss the rich treasures available to us through them. They give us an extraordinary vision of the goal of Christlikeness and a root understanding of sin – largely lost to our postmodern world – in terms of a profound psychology of human nature, sinful impulses, temptation, demons and spiritual warfare.

Despite the emerging East and West spiritual traditions, there was cross-pollination from early on, resulting in a fairly common understanding and practice of the threefold path. Though distinctive elements emerged in Greek (Orthodox) and Latin (Catholic) spiritualities, we can say that the threefold way is *the* most enduring common spiritual tradition of the Christian Church to this day. The fathers and mothers taught that it was not only for monks, but also for ordinary Christians in daily marriage, family and work, in the required context of right doctrine and participation in liturgical and sacramental life, i.e. accountability in community and spiritual direction. There is no such thing in Christianity

---

246 Maloney, *Pilgrimage of the Heart*, 10.
247 For example, Martin Luther said, "I admonish you to shun like the plague that 'Mystical Theology' of Dionysius and similar books which contain such idle talk", Johnston in *Mystical Theology*, 23. True Christian mysticism is simply living the Gospel at the deepest levels of consciousness. The New Monasticism is a contemporary movement that brings *the good* of monastic values and practices to ordinary Christians in everyday life. See their resources in my Bibliography, The Rutba House (ed.), Augsburger, Jamison, and Workman.

as spiritual elites exempt from the discipline and commitment of local church belonging and membership.

Therefore, part of my motivation in this chapter is to introduce this path to Protestant-Evangelicals and Pentecostal-Charismatics (my root traditions) in order to broaden the rich knowledge and experience of classic Christian spirituality.

Introducing the three stages

The purpose of stage one is *to purify* us from sinful vices by Christ's virtues. This active phase of the *praktiki,* the virtuous-practitioner, is to cooperate with the Spirit's work of grace in *cataphatic* knowing of God via the senses.

Stage two is *to illumine* the purified mind by the Spirit with the vision of God, a transition from active practices to passive enlightenment. In this active-passive phase, the *physiki,* the natural-contemplative, meditates on God via nature, receiving mediated spiritual knowledge of God. "The light of the knowledge of God's glory" (2 Cor 4:6) shines brighter as the senses are darkened to see God by faith – the entrance to the third stage.

The third stage is *union* with the Father. In this passive phase the *theoretiki,* the theological-contemplative,[248] contemplates God directly, experiencing unmediated mystical knowledge of God in *apophatic* union with the Father – in mature faith and love. God is not so much the object of our knowledge as the cause of our wonder. As we advance in The Way, God becomes ever more intimate yet ever more distant; known by the smallest child yet incomprehensible to the most brilliant theologian.

These stages, however, are not fixed. Prayer is a living relationship that defies neat categories. The stages are a yo-yo journey of overlapping movements back and forth till maturity; of interdependent, deepening levels that are more simultaneous and coexistent than consecutive. For

---

248 Both contemplation (*theoria*) and theology (*theologia*) is knowing God experientially. The West translated *theoria* into Lat. *contemplatio* (contemplation, the *apophatic* method) to differentiate it from *meditatio* (meditation, the *cataphatic* method).

example, beginners can have glimpses of divine glory as sheer gift while the most mature saints still fight temptation, seeing themselves at the very beginning. Indeed, though we *are* saints in Christ and *become* saints by sanctification of the Spirit, we *remain* sinners till our last breath – still capable of sinning!

A disclaimer: To *responsibly* explain the threefold path it is necessary for me to go over and dig deeper into some of the ground already covered in this book.

Way of purification for beginners: *Via purgativa*

Christians follow Jesus, who is The Way, by the Spirit, to the Father. The Way begins with purification: "Whoever wants to be my disciple must deny themselves and take up their cross and follow me" (Matt 16:24). Jesus walked the way of self-denying purification and death, not for his own sins – for he was without sin – but for humanity's sin(s). We follow him in the way of purification because our sins *have been* forgiven. This first step, or novice stage *assumes* salvation; as John says, "I am writing to you, dear *children*, because your sins have been forgiven" (1 Jn 2:11).

In the tabernacle and later Temple, the path to God's immediate presence was from the outer court, through the Holy Place, into the Holy of Holies. The first step, the outer court, was the removal of all obstacles to enter God's presence by the laver of washing and altar of sacrifice. Messiah Jesus is the laver and altar that cleanses us from our sin by his once-for-all sacrifice on the cross (Heb 9:26, 10:10). *This* is the basis, not only of salvation, but also of *our* ongoing sanctification and sacrifice of worship: the self-denying offering of our body to God in the washing and renewing of our mind (Rom 12:1–2), purified and transformed at ever-deeper levels of being.

Forgiveness and cleansing of our sins faces us with our *sin*: the sin-principle at work in us. Though it was put to death in our union with Christ on the cross, we are to enforce its death *in real terms,* which is an

Part Three: Praxis

ongoing battle as Peter says, "abstain from the desires of the flesh that wage war against the soul" (1 Pet 2:11). *Via purgativa* is to purge sin out of us by imitating Jesus. We deny ourselves by taking up our cross daily, dying to sin-filled tendencies that govern our corrupted thoughts and desires, words and deeds. The fathers spoke of this dying to self for Christ's sake as *white martyrdom* that all Christians undergo daily, which enables us to joyfully undergo *red martyrdom*, physical death for Christ's sake, if God gives us that gift. In white martyrdom we acquire the virtues that fortify our new nature to obey God's commands, by which we put off the old nature that died with Christ in baptism, and put on our new nature raised with Christ in baptism. The foundation principles of repentance, faith and baptism (Heb 6:1–2) are not one-off for salvation: they help us to *"work out* your salvation with fear and trembling" (Phil 2:12) as the way of purification.[249] We participate in Christ's death and resurrection *in real terms*. And likewise, regular breaking of bread reminds us to live death and resurrection.[250]

After his baptism, the Spirit drove Jesus into the desert for solitude and prayer, and three centuries later drove thousands of Christians to *literally* follow Jesus' example. The same Spirit leads every born again and baptized believer into the wilderness of solitude and prayer, where our "untamed savage soul" is transformed in God. The church fathers saw *prayer* as the symbolic reality of our whole-life, life-long relationship with God. They saw the *desert* as the landscape of the soul where we are stripped – the *kenosis* of self-emptying – of all reliance on wrongful attachments, laying bare our naked need of God. Indeed, the monks saw prayer as a remembrance of death: the daily practice of

---

[249] John Climacus, 7th cent. monk, said, "Greater than baptism itself is the fountain of tears after baptism" that purifies at ever-deeper levels. Cited by Maloney, *Pilgrimage of the Heart*, 34.

[250] Isaac the Syrian (613–700) said, "Blessed is he that has eaten the Bread of Love which is Jesus. While still in this world, he breathes the air of the resurrection, in which the righteous will delight after they rise from the dead." Cited in Ware, *The Orthodox Way*, 109.

solitude and silence before God is the stripping of self in surrender to Transcendent Reality; a regular rehearsal for the day of our death when we (have to) surrender ultimate control to God in total trust and final stillness.[251]

Prayer, even at the best of times, is not easy. It's a daily dying to self. In learning to pray honestly – to become a living breathing prayer, praying our living and living our praying – we enter a desert of demons that breaks the denial of, and the blindness to, the false self we have built up. We then face and overcome what arises: temptations, vices and passions, brokenness and attachments to things other than God; all to be stripped from us by the Spirit. This ongoing desert battle is to test, establish and transform us in our (new) identity in Christ that the devil challenges: "If you are *God's beloved child*, then prove it by…" (Matt 4:3, 6 RAP). To overcome the evil in and around us, *we have to face it* with prayerful use of, and obedience to, God's word, as Jesus did. As we do so, the Word becomes our flesh – living in us, making us strong in God. "I write to you, *young people*, because you are strong and the word of God abides in you, and you have overcome the evil one" (1 Jn 2:14 NRSV).

In short, the way of purification is imitating Jesus *in his spiritual practices* by which we participate in his death and resurrection. Church fathers called it *askesis:* the asceticism of inner striving or struggle via *classic spiritual exercises* like solitude, silence, prayer, fasting, meditation, simplicity, service, and so on (in chapters 11 and 12). The purpose of these practices is freedom from sinful conditioning by training or reconditioning ourselves for full fitness in running the race of shared life and co-working with God.[252] Thus the athlete (ascetic, *praktikos*) of the first stage had two *daily* foci: a) the regime of spiritual disciplines

---

[251] Evagrios said, "the way of stillness teaches (you to) remember the day of your death, visualize the dying of your body… remember too the day of your resurrection and how you will stand before God", *On Asceticism and Stillness,* in Palmer *et al., The Philokalia,* Vol. One, 35–36.

[252] Modeled and taught by Paul, 1 Cor 9:24–27; Phil 2:16; 1 Tim 4:7–10; 2 Tim 4:7. Also Heb 12:1–2.

as *the necessary context* that enables, and b) the regular resisting and overcoming of evil *in the required moment*. The spiritual exercises create *the right conditions or environment* that grows Christ's virtues in us. They form the moral muscle and character to make the right choices *in the moment*, that we might fulfil "the righteous requirement of the law" as we live "according to the Spirit" and not "according to the flesh (sinful nature)" (Rom 8:4).

The ascetic pursuit of *both* a) and b) is only possible by the grace of our Lord Jesus Christ, with the love of our Father and enabling life of the Spirit (2 Cor 13:14). The church fathers taught salvation – purification, enlightenment and perfection – as pure gift, as total grace, not earned by our efforts. However, paradoxically, they also taught serious co-operative effort with God's grace-full work: itself a grace by the power (*dynamis*) and energy (*energia*) of the Spirit. "We are to hold in balance two complementary truths: without God's grace we *can* do nothing, but without our voluntary co-operation God *will* do nothing"[253]

Sadly, the not yet consciousness of this continuing evil age with the emphasis on human effort in the ongoing spiritual battle led some into legalism and performance. They sought to *earn* salvation and sanctification by their efforts in the spiritual quest. When disciplines are viewed or used for spiritual reward and/or bodily punishment in order to merit God's favour and holiness, it leads to unbiblical and extreme practices motivated by performance and guilt, and/or pride and elitism. But to put no co-operative effort into our sanctification by the Spirit, in the name of (extreme) grace, leads to lose liberty and licentiousness – an equal opposite heresy.

---

[253] Kallistos Ware (his italics), *The Orthodox Way*, 112. Diadochus of Photiki (400–486) said, "Divine grace confers on us two gifts… the first gift is given to us at once when grace renews us in the actual waters of baptism… the second – our likeness to God – requires our co-operation", *On Spiritual Knowledge and Discrimination,* in Palmer *et al., The Philokalia,* Vol. One, 288.

Praxis of purification – overcoming vices and passions
English "vice" or "vicious" (full of vice) comes from Lat. *vitium*, meaning defective or failing. Vice was a technical term for the common failures or defective sinful impulses ingrained in fallen human nature. The equivalent in the Greek fathers was "passions", *pathi* or *pathos*; literally that which we suffer, which happens to us, which makes us passive (not the English "passion" as in love). Passions are the corrupted avenues and faculties of disordered thoughts, desires and appetites, by which demons tempt and enslave us. They weaken and overcome our will and make us passive, i.e. we are ruled by our passions. The East had *eight* primary passions, known in the West as the *seven* deadly sins or capital vices (they joined vainglory and pride). The passions or vices move from the physical sensibilities to the deeper levels of soul and spirit:

- *Body:* gluttony (food), lust (sex), avarice (greed of money, things).

- *Psychological:* anger (wrath), envy (sadness and jealousy at other's good fortune), dejection (*acedia* – sloth or listlessness with the spiritual life).

- *Spiritual:* pride (wrong self-esteem, egotistical self-love and selfishness).[254] Vainglory means unjustified or futile boasting, a form of pride. Pride was seen as the original temptation and sin, the source of all the vices.

These are the *primary* or *capital* vices, i.e. each opens the door to other related passions.[255] Beside primary and secondary passions, they distinguished between natural and unnatural passions. Natural passions are God-given faculties enslaved by evil via original sin and our fallen human nature. Salvation frees them to be sanctified and rehabilitated into

---

254 Pride has its "root in *philautia*, egotistical love of self as an autonomous and independent absolute", says Dumitru Staniloae (*Orthodox Spirituality*, 81) in the context of quoting Maximus the Confessor, "It's clear that he who is egotistic has all the passions." So true!
255 It was common to list numerous related passions of the body and soul, each divided into categories; Gregory of Sinai (1265–1346), in Palmer *et al, The Philokalia*, Vol. Four, 226–227.

godly passions for the spiritual life. For example, the *natural* appetites for food and sex are corrupted by sin to enslave us in gluttony and lust, now become *unnatural* passions foreign to our spiritual nature. However, retrained by the discipline of fasting and chastity they become spiritual hunger and pure love, now *godly* passions expressing our new nature in Christ. Anger is a natural passion alerting us to wrongdoing. Indulging unresolved anger can lead to bitterness, hatred and rage – all unnatural passions. Rehabilitated anger becomes godly indignation against all forms of evil, thus motivating compassion. And so on… applicable to all the passions… till all God-given faculties and natural passions are perfected in the resurrection.

Neoplantonic ideas led some to teach: all passions are inherently unnatural, i.e. extrinsic evil to be eradicated, not rehabilitated and integrated. The avenues of enticement were themselves seen as sinful and evil, leading to denigration of the body. Spiritual disciplines were punitive.[256] They did not distinguish between the sinful enslavement of our human faculties and *the faculties themselves*, which need redemption and transformation. Any suppression of *legitimate* bodily appetites and psychic needs – "put them to death, cast them out" – results in those "parts" being split off from the whole of us. To the degree they are separated and alienated from the whole of who we are, their unfulfilled needs seek attention and reintegration by "acting out" with increasing corruption of appetites and desire, known as addictions in modern terms. Thus, legitimate appetites and needs become demonized and drive us with guilt, producing a shame-filled secret life of sin. Then *outward* performance in spiritual practices becomes key *to be seen* to be okay, to have the high moral ground. Such moral legalists (moralism as opposed to healthy morality) often have to hide a dark double life of immoral enslavement by shamelessly imposing their guilt on others.

---

256 "Penance", correctly understood, is deeds or fruit of repentance (Matt 3:8; Acts 26:20; 2 Cor 7:10–11). But penance as punishment and flagellation of the body derives from the Gnostic axiom, "my body kills me, therefore I kill it", cited in Maloney, *Prayer of the Heart*, 39.

In short, the passions are to be educated, *not* eradicated; transfigured, *not* suppressed or cut off. This is how we attain "dispassion" (*apatheia*) for enlightenment and union with God (discussed below). The question is: *how do we overcome our sinful nature, our vices, our corrupted passions?* By "putting on" the virtues, the moral practices and character strengths that overcome the vices. The influential Maximus the Confessor (580–662) said, "Virtue may be defined as the *conscious* union of human weakness with divine strength" via *intentional* spiritual practices.[257]

Primary virtues and practices

Ongoing repentance and faith: It begins with repentance (*metanoia*), literally a change (*meta*) of mind (*noia*) about sin, self and God. "God requires us to go on repenting till our last breath."[258] We turn *away from* vices by seeing their true sin-filled nature. We change our minds, turning *to* virtues as the beauty-full vision of Jesus that ravishes us to love and obey God. Inseparable from this is faith (*pisteou*). Faith is not belief *about* God: *that* he exists, *that* we believe what is true about him. Faith is belief *in* God: to trust him in personal relationship just as we turn to and rely on a friend we trust. "Faith is not the supposition that something might be true, but the assurance that someone is there."[259] We change our thinking by turning to Jesus in all things, *en*trusting ourselves to his enabling Spirit in the sacrament of the present moment, choosing to resist evil and obey God.

Spiritual poverty and sorrow: By repentance and faith we face and own our spiritual bankruptcy before the Holy One. The clearer we see our desperate need for God, the greater our appreciation of his love and

---

257 In Palmer *et al, The Philokalia*, Vol. Two, 230. See 53 for Maximus' seven virtuous practices to overcome the vices (I discuss most of them) and attain dispassion. The fathers had various overlapping lists of virtues or "steps of the ladder" – a common term not meant as pride or elitism, "I'm higher up than you are!" It was to ascend Jacob's ladder of spiritual life, to live heaven here on earth.
258 Said Isaiah the Solitary, of Sketis (420–491), cited by Ware, *The Orthodox Way*, 114.
259 Ware, *The Orthodox Way*, 16.

mercy in our salvation. Knowing our need for mercy opens us to receive mercy, and to be merciful. The fathers spoke much of the gift of tears in prayer, the *penthos* (sorrowing, mourning) of crying out to God for our hearts, the aspects that are still "deceitful above all things" (Jer 17:9).

They discerned between godly and worldly tears, true and false repentance (see 2 Cor 7:9–11). Tears of *godly* sorrow tame what is savage in our souls. God will never despise the acceptable sacrifice: the excellency of a broken and contrite heart (Ps 51:17). An example is the penitent tax collector who prayed beating his breast, "God, have mercy on me, a sinner" (Lk 18:13). This is the basis of The Jesus Prayer of the Orthodox, explained below. Jesus said, "Blessed are the poor in spirit"; to know our spiritual poverty leads to the blessing of mourning (*penthos*) that repents, and such repentance purifies us from the vices and their effects.[260] Wet eyes and a soft heart make for a pure soul.

Watchfulness: The fathers taught that *penthos* (sorrow) produces *nepsis* (sober vigilance – from *nepo*, to be sober, not intoxicated). We cultivate constant attention to diligently guard our heart and mind above all (Prov 4:23; Phil 4:7). *Nepsis* is "the state of inner alertness necessary to check every thought at the entryway to our consciousness."[261] This is how we grow in self-knowledge, healthy self-awareness, and conscious mindfulness as a sacrament of the present moment. God's Spirit is our Joshua Sentinel standing guard at the door to our mind and heart, challenging every thought: "Are you for us or for our enemies?" (Josh 5:13).

The more we cultivate *nepsis* the more our conscience is sensitized to the Spirit's consciousness – responding to, not grieving the Spirit

---

260 The fathers saw the beatitudes (Matt 5:2–10) as the blessed beauty of spiritual growth: from spiritual poverty to mourning, leading to humility and meekness, then hunger and thirst for justice and holiness, making us merciful and pure in heart to see God in all things, becoming peacemakers as God's children who reflect his nature, resulting in certain persecution (contrary to my interpretation in chapter 6).

261 Maloney, *Prayer of the Heart*, 107. *Nepsis* is similar to "mindfulness" in modern psychiatry and psychology, as in Daniel Siegel, *Mindsight: The New Science of Personal Transformation*.

(Eph 4:30). English "consciousness" is from Lat., *conscire*, "to be aware with". Consciousness is *shared awareness* of the self and its living context, a participation in the Spirit's awareness. Then we see reality as it is, through eyes larger and clearer than our own, with immediate knowledge of what is really happening in the present moment, and how to respond accordingly. Consciousness formed by another spirit and/or dominated by our passions, sees people and things as objects to serve and satisfy our ego, the self.

Discerning "passionate thoughts" (*logismoi*): These are the seven/eight *primary* passionate thoughts (vices) and their related subordinates. *Noema* refers to mere thoughts. *Logismoi* are thought-images and sensible-phantasms that arouse the passions, to be discerned as good or bad (Heb 5:14). They become evil as we respond to their allure, accepting them into our consciousness to feed our (unnatural) passions – the cancer of self-love. *Logismoi* distract and scatter our attention from God to self-indulgence, to be countered and defeated by silent prayer. That stills us with *hesychia*, tranquility and rest, focusing and centring us on God's immediate loving presence.

Nepsis (vigilant watchfulness) is the food that feeds the gift of discerning (*diakrisis*) of spirits, which enables us to distinguish between thoughts – both *noema* and *logismoi* – that come from evil spirits, or self, or God. This is how we recognize and resist temptation, and how we hear and obey God. We discern revelations, thoughts and experiences by the fruit they produce. If they are clear and simple, with an authority that witnesses in us, convicting us of truth that can be trusted – and if it leads to faith, hope and love – then it's consolation from "the good Spirit". If, however, it distracts and lures us, resulting in fear, anxiety, guilt and condemnation, then it is certainly desolation from "the bad spirit."[262]

Overcoming temptation: The word for temptation, *peirasmos*, also means trial or testing. Every temptation is a test or trail of our faith

---

[262] Ignatius' words in "Rules for the Discerning of Spirits" (numbered 313 to 336), in Ganss, *The Spiritual Exercises,* 121–128. See also footnote 76.

for spiritual growth, allowed by God, though he never tempts us with evil (Js 1:13). Sin is wrong-doing (sins of commission) that stems from wrong-thinking, and hence wrong-being. But it is also *not* doing the good we know we ought to do (sins of omission, Js 4:17), i.e. we *refuse* right-doing that stems from right-thinking, and hence we refuse right-being. The Greek fathers describe *six steps of temptation and sin*:[263]

1. A thought (*noema* and/or *logismoi*) enters our mind as normal, then...

2. *Subtly suggests* an image-fantasy, momentarily stirring and enticing the presence of a sin-inhabited impulse, desire or appetite. This is a *logismoi*, a temptation. Demons cast passionate thoughts as bait into our mind to lure us. Paul says they shoot "flaming arrows" that "the shield of faith" extinguishes (Eph 6:16). In our watchfulness (*nepsis*) and discernment (*diakrisis*) of the Spirit – our Joshua Sentinel – we recognize the *logismoi*, challenge and reject the temptation. We also call on the name of Jesus, restoring the cleansing memory of God to our mind. We even avoid what is called "the occasion for sin": any situation or context that we know, from past experience of vulnerability, will lead us into temptation.

3. *Twilight transition* from temptation to sin: pondering or entertaining the suggested thought-image, even for a second, arouses the particular passion it is enticing. This is called *communion* with the *logismoi* (rationalizing and justifying) and *coupling* with the passion (prompting promised pleasure). Playing with the temptation, nibbling at the bait, weakens the will; setting the intention of the heart to sin, which,

---

[263] For example, Mark the Ascetic (early 5th cent.), *On the Spiritual Law*, in Palmer *et al*, *The Philokalia*, Vol. One, 119–120. They expanded on Js 1:14: "each person is tempted when they are dragged away by their own evil desire and enticed. Then, after desire has conceived, it gives birth to sin; and sin, when it is full-grown, gives birth to death." As the LORD said to Cain, "sin is crouching at your door; it desires to have you, but you must master it" (Gen 4:7). The West taught three steps: suggestion, entertainment, and consent; e.g. Luther's famous "we cannot stop birds flying over our head (thoughts come to us), but we can stop them building a nest in our hair (do not entertain them... chase them away)."

as Jesus taught, is tantamount to the sin itself (Matt 5:28).

4. *Consent* to sin: we choose to bite and are hooked. We "do it" with a sense of relief and pleasure – to be followed by regret and remorse, guilt and condemnation.

5. *Reinforcement* of previous sins: each occasion of yielding to temptation and consent to sin strengthens existing patterns of sin that further inhabit the passions.

6. *Resulting in enslavement* to unnatural passions, coming under their power.

To recognize and defeat temptation is to repent and believe by the Spirit's vigilance and use of God's word. We humble and submit ourselves to God, then resist the devil, and he flees from us (Js 4:6–7). Every "no" to evil is a "yes" to God; a long obedience in the same direction that rehabilitates our passions to perfection.

Attaining dispassion: *Apatheia*, the goal of purification, is not indifferent apathy. Dispassion means we still feel passions but are no longer controlled by *unnatural* passions. Evagrios called it "passionate passionlessness": free from passions to the degree they are tamed and trained to serve and energize our spiritual life by the practice of virtues. The dispassionate person is characterized by: a) a state of spiritual rest, peace and quiet; that b) routinely defeats temptation by habit of our new nature in Christ, our true self; where c) the mind is no longer cluttered, distracted, dominated by the passions, but is free to contemplate God; and d) the will – via our sanctified thoughts, impulses and appetites – is preoccupied with God as the sole object of desire; and e) where love rules.

Altruistic love for God, others, and all God has made, grows and burns with passion in the degree to which we progress in dispassion.[264] This is a return to the original Garden of Delight and an anticipation of

---

[264] "The dispassionate person no longer sees and thinks of things (and people) through the prism of passion which wants to be satisfied by them… they appear as having their own purpose independent of his egotism… as gifts of divine love and wisdom", Staniloae, *Orthodox Spirituality*, 189.

the future resurrection state in which body, soul and spirit are totally integrated and united; needing no-thing in full-face-fellowship with the Father and Son, completely possessed by the Spirit of love, radiating the glory of eternal life.

Love: The way of purification by moral effort should not be seen as exhausting religious legalism, but rather as the grace of liberating love – which it is. *Love* is the source and crown of the virtues (Col 3:14), as *pride* is the source and chief of the vices. Fall in love with Jesus by discovering his personalized love for you, and stay in love on this journey of love, and it will decide everything. The rest will take care of itself. Over the centuries, spiritual mothers and fathers focused on love as the spirit and heart of *via purgativa, illuminativa* and *unitiva*, often by using the Song of Songs.[265] Here is my summary typology-parable of the journey of love from Solomon's Song.

It is night. The bride is in bed. Asleep. Yet her heart is awake, aware. Longing for her Lover. Listen. My Lover! He comes! He stands behind her wall, peering through the lattice. Knock! Knock! "Arise my beloved, my beautiful one, come away with me. The winter has passed. Spring is here." But she has taken off her robe, must she put it on again? She has washed her feet, must she soil them again? Then he put his (nail-pierced) hand through the latch-opening. Her heart pounds for him. "O that his left arm was under my head and his right arm embracing me." She arises. Perfumes herself. Opens the door. But her Lover has gone.

She faces the dark night of nothingness. Alone. Then she abandons everything for love. Only with the light of love burning in her heart to guide her. She goes out into the streets, awash with tears, looking for him. Everywhere. But does not find him. Instead, the watchmen of the walls find

---

[265] For example, Teresa of Avilla, Julian of Norwich, John of the Cross, Hannah Hurnard – see my Bibliography. *Allegorical* interpretations of Song of Songs tend to neoplatonic dualism where human sexuality is wrongly "divinized" into sacred sexual intimacy with (G)god, or discounted as "of the flesh" – both are pagan views. See Davidson, *Flame of Yahweh*, 545–632. His *literal and typological* interpretation does justice to both human sexuality *and* godly spirituality without confusion – see footnote 294.

her. She asks them where her Lover is. Where has he hidden himself? They laugh and mock her, beat and bruise her, taking her robe. Naked, stripped of everything, lost in the night, she desperately cries out to her friends, "If you find my Lover, tell him I'm sick with love for him!" All hope is gone. Now completely alone. Deepest darkness.

Suddenly he appears. She sees him in the darkness. Night is light. She clings to him. Does not let him go till she brings him to her mother's home. But he does not awaken love till it's ready. "Come away with me my beloved!" He takes her to his vineyard to taste the first fruits. To his locked-up garden, fragrant with beds of spices. To gather flowers and unseal fountains to flow freely. There to consummate love, to skip on the hills, dance on the mountains. For the bride is his unlocked garden of delight, the seal of love over his heart. Oceans of tsunamis cannot quench the holy flame of love that burns like a mighty forest fire – jealous love – stronger than death.

Way of enlightenment for proficients: *Via illuminativa*

The Temple outer court is the way of purification by *natural light*, via the worshipper's natural senses, through Christ's altar of sacrifice and laver of washing. Then the worshipper in the Holy Place contemplates God by the *mediated light* of the oil-fed candelabrum: Spirit-revelation via spiritual senses, the way of enlightenment. The third stage is through the thick curtain, the complete darkening of our senses, into the Holy of Holies, which has no natural or mediated light. God dwells in a dense dark cloud (of incense) to protect us from direct exposure to his immediate presence (Lev 16:13). Those who enter, however, discover the darkness shines bright with *numinous light*. They see (by) the *Sh'kinah*, the glory of the Father, enthroned on the mercy seat sprinkled with the blood of his Son – his body torn from top to bottom – giving free entrance to all worshippers (Heb 10:19–22).[266] This is the place, between the cherubim,

---

[266] The torn veil is also God's exit to encounter all who call on him wherever they are: God's *ekstasis*, "going out from him/herself" in ecstatic self-giving love in Jesus and the Spirit.

of the most intimate communion (Ex 25:22), a vision of God by pure faith and love beyond all our senses. The full vision of all the divine glory, however, is reserved for the coming age – only resurrected glorified bodies can handle that!

The symbol of *via purgativa* is *the desert* of prayer, through Jesus' death and resurrection. *Via illuminativa* is up *the mountain* of prayer, for transfiguration by the Spirit's light, as in Moses on Mount Sinai and Jesus on Mount Tabor. "Who may ascend the mountain of the LORD? Who may stand in his holy place? The one who has clean hands and a pure heart, who does not trust in an idol or swear by a false god" (Ps 24:3–4). The degree to which we are purified from the idols we worship via our corrupted passions, is the degree to which the Spirit enlightens us to contemplate and know God by faith. Hitherto quenched by the passions, the *charisms* (grace-gifts) of the Spirit now blaze into our consciousness, shining from within our dispassionate heart in all their brilliance.

Maximus taught from Is 11:1–3 that the Spirit's gifts shine from the *fear of the Lord* (purification), to *strength* (practice of virtues), to *counsel* (discern the good and evil in all things), to *understanding* (spiritual insight into how to do good), to *knowledge* (spiritual grasp and affective identification with the divine purpose in all things), and to *wisdom* (simple contemplation and celebration of the truth resulting in union with God).[267] These graces illumine our consciousness to know God and live by the Spirit's revelation, as in Jesus, who did not judge by what he saw with his eyes, or decide by what he heard with his ears (Is 11:3 cf. Jn 5:19–20, 30).

Purification leads to illumination: a clear vision of God. "Blessed are the pure in heart, for they will see God" (Matt 5:8), not only in heaven when they die, but here and now in all things. To be pure in heart is to be "undivided" (Ps 86:11; Ezek 11:19–20), *not* "double-minded" (Js 4:8), but focused and centred on God in Christ.

---

[267] Palmer *et al*, *The Philokalia*, Vol. Two, 218–220. Staniloae, *Orthodox Spirituality*, 195–198.

The Greek fathers taught, as per John's Gospel, Jesus is The *Logos*: God's Word – his self-revelation of reason and purpose *in creation* – through which we see and know God. However, there are also *logoi*, words or reasons, in every visible and invisible created thing, i.e. their particular purpose in relation to God and all other things. Every created thing is holy, not in the pagan sense of being divine (pantheism), but in the biblical idea of each thing having its rightful place and unique reason under God. A mountain gives glory to God by being a mountain, likewise a tree or a cat!

Logoi are expressions of the *Logos* in all the magnificent fecundity – exploding fruitfulness of rich diversity – of the Maker and Sustainer of all things (Heb 1:3). So, we "find God in all things"[268] as the Spirit lights up their hidden *logoi,* their unique God-given essence, meaning and intention. That gives us an ever-clearer vision and personal knowledge of God. The meaning(s) of the *logoi* are objectively true in themselves no matter how we subjectively see or interpret them. They yield to ever deeper meanings in God, not because they change, but because we change and see differently.[269] By our contemplating God in creation, the Spirit shines in our hearts giving us the light of the inexhaustible glorious knowledge of God in the face of Jesus Christ (2 Cor 4:6). Jesus is the face of the Father: to see him is to see the Father.

Contemplating God in creation – his shining self-revelation in each *logoi* intuited to us by his Spirit – is not only through 1) animals, birds, fish, flowers, stones and the stars (Ps 8:1, 5–9; 19:1–6). Finding God *in all things* includes 2) *human creation*: each person is God's *eikon* (image), a living *logoi*, through which we can encounter God, if we have eyes to see by the Spirit. And 3) *every daily situation, circumstance and happening*: God is present and active moment by moment in our lives, working in all

---

268 Ignatius' famous phrase, see Gerard Hughes and William Barry in my Bibliography.
269 Merton says (*New Seeds of Contemplation,* 21) we do not detach ourselves from *things* to attach ourselves to God – there is no evil in anything God created, thus it cannot *per se* become an obstacle to union with God. We become detached *from ourselves to see and use things in and for God.*

things for our good as we discern his love and purpose in each moment (Rom 8:28–29), always giving thanks to him in everything (Eph 5:20; Col 3:17; Heb 13:15). This includes 4) the spiritual awareness to discern the *logoi* in *invisible realities behind visible phenomena* as in visions and dreams, gifts of the Spirit and ministering angels – also enticing demons and evil attack. And 5) *scripture:* hearing God in the particular text. The Spirit reveals God's meaning and intention (*logoi*) for us personally as we read, study, meditate and memorize God's word. Lastly, 6) *church and sacraments:* experiencing God in and through the Body of Christ, especially in regular partaking of the Lord's Supper.

All six are symbols and sacraments of God's holy presence, or what Merton calls "seeds of contemplation".[270] All six are the face of Jesus. This kind of prayer-full-ness is marked by intense affection and ardent longing for more intimacy with Jesus and the Father. This second stage brings surprises and consolations with an affective finding of God by the Spirit where we have not "seen" him before.

The praxis of illumination

We come to know God in creation by ongoing virtuous practices, especially *nepsis* (watchfulness) and *diakrisis* (discernment). While vigilance and discernment of the *logismoi* continues in our overcoming demonic thought-temptations; positive watchfulness in discerning the *logoi* takes over. We begin contemplating God's truth in all things. The mind once scattered and dominated by the passions – seeing people and things as objects to satisfy our desires – is now centred and focused on seeing and celebrating God in all things. It is the mind dominated by the flesh versus the mind governed by the Spirit, each with their own fruit (Rom 8:5–8).

---

[270] "Just as the wind carries thousands of winged seeds, so each moment brings with it germs of spiritual vitality that come to rest imperceptibly in (our) minds and wills. Most of these unnumbered seeds are lost, because men are not prepared to receive them", *New Seeds of Contemplation*, 14.

The shift from flesh to Spirit is the ease of the Spirit's organic sanctifying work in us as we surrender co-operatively to the Spirit. If it's an anxious or driven process, it's a sure sign of evil spirit at work. If the demons cannot stop us from finding God in all things, they will push us by anxiety and guilt to perform, to make it happen. Rather, we *allow* it to happen by slowing down, learning to live the unhurried life. We cultivate inner stillness and presence. We stop, look, listen and en-joy (enter into joy). "I cannot contemplate either nature or God without learning to be present where I am, gathered together at this present moment, in this present place."[271]

To become present to God, self, people and things, in the sacrament of the present moment, is the beginning of contemplation. Then our eyes are opened literally and spiritually *by the Spirit* to see *God's* extraordinary world in and through the ordinary world we see all around us. We discover the childlike astonishment and joyous wonder of "bifocal" vision not distorted by sin. In fact, we see with God's eyes, seeing all things in God, not only God in all things.

Like Moses, we see God in the ordinary bush, beside other things. What drew his attention was not that the bush was burning. The desert heat ignited bushes from time to time. It was that the bush did not burn up (Ex 3:2–5). *Only when God saw Moses stop to consider, and approach, did he reveal himself.* God told him to take off his shoes, stripping him of the deadness of familiarity so as to recognize the place where he was standing was holy ground. In this way we become aware of sacred space and sacred time – where true transformation happens – in *this* material object, in *that* person we meet, *this* moment, *that* incident, *this* text. Each is unique, unrepeatable, of infinite symbolic value as a window into eternity. We begin to see with excitement the extraordinary in the ordinary all around us. It's like either looking *at* a pane of glass or looking *through* it to the world beyond.

---

[271] This quote and the next paragraph are from Ware, *The Orthodox Way,* 117–118.

Symbol(ize), *symballein*, is to throw together with, to unite two things without confusing them. A symbol is a visible reality that not only represents an invisible reality, but also makes it visible. Symbols show two things simultaneously, joining matter and spirit, without confusing them – a bridge between two worlds. Symbolic consciousness sees material objects as symbols of God, signs and representations of a more profound reality by revelation of the Spirit.

Planet earth, and the entire expanding universe, is a cosmic symbolic Burning Bush filled with Divine Fire, yet not consumed. It is a theophany that mediates God's presence for all who slow down, stop and see, listen and learn.

Indeed, *the world is charged with the grandeur of God / It will flame out, like shining from shook foil / It gathers to a greatness...*[272]

Or as Elizabeth Barrett Browning poetically observed in 1856:
Earth's crammed with heaven,
And every common bush afire with God;
But only he who sees, takes off his shoes,
The rest sit round it and pluck blackberries,
And daub their natural faces unaware.

Three important clarifications

To understand the above we need a *right view of God in relation to creation* as summarized in footnote 26. Beside the *Logos* and *logoi* of God and creation, the Eastern fathers taught that God is unknown yet known, hidden yet revealed. They drew a distinction between God's *essence*, the unknowable eternal mystery of God's inner being; and God's *energies*, the self-revealing actions and loving presence of God in creation. For example, the sun in *essence* is unapproachable and inaccessible; we cannot even look into the sun without being damaged. Yet we know the sun by

---

[272] The opening lines of Gerard Manley Hopkins' sonnet, *God's Grandeur*, in 1877. And what follows is from http://www.notable-quotes.com/b/browning_elizabeth_barrett.html.

its radiating *energies* that penetrate and give life and light to all things within its orbit – earth in particular. To experience the sun's energies is to experience the sun itself, but not in its essence or we would die – likewise with God. The Son, through whom God made the universe, is the *radiance* of God's glory, the exact *representation* of his being, *sustaining all things* by his word, through the *energizing power* of the Spirit (Heb 1:2–3 cf. Ps 33:6). We know and experience God through God's *uncreated energies of love* in creation by the Son and the Spirit – Irenaeus' (130–202) "right and left hand of God" – through whom we are divinized into God's glorious likeness.

Secondly, we need *correct accountability* in our contemplation and experience of God. This is for protection and guidance, particularly in our interpretation of the Spirit-intuited meaning of things in nature and scripture. The spiritual quest is a warfare of (attempted) deception, hence the need for discernment and hermeneutics – the doctrine of revelation and principles of (biblical) interpretation. Simply to say: we can be seriously misled by what we believe is – and the misinterpretation of – the Spirit's enlightenment.[273] Satan comes as an angel of light to deceive and destroy us (2 Cor 11:3, 14; 1 Tim 4:1f). The stories of such deception are legion in church and monastic history. The fathers taught the absolute importance of church belonging, right doctrinal instruction and biblical interpretation, submission to pastoral care, and accountability to wise fathers and mothers in spiritual direction.

Thirdly, we need to undergo the shift from natural-rational knowledge of God, to symbolic-spiritual, and then mystical knowledge of God. It's the movement from *cataphatic* to *apophatic* experience of God. This is the transition of the second stage, simply put: from mediated to direct unmediated knowledge of God. The latter is the third stage of perfection. The one is not inferior to the other – merely different methods of

---

[273] See Morphew, *The Spiritual Spider Web*, a study on Gnostic deception in Pentecostal, Charismatic, Evangelical circles. Also Jones, *Spirit Wars,* and Keener, *Spirit Hermeneutics*. See Appendix 1.

experiencing God in the journey of knowing him ever more intimately.

The fathers explained this shift symbolically: Moses first experienced God as light in *the burning bush*, the affective and rational knowledge of God via the natural senses and reason-able mind. Then he experienced God in *the fiery cloud* that led Israel out of Egypt, a mix of light *and* darkness, of rational *and* spiritual knowledge of God. Discursive logic, images and words find their limit, becoming silent and darkened in the face of growing mystery. Here intuitive contemplation takes over. The more we really know God as God knows him/herself, the more we realize the less we know him in the limitation of our faculties. So, we rely on flashes of intuitive revelation by the Spirit, moving us beyond thoughts and senses to direct contemplation, infusing us with true spiritual knowledge of God.[274]

Finally, Moses experienced God on Mount Sinai *in thick darkness*, a cloud of blinding smoke, God's fiery presence. God is *not* "thick darkness", but dwells in it (Ex 20:21, 24:15–18). The darkness, in fact, is in us, denoting *our* human inability to grasp God's inner nature. On entering the cloud, Moses' natural and rational senses were disoriented and darkened. That paradoxically led to "face to face" encounter with God (Ex 33:11), a burning light of unmediated (S)spirit union. This is direct contemplation of God – *the* most transformative. Moses was *unconsciously* transfigured by intense light into radiating light. He only became aware of it by its effect on the people. They asked him to cover his face, to dim his ultra-bright headlights, because they were unable to look at him! True spirituality is truly unconscious spirituality. More

---

[274] Gnostic revelation knowledge is both *anti-rational* (opposed to logical reason, which is seen as inferior humanism) and *irrational* (renouncing reason in a leap of faith for revelation knowledge). True spiritual knowledge is *supra-rational,* as Staniloae says, "The supreme knowledge of God… activates and uses all the resources of reason to the fullest exercise of its powers. We are raised to a supra-rational knowledge of God; after our reason itself is exercised to the maximum, we understand that the domain into which we have penetrated surpasses our limited rational powers, by a plus of light, not by a minus", *Orthodox Spirituality*, 208.

accurately, unselfconscious spirituality.[275]

Similarly, we ascend Mount Tabor with Jesus in prayer (Lk 9:28–29) where we are transfigured by light into light in the cloud of unknowing. Jesus, in prayer, became light from light in the most intimate interpenetration of his being with his Father. As we pray with Jesus our senses are darkened by the cloud of unknowing. We are filled with light, divinized to hear and see "no one except Jesus" (Matt 17:8), and thus the Father. The *terror* of the cloud, God's holy presence, on Tabor (Lk 9:34) and Sinai (Ex 19:16) is taken away on Mount Golgotha. There Messiah removed all fear of judgment for those who believe. Golgotha is the ultimate place of deepest darkness where God's glory shone brightest, as per John's paradoxical theology in chapter 7. The divine Taboric Light is nothing other than the uncreated energies of God's love that increasingly shines in those exercised in this form of prayer. Our soul *and* body are unconsciously "Christified" with the glory that our spirit contemplates (2 Cor 3:18), in growing anticipation and actual foretaste of our resurrection. "Then the righteous will shine like the sun in the kingdom of their Father" (Matt 13:43).

Way of union for the mature: *Via unitiva*

To be a *theoretiki*, contemplating God *directly* and not via any created thing, we apply the way of negation to the life of prayer. As the positive *cataphatic* way of images, words, senses and symbols find their limit, the negative *apophatic* way takes us further. More than a method, it's an attitude of pure faith and humility in realizing the divine incomprehensibility. The mind no longer forms abstract ideas and rational concepts of God, reducing the infinite mystery of God's nature and wisdom to human thought. The more we know we cannot know God by representative

---

275 Real transformation is not a self-conscious arrival; *others* see the changes in us that we are not aware of. They then receive and walk in the light that shines through us; or they cover it, or even put it out as they did with Jesus, because it exposes the moral darkness of their golden-calf idolatry.

ideas and images, the more we know him by faith and love. Ultimately, God cannot be known except by God. God does not know him/herself by any representation of God. Thus, we can only truly know God by being transformed in some sense into God – united in faith and love to who/what God is – to know God as God knows him/herself.[276]

Apophaticism, as in contemplation, is "an existential attitude which involves the whole man: there is no theology apart from experience; it is necessary to change, to become a new man."[277] The result is a *wisdom* from God beyond knowledge, by an experiential union of love in purified faith, which divinizes us into the likeness of God. This is the way of the mature, the spiritual fathers and mothers who know the Father in perfected second innocence, having grown up from the child stage in which we know the Father in naïve first innocence (see 1 Jn 2:13–14).

The *apophatic* method is the practice of silence in which we negate and set aside all our faculties to encounter God in growing stillness: "Be still and know that I am God" (Ps 46:10). In the context of the psalm it means (my RAP), "Stop fighting and striving! Let go! Relax! Be still, silent, and let *God* be God! *Then* you will see and know I AM." To become still and silent in complete trust and loving surrender – where we discover God *is* God, God *as* God – is not easy. It goes against all our natural inclinations. Words now fail to explain the inexplicable, the mystery of direct intimate participation in the divine nature, the Holy of Holies.[278] What follows builds on my introduction to the mystic and ecstatic traditions in chapter 3.

The East calls *apophatic* contemplation *hesychia:* inward tranquility of concentrated silence. The one who practices it is called a *hesychast.* The primary method to attain *hesychia* is The Jesus Prayer: *"Lord Jesus*

---

276 See Merton, *New Seeds of Contemplation,* 132. Jesus is the *only* "exact representation of (God's) being" (Heb 1:3) – we know God *as* God through Jesus by his Spirit.
277 Lossky, *The Mystical Theology of the Eastern Church,* 38.
278 Isaac the Syrian said, "Speech is the organ of this present world. Silence is a mystery of the world to come" in Ware, *The Orthodox Way,* 133. By practicing silence, we enter the world to come. Then our lived lives – our thoughts, words and deeds – echo silence, we echo heaven on earth.

Christ, Son of God, have mercy on me, a sinner."[279] The ever-active mind is not easily quieted. If our approach is entirely negative, eliminating all thoughts without offering the mind an alternate activity, we will likely end up day-dreaming. By giving the mind a task like praying the Jesus Prayer – or any other phrase or short prayer – we enable it to slow down and focus on Jesus, moving the mind beyond itself into silence, then stillness and restful repose in God's presence. By focusing on the words as an actual invocation of our Lord Jesus, we progressively put aside – in fact, move beyond – all our senses.

As mentioned in chapter 3, it begins as *prayer of the lips* (purification). Then it grows inward to mental prayer, prayed phrase by phrase in the rhythm with our breathing: *prayer of the intellect* (enlightenment). By constant practice it descends into the heart – our spirit and will – and is united with it: *prayer of the heart* (union). It is no longer something we do or say or think, but who we are. We no longer *say* prayers from time to time but become a person who *is* prayer all the time. Acts of prayer lead to a spirit of prayer: unconscious heart prayer. Our spirit prays unceasingly in the Spirit and the Spirit prays ceaselessly in our spirit, in the midst of all activities, even in our sleep. To the extent we live in this inner communion of transforming light, an unconscious union of love, we naturally overflow in unselfconscious acts of loving service to others – *or else it is spurious!*

The West calls it contemplative or centring prayer:[280] the practice of silent prayer in suspense of all our senses for direct union with God. *How do we do it?*

---

279 Ware, *The Orthodox Way*, 122–123, and Gillet, *The Jesus Prayer*. It's based on Lk 18:14, 38, the cries of the publican and blind Bartimaeus for mercy. And rooted in Jesus' Name as an invocation of his immediate presence (Acts 4:12; Phil 2:9–10; John 14:13–14; Luke 10:17). *The Way of a Pilgrim* by an unknown Russian peasant tells his story of a life-long pursuit in praying The Jesus Prayer.
280 See *The Cloud of Unknowing*; Keating, *Open Mind, Open Heart*. Merton says, "Contemplation is the highest expression of a man's intellectual and spiritual life", in *Contemplative Prayer*, 1.

We find a secluded place and make it our daily sanctuary. We sit in a chair or kneel (on a prayer stool) in a comfortable posture for protracted time with God. Then we start with ten to fifteen minutes a day of silent contemplation. With practice it can be lengthened. We begin by consciously relaxing our body, mind and emotions. We do not picture God or dwell on revelations, thoughts, noises, feelings or sensations. As we sense *any* stimuli, we gently but immediately usher it out of our consciousness, even writing down things that come to mind that we need to do. We wait on God long enough till all stimuli subside. Then our consciousness moves beyond awareness of, and response to, any stimuli. It becomes perfectly still, entering a state of concentrated rest that can be even deeper than that attained in sleep. They suggest we repeat a prayer-word (like "Jesus") with our rhythmical breathing as a means of attaining this state, in which we surrender to God in pure faith and adoring love. This kind of breath-prayer fulfils the same function as in the Jesus Prayer above.

By regular practice we reach the still point of being, a state of being-in-love, the twilight of conscious unconsciousness in which we mystically experience (S)spirit union with God. Like sleep, we only know afterwards we experienced it. While asleep, we are not conscious of sleeping. On waking we know we slept. We feel rested, refreshed and renewed. If not, we need more sleep, knowing that it's not the quantity but the quality of sleep that is transformative. Thus contemplation, centring prayer, is an exercise of rest-full encounter with God's transfiguring love – by love, in love, for love – known on reflection after the experience. This daily practice overflows into our day, growing a moment by moment consciousness of being-in-love, living from the depths of being centred in God's love. Again, its authenticity is seen in lived love, the fruit of the Spirit (Gal 5:22), not in manifest mystical ecstasy itself.

The above is *acquired* contemplation by discipline and practice. *Infused* contemplation is a surprise intuitive experience of the Spirit given as God sovereignly wills – even to the novice – affirming that the three stages in the spiritual journey are more simultaneous than consecutive. *Both* acquired and infused contemplation are pure grace-gift, thus the distinction between the two is merely theoretical.

Contemplation is a unitive state of intuitive mystical union with God, self, others and nature, in which ecstasies of the Spirit most naturally occur.[281] For example, the gift of tongues by the Spirit is *both* an entrance into *and* a transcendent ecstasy of contemplation. I praise and pray in tongues "with my spirit" as a willing act of faith, just as I, by my will, "pray with my understanding" (in English, in my case, 1 Cor 14:15). However, I also pray in tongues as an out-going (*ekstasis*) of joyful praise (1 Cor 14:16) and/or inarticulate groaning (Rom 8:26–27). In praying in tongues our spirit prays "mysteries by the Spirit" *directly* to God and our mind is "unfruitful", i.e. darkened and transcended in unmediated union with God (1 Cor 14:2, 14).

This is similar to the above two methods, among other means of direct contemplation of God. Paul derived great benefit from speaking in tongues because he did it "more than all of you", referring to his personal practice of prayer (vv.18–19). The *apophatic* practice of tongues as direct unmediated communion with God by the Spirit – in faith and love beyond our understanding – is the primary principle or method underlying how we experience all the ecstatic divinizing gifts of the Spirit.

Therefore, these are *three* tried and tested historical Christian *apophatic* methods of *via unitiva* that we can practice daily, throughout the day.

The dark night(s)

Is the above darkening of the senses the same as the well-known, but little

---

281 I must qualify this by saying the mystical is not a special event *per se*, nor reserved for the special few. In Galatians, Paul says the reception and experience of the Spirit confirms we are justified *by faith* in Christ, not by the works of the law. In other words, *all believers*, in that sense of salvation, experience mystical union with Christ by the Spirit. The challenge is to grow into its subjective reality and to live in it.

understood, dark night of *the senses* ("the first night") and the dark night of *the soul* ("the second night") – as per the teaching of Spanish mystic John of the Cross (1542–1591)? And is there a difference between these two nights?

Simply put, the dark night of *the senses* is the Latin tradition of purgation with the transition to the second step of illumination. The "exterior senses" – our five bodily senses and appetite-attachments – are purified and disciplined to live by faith and not by sight. "This dark night is a privation and purgation of all sensible appetites for the external things of the world, the delights of the flesh, and the gratifications of the will."[282] This includes God withdrawing *sensible* consolations of the Spirit to wean us from attachment to the affective and visible so that we abandon ourselves to God in faith. In fact, the spiritual masters say these consolations are given to beginners for encouragement, and those that had physical affects or manifestations had to be transcended, or they became obstacles to the love and service of God.

We become detached and "indifferent to all created things", only using them "to the extent that they help us in the pursuit of the end for which we are created… to praise, reverence, and serve God our Lord."[283] The dark night of the senses is not due to disobedience, laziness, lukewarmness, injury or illness. It happens as we continue to grow in love, patience, humility, and other virtuous practices. If the dark night of the senses is like pruning the tree (for more fruit), the dark night of the soul is pulling up the roots (for transplant) – a much more excruciating process!

The second night, the dark night of *the soul*, also called dark night of *the spirit*, is the transition from the second to the third step, *via unitiva*. Here the "interior senses" – our *psycho-spiritual senses* of seeing, hearing, smelling, tasting, touching and desiring God – are purified to the core for spiritual marriage, the unitive state of being-in-love. "This dark night is an inflow of God into the soul, which purges it of its habitual ignorances and

---

[282] John of the Cross, *The Ascent of Mount Carmel*, 1.1.4, in *The Collected Works*, 119.
[283] Ignatius in his Principle and Foundation, in Ganss, *The Spiritual Exercises*, 32.

imperfections – natural and spiritual – and which the contemplatives call infused contemplation or mystical theology. Through this contemplation, God teaches the soul secretly and instructs it in the perfection of love without its doing anything or understanding how this happens."[284]

This takes place through a much more crushing desolation of the soul and spirit that is purged of the deepest roots of imperfections. We experience a state of extreme inner aridity, an (apparent) abandonment, even rejection, by God. Some in this state have feared they would be eternally lost. It's even more painful because one loves God, longs for him, wants only him. Our Lover withdraws from us into the dark night. We, his beloved bride, forsake all for love and go into total darkness seeing nothing, seeking only him, but not finding him – only to be severely attacked by evil (which often comes through our closest friends). The more intense the darkness and longer the night the more our spiritual senses are refined and transformed by the fire of love. In this way God's burning love penetrates our being to the core, uprooting and defeating evil, uniting us with God.

Jesus, in his humanity, went through this night in an ultimate sense in Gethsemane and Calvary: "*Abba,* Father, all things are possible for you. Remove this cup from me… *My God, my God, why have you forsaken me?*" (Mk 14:36, 15:34) In his moment of deepest darkness, utterly forsaken by God, evil did its worst work. But ironically, in that very moment Jesus was *most united* to God and his work of world redemption, overcoming evil. Our greatest participation in maturity is in Christ's abandonment experienced on the cross, the darkest of all nights, of the soul and spirit. Those who experience this dark night enter and make up what is lacking in Christ's afflictions (Col 1:24). Not as in ultimate redemption (only Jesus can do that), but in mystical participation and compassionate union with Jesus' suffering love for this lost world, which in some sense is redemptive. Is this not part of Paul's threefold "inarticulate groanings" of creation, ourselves and the Spirit in Rom 8:18–27, 34b? The Spirit feels

---

[284] John of the Cross, *The Dark Night,* II.5.1, in *The Collected Works,* 401.

and expresses all these groanings *in and through us as a living prayer* to the Father and the Son for the fulfilment of God's redemptive purposes.

We all experience the dark night of *the senses* to one degree or another, in one form or another, for purification of the exterior senses. But only some experience the dark night of *the spirit* – at least in its extreme form. It can happen once or a few times, and can last a few days, or weeks, or months, even years. It is not due to, nor the same as depression, though some undergo depression in this darkest of nights.

Mother Teresa experienced this dark night throughout her last 45 years of ministry, known only to her spiritual directors. Reading Mother Teresa, *Come Be My Light,* affected me deeply (for good). To elaborate I would have to address, among other things, the controversial decision by Brian Kolodiejchuk to edit and publish her most intimate disclosures. I felt like a spiritual voyeur intruding on holy ground. Sufficient to say her writings reveal her closely guarded secret of "profound interior suffering, lack of sensible consolation, spiritual dryness, an apparent absence of God from her life, and, at the same time, a painful longing for Him" (21-22). How does one make sense of this in light of her astonishing humility, being fully at God's disposal, fulfilling her call as Jesus' light to those in darkness, living out her desire to "satiate the thirst of Jesus on the cross for Love and Souls" (41)? All in serving the poorest of the poor? Her light shone brighter and brighter through those dark years. As Fr. Neuner concluded, "her work had its roots in the mystery of Jesus' mission, in union with him who dying on the cross felt abandoned by his Father" (9).

Therefore, the darkening of *the senses* in the practice of contemplative prayer has similarities with, yet is qualitatively different to, the two dark nights as described.

The living flame of love
The source of both dark nights that lead to union with God is *love*: God's initiating love and our responding love. Christian spirituality, from beginning to end, is loving God by being in his love for us. The primary

image for this love is fire: "It burns like blazing fire, like the very flame of Yahweh" (S of S 8:6 NIV, margin). John of the Cross described the spirituality of love as *The Living Flame of Love*:

> *O living flame of love*
> *that tenderly wounds my soul*
> *in its deepest centre! Since*
> *now you are not oppressive,*
> *now consummate! If it be your will:*
> *tear through the veil of this sweet encounter!*[285]

He called it "the science of love",[286] meaning the *experience* of mystical theology: the union of being-in-love with God and *reflecting* on it in order to *teach and initiate* others into it. This science is a love story initiated by God in pure passion, a journey of ever-deeper agony and ecstasy of the human soul in love with God.

It begins with God's initiating burning love that ignites the living flame of love in our hearts. At first it is intense and intoxicating, the **wine of love** spoken of in S of S 1:2, "Your love is better than wine" (NRSV), with the reply that her kisses are "like the best wine that goes down smoothly" (7:9 NRSV). John says of this sweet encounter in Solomon's song: "Sometimes without doing anything on their own, persons feel in their intimate substance that their spirit is being sweetly inebriated and inflamed by the divine wine."[287]

Then the flame grows stronger and we experience the **wound of love** – the paradox of pleasure and pain that purifies and transforms those who truly love. God's love tenderly tears through the veil of our imperfections

---

285 The first of four stanzas of his poem by that title, in *The Collected Works*, 639–640.
286 *The Collected Works*, 437, 440. Bernard Lonergan gives a transcendental *method* for knowledge beyond experience, understanding and reason: a kind of knowing – a mystical wisdom – by God's *love* and our responding *love*. He calls it the grace of self-transcendence that "becomes an actuality when one falls in love. Then one's being becomes being-in-love… once it has blossomed forth and as long as it lasts, it takes over. It is the first principle" from which all else flows, in *Method in Theology*, 105.
287 *The Spiritual Canticle*, 25.8, in *The Collected Works*, 572.

and inability to know him and penetrates to our deepest centre. It fires us into, and through, the dark night of the senses, and then of the soul. In our darkness and dryness our ugly sinfulness is fully exposed. God's apparent withdrawal makes us ache for love of him, drawing us out beyond ourselves through trials and tribulations to trust him in pure love. The wound of love is death to all corrupted appetites and idolatrous attachments to created things, in a consummate resurrection of being-in-love with God in the beauty of holiness.

That, in essence, is the ***wisdom of love*** fired and infused into our spirit, mind and body. It's a dark-light diffused-formless wisdom beyond knowledge in a cloud of unknowing – seen in the cross, the wound of love. *That* is the mysterious wisdom of love that glorifies us with the Lord of Glory (1 Cor 2:7-8). Once hidden from the powers and people of this world, God's secret wisdom of love is now revealed in Jesus and his followers. "The wise" of this world see it as foolishness and "the powerful" as weakness. In truth, it is the Spirit's inflow of God's highest wisdom in his deepest thoughts. These sublime disclosures teach and instruct us in the perfection of love – the wise mind of Christ in the Father's wise will by the Spirit's revealed wisdom – divinizing us into the light and love of the Trinity.

The result is the ***wonder of love***, a moment by moment being-in-love *in real terms*. Wonder is worship, a life of consummated love and beauty. Overtaken by the sheer wonder of God, we worship God for who God is, not for what he means to us by virtue of what he does for us. We see God *is God* and know God *as God*. We are ravished and transformed by God's beauty.[288] This is worship in (S)spirit and truth.

This is evidenced in its finest fruit, the ***works of love***: laying down our lives in love of God and others in deeds of self-sacrificing service as Jesus did (1 Jn 3:16). The works of love are the full and final test of

---

[288] John of the Cross says to Jesus, "That I be so transformed in your beauty, that we may be alike in beauty... I shall see you in your beauty, and you shall see yourself in me in your beauty", *The Spiritual Canticle*, 36.5, in *The Collected Works*, 611.

the authenticity of the living flame of love that divinizes us into Christ's likeness. It is the *ekstasis,* ecstatic joy, of self-transcending love that energizes us to love as God loves, to dance with delight while weeping with pain. Even our sexuality is transformed and divinized to love with the fire of God's love, the pure passion of heaven. And all of this, from beginning to end, is the **work of love** by the Holy Spirit in us and through us into the world around us.

John's words summarize this science of being-in-love – the living flame of love: *"The soul is purged and prepared for union with the divine light just as the wood is prepared for transformation into fire. Fire, when applied to wood, first dehumidifies it, dispelling all moisture and making it give off any water it contains. Then it gradually turns the wood black, makes it dark and ugly, and even causes it to emit a bad odor. By drying out the wood, the fire brings to light and expels all those ugly and black accidents that are contrary to fire. Finally, by heating and enkindling it from without, the fire transforms the wood into itself and makes it as beautiful as it is itself."*[289] And *"so the wood becomes much more incandescent and inflamed, even to the point of flaring up and shooting out flames from itself."*[290]

In conclusion: union, divinization and the garden of God

What is the nature of this union with God and our consequent divinization? From the theology of God's essence and energies, the Eastern fathers differentiated three kinds or models of union, each equally a unique mystical oneness or union-in-love:

- Union according to *essence*: God as Trinity – three Persons in/with one nature, without confusion of Persons.

- Union according to *hypostasis* (*personal* union): Incarnate Christ

---

[289] *The Dark Night,* 2.10.1, in *The Collected Works,* 416.
[290] *The Living Flame of Love,* Prologue. 3, in *The Collected Works,* 639. Another common illustration of divinization that Christian mystics used is an iron stake placed in the fire. It absorbs the fire till it glows as fire, becomes fire, yet remains iron, with refined integrity of its own properties.

- one person with two natures (human and divine), without confusion of natures.

- Union according to *energy*: The believer and God – two persons in one (S)spirit (1 Cor 6:17). More accurately, four persons (Father, Son, Spirit and the believer, Jn 14:23) in a union of uncreated energies of love, without confusion of (S)spirit, nature, or persons.

Believers do not become *one essence* with God – we are not divine and will never become divine. Nor do we become *one person* with God by participating in Christ's hypostatic union, having two natures, human and divine. In following the person of Jesus – we do not follow a (divine) nature – we have union with God by our regenerated spirit/nature in Christ. To "participate in the divine nature" (2 Pet 1:4) means we, *as human beings,* have *koinonia* – common participation, shared life and partnership – with the Trinity. We partake in God's nature by the transforming grace, power and glory of the indwelling Son and Spirit. These are the uncreated energies of God's *love*, the divine passionate *eros* that is the basis of Christian spirituality, which unites and perfects all things in God.[291]

The more we mature in this union of love the more we undergo *theosis*, the divinizing transformation of our *character* – not of our (human) *essence* – escaping the corruption in the world that is caused by evil desires (2 Pet 1:4). We progressively produce the character of Christ, "the fruit of the Spirit" in contrast to "the works of flesh", which are diametrically opposed (Gal 5:16–22). Deification is like exposing ourselves directly to the sun while working or playing or lying on the beach. Our bodies absorb the sun's rays and become radiated till we glow

---

[291] Pseudo Dionysius said, "Divine *eros* is expressed outside of itself (it is ecstatic), for it does not permit lovers to remain by themselves, but with those who they love", cited by Stavropoulos in *Partakers of Divine Nature,* 83. Stavropoulos concludes (90), "Each person finds perfection within the love of God. Perfect love establishes the individual in the likeness of Christ. For this reason the life of love is the life of perfection."

with heat. To participate in the divine nature is to absorb and radiate God's eternal life, light and love. We become *like* God, truly godly, but *not* God.[292]

Beside the above three models, there is the union of believer and believer (as in Jesus' prayer, Jn 17:22–23), and the believer and creation – also unions of God's uncreated energies of love by the Spirit without confusion of persons and/or creation. We do not reject this world to become one with God, but we enfold it – in all its brokenness – into our (God's) love so that by God's grace it too may be finally transfigured. And by experiencing union with God, others and creation – Hebraic *Shalom* – we become our true selves made new in Christ Jesus.

Biblical oneness is *not* assimilation into the other with a loss of self. As the two become one, paradoxically, love differentiates and matures each in their uniqueness. This is true of our union with God, our unity with one another as husband and wife, as believer with believer, and with creation. To the degree of union with the Ultimate Other we are completed and perfected as fully human, and in some mystical sense God is completed as fully God, though God is eternally complete. We become the best version of ourselves that God intended before creation – his perfect image – and God is fully manifested as the brightest heavenly reality of that shadow earthly image (us). Though God in essence never changes he is not left unchanged by union with us. What this means will only be known in the resurrection, just as Jesus in his resurrected human body has in a certain sense forever "changed" the Trinity.

---

[292] This is how we must interpret Ps 82:6, "You are 'gods'; you are all sons of the Most High" (cited by Jesus in Jn 10:34–35), and Irenaeus' words, "God the Logos became what we are, in order that we may become what he himself is", famously repeated by Athanasius (296–373), "God became man so that man can become God". Otherwise, taken literally, these statements would be heresy. The fathers used *theosis,* strictly avoiding *apotheosis,* used by the Greeks to mean that people, like heroes and emperors, attain the rank of deity – become divine and cease to be human – a change of essence, not of form. See Christensen & Wittung, *Partakers of the Divine Nature,* 23–31, 95–131.

This brings us full circle back to the *perichoresis* discussed in chapter 1, the mutual interpenetration and indwelling of the Trinitarian God, the Eternal Com-Unity of Love. All "born agains" in Jesus are caught up by the Spirit into *that* most holy of all communions: actual participation in the mutual interpenetration and relational indwelling of the Father, Son and Spirit. This is the divinizing dance of love that will finally be fully consummated in God's new garden: the new earth with new heavens.

The biblical vision begins and ends in God's Garden of Delight.[293] In the beginning (Gen 1 & 2) it was a pristine Garden-Temple, the place of the marriage-enthronement of God and his differentiated human image as male and female. It was the place of Adam and Eve's marriage-enthronement under God. They exercise God's Reign of *Shalom* over his creation in consummated nuptials of union with God and each other. Then all goes wrong. But the promise is that in the end there will be a union of new heavens and a new earth (Rev 21 & 22), with a new Garden-City, the New Jerusalem. The Trinitarian God will be the Temple, in which a new marriage of God and his people will take place, consummated in a new enthronement to rule and reign in *Shalom-Love* over God's new creation throughout the eternal ages.

This future promise has already been realized in principle in Jesus inaugurating the new creation in the midst of the old. In Christ we *are* a new creation: through union with God in Messiah by his Spirit we already enter and experience that future Garden of Delight, as a tantalizing and transfiguring foretaste of its future fullness. If the symbol for *via purgativa* is the desert of prayer, and that of *via illuminitiva* is the mountain of prayer, then the symbol of *via unitiva* is the garden of prayer.

---

[293] Ephrem of Syria (306–373) is famous for using God's Garden as the landscape to understand deification, well summarized by Thomas Buchan, *Paradise as the Landscape of Salvation in Ephrem the Syrian,* in Christensen & Wittung (eds.), *Partakers of the Divine Nature,* 146–159.

The ultimate goal of the spiritual life is the fruitful union of mature love: our completion in perfect unity of will, mind, emotions, words and actions with God – evidenced, again, in the fruit of the Spirit, our "Christification". This is nothing less than face-to-face consummated nuptials with God, each other and creation. It's the dance of love in God's new Garden of Delight – lived out in the desert of this age.

That is why Jewish and Christian mystics say the Song of Songs is the Holy of Holies of God's relationship with his people, not only of human sexual love.[294] The evocative imagery of the sensuous garden of love is analogous to the sublime heights of rapture with God to which humans can possibly attain this side of heaven and resurrection. Ultimately words and images fail to describe this beautiful mystery of love. We know it by experience as we live our marriage-enthronement with God daily in anticipation of its future consummation. To the degree we live into that profound mutual intimacy with the Father moment by moment by the Spirit, we rule and reign with Christ *in real terms in this life*, at all levels of personhood and created reality.

QUESTIONS FOR REFLECTION AND DISCUSSION

1. Had you heard (or known) of this classic Christian spiritual tradition before reading this chapter? What is your impression of the threefold spiritual path?

2. What do you struggle with most in this chapter? Why? What can you do about it? Where do you think you are at this time in your spiritual journey *viz-a-viz* these stages?

---

294 Space does not allow for discussion of the Song. Richard Davidson (*Flame of Yahweh*, 545–632) shows its *literal* meaning: a poetic instruction and celebration of human sexuality as created and blessed by God. The climax is 8:6, "love… burns like blazing fire, like the very flame of Yahweh" (NIV, margin). This conclusion affirms God as the *source* and *spirituality* of all human love, especially sexual, which can then be legitimately read back into the Song as an *analogous typology* (different to *allegorical spiritualisation*) of the drama of love and intimacy between God and his beloved people.

Part Three: Praxis

3. What vices do you need to rid yourself of? What virtues do you need to practice cooperating with the Spirit in purifying and freeing yourself from those vices?

4. In reflecting on *via illuminitiva*, what experiences have you had of what is described in this stage of spiritual growth?

5. How would you explain, in your own words, what union with God means?

6. What in particular do you feel God has said to you through this chapter? What are you going to do about it?

CHAPTER 10

TRANSFORMATION: THE SPIRIT OF THE DISCIPLINES

*"Train yourself to be godly.
For physical training is of some value,
but godliness has value for all things,
holding promise for both the present life and the life to come."*
Paul – 1 Tim 4:7–8

The context of this verse is "how people ought to conduct themselves in (and beyond) God's household… the pillar and foundation of the truth" (3:15–16). The local church is, and ought to be, the bastion of embodied truth in a corrupt post-truth world. Paul then says that Jesus is "the mystery of godliness" (v.16): *the revealed secret to God-like-ness*. In other words, it's an open secret that the real source of godliness, defined as incarnate truth evidenced in godly character, is Jesus – not other ideas, beliefs, spirits or philosophies. The quality and character of *his* incarnate life, vindicated by the Spirit in bodily resurrection and proclaimed among the nations, is *the* Saving-Life that (trans)forms into true godliness all who believe.

This does not mean that we sit back and "just believe". If we *really* believe, we *will* prioritize training in *that* godliness to be spiritually fit for life with God in this age and the age to come. The life of the coming age, "eternal life", is "*the* life that is *truly* life." Hence, we must "take hold of" it here and now (6:12,19), *training* ourselves to live the future in the present, to do God's will on earth as it is in heaven. And this involves our bodies. Paul is not dualistic, pitting physical training against spiritual training (4:7–8), but says the former has relative added value to the latter. The Greco-Roman world of athletes, gladiators and soldiers well knew of the mutual benefit of bodily *and* spiritual fitness and wellbeing.

Over the years I have come to understand *the absolute importance of the body in relation to the spiritual life*. And thus the importance of what I call the holy trinity of daily spiritual *and* physical exercise, *and* a healthy diet. I have found these three daily disciplines essential for fitness in life with God, more so the older we grow. Our decaying bodies are key to our spiritual maturing for the life to come. We have to trust God more and more – his power is perfected in weakness. In their growing weakness our bodies become translucent with the power and glowing glory of eternal life, anticipating our resurrected spiritual body (1 Cor 15:42–44). "From hour to hour we ripe and ripe, from hour to hour we rot and rot."[295]

This chapter is closer to a practical *Evangelical* theology of sanctification. How does spiritual transformation take place *in practice*? How does God actually form and transform us toward Christ-like-ness? Here I can do no better than to summarize Dallas Willard on spiritual transformation, on what he called *the with-God-life in apprenticeship to Jesus in his kingdom of the heavens*. As a Christian philosopher he was profoundly insightful, truly biblical and intensely practical.

I begin with Willard's *key assumptions* captured in his concise definitions *italicized* below – *the Spirit* behind the practice of spiritual (trans)formation.[296] Then I unpack *the praxis* by which it takes place. He rightly framed the with-God-life – the God-with-us life seen in the embodied Immanuel – in Jesus' message and mission of God's kingdom.

---

295 Fulton Sheen, *The Divine Romance*, 13.
296 See *The Spirit of the Disciplines*, *The Divine Conspiracy* and *Renovation of the Heart*, from now on *SD, DC* and *RH* respectively. I use them as primary sources, citing quotes. This is my *interpretation* of Dallas with some added material of my own. I use his first name rather than his surname.

Though Dallas understood the mysterious tension of the already and not yet of the kingdom, he did not use those terms. He taught it as the experiential process of how God's Spirit *actually* transforms us. That happens primarily – though not exclusively – through training, as in our response-able actions in apprenticeship to Jesus. His focus was on being *practitioners* of God's rule and reign in our own lives and the world around us: "Practical theology's overall task is, in effect, to develop for practical implementation the methods by which women and men interact with God to fulfil the divine intent for human existence."[297]

Assumptions and definitions

Spirit is power. More precisely, *spirit is unembodied or nonbodily personal power.*[298] Ultimate reality is (S)spirit. Capital S is God, the Creator-Source of reality (Jn 4:24). Small s is spiritual reality, other spirit-beings God made. Material creation is "of the (S)spirit" (Col 1:15–17; Heb 1:2, 11:3), owing its existence to the spiritual or super-natural. We live in *one two-dimensional reality*: unseen and seen, spiritual and material, existing hand-in-glove. Spirit is not empty space or "thin air". It is actual substance, albeit spiritual. Spirit is substantial *personal presence:* the power of free will, mind and feelings, but without materiality (a body); whether it's *holy* Spirit in service of God or *evil* spirit in opposition to God. It interacts with and can inhabit matter, characteristically manifesting itself to those who seek it, incarnating itself in those who worship it. Therefore, (S)spirit is the primary power or energy of formation of physical reality, more so of human persons, and especially our bodies.

This kind of power or energy must be distinguished from *arbitrary* power or force, as in matter – like gravity, magnetism or electricity. Though neither spiritual nor personal, such power can equally benefit or harm (even kill) us, depending on how we relate to it. *Matter is potential power.* More precisely, it is *embodied non-personal power* to be released,

297 *SD*, 15.
298 *SD*, 64. *DC*, 93–94.

Part Three: Praxis

harnessed and worked with for the good of creation, *by those in right relationship with it.*[299] God made humanity for this very (earthly) purpose.

Human beings are embodied or bodily personal power.[300] That is, we are unique spirit-body beings made in God's image, the climax of his creation, to rule on his behalf. This means we are of – live in and from – God's one reality; straddling both spiritual and material dimensions: "a great human contradiction, dust and divinity."[301] Only God is fully self-determining and self-generating life and power: what he says is (Ex 3:14). We are partially self-determining: what we say becomes, more or less! We are made for *interdependent* life with God, to live by a power beyond ourselves. By relating rightly to *divine* power, living interactively with, and operating in, *God's* Spirit, we image God. We fulfil our created purpose. We govern under God in his likeness, implementing his heavenly kingdom (will) in the natural order entrusted to us.

However, humanity in Adam and Eve fell from this divine purpose, this creation design. Deceived by evil spirit in rebellion against God, humanity also rebelled, resulting in separation from the Source of Eternal Life.[302] That death, in Gen 3:1f, led to alienation from God

---

299 *SD*, 64. (S)spirit, holy or evil, can interact with matter (beside human beings) to use its power and energy for good or evil; e.g. the evil intent behind the storm that Jesus "rebuked" – the same way he rebuked demons out of people's bodies (Mk 1:25, 4:39). The multiplication of the five loaves and two fish to feed the multitudes was by *Holy* Spirit (Mk 6:35–44). However, *all* spirit-matter interaction is limited to the sovereignty of the one Creator-God who has no equal or opposite other.

300 *RH*, 34–35, 160–161.

301 *SD*, 52. This does *not* mean we pre-existed as (divine) spirit-souls before our biological conception and birth as physical bodies, as in Gnostic and Hindu belief.

302 Adam and Eve grasped for a power, the knowledge of good and evil, for which they did not have the character. If they had chosen a long obedience in the same direction, they would have come to know all they needed to know when they needed to know it, routinely discerning and choosing good over evil. They would be alive today by God's Spirit, their bodies radiant with eternal life and the earth filled with the kingdom, glory and knowledge of the Lord as the waters cover the sea. God reveals true knowledge commensurate with character development that can responsibly use its power for the good of creation, *God's* glory. Knowledge is power, but without selfless love of God and others it is the self-serving power of human pride that ultimately destroys (see 1 Cor 8:1–3).

(spiritual), from ourselves (psycho-physical), from others (social), and from creation (ecological). Hence the radical evil in the ruined soul. It rules through death in a progressive spiritual, psycho-physical, social and ecological formation, molding the world into its image of the corrupted character of self-worship.

But God comes to seek and save the lost. *Salvation is a life, a new order of spiritual life.*[303] It is *God's* eternal kind or quality of life, given by Jesus through his death and resurrection Spirit, and received by faith in him – consequently our human spirit comes alive, is regenerated, with God's eternal Spirit-life. This wholistic salvation is a progressive spiritual, psycho-physical, social and ecological re-formation from the inside out. It restores us to our original created purpose – and more.

Life is the power to relate and assimilate.[304] The nature of created life is its dependence on "the other." It relates beyond itself to assimilate what it needs to sustain, grow and enhance its own properties of life. A seed has life but remains dead as long as it is separate from its source of life. If planted in soil it comes to life by drawing in surrounding moisture and nutrients to grow into a plant or tree. Soil is the seed's natural element to express its life to the full. Humans breathe to live. We live because we breathe. Oxygen is our natural element for physical life. God's Spirit – future age or heavenly "oxygen" – is our (super)natural element for *spiritual* life. In other words, we relate to and assimilate *Holy* Spirit via instinctive practices *and* intentional exercises. For example, we take our first breath of eternal life when we are born again by God's Spirit (Jn 3:3–6) and instinctively cry "Abba! Father!" (Gal 4:6). Then we continue exercising our spiritual lungs with God's oxygen, called prayer and worship, to live God's kind of eternal life in this evil age.

Do not think, however, of spiritual and physical life as separate. The spirit-body life and relationship is a seamless garment that cannot be divided without destroying the whole. God designed the human body

---
303 *SD*, 28–34.
304 *SD*, 57. I introduced this idea of life in chapter 6.

for eternal life: it can only mature into its created purpose when filled with God's eternal Spirit-life. Our body is our whole person, including, of course, our will, mind, emotions and relationships. Let me illustrate the wonder of this nature of life.

There are orders of life and types of bodies (1 Cor 15:37–44) perfectly suited to one another in the various kingdoms God made: from the mineral, to the plant, to the animal, to the human kingdom. For example, a cabbage has a certain kind of life in a vegetable body adequate to the life it carries. Imagine *that* life poured into a body in the mineral kingdom, like a rock. Would the rock adequately express the properties of life – the growth, colour, texture and taste – of the cabbage? No! It's inconceivable! If the life of a playful kitten were poured into the cabbage, its cabbage body might well explode with energy! Or the order of life in the kitten would be restricted to death in the body of the cabbage! What will happen if we could pour human life, in all its sophisticated properties and faculties, into the kitten? How incredibly limiting and ludicrous that would be for human life? It is not designed and suited for such an animal body.

Now the amazing mystery of *God's* order of life: eternal Spirit-life. It is so infinitely superior to finite human body-life that we cannot even begin to compare it with the crazy contrasts of the mineral, plant, animal and human kingdoms. Yet God, not localized in a body, lovingly designed the localized human body to receive God's life – to literally "be filled with all the fullness of God" (Eph 3:19 NRSV). Our body is fully suited to God's eternal life, to share in and express it to the full, in all its mysterious properties, power, beauty and glory. Our body – with spirit, will, mind and emotions – yearns for this incarnation of God's Spirit, for our completion as human beings. God not only *designed* our body for this purpose but also *desires* to pour him/herself into us. God is in no way limited or diminished by being "localized" in us, completing us as his radiating image for all creation.

A correct theology of the body is critical. The body is *potential power/ energy*, depending on its formation and use. "Roughly speaking, *God relates to space as we do to our body*."[305] Just as God fills and upholds creation, so the spiritual life is the body's fulfilment. Our body, in turn, is our greatest resource for the spiritual life – in preparation and anticipation of a Spirit-saturated, trans-physical resurrected-body. Though a decaying "jar of clay", the body is a lightning conductor between heaven and earth; a storehouse and transmitter of God's presence and power. Such a body, disciplined in right relationship to God, communicates God in real terms. Thus, there was real power in the laying on hands by Jesus and his first followers.

When our children were little, they loved to look in rock pools for small sea creatures like red starfish – to keep them as pets! On their first day in captivity the starfish lost their colour. The second day they were slimy. The third day they stank. Then they died! All because they were taken out of their natural element. The (super)natural environment for human life to thrive to the full, is God's person and presence: his Spirit-life, kingdom, grace and glory. To the degree we alienate and separate ourselves from *that* reality we lose colour, become slimy and smelly, living death in the whole of who we are: spiritually, psycho-physically, socially and ecologically.

Dallas illustrates the positive side of this with a different metaphor: "The light bulb is dead when disconnected from the electrical current, even though it still exists. But when connected to the current, it radiates and affects its surroundings with a power and substance that is *in* it but not *of* it" (his italics).[306]

---

305 *DC*, 87. Dallas' italics.
306 *SD*, 64. A similar (Orthodox) illustration of divinization: the filament in the light bulb curls round and round to slow down the current that enters, so that, infused with an energy beyond itself, it lights up and radiates light. We must slow down to linger and wait in God's presence to be infused with his uncreated energies of love that radiate the Taboric Light of God's *Sh'kinah*.

The gospel of the kingdom and discipleship to Jesus

This is the good news of life in God's kingdom *of heaven*. Heaven is not "space" beyond the sky. It's *substantial spiritual reality* in the atmosphere around us, available and interactive with us. The coming of Jesus and the Spirit "opened" the heavens (Mk 1:10) to inaugurate God's spiritual kingdom on earth – "the kingdom alongside" (Dallas' phrase) that we step into and live from. Jesus embodied *that* kingdom, *that* spiritual life, as the model and means of life for all his apprentices. As we trust him, relying on him daily, we experience *that* reality – kingdom life.

God's kingdom is the range of his effective will.[307] Where and when God's will is done, his kingdom has effectively come (Matt 6:10). We all have our kingdoms, limited in power and range in terms of our will being done. When God's kingdom (will) clashes with our kingdom (will), what do we do? To follow Jesus is to enter and live under *God's* kingship. To pray, "Your kingdom come" means "my kingdom go". We seek *his* kingdom *first and foremost,* and all we need is given to us (Matt 6:33). We deny ourselves and take up our cross (Matt 16:24), just as Jesus carried his cross, yielding his will to God, "not my will, but yours be done" (Matt 26:39). Our cross is when our will and God's will cross, then we choose. If we die to self, our will comes alive to God's will and its power. In this way, God's kingdom Gospel is the power of wholistic transformation for all who believe: for persons, society, and creation.

The alternative "gospels of sin management"[308] in current Christianity are about our "sin problem", i.e. God is an anti-dote to sin – without sin we would not need God! On the right, there is the conservative (spiritual) evangelical gospel of personal sin management, a private vampire gospel: "Jesus, give me some of your blood to forgive my sins, so that I can get into heaven when I leave the earth!" On the left, there is the liberal (liberation) social gospel of structural sin management, a utopian empire gospel:

---

307 *DC,* 29.
308 *DC,* 43–64. I have somewhat caricatured them with my wording.

"Jesus, as you shed blood, we too will shed blood – ours and others – to remove systemic injustice and get heaven to earth, no matter the cost!"

Both are *human*-kingdom gospels that cannot make disciples, they have no power for wholistic transformation. They produce the salvation-sanctification gap, and the authority-power gap. The first is the gap between being converted and being a daily disciple, between good Christian intentions and our unchanged readiness to sin. The second is the gap between our words and unchanged reality around us, between using the name of Jesus and its distinct lack of effect. This is the unsanctified powerless state of the contemporary church – with some pockets of renewal.

The Gospel of the kingdom is "the keys of the kingdom" (Matt 16:19). Jesus gives us, his followers, the keys (authority) to open the kingdom to others. Entering the kingdom, we are transformed to exercise a spiritual power way beyond ourselves. Imagine being given the keys to a future-age super-car. By stepping into the car, we entrust ourselves to a power-zone of the future made present. We use the key to initiate and interact with a movement of supernatural enablement way beyond our own strength and capacity. We are carried around in it – by it – to fulfil our collaborative purpose, without ever exhausting our own resources, till we reach our destination. This is life in God's kingdom as a daily disciple of Jesus.

To be Jesus' disciple is to be his student, his apprentice; a disciplined learner, learning from him how to live the life he lived in his Father's kingdom. We must distinguish between his life and our life: to be Jesus' apprentice *today* is to live interactively with him, learning from him how to live *my* life as *he* would if *he* were *me* (to make it personal). I cannot live his life as a rabbi 2000 years ago, nor be with him as his disciples were back then – both are unrepeatable. However, I certainly can learn from him daily how he would live my life in the power of God's kingdom, if he were me, in my particular life context.

How do I do this? Through interactive relationship and purposeful training by his indwelling Spirit. Apprenticeship to a master is to arrange one's life to become like the master – to learn their way of life, their vocation and trade – in a disciplined and structured life formation. To be an apprentice of Jesus, the Master of God's kingdom, is to be fully committed to, live interactively with, diligently learn from, to purposefully become like him. In so doing, we incrementally live the life and vocation of God's kingdom in the Spirit's power and character, just as Jesus did. This is (ought to be) our whole-life, life-long pursuit, in all dimensions of our personhood.

(Trans)formation in all dimensions of human personhood

God's human image is a multi-dimensional unity of personhood. God is Three in One. We are spirit, soul and body as one person. Paul uses Greek language categories but teaches Hebraic wholism: "May the God of peace sanctify you through and through… your *whole* spirit, soul and body" (1 Thess 5:23). Paul's "peace" is *Shalom:* we are a dynamic interrelated whole, not an amalgam of functioning "parts".[309] To the degree we are *de*formed by sin and death, we disintegrate into fragmented "parts" at war with each other. To the degree we are *re*formed in Christ we are reintegrated, recalibrated, into a whole *Shalom* person: all interrelated dimensions of personhood working harmoniously as one under God's loving rule.

The reality is, whether we know it or not, we all live from our hearts for better or for worse, depending on its condition and formation (see Prov 4:23 cf. Matt 15:18–19). Biblically, the *heart* is the fountain from which life flows – heart is synonymous with *spirit* and *will*; the power of choice at the centre of our being. It's our spiritual nature, the primary

---

[309] We have seen *and* unseen "parts" that exist as one seamless garment of life. If you open up my body, you will not find my spirit in there; if you open my brain you will not find my mind. Paul endorses the idea that we are one spirit, soul and body – the soul seemingly being the psycho-emotional interface between spirit and body. On *Shalom* see footnote 98.

means of (S)spirit interaction that gives definite form and character to our spirit, our whole being. Thus, the *human* concept of spirituality, the *humanistic* project of formation, is our relationship to what's most important to us, what's of ultimate value, "to become a happy successful *spiritual* person", as is often said.

The strictly *Christian* or God-project of spirituality is *the redemptive Spirit-driven process of forming the inner world of the self* – in all its governing inclinations – *to take on the character of the inner being of Christ himself.*[310] The more this happens, our outer life becomes the natural expression and outflow of Jesus' inner life and character. He lived and taught *that* quality of inner-outer life in the Sermon on the Mount (Matt 5 to 7), i.e. "to obey everything I have commanded you" (Matt 28:19). But, if the outward behaviour of obedience becomes *the* focus, the process of spiritual formation is defeated; falling into crushing legalisms, guilt performance and small mindedness. Conversely, focus on the inner formation of the spirit, will, mind and feelings, leads to bodily obedience as the natural outflow of a renovated heart – who we are – not obedience from white-knuckled determination and discipline in the moment, which predictably fails.

Dallas presents six dimensions or aspects of human life and personhood:[311]

Choice – the spirit, heart, will, decision, character.

Thought – images, concepts, judgments, memory.

Feeling – emotions, sensation.

Body – behaviour and action, interaction with the physical world.

Social – context of personal and structural/systemic relations to others.

Soul – the factor that integrates all of the above to form one life.

---

310 RH, 22. God transforms evil governing inclinations of our heart from childhood (Gen 8:21 cf. 6:5).

311 RH, 30. For lack of space I do not explain these dimensions and how they are (trans) formed in Christ – discussed in detail in RH. One can debate the extent to which Dallas distinguishes between *soul* and *spirit*, compared with the synonymous use of *nephesh* and *ruach* in the OT.

Part Three: Praxis

Life *with* God flows from "above inside out": an order of (trans)formation from God into the human spirit, to the mind and emotions, then the soul, the body and the social context. This is true worship; the reign of *Shalom*, where God's will is done as it is in heaven. Life *apart* from God is a reversal of this order, flowing from "beneath outside in": whereby evil and other forces in the social context and the body dominate and disintegrate the soul, scatter the emotions, disorder the mind, enslaving and forming the will/spirit in the image of the god being served. This is functional *idolatry;* the reign of death and chaos, where Satan's will is done as it is in hell. Tolstoy said, "the God that people generally believe in *has to serve them*... in very refined ways, say by merely giving them peace of mind. This God does not exist. But the God whom people forget – *the God whom we all have to serve* – exists, and is the prime cause of our existence."[312] Jesus teaches the same contrast: the *good tree* naturally bears good fruit from the good it is rooted in, just as the *bad tree* is known by its consistently bad fruit-root reality (Matt 7:16–18, 12:33). James has the same contrast in the context of *wisdom* "from above" and "from beneath" (Js 3:13–18).

I illustrate this in Figure 10 below.[313] Spiritual formation ("SF" in the diagram) is wholistic, whether from above or beneath, from within or without. In other words, *God, the Word and Spirit,* and/or *the world, the flesh and the devil* – and a mix of benign forces between – forms the whole person, directly leading to action that comes from the whole person. Our outward *attitude* and *action* do not arise solely from our inner *will* (heart/spirit). It is more complex: the will both acts on and is acted on by multiple aspects of personhood. In reality actions *always* arise out of the *interplay* of universal factors in human life: spirit, mind, emotions, body, soul and social context. Good intentions alone are inadequate to ensure proper action, as Jesus said, "the spirit is willing but the flesh is weak" (Matt 26:41). The disciples intended to pray with Jesus but fell asleep.

---
312 Cited in *RH*, 40. Tolstoy's italics.
313 Adapted from Dallas' diagram in *RH*, 40.

Peter intended *not* to deny Jesus, even vowing to die with him, but he denied Jesus. We are all sincerely willing to do good, but ready to do wrong – just given the appropriate situation or temptation!

Figure 10. "SF" Actions and the Whole Person

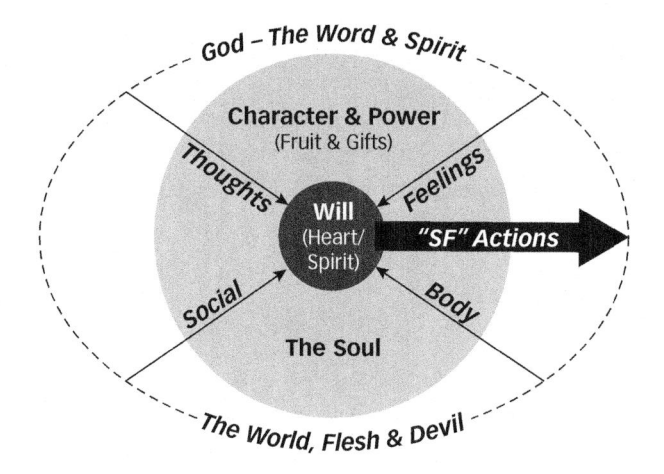

God – The Word & Spirit

- Character & Power (Fruit & Gifts)
- Thoughts
- Feelings
- Will (Heart/Spirit)
- "SF" Actions
- Social
- Body
- The Soul

The World, Flesh & Devil

If the six dimensions are properly aligned to God and each other, our actions will simply be the good fruit of the good tree. If not so aligned, they will inevitably be the bad fruit of the bad tree. Attitudes and actions are not *imposed* on who we are; they consistently *express* who we are – our character, our relatively consistent will. The God-intended function of the will (spirit/heart) is *not* to be at the mercy of forces playing upon it from the larger self and beyond – the world, the flesh and the devil – but to reach out to God to receive the grace that properly reorders and reforms the soul, along with the other aspects of the self. These faculties are transformed and trained through faith that "relates and assimilates" God's Word and Spirit, via appropriate spiritual practices, to reinforce the will to routinely choose God and naturally do good. These acts of obedience become a pattern, then a habit. *That* then is our character: consistent integrity of inner and outer being – the character *and* power, fruit *and* gifts of the Spirit of Jesus in us.

What is transformation and how does it take place?

The NT word *metamorphoo* means to transform, change or transfigure into another form or image. It appears twice in Jesus' transfiguration (Matt 17:2; Mk 9:2) and twice in Paul (Rom 12:2; 2 Cor 3:18). Luke uses another word (9:29), avoiding *metamorphoo,* probably to not invite comparison with pagan ideas. It was commonly used in the Greco-Roman world, especially for idealized religious change: spirits of the gods manifested ecstatic momentary transformation in the worshipper. Today we "morph" faces from old to young and *vice versa* on TV or computer screens.

Behind Jesus' *metamorphoo* and Paul's use of it in 2 Cor 3:18, stands Moses' transfiguration. After forty days in God's presence, his face shone with glory in mediating the covenant. However, the *new* covenant in Jesus, in Paul's interpretation, is not merely outward change that fades away. God's indwelling Word and Spirit regenerates and transforms the spirit/will to naturally obey God's commands – the glory of behavioural change that is incremental and lasting, even eternal.

These texts show a two-sided reality: a) *only God* can and does change us for good. We cannot change ourselves, as in biblical *metamorphoo*. God transforms us from within, from one degree of glory to another, *seen in outward behavioural change*. God does it by his Spirit in union with our regenerate spirit (1 Cor 6:17). And yet, b) it clearly happens *with* human participation via spiritual practices: *as Jesus prayed* he was transformed (Lk 9:27); *as we renew our minds* we are transformed (Rom 12:2); also, *as we contemplate* the Lord's glory (2 Cor 3:18). In other words, God does not sovereignly or unilaterally change us by Spirit-pulses remotely controlling us like a TV or robot. Nor are we changed by our own effort in disciplines, a humanist project of the self-made person. Rather, it's a delicate dance of the divine and human.

Transformation is a divine dance of God's graceful action by his Spirit and our responsive participation in those movements via spiritual practices. Jesus was formed by the Spirit in his human nature and body in relational interaction with his Father via extensive spiritual practices till his death. We see the same in Paul and the Early Church: the practice of classic spiritual disciplines was fundamental to their sanctification by the Spirit. This is Hebraic bi-polar thinking, where apparent contradictory opposites are held in tension, as the rabbis say: "When you pray, pray as if everything depends on God, and when you work, work as if everything depends on you." Both are simultaneously true without contradiction.

Noted earlier, human nature does not like both/and tension and seeks either/or resolution – *either* Spirit miracle *or* human effort! Various understandings of sanctification and transformation can be mapped on the either/or continuum, and in kingdom terms from "kingdom now" to "kingdom not yet" extremes:[314]

- *Total sanctification:* God transforms us at salvation, or by a subsequent "second blessing", making us holy, as in literal "sinless perfection." It's instant sanctification like instant coffee – no work involved. But experience and scripture (e.g. 1 Jn 1:8–10) tells us this is not true.

- *Power-encounter:* God transforms us by spiritual experiences, ecstatic manifestations, supernatural gifts – notorious for its limited effect for lasting character change.[315]

---
314 This is a stereotypical list. Space does not allow me to discuss each in detail.
315 Though rich in Spirit-gift-manifestations, Paul challenged the Corinthian Christians (they were like modern Spirit-chasers who seek regular power encounter as their spiritual fix) regarding their carnal and unspiritual behavior. Many in my congregation experienced regular power encounters in the "Toronto Blessing" years; yet, as their pastor, I know most still struggled with their same besetting sins years later.

Part Three: Praxis

- *Grace and faith alone:* God saves *and* continues to sanctify us only by grace – simply believe what Jesus has done and transformation happens. This misunderstands grace and faith by setting it in a wrong opposition to effort and discipline, which tends to licenciousness, as in Rom 6:1.

- *Spiritual insight and revelation knowledge:* moments of revelatory insight and/or the right kind of spiritual or theological knowledge transforms us. Knowledge can create a desire for change, but does not sustain it. And knowing something is true does not change the inclination of the will.

- *Liturgical ritual practice:* we are transformed by doing the required religious observances, especially church attendance and the sacraments. However, no spiritual practice in and of itself has the power to produce change, unless God's Spirit works through it.

- *Personal vision and discipline:* we are transformed by our new identity and destiny in Christ, as in the vision and goals we have of our being and becoming, with the disciplined strategic effort to attain it. Without genuine and total reliance on God's Spirit this is a form of humanism.

There may be more. All have aspects of truth, but each is inadequate on its own, lacking the power of biblical transformation. And if pushed to an extreme, each of the above teachings can end up in heresy.

In summary: Only God can and does change us, by the grace of his Spirit, progressively transforming our heart, character *and* behaviour into who we really are, our new nature in Christ. And it happens as we respond to God. It is a dance of love in apprenticeship to Jesus as we respond in faith to the grace-full initiative of the Spirit. The Spirit works in spontaneous moments *and* structured practices, as event *and* process. *Both* moments and practices constituted the spiritual disciplines of Jesus and his followers – and by such the Spirit *meta-morphs* us into Christ's likeness.

Golden triangle of transformation

Dallas' diagram (Figure 11) shows how this happens in practice – a threefold dynamic in spiritual transformation, and fourfold if one adds community context.[316]

Figure 11. Golden Traingle of Transformation

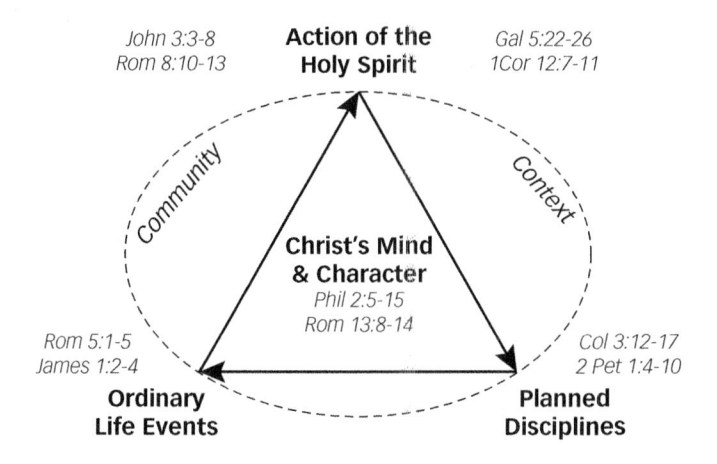

```
              John 3:3-8    Action of the    Gal 5:22-26
              Rom 8:10-13   Holy Spirit      1Cor 12:7-11

                         Community    Context

                          Christ's Mind
                           & Character
                            Phil 2:5-15
                           Rom 13:8-14
         Rom 5:1-5                                Col 3:12-17
         James 1:2-4                              2 Pet 1:4-10
              Ordinary                         Planned
              Life Events                      Disciplines
```

This is not a magic formula or telephone booth for instant transformation into a Super-Christian! Rather, it represents slow but sure transformation into Christ's mind and character – a life-long whole-life process – a long but incrementally joyous obedience in the same direction.

Most important is the top of the apex, the work of God's Spirit. The texts say we are born of the Spirit – and filled with the Spirit; growing/ transformed by the Spirit into the fruit of Christ's character; and are given

---

316 *DC*, 380. I added the dotted circle to represent the community context in which it takes place.

gifts of the Spirit as needed. This is the already of God's rule and reign breaking into the not yet of our lives by the Spirit's power, working the fullness of future-age life in us. This is purely God's action of grace. We cannot make it happen. We can ask, desire and seek it. We can discern and recognize it. We can believe, respond and work with it. *Or* be ignorant and blind, unbelieving and hardened to it. We can ignore, neglect or reject it.

The "kingdom come" action of the Spirit is always at work, whether we see and feel it, or not; whether we are awake watching or asleep resting (Mk 4:26–29 cf. Ps 121). Jesus knew that. By training and practice he grew into the joyful ease of recognizing and working with the Spirit, till his whole life was a co-working with his Father (Jn 5:17–20). How then does the Spirit work? How do we recognize and respond to it? In two ways: a) the Spirit is active in – *and we respond through* – the ordinary daily happenings of our lives; b) the Spirit is also active in our practice of planned spiritual disciplines. And I would add: in the context of faith community belonging.

The Spirit is present and active in *daily events and joys, in trials and temptations*.[317] They are sacraments (means of grace) of the present moment, depending if we respond or react. If we respond to the Spirit in the event it's a stepping-stone to transformation. If we react to the situation it's a stumbling-block to anger and other carnal reactions. Jesus' younger brother said we must consider it pure joy whenever we face trials of many kinds, because we know that the testing of our faith produces perseverance, which matures and completes us in God's reign (Js 1:2–4). Paul says we can even boast in trials and sufferings because *we know* it produces perseverance, which develops character and resilient hope. *We know* this because God pours his love into our hearts by the Holy Spirit

---

[317] Ignatius' discernment of consolations of the good Spirit and desolations of the bad spirit, finding God in all things, responding to what he is doing in each moment – see Barry, *Finding God in all things*. Fellow Jesuit, Jean Pierre de Caussade, said, "There is no moment in which God does not present Himself, under cover of some pain to be endured, some consolation to be enjoyed, or some duty to be performed", *Abandonment to Divine Providence*, 19.

in all these things (Rom 5:3-5). *We know* that God works in all things for our good because we love him and are called according to his purpose (Rom 8:28). *Nothing* that happens or comes upon us is out of God's orbit of good work or control. The ordinary daily stuff of our lives is indeed the means of the Spirit's work in us, as we interactively respond to the Spirit.

The Spirit is equally present and active in our *planned spiritual disciplines,* working the already kingdom into our not yet reality. These are activities *we* plan, practice and pursue! *They* do not simply happen to us! The classic spiritual disciplines are also sacraments: primary means of the Spirit's sanctifying and transforming grace in and through us. Paul teaches us to think through, plan and practice appropriate disciplines to "put off" the old sinful nature and "put on" our new nature in Christ.[318] Christian practices, correctly understood, are not to be done *in order* to make something happen, or to do them as duties to obey God. They are acts of worship as a participation in Jesus' practices; *connecting points* to God's presence and power.

Peter spells it out (2 Pet 1:3-11, my italics): *because* we "participate in the divine nature (we) escape corruption in the world caused by evil desires. *For this very reason, make every effort to* [he does not say sit back and relax, you can add nothing to your salvation] add to your faith goodness; and to goodness, knowledge; and to knowledge, self-control; and to self-control, perseverance; and to perseverance, godliness; and to godliness, mutual affection; and to mutual affection, love. [These are virtues, spiritual practices that facilitate growth and transformation to maturity]. For *if you possess these qualities in increasing measure,* they will keep you from being ineffective and unproductive in your knowledge of our Lord Jesus Christ. But whoever does *not* have them is nearsighted and blind, forgetting that they have been cleansed from their past sins. *Therefore... make every effort* to confirm your calling and election. For *if you do these things,* you will never stumble, and you will receive a rich welcome into the eternal kingdom of our Lord and Savior Jesus Christ."

---

318 Rom 13:12-14; Col 3:12-17; Eph 4:17-32. I discussed these texts in chapter 8.

That says it! It cannot be clearer than this! We have no excuse!

Then there is the dynamic interaction between planned spiritual practices and daily happenings. As noted earlier, *both* constitute spiritual discipline to respond to the Spirit. The more we give ourselves, in a planned and paced manner, to appropriate regular spiritual practices, the more we will recognize and respond to the Spirit in everyday events, no matter *how severe* the tests may be. And the more we discipline ourselves into discerning and responding to the Spirit's movements in the moment, in *whatever* happens to us during the day, the more we will desire – be drawn back to – focused time with God, for sheer love of him, in planned spiritual practices.

The added circle of local community belonging, support and accountability is equally important. These dynamics of spiritual transformation are reinforced, deepened and directed with brothers and sisters, and spiritual leaders, in committed faith community. From beginning to end, scripture is about the Trinitarian God, the Eternal Community, creating and living and working with family. The Spirit works transformation of individuals in and through community. The local church is, ought to be, was designed to be, God's hothouse of spiritual growth. Without the love and protection, discipline and direction of local church, we become disconnected and vulnerable spiritual lone rangers – not heroic at all.

Grace, discipline and training

Dallas cleared up the confusion between grace and effort. Grace denies *merit and earning*, but not *effort*. We cannot earn salvation or transformation. It's all by God's free grace, available to all. The air is free, not earned or merited, but we must breathe to benefit from it. Breathing is faith that works, that responsively participates. God's kingdom seeds are generously sown in the world but are lost on most people due to their inadequate heart response (Matt 13:18–23).[319] Grace does not robotically

---

319 Jesus describes four heart responses – attitudes and conditions. We are responsible –

change us; it requires response for us to benefit from it. It motivates participation. Sadly, God's grace is "without effect" for many people (1 Cor 15:10).

If we receive the costly grace of our Lord Jesus, it *will* motivate effort and disciplined learning in Christian living. The devil tries to keep us from Peter's "make every effort" – the cheap grace of the "extreme grace" teaching that leads to graceless living. Otherwise the devil pushes us into performance and legalism – we see our efforts in spiritual practices as a means of impressing God, to merit and earn, even manipulate and demand his favour and blessing. The radical middle is to see and receive it *all* as pure grace-gift – grace (*charis*) is gift (*charisma*) – drawing more and more on grace *in* making every effort via regular spiritual practices to co-work with God. We "use up" grace till we end up living entirely by grace and grace alone.

A discipline is well-directed effort, not random responses to feelings, desires or wishes. If we see grace as the freedom to flow with whatever we feel or happens, discipleship will be at the mercy of our moods and circumstances. Desire for God is a manifestation of grace, but without discipline – being fed as in "relating and assimilating" – it soon dies. Desire that is disciplined and reinforced by spiritual practices deepens into sustained godly passion, fueling the fire of discipleship.

The word "discipline" has negative association and prejudice that must be overcome to correctly understand it in relation to spiritual practices. "The phrase 'the discipline' was for centuries used to refer to a whip, to chastise the body during acts of penance" – the idea of self- or other-inflicted pain for spiritual acceptance and purification.[320] This originated in Middle Ages monasticism, was rejected by Luther and Protestantism, despised by Enlightenment rationalism. "Asceticism" associated with

---

not God – to plough up the fallow ground, the rocks and weeds, of our hearts (see Hos 10:12), *so that* when the grace of God, the word of the kingdom, comes to us, it is not lost, but is maximised in us.

320 *SD*, 135. See the historical view, then correct meaning of discipline and asceticism, 135–154.

"the discipline", was also rejected, and still carries prejudicial baggage for Evangelicals. I trust, however, that my previous chapter has suitably explained and redeemed *the true meaning and use* of both words. Biblically, God disciplines *his children* for their good, which is corrective training, not punitive punishment. We all engage daily in "natural" practices and ordinary activities that are actual disciplines – whether we know it or not – which enable us to live life, to grow and do well.

A discipline is an activity within our power that enables us to *indirectly* achieve what we cannot otherwise achieve by *direct* immediate effort. For example, if I want to become a pianist, I cannot sit down and play the piano by direct immediate effort. But if I yield to the discipline of daily practice, I will indirectly eventually achieve what I cannot otherwise achieve by trying in the moment, i.e. become a pianist. The same applies to our desire to become like Jesus (the Spirit being the "maestro-teacher"). It's the difference between *trying* and *training*, between performance and practice. Note that discipline for its own sake is meaningless. It must be well-directed (strategic) effort, or else it leads to pride, self-absorption or masochism.

Paul instructed Timothy *to train himself* to be godly, for fitness in shared-life with God, in this life and the life to come (1 Tim 4:7). Paul's *gymnazo*, "train",[321] is the root word for English gymnasium with its familiar associations of sport and battle, images that Paul loved and used to describe the spiritual life. The idea of training is that we engage in exercises and practices, well-directed effort, to equip ourselves with the fitness that is needed to do what we need to do, when we need to do it. Training "off the spot" incrementally conditions us with the capacity and readiness to perform "on the spot" when needed. We can only *be* on the spot who we are *becoming* off the spot. We no longer try, we simply are – we naturally deliver.

---

321 Also used in Heb 5:14, 12:11, and 2 Pet 2:14, false teachers "*trained* in greed" NRSV. Luke uses *asko,* from which "ascetic" is derived, in Acts 24:16, "herein do I *exercise* myself…" (KJV).

Jesus taught his disciples in Matt 6:1–18 to give, pray and fast regularly "in secret" (off the spot), and God's unseen presence and power will be "openly" seen in them (on the spot).[322] Building a "secret history" with God in such practices will enable and ready us to do all God requires when he requires it of us. Our will, mind, emotions and body, will be (re)trained to naturally do God's will as it is in heaven. Jesus told his tired and fearful friends in Gethsemane: "watch and pray so that you will not fall into temptation. The spirit is willing, but the flesh is weak" (Mk 14:38). But they fell asleep. Their spirit was willing, turned to God, but the governing tendencies of their bodies took over. They were not sufficiently (re)conditioned by the (S)spirit through the practice of watchful prayer to do what was needed. They tried to perform on the spot, not having done the training off the spot. In his darkest hour, when Jesus needed his closest friends the most, they failed him.

In short, the NT idea of training is *not* to gain techniques in doing, but to grow transformation in being. Training is the practice of discipleship, being apprenticed to Jesus to become like him. The fruit of such training – spiritual formation – is that we have the character to naturally and routinely do what we need to do when we need to do it, as Jesus would if he were us. In this sense the disciple – disciplined learner – becomes able "to obey everything I have commanded you" (Matt 28:20).

Introducing the classic spiritual disciplines

For millennia God's people – from Abraham to Jesus, the Early Church, and throughout church history – have given themselves to worship, prayer, fasting, giving, service, and other spiritual disciplines. In so doing, the church has seen it all in terms of both healthy *and* aberrant spirituality. On a continuum from Gnostic and legalistic beliefs on the one side, with extreme unbiblical practices; through the radical middle of

---

322 "Openly" in Matt 6:4, 6, 18 (KJV; the NIV and NRSV have "will reward you") echoes 3:16, the heavens "opened" in the Spirit's coming – meaning kingdom breakthrough as in 4:16, 23–25.

a healthy view and balanced practice of the disciplines; to the other side, rejecting the disciplines as unnecessary religious ritual due to "grace". The errors and excesses, pointed out in the previous chapter, must not deter us. The major part of the history of Christian spirituality has predominantly been good. We have seen in recent decades an unprecedented renewal of interest in classic spirituality and spiritual disciplines. Protestant-Evangelical prejudice is being overcome, and the good of classic Christian spirituality is being explored like hidden treasure – thanks to Dallas Willard and others of his kind. The disciplines are a rich resource for a deeper, more authentic (even mystical) experience of spiritual growth and transformation.

In kingdom terms, these classic spiritual disciplines are activities designed to bring us into more effective co-operation with God and his kingdom. They are the tried and tested *practical ways* through which Jesus companions and apprentices us today by his Spirit. They are the menu or set of core exercises, essential tools and aids, that train and equip us with the faith, character and power that is needed to share in God's rule and reign *in real terms*. Note that I use the words disciplines, exercises, practices, tools and aids, synonymously. They are *a means* to an end in this age; not needed when the future age fully comes, and God's will is done as it is in heaven.

However, the disciplines and the extent to which we practice them are *not a measure* of our spirituality – an error of Christian asceticism from the desert fathers to the Reformation. They are not the purpose of the spiritual life itself, having no value in themselves. "The aim and substance of the spiritual life is… the effective and full enjoyment of active love of God and humankind in all the daily rounds of normal existence where we are placed. The spiritually advanced person is not the one who engages in lots and lots of disciplines, any more than the good child is the one who receives lots and lots of instruction."[323] The more God rules and reigns in

---

323 *SD*, 138. *But*, beware of self-deceiving pride that says you no longer need disciplines. While some naturally fall away as they achieve their purpose in us, other "staples" will be needed till we die.

us, the less we need the disciplines; the younger we are in the spiritual life, the more we need them. And, as I have often stated; a) without a regenerate spirit/heart indwelt with God's Spirit working God's kingdom in us, spiritual disciplines will have limited effect for transformation, ending up as empty ritual in a "religious spirituality"; and b) if practiced for their own sake, spiritual disciplines will end up in a "narcissistic spirituality" like the sweaty ego parade of pure muscle mass in the gym.

In the way the list or menu of the classic spiritual disciplines is divided and set out, I follow Dallas' presentation,[324] with my own adjustments and additions.

In the next chapter I explain the disciplines *of engagement* – eight practices that directly engage us with *the already* of God's kingdom come. This is our intentional *attachment* to God and his kingdom enterprise.

In chapter 12 I discuss the disciplines *of abstinence* – eight practices that complement the disciplines of engagement, helping us to directly discipline *the not yet* aspects of the kingdom in our lives. This is our intentional *detachment* from the world, the flesh and the devil.

In chapter 13 I give an overview of some other classic tools and aids that have been used in the Christian tradition for spiritual growth and transformation.

In the final chapter I conclude by offering a framework of practical proposals for living a balanced and integrated spirituality in ordinary everyday life.

Key questions before engaging in the disciplines

Dallas wisely listed a number of key questions that we need to ask *before* we engage the disciplines, before we do a particular practice, so that our practice is not mindless or naive. This is more important when we venture *beyond* the "classic core" disciplines and decide to engage in more tailored, peripheral or exotic spiritual practices. Paul expected and taught the early churches and individual followers of Jesus to *think through* what

---

[324] *SD*, 156–192.

they are doing, why they do it, and how they do it – even with whom they do it. Paul himself was a good example of this. Slavish imitation, or mindless practice of spiritual exercises by rout, out of obligation, or to please someone, or to be "in" with a group, is to be seriously avoided. Here are the questions – with some overlap among them – that we need to ask ourselves:

What is the discipline? I must make sure I know what the discipline is, and not blindly engage in what I know little or nothing about.

What is its biblical basis? Is it part of the biblical teaching in spirit, if not in letter? I do not need a proof text for each discipline; but I need to see the discipline illustrated in God's people in the OT, and/or in Jesus and the Early Church. This is easy for the classic disciplines, but applies more to discerning extra-biblical practices.[325] They are not to be dismissed out of hand. Each is to be carefully evaluated in accountability to respected spiritual leadership for protection, in my view, because they tend to the appeal of "different", of novelty, extra-ordinary, exotic, the heroics of "extreme spirituality." These are of no value in the kingdom, though some people today value them, often to bolster their identity and ego.

For whom am I doing it? I must consciously do it for God, with God, before God as the audience of One, "in secret", my hidden history with God. Doing it for myself is good if it is prioritizing my growth, training and transformation *with the Spirit*. But doing it for myself to assuage guilt, to punish myself, to feel good about myself, to prove myself to myself, or to God or others, is self-defeating. And doing it to please others – to meet requirements of acceptance or belonging, is dangerous.

Why am I doing it? What is it designed to do? What is its spiritual benefit? I must know what the particular discipline promises to produce in me. The following chapters will clearly show how each discipline is aimed at addressing a certain aspect of receiving the kingdom ("engagement"),

---

[325] *Extra-biblical* is beyond or not in scripture, to be discerned if helpful or not. *Non- anti- or un-biblical* is *against* what scripture teaches, or clearly *not* what scripture teaches – to be rejected.

and/or rehabilitating and retraining "parts" of my personhood where the kingdom has not yet come ("abstinence"). Once again, it is pointless to practice a particular discipline purely for its own sake.

How does it relate to my physical body? Discussed earlier, a correct theology of the human body explains why the spiritual life is the fulfilment of my body, and why my body is my greatest resource for the spiritual life. Each discipline relates in one way or another to my body in the sense that it is the whole of me, including my spirit, will, mind, emotions, desires, bodily appetites, and social-environmental relationships. An exercise or discipline, if it is a *spiritual* practice, will always involve my body in respect of the fulfilment of one or more aspects of who I am.

How does it relate to God's kingdom and ministry in my life, in the church, and in my world? Spiritual practices are not only for personal transformation. They are also for community growth and missional witness (social transformation). The disciplines are both personal and corporate, exercised as part of the practices of local church belonging. Thus, spiritual practices are *personal* but not *private*: I personally do them before God – others cannot do them for me – but they are never private as in being unquestionable, unaccountable to local Christian community. The disciplines bring me into more effective co-operation with God and his kingdom, to advance his rule and reign to the ends of the earth. So, I ask how the particular discipline will help to equip and enable me to minister more effectively with God in his kingdom work, both in my local church and my missional involvement in the world.

What are the practicalities involved? I need to be aware of how to do the discipline and what is involved in doing it. This implies being initiated or discipled into the disciplines by community and/or a spiritual mentor. I learn best by modeling, by watching others do it. So, before I engage in a particular discipline I need to know how I must do it, when I should do it, and for how long I should do it. And also, with what other discipline(s) should I do it? Some disciplines are best practiced in conjunction with others because of their complementary benefits.

What are the dangers, if any? Each exercise has a point of danger in its own way. More so if it's a practice *beyond* what I will detail as the classic spiritual disciplines. However, we need to be aware of dangers like unworkable practicalities that negatively affect us, spiritual excess, ideological pressure, spiritual pride, over extending our capacity, boredom, deception, and depression. For example, if I fast and I am on chronic medication, then it would be wise to consult my doctor for guidance as to the kind of fast, the duration of the fast, and its compatibility with my medicine, so that I do not endanger my health. This also raises dangers around the extent to which we practice certain disciplines that may trigger unhealed psycho-emotional and mental-health issues. I need to know myself and learn what works for me, and what does not work for me at this stage in my personal growth. Therefore, once again, the importance of community and accountability, of spiritual direction and pastoral leadership, in the practice of spiritual disciplines.

These questions will guide my discussion of the disciplines in the next three chapters, without necessarily answering each question for each spiritual practice.

QUESTIONS FOR REFLECTION AND DISCUSSION

1. In what ways does this chapter differ from the previous chapter?
2. How would you explain Paul's instruction to "train yourself to be godly"? What would that entail for you personally in your life at this time?
3. Did you find Dallas' definitions (in italics) helpful or difficult to understand? If you go over them again, how would you put them into your own words?
4. Can you agree with Dallas' basic assumptions as I have

summarised them? Have they changed your view of anything? What do you not agree with?

5. How did you understand spiritual transformation and God's way of changing us, before reading this chapter? Has anything now changed in your view?

6. Do you experience, or intentionally practice, the golden triangle of transformation? What do you need to do in order to experience it?

7. How would you define (spiritual) discipline? Are you a disciplined person?

8. What do you think of the questions that we should consider before we engage in the disciplines?

CHAPTER 11

PRACTICES I: DISCIPLINES OF ENGAGEMENT – THE ALREADY

Jesus said to the man (with a withered hand), *"Stretch out your hand." He did so, and his hand was completely restored.*
Lk 6:10

"A discipline for the spiritual life is, when the dust of history is blown away, nothing but an activity undertaken to bring us into more effective cooperation with Christ and his Kingdom."
Dallas Willard[326]

In classic Christian spirituality there is a set or menu of commonly accepted practices that connect us directly with God's kingdom, known as the Disciplines of *Engagement*. They are practices of *attachment* to God. In practicing them we engage God through Jesus by his Spirit, entering ever more fully into the Trinitarian Life, the Rule and Reign of Love. These positive and proactive *virtues* complement the set of spiritual practices that are more negative and reactive, known as the Disciplines of *Abstinence*. They are practices of *detachment* from the *vices* of the world, the flesh and the devil, designed to help us abstain from satisfying our

---
[326] *SD*, 156.

psycho-bodily appetites in order to discipline and retrain them. These disciplines create space and make way for engagement with God and his kingdom.

The traditional order is first disciplines of abstinence, as they *indirectly* make room for us to encounter God *directly* via disciplines of engagement. The former counteracts tendencies to sins of *commission*; the latter counter tendencies to sins of *omission*. Jesus' parable of the seed falling on different types of ground – conditions of the human heart – conveys this idea (Matt 13). The hardness of our heart, the rocks of superficiality and the weeds of life's worries are ploughed up by the disciplines of abstinence. To the degree we do this we are like prepared soil, ready to receive the kingdom through disciplines of engagement. Then the kingdom is not lost on us, its work is not cut short; rather, its fruit is fully maximized in us. In classic spirituality it's commonly illustrated as first breathing out foul air (disciplines of abstinence – purification) to make "the space" to then breathe in God's pure oxygen (disciplines of engagement – enlightenment and union).

These two sets of disciplines were classically framed in an ascetic-liturgical paradigm. The distinctive feature of this book is framing Christian spirituality within the kingdom worldview of Jesus and working out the implications. Therefore, from a kingdom paradigm we can reverse the above order. Jesus came announcing, enacting and inaugurating the kingdom of heaven as a Spirit-baptism: God encounters us in "open heavens." As quoted above, Jesus said to the man, "stretch out your hand", to receive the kingdom that is *at hand*. As we reach out in faith, via practices of engagement, we experience the kingdom come. The engagement enables us to actively reach out and directly receive *the already* of the kingdom in Jesus and the Spirit. We are born again by God's Spirit, we take our first breath of eternal life. Then we continue to breathe God's Spirit by proactively engaging the kingdom, relating to and assimilating the life and powers of the coming age.

The *message* and *ministry* of Jesus was "the kingdom has come." People experienced the kingdom and entered it by following Jesus. Only then did they become aware of *the mystery* that Jesus taught: the kingdom has come but is yet to come. The kingdom is here in principle as Spirit-power but will come in fullness and finality at Jesus' return. The first is open heavens; the second is heaven actually come to earth. Where God's will is done, his kingdom *has* come. So, the disciplines of engagement enable us to proactively engage God to do his will. But where his will is *not* being done in our lives – where his kingdom has *not yet* come – the disciplines of abstinence reactively help to bring that aspect under God's rule and reign.

Therefore, disciplines of engagement with the "open heavens", with the in-breaking availability of the kingdom, grow our new nature and identity in Christ. They also expose and confront the not yet aspects in and around us, working in tandem with disciplines of abstinence to bring them under God's will. Once again, it's not *either* kingdom now (engagement) *or* kingdom not yet (abstinence). It is both/and at the same time, working together in creative tension, engaging to "put on the new" and abstaining to "put off the old", in Paul's language.

A note on attachment and detachment: we move from unconscious attachment to created things and ourselves (needs and appetites), to awareness of those attachments, to conscious detachment by abstinence, then to attachment to God by engagement. However, maturity is *indifference to all things,* whereby we transcend even our attachment to *our experience* of God and his kingdom. We can subtly replace attachment to self and things with attachment to experiences, manifestations and consolations of the Spirit, to practices that we enjoy. To be attached to them as our security, meaning, and even identity, blocks true union with God. Union is unconscious attachment beyond our conscious experience(s) of God, though the latter leads to the former – attained by genuine indifference to all created things, our body-self, *and* spiritual consolations. We then see *all* these "things" as given by God, not as an end, but to be *used* to the extent they enable our pursuit of God. *And* to free ourselves from them to the degree they hinder us from union with God by pure faith in perfect love, beyond all conscious sense experience of God.[327]

Here is the list of the eight primary disciplines of engagement. Each addresses a particular dimension of encounter with God and his kingdom, which in turn relates to one or more dimensions of our personhood that the Spirit transforms in God's rule and reign. And each discipline, though practiced personally, has a communal dimension to it.

Study – The Word
Worship – The Presence
Celebration – The Joy
Prayer – The Friendship
Service – The Ministry
Fellowship – The Community
Confession – The Forgiveness
Submission – The Authority

Study – The Word

The discipline of study directly engages us with The Word of The King. The King's word is authoritative and powerful, speaking creation into being. God rules and reigns by his word, which is living and active, sharper than any two-edged sword, penetrating the deepest recesses of our being, judging the thoughts and intentions of our heart (Heb 4:12). God's word is his revealed mind, will and truth, that exposes and confronts all untruth in us and in the world at large. It liberates us – our will, mind and emotions – from the kingdom of darkness into the kingdom of light.

By *The Word of God* I mean the Spirit-inspired *written word*, the Bible. But also the *living word*, King Jesus, who works and speaks by his Spirit in our thoughts and heart, in creation and other means already discussed.

---

[327] See Merton on detachment and attachment in *New Seeds of Contemplation,* 203–213. On Ignatian indifference to all things, see footnote 283 and the quote it cites.

Part Three: Praxis

By *the discipline of study,* I mean the regular practice of immersing ourselves primarily in scripture, and in God's ongoing words and works in our lives and world.

This first and primary discipline of engagement is the counterpart to, working in tandem with, the first and primary discipline of abstinence: solitude (see next chapter). We practice the discipline of study – listening to and learning of God in scripture – in daily times of solitude and silence alone with God. And also when we make time for extended Bible study outside of our daily devotions.

The discipline of study goes back to our Hebrew roots from Moses to King David, from the prophets to Jesus and the Early Church. They all gave themselves with singular devotion to read, study, meditate on, and memorize God's word. Torah commands it, as seen in the *Sh'ma Israel* (Deut 6:4–9). A careful reading of the Gospels shows Jesus steeped in scripture, alluding to and quoting Hebrew texts all the time. It formed the very texture of his thoughts, words and deeds. The writings of the apostles (the NT) and the church fathers – even their most philosophical thinkers – evidence an enviable verbal command of scripture. They express thoughts and ideas in biblical language, seldom above it; whereas many modern Christian writings merely cite the Bible, usually in a footnote, in support of their theological ideas.

This discipline of study is most needed – must be intentionally cultivated – in the early part of our spiritual journey. It's our spiritual food and drink for life and growth. "The milk" of the word feeds us as babes in Christ. Then, in order to grow in the true knowledge of God, to be formed in Jesus' worldview – the mind and heart of Christ – "the meat" of the word becomes our diet (1 Cor 3:2; Heb 5:12–14; 1 Pet 2:2). Hence Paul says to Timothy and all of us, "study to show thyself approved of God… rightly dividing the word of truth" (2 Tim 2:15 KJV). Indeed, God's word protects and sets us free by renewing our minds, transforming and enabling us to discern and do God's perfect will in our every thought, word and deed (Rom 12:2).

This primary discipline of engagement has four aspects: to *read, study, meditate* on, and *memorize* scripture.

There is great value in simply *reading* the Bible as a book, to get an overview of the contents and stories, allowing it to wash over us, hearing God speak to us through the text. We can read the whole Bible in one year if we read two chapters of the OT and one of the NT *daily.* The One Year Bible lays it out as daily readings. I have been so enriched by simply reading the Bible cover to cover, again and again.

Studying the Bible takes us further. We think through the passage. We look up cross-references, use Bible Dictionaries and commentaries to understand the biblical author's intention and meaning in the text. Then we apply *that* (correct) meaning to our life-context. Doing formal biblical studies at a respected seminary or institute is part of this discipline. One quickly realizes the Bible is an absolute treasure chest that will take us the rest of our lives to unpack, be enriched by, and share with others.

Meditation is a further form of the discipline of study. Here is where "The Word" becomes our flesh (Jn 1:14). Scripture itself prioritizes meditation on God's word, both "day and night", with its profound benefits.[328] Described in chapter 3, *Lectio Divina* is a practical seamless way of meditation with silence, prayer and contemplation – noting the difference between meditation and contemplation. But the most natural and effective form of meditation is *memorization* of the text.

Hebrew meditation *is* memorization and memorization *is* meditation. It is a mind, heart and verbal discipline (e.g. Josh 1:9, Jews had to have God's word on their foreheads and lips, Ex 13:9). This kind of meditation, especially in the Psalms, was the primary means of prayer for God's people.[329] We take a text with us from our morning devotional reading by writing it on a card or recording it in our phones. We learn the text

---

328 Josh 1:9; Ps 1 (the whole psalm), Ps 77:12, 119:15, 27, 48, 97, 148, 143:5, 145:5; Is 50:4–5.
329 See my book *Praying the Psalms,* teaching the Hebrew root method of word-prayer-meditation. There are other accepted methods of Christian meditation that I cannot detail here. We should not be restricted to one or other method, but learn to practice them all.

by heart and recall it to mind through the day, reading it if necessary, repeating it (aloud) to ourselves. We use the words to pray, to ask God about its meaning, chewing and ruminating, feeding on the revelations and insights, digesting its spiritual nutrients and nuances. Memorization of scripture holds God and his truth constantly before our minds, keeping us in perfect peace (Ps 16:7-8; Is 26:3). Over time, consistent meditation by memorization disciplines our thoughts and imaginations, our hearts and emotions, words and deeds, giving life and health to our bodies (Prov 4:20-22). We catch ourselves thinking God's thoughts, feeling his emotions, speaking his words, doing his deeds, living and being his truth.

The community dimension of the discipline of study is local-church teaching and accountability to respected leadership and wise direction. We participate in regular *biblical* teaching and worship (1 Tim 4:13). As Bonhoeffer said, the church gathers *under* and is *formed by* the authority of God's word.[330] This corporate discipline keeps us from being victims of our own whims and fancies, reading the Bible only when we feel like it, reading only our favourite texts. It protects us from overly subjective and introverted hearing from God in our interpretation of scripture in our lives. Sincere Christians can stray into spurious ideas, mixed beliefs and false doctrines. We can be spiritually deceived into a wrong reading and novel use of scripture that results in forms of unaccountable super-spirituality or humanist rationalism, immoral license or moralistic legalism.

Worship – The Presence

The discipline of worship directly engages us with The Presence of The King. In times past when people entered the presence of a king and/or queen, seeing them in all their glory, they would bow, even prostrate themselves in humble homage. "Come, let us bow down in worship, let us kneel before the LORD our Maker" (Ps 95:6). Study engages us with

---

330 In *Life Together*, 40–66.

God's future self-revelation made present by his Word and Spirit, and this naturally results in worship. And the more we see and know God, the more we worship in awe and wonder, gazing on his beauty (Ps 27:4). Worship is our only adequate instinctive response to God, to his self-revelation.

Willard says, "In worship we engage ourselves with, dwell upon, and express the greatness, beauty, and goodness of God through thought and the use of words, rituals, and symbols… to worship is to see God as *worthy*, to ascribe great worth to him."[331] Thus the old English word "worth-ship": to lift up, dwell on and make known God's *worth* – the eternal beauty of ultimate goodness. We see it in John's revelation of untold numbers of beings continually worshipping God around his throne, crying, "You are *worthy*, our Lord and God, *to receive* glory and honor and power… *worthy* is the Lamb, who was slain, *to receive*…" (Rev 4:11, 5:9, 12).

We were created to worship the Triune Person and Presence made manifest in space-time reality through The Word and The Spirit. When we worship in spirit and truth, we enter and participate in the heavenly worship of saints and angels. The veil or barrier between heaven and earth, this age and the coming age, has been torn in Jesus and God's future ruling presence manifests in our worship. To worship is to give God praise, glory, honor, might, majesty, wealth and wisdom. We give all we are and have, and represent, in response to all God is and has done for us. In so doing we express our true human nature as God's image-bearers; we fulfil our role as priests of God's creation, bringing and articulating *all* of creation's praise to God.[332]

Therefore, while worship is essentially *our response* of returned love to God's loving self-revelation, it is also a *proactive faith practice* that engages us with God's immediate presence. Acts of worship teach us to recognize, receive, and be filled with his manifest presence – then we live as fragrant carriers and instruments of God in the world. We are (ought

---
331 His italics, *SD*, 177.
332 This paragraph: Eph 2:18; Jn 4:22–24; Heb 10:19–22, 12:22–24; Rev 5:12; Ps 8 cf. Ps 148.

to be) the people of The Presence. *This* is what distinguishes us from all other people, as Moses prayed (Ex 33:14–16). Worship transforms us ever more deeply, purifying our hearts to see God ever more clearly, to know him ever more intimately, and be sent by him ever more willingly, as seen in Is 6:1–8.

Practically, by worship I mean both *acts* and *lifestyle* of praise and thanksgiving, of adoration and contemplation of God.

We do *acts* of praise and adoration in our devotional times and in church gatherings, through music, song, dance, words, rituals, sacraments, symbols and art, as well as in silent contemplation of God beyond images, thoughts and words.

Worship is also our *lived life* of service in ministry and mission. All we think and say, do and become, for God and others, is our reasoned and intentional worship, our only worthy response to God's worthiness. Hence the first commandment, "I am the LORD your God... You shall have no other gods before me" (Deut 5:6–7). Any act or lifestyle of idolatry – worship of another god – denies and destroys our very nature as human beings. This includes both the temple of our body and of God's creation, for which he holds us accountable. We become what or who we worship: it-her-him acquires power over us, and in time incarnates itself in us; either God by his Spirit through Jesus, or another god by its own spirit and character.

Again, we must avoid the danger of two extremes. *Traditionalism:* overly ritualized acts of worship that become empty and meaningless – an end in itself – "dead works" that mean nothing to God. *Experientialism:* esoteric or exotic acts of worship in the name of experimental creativity that are no longer biblical, that do not glorify Jesus. Worship that magnifies our experience, focusing on how good or bad it is, how it makes us feel, what we get out of it, is more about me and my needs than about God and his worthiness. Using God for our purpose, to make us happy, is ultimate self-worship: we are our own god – the greatest deception of all.

Celebration – The Joy

The discipline of celebration directly engages us with The Joy of The King. As study of God's word and his self-revelation leads to worship, so worship of God's person and presence leads to celebration. To celebrate is to enjoy, to enter into the joy of God and his kingdom come. Celebration is the completion of worship in the sense of enjoying our lives and world as God's good work and gift to us. It has to do with remembrance and retelling, thanksgiving and gratitude, joy and community. We celebrate past God-events and enjoy present God-gifts. But more so, celebration anticipates the future fullness of God's joyous kingdom consummated on earth.

The practice of celebration goes back to ancient Israel when God became their King and commanded them to celebrate various feasts through the year. Intended to commemorate God's intervening acts of deliverance and their covenant relationship, they were feasts of rejoicing in God's presence: "buy... cattle, sheep, wine or other fermented drink, or anything you wish. Then you and your household shall eat there in the presence of the LORD your God and rejoice" (Deut 14:26). For the feast of Passover God said, "you shall celebrate it as a festival to the LORD... Do no work at all on these (seven) days, except to prepare food for everyone to eat; that is all you may do" (Ex 12:16). That is all you may do? Just prepare food and feast for seven days? These are astonishing instructions for festive celebration!

The prophets envisaged a time when YHWH will come in his Messiah-King in a new Passover Exodus, fulfilling the feasts of Israel, to dwell among his people and celebrate face to face: "On this mountain the LORD Almighty will prepare a feast of rich food for all peoples, a banquet of aged wine and the best of meats" (Is 25:6).

Jesus consciously fulfilled this in his ministry, marked by table fellowship, feasting with people, to the point of being associated with drunkards, prostitutes, sinners and tax collectors. His first miracle in

John's Gospel is his enjoyment of a marriage feast, turning over 500 liters of water into the best wine. Imagine that? The wedding parties went on for days! Jesus enacted an image of God as a welcoming, embracing, partying and dancing Father, in his scandalous prodigal love for his returning people (Lk 15:20-24). God is not a party-pooper angry Judge! He is a positively joyous and generous Being filled with holy delight.

This unashamedly "sensual and earthy character of celebration or jubilee… will seem far too hedonistic for many of us. But we dishonor God as much by fearing and avoiding pleasure as we do by dependence upon it or living for it."[333] It stumbles the "older brother" in us, and certainly the pharisaical and/or gnostic Christians who deny the goodness of God and his creation. Unable to enjoy it they judge and condemn those who do. Not that celebration is a license for loose living, for gluttony and drunkenness – behaviours that are perversions of true celebration.

This biblical background to the discipline of celebration guides us in its practice, both individually and corporately. There is indeed "a time to weep and a time to laugh, a time to mourn and a time to dance" (Eccl 3:4). We need to build into our lives those times and ways of enjoying the blessings of God. How do you – or can you – *personally* do this? By celebrating birthdays and anniversaries, taking time out to walk in the country, to read a good novel, do one of your favourite things, treating yourself *with God's enjoyment*. Celebration is, however, best expressed and practiced *in community* with family and friends. We celebrate in local church through events and concerts built around victorious worship, in song and dance, story-telling and drama, eating and drinking, and other means of unbridled joy and laughter. A God-given way of doing this is to follow the Christian calendar and celebrate the Messianic fulfilment and meaning of the biblical feasts.

Paul commands us to "rejoice in the Lord always. I will say it again: Rejoice!" (Phil 4:4). That is a decision, a discipline of celebration that produces a positive attitude, a joyous state of being – buoyancy in all

---

333 Willard, *SD*, 179-180.

of life's turbulence – because God's goodness and generosity *has become real in us*. Indeed, "the joy of the LORD is your strength" (Neh 8:10). It overcomes anxiety and discouragement, negativity and sadness. Joy is different to happiness: it is a cultivated condition of the heart and mind; while happiness is more circumstantial, dependent on external factors.

Prayer – The Friendship

The discipline of prayer directly engages us with The Friendship of The King. Prayer is the means by which the sweetness of future face-to-face friendship and co-working with God breaks into our lives in the present. By prayer I mean relationship. It's conversational relationship with God, not just "saying our prayers", not just talking to God in a monologue. Prayer is interactive dialogue and responsive listening in intimate friendship and co-working with God. Prayer is "being with" God in unbroken companionship *and* collaboration – authentic mutual friendship.

As the discipline of study leads to worship, and worship leads to celebration, so these three naturally lead to prayer: a life of interactive friendship with the Father and the Son by the indwelling Holy Spirit. By definition prayer works together with these and other disciplines, such as solitude, silence and fasting in the next chapter.

We see Adam and Eve walking and talking with God in the cool of the evening in the Garden of Delight – transparent face-friendship with God. Enoch walked with God so faithfully every day that one day God took him home to be with him forever (Gen 5:24). That's how much God enjoyed his company! Abraham walked interactively with God in trusting relationship, so much so that scripture calls him "the friend of God" (Js 2:23 cf. 2 Chron 20:7; Is 41:8). God shared his intimate thoughts, feelings and plans with Abraham, and this led to extraordinary intercession and bold negotiation with God on behalf of two cities (read Gen 18:17f). Moses spoke "face to face" as friend to friend with God

Part Three: Praxis

(Num 12:8). We see the practice of prayer from Abraham to Moses, to David (Hebrew tradition attributes Israel's prayer book to him – 150 psalms) and the prophets, culminating in Jesus and the Early Church.

Much of this book is about prayer, so simply to say: Jesus is our ultimate model of the discipline of prayer. He engaged in personal private prayer, as well as corporate prayer, on a daily basis. *That* became his very being-in-love with his Father by the Spirit, moment-by-moment companionship and collaboration: "My Father is always at his work, to this day, and I'm living and working with him. The truth is, though I'm his son, I do nothing on my own initiative. I only do what I see my Father doing, I only say what I hear my Father saying" (my RAP on Jn 5:17–20).

Jesus imparts this *same* prayer-relationship to his followers, calling us his friends, as he discloses the Father's intimate thoughts, feelings, words and deeds by his Spirit (Jn 15:15). Prayer is encounter with God as *a real person* with real emotions, mind and will. Prayer is identifying with God in personal knowing as *that* Person identifies us in his/her image.[334] Prayer does not change God; it changes us, aligning us in harmony with his desires, will and actions. Prayer instills a growing confidence of being, of peace and power grounded in God's real companionship with us, so that we live in full trust of his loving care no matter what happens.

Thus, there are two *ways* of practicing prayer: *acts* of prayer with others, and more especially in personal daily times alone with God. Jesus said, when we pray we must go into our room, close the door and talk to God without interruption "in secret" (Matt 6:6). Secondly, we cultivate the *attitude* or *spirit* of prayer by training ourselves to pray continually through the day (1 Thess 5:17), invoking God's presence and will in our every thought, word and deed. Both acts and attitude of prayer are the wings on which we soar like an eagle on the wind of God's Spirit (Is 40:31).

---

[334] See Robert Marsh SJ, *Looking at God Looking at You*, on mind-blindness and spiritual autism: we pray to our notion of God, a projection of self, not to the real God *as a real person*. Unable to identify with God – he does not actually hear, speak, feel, think, interact – prayer becomes all about us.

There are four basic *forms* of prayer in Christian tradition, described in chapter 3: verbal, meditative, contemplative and ecstatic prayer. You would do well to re-read them with a view to practicing the kinds of prayer you do not normally exercise. This will certainly grow new and deeper dimensions of friendship with God in your life.

The various *kinds* of prayer flow as one river of life. We pray spontaneously what is in our heart and mind. We pray set prayers, as in David's psalms – the age-old tradition of God's people – and *the* prayer Jesus gave us in Matt 6:9–13. Words given to us, especially those inspired by the Spirit, teach us how to pray, to express our emotions and perceptions, joining our longings and hopes with God's desire and will. We pray by listening in silence. We pray with thoughts, words, sighs, sounds, inarticulate groans and other tongues by the Spirit. As Paul says in Eph 6:18, "pray in the Spirit on all occasions with *all kinds of prayers…*", like praise, thanksgiving, request, petition, supplication, intercession, protest, lament, weeping, and worship. That covers all of life's realities – we pray our living and we live our praying.

A closing comment on the challenge of prayer. Prayer is a battle, even at the best of times. If the devil cannot keep us from prayer, he disrupts us in prayer. All the distractions of wondering thoughts, intruding images and other phenomena, are best dealt with by directing our will to remain attentive to God in simple desire of him. When the will is set, the disruptions of the mind, imagination and memory come and go harmlessly in the background, till they come to peaceful attention before God. However long that takes, the will remains steady. If the will is drawn away from it's holy work, then the distractions harm prayer. Prayer is indeed a battle of the will.

Service – The Ministry

The discipline of service directly engages us with The Ministry of The King. By practical acts of service to God and others we participate in *Jesus'* ministry and mission of *the* kingdom. It's never about "*my* ministry" or "*my* mission." It's always about "*his* ministry." We are in the service of the King, continuing to do Jesus' kingdom ministry to the ends of the earth. We do it in anticipation of, and preparation for, our joyous service in the coming age when every atom of our resurrected bodies will naturally do the will of King Jesus in complete love of him.

Therefore, acts of service that *could* be done as a discipline, to enhance our spiritual life, *need* not be done as such. They can be done as acts of love from a heart spontaneously overflowing with *God's* love, unrelated to any benefit to us. Then the future kingdom is a present presence that operates in us as the loving service of our Servant King. However, service as a discipline trains us in humility and trust, away from pride and possessiveness, away from our natural inclinations to selfishness. In fact, the principle of *could* be, but *need* not be done as a discipline, applies to all the disciplines to the extent the kingdom actually reigns in us.

By the discipline of service I mean doing good by using our time and energy, resources and gifts – natural and spiritual – in service of others. Willard says, "In service we engage our goods and strength in the active promotion of the good of others and the causes of God in our world."[335] The NT word for service is ministry, and ministry is service. God's kingdom subverts, even inverts, the general perception that service is for lower society. We are all called to practice the discipline of service, no matter what place or position in life we hold. But Jesus especially calls those among us who have resource, privilege and power – especially leaders – to use it to serve the least among us (Matt 20:25–28). Indeed, "to live as a servant while fulfilling socially important roles is one of the greatest challenges any disciple ever faces… this alone will train them to exercise great power without corrupting their souls."[336]

Furthermore, acts of service, if done for the audience of One, free us from bondage to others and what they think of us. Doing acts of service

---

335 *SD*, 182.
336 *SD*, 183.

as people-pleasers, to be seen by them, gives them power over us. Even the lowliest form of work is in truth *service to God* in that it serves others; it dignifies the server by giving meaning and purpose to the service (Col 3:22–24). Without condoning slavery and systemic injustice, what Paul says to these (Christian) slaves in Colossae can be applied as a daily spiritual discipline to many forms of seemingly lowly work in our world.

The point is that service in the spirit of Jesus frees us in genuine humility to be whom we are in God, without having to keep appearances or uphold our reputation. We live in the joy of completely forgetting ourselves in service of God for his sake alone. All service is doing the ministry of the King for the good of his kingdom purposes. Jesus simply "went around doing good" in his daily life ministering the kingdom by the power of the Spirit (Acts 10:38) – service in practice.

It generally takes the form of spiritual and practical ministry to others through our particular calling and spiritual gift-mix as we serve in various ministries in our local church and beyond. It also takes the form of both random and planned acts of kindness like visiting the sick, feeding the hungry, clothing the naked, i.e. doing "good deeds" as Jesus instructed (Matt 5:16 cf. 25:31–46).

Fellowship – The Community

The discipline of fellowship directly engages us with The Community of The King. I have already noted the community dimension of the disciplines. However, this discipline of fellowship is itself the practice of community, i.e. relational belonging in common activities. The old English word fellowship, translated from the NT *koinonia*, means to share life in common, to participate communally. In the NT it refers to *God's* community; Jesus' (local) church, both in its organized form via meetings and activities, and organically in relational caring and sharing.

Belonging and participation in blood family, in the home, is naturally organic. But we quickly discover it is also a commitment and a structure

– a discipline. God's design is family, biological *and* spiritual family: "God sets the lonely in families" (Ps 68:6). Many opt out of family practice – the yoke of formation – when the discipline, or whatever perceived pressure or hurtful dysfunction, becomes too much.

The same applies to church, "the local fellowship", as it used to be called. It's *both* spiritually organic *and* a formal discipline of belonging and participation – from which, sadly, many have withdrawn. The local church is God's plan despite its failings and troubles, even abuses – as a community of recovering sinners. Hence community involves the discipline of healthy conflict resolution, forgiveness, correction, reconciliation and growth (next two practices). God has *no* plan B, no second Bride of Christ. Besides, he promises to perfect his church for Jesus' coming. I choose to believe God more than our inadequacies and failures.[337]

In short, by the discipline of fellowship I mean committed belonging in the local church and participation in its regular practices and activities like worship, prayer, teaching, celebration, services and ministries. By doing this we engage the actual Community of God: the heavenly Trinity of the Father, Son and Spirit; perfect in relational love. *That* Community is present within the earthly – earthy, ordinary, human, mundane, structured – local church. Jesus' church is divine *and* human, the community of both the already *and* not yet of God's kingdom.[338] The Trinitarian Community is the *already* revolutionary treasure in the church, which we encounter and enter as we practice *koinonia*. It shines through all the weaknesses and cracks of the *not yet* traditional clay jar of

---

[337] Marriage fails and ends in divorce because people fail, not because the God-ordained institution of marriage-covenant does not work. Unresolved hurt and disillusionment leads to living together, a change of belief due to, or to justify, a change in life praxis in all the permutations of "friends with benefits". The same applies to church. I went through a painful divorce in 1984, yet I believe more now in marriage than ever before. Having been through all sorts of pain and divisions in church and in leadership since 1968, I believe more in God's local covenant community than ever before.

[338] Merton says, "The biggest paradox about the Church is that she is at the same time essentially traditional and essentially revolutionary... (the) Christian tradition, unlike all others, is a living and perpetual revolution... a constant, quiet, peaceful revolution against death." *New Seeds of Contemplation,* 142.

imperfect local church. Often the 'crack-pots' in the family are the most challenging, but they are a primary means of Jesus encountering us and working his character into us – if we do not withdraw from church.

As we worship and work side by side in serving one another and God's world, we encounter the Father, Son and Spirit. All God's diverse grace-gifts, generously distributed in his local church, shine through all of us, to enrich us all, by the activity of the Spirit. It never ceases to amaze me as I catch glimpses of Christ's glory, often in the most insignificant, even difficult, member of the church. There is something supernatural and enriching about unadorned honest fellowship in Christ. Furthermore, by the practice of *koinonia* we engage the Communion of Saints; not only those alive in the broader worldwide church, but those who went before us, now in the presence of God, with whom we worship (Heb 12:22–23). Whether in heaven or on earth (Eph 3:14), all in God's family profoundly belong, are spiritually/mystically joined, nourished and built up by, and into, the Trinitarian Community of Eternal Love.

Confession – The Forgiveness

The discipline of confession directly engages us with The Forgiveness of The King. By the discipline of confession I mean living an open and disclosed life, holding ourselves accountable to God in his local covenant community. Or reactively allowing one or two trusted friends or respected leaders to hold us accountable – without reacting! It means walking in the light of the King. It means mutual sharing whenever we meet in Jesus' name as two's or three's,[339] as home groups, as local church. We practice confession, as in disclosure, at two levels.

Confession is facing and making right specific wrongdoing with God and each other. It means agreeing together, keeping short accounts for healthy relationship with God and one another. At a deeper level, it's opening ourselves up to be known, ideally and ultimately to Trinitarian

---

[339] Matt 18:20. The context is about sin, confession, forgiveness, reconciliation, church discipline.

transparency. Confession begins with our failings, then moves to disclosure of our "stuff", to know and be known for whom we are, to receive and give God's forgiveness and grace. We can belong and participate, yet *not* be accountable, let alone making ourselves vulnerable to be known. We can duck and dive, play-act and perform, wear masks, live a double life. Or we can withdraw, as mentioned earlier, in the name of hurt, or for whatever reason. Hence, spiritual leaders are responsible to nurture and maintain a safe environment of love, acceptance and forgiveness, of confidentiality for healthy disclosure and growth.

Imagine living a life that is totally transparent with nothing to hide, no guilt or shame? Being real, honest, true to the core? What you see is what you get, no games-play. That person is truly free. At the end of his ministry Jesus said, "the prince of this world (Satan) is coming (but) he has no hold over me" (Jn 14:30). Literally no "handle" or foothold (Eph 4:27) as in a sin, unresolved issue or unsettled claim, that the devil can take hold of, to access him, to accuse him of guilt, to shake him with condemnation. The discipline of confession is the door to the radical freedom of a clear conscience, spiritual security and psycho-emotional health.

Many Protestants, more so Evangelicals, Pentecostals and Charismatics, reject formal "Confession" as a perceived abusive Catholic and Orthodox tradition. We throw the baby out with the bathwater, losing something powerful.[340] The shift from communalism to individualism via the Reformation and Enlightenment has resulted in a fiercely guarded *personal and private* relationship with God whereby we confess *only* to God *alone* – "it's none of your business, thank you!"

James says, "confess your sins to *each other* and pray for *each other* so that you may be healed" (5:16). The context (vv.13–20) is the faith community, where those in trouble, those who are happy, who are sick,

---

[340] Willard says, "Confession... is one of the most powerful of the disciplines for the spiritual life. But it may be easily abused, and for its effective use it requires considerable experience and maturity, both in the individual concerned and in the leadership of the group." *SD*, 189.

who have sinned, have wandered from the truth, fallen into error, can come and confess and process.[341] Then to pray for each other, ministering God's forgiveness, healing, encouragement and joy. James links some sickness to sin (v.15, though clearly, not all sickness is due to sin), alluding to the cost of unconfessed sin that we pay for in various ways.

The discipline of confession not only removes that heavy burden, but also helps us to avoid sin and wrongdoing. Meeting a close spiritual friend regularly (the twos and threes, and even the home group – if it's safe and intimate enough to share deeply), makes it difficult to sin because one knows they will ask accountability questions and you cannot lie (see chapter 13). As John says, God is light; there is no darkness in him. If we walk in *the* light, as he is in the light, we have *koinonia* with *one another* and Jesus' blood keeps purifying us. When we do sin, and confess it, God is faithful and just to forgive us and purify us (1 Jn 1:4–9). Therefore, confession is in the context of walking in the light community (*koinonia*) of God and each other. It's not *either* confessing to God *or* to each other, it's both/and.

We also must bear in mind that confession involves repentance – turning away from sin and toward newness. "Whoever conceals their sins does not prosper, but the one who confesses and renounces them finds mercy" (Prov 28:13). And depending on the nature of the wrongdoing, it may involve restitution, for redress and restoration.

This discipline of confession engages us with the power of God's forgiveness and all that comes with it. This is direct engagement with the already of God's future *pronouncement of acquittal* at the end-time Judgment Day, now available in Christ. In that sense confession is truly a sacrament, a means of future kingdom grace given now as unmerited

---

[341] The human (sinful) instinct to withdraw from the light of community – as Adam and Eve did in the garden – allows our hearts to deceive us in private confession on our own T&Cs (Terms and Conditions). The godly instinct is to always go to community when in trouble. The church is a messy hospital for repenting sinners, not a five-star hotel for comfortable saints!

forgiveness, whenever we need it. God's forgiveness is full and final: "As far as the east is from the west, so far has he removed our transgressions from us" (Ps 103:12). When God forgives, he forgets: "I will remember their sins no more" (Heb 8:12). In a world where multitudes suffer from feelings of guilt and shame, to know God's unconditional forgiveness is truly liberating, and to live in his forgiveness is absolute freedom and psycho-emotional health.

The key is living in God's forgiveness, which means practicing confession. I need it pretty regularly, because, besides my ongoing failures and sins, I am far from whole. Some teach that once you are born again you are a saint, *not* a sinner: to say you are a sinner is to "undo the finished work of Christ on the cross." This is an absolutist kingdom-now statement that denies the not yet reality. The truth is that *every* saint, no matter how mature and holy, still sins this side of heaven. Yes, we should sin less and less. But till our last breath we are still capable of sin. So, if we still sin, we are sinners, yet saints in Christ. Both are true at the same time.[342]

I do not believe "once forgiven, always forgiven" if it means: "at salvation every future sin is already forgiven, *so you can never be guilty or unforgiven*" (as some teach). This is another absolutist kingdom-now statement in denial of the not yet. The reality is that if I do not keep short accounts with my wife, asking her forgiveness when I do wrong, I undermine our relationship and eventually it will be destroyed by unresolved issues. Likewise, we can grieve the Holy Spirit as Israel did in the wilderness (Eph 4:30 cf. Is 63:10). God can hold us in unforgiveness (Matt 6:15). We too can hold others in unforgiveness (Jn 20:22). Then our "guilt remains" till we confess our sin and blindness, and make right (Jn 9:41). So, when we do sin, let alone when our weaknesses and brokenness manifest, we need to practice confession.

---

[342] See the first section of my story in chapter 1. Also footnote 102.

Submission – The Authority

The discipline of submission directly engages us with The Authority of The King. This is an extension of the NT practice of confession (*homologeo*), which is "to speak" (*logeo*) "the same" (*homo*). To submit (*hupeiko*) is "to yield" (*eiko*) "under" (*hupo*) the authority of another. Therefore, to confess is to agree with, by submitting to others in relational accountability. Practically it means humbly yielding to correction, counsel, instruction and direction, especially from spiritual leaders.

Submission is a kingdom reality: God in Christ is our King and we are his subjects. By submission I mean placing ourselves under God's authority in heartfelt yielding to, and joyful cooperation with, his rule and reign. More so when it goes against our wants, desires and will: "Father, not my will, but yours be done." We submit to God, trusting his greater purpose for our good. The value of submission is that we do not always get our own way, in an age of extreme individualism that devalues community and authority. We learn to yield to God and others in service of his purposes – at times beyond our understanding. That is precisely why it is a spiritual discipline, which engages us with God's authority over all things.

As in confession, it is easier to submit directly to God (privately) than to other people. However, the way God's kingdom works is that he invests and delegates his authority in people and structures, which he ordains for the good of all. So, to submit is to yield to the authority of people and structures God has placed in our lives, in respect and faith of the greater good they have responsibility for, under God. To the extent we practice submission to *that* authority, we participate in God's future kingdom authority now. God shares and imparts his heavenly authority (i.e. we exercise spiritual authority in real terms) to the extent we place ourselves under earthly authorities that he ordains, as seen in Matt 8:7–13, 28:18–20.

But here, as Dallas warned, is the human danger, quoted in footnote 340. The word "submission" (including "authority") is almost a swear word due to its misuse and abusive practice – often upheld by incorrect traditional hierarchical interpretation of biblical texts. Broken people and leaders can manipulate and control, bind and disempower others through spiritual and structural authority in God's name.[343] That is not *God's* authority, which liberates and empowers, bringing his kingdom on earth as in heaven. Rather than throw the word and concept out, we must redeem its biblical meaning and practice, as witness of God's kingdom in an unruly and rebellious world. Therefore, the effective practice of willing submission and use of gentle authority requires sensitivity and respect, experience and maturity in the church corporately, and as individual followers of Jesus in society.

We practice the discipline of submission as the apostles taught:[344] believer to believer, wives to husbands, children to parents, workers to employers, citizens to governing authorities; and in God's community, congregants to spiritual leadership. Paul teaches in Eph 5:18–6:1-9 that all practice or levels of submission stem from "be filled with the Spirit" (v.18, submission to God's Spirit). In practice this results in submitting "*to one another* out of reverence for Christ" (v.21). Being filled with the Spirit means respectful submission to Christ's headship *by submitting to one another*. This *mutual* submission of all to all under Christ's governing Spirit (see Phil 2:1-6), is the foundation that qualifies all practice of submission and exercise of authority that follows (v.22f, wives to husbands, children to parents, and so on).

The same applies to the texts that address church members and their leaders, regarding the practice of submission and exercise of both

---

343 When submission entails/requires wrongdoing, disobeying God, then we respectfully disobey the authority and non-violently submit to the consequences, entrusting ourselves to God (Acts 4:18–20).

344 They interpreted the common Greco-Roman household and societal rules in light of Messiah Jesus, see Rom 13:1-7; Eph 5:18–6:1-9; Col 3:18–4:1; 1 Pet 2:11–3:1-7. I cannot exegete these texts here.

spiritual and structural authority in the kingdom community. What is clear in the instructions is that those older in The Way of Jesus, the wise elders, lead by example "of *their* submission to *servanthood*... not of the *drivership* that so often prevails..."[345] Then submission is freely given to accountable authority that truly sets us free to do God's will.

QUESTIONS FOR REFLECTION AND DISCUSSION

1. Why are there two sets of disciplines (engagement and abstinence)? And what is the difference between them? Why is that important?

2. How do the disciplines of engagement relate to the reality of God's kingdom, and how do we experience the kingdom through practicing them?

3. Having read through these eight disciplines...
   a) What few things in particular strike you? Why?
   b) What new things have you learnt?
   c) What do you *not* agree with? Why

4. Go over each of the eight disciplines and ask yourself:
   a) Which ones do I particularly struggle with? Why?
   b) Which ones am I practicing on a regular basis?
   c) How can I practice – or plan to practice – the others from time to time?
   d) How can I practice these disciplines in creatively different ways, to refresh them for fresh experiences of God?

---

345 Willard's italics, *SD*, 190. See 1 Pet 5:1–5; Heb 13:7, 17; 1 Thess 5:12–13; 1 Cor 16:15–16.

CHAPTER 12

PRACTICES II: DISCIPLINES OF ABSTINENCE – THE NOT YET

*"Dear friends, I urge you, as foreigners and exiles,
to abstain from sinful desires, which wage war against your soul."*
Peter – 1 Pet 2:11

The Disciplines of Engagement are proactive practices, or virtues, that engage us directly in various dimensions of the kingdom already come. They attach us to God and his kingdom. The complementary Disciplines of Abstinence are reactive exercises that address vices, those aspects in us where the kingdom has not yet come. They enable us to abstain from satisfying certain needs and demanding desires in various dimensions of our personhood. This detaches us from the world, the flesh and the devil, making space for engagement with God and his kingdom.

While disciplines of engagement are directly related to God, disciplines of abstinence are directly related to our body, in and through which we live. They are designed to discipline normal needs, desires and motivations, such as those for food, sleep, sex, companionship, activity, material comfort, security, reputation or fame, and so on. By abstaining from them, to some degree for certain periods, we become detached from the drive to satisfy them, and from their improper uncrucified attachments (vices) lodged in our bodily appetites and psycho-emotional needs. These manifest as sinful habits, hurtful entanglements, co-dependencies and addictions that house the sinful desires *from which we must abstain* – as Peter exhorts us. The disciplines of abstinence enable us to do precisely that.

Therefore, by disciplining the need to satisfy *legitimate* psycho-physical-social drives, we negate – crucify and put to death – the abnormal *illegitimate* sinful desires that still inhabit them. In so doing, we positively retrain and re-inhabit these faculties for availability and service in God's kingdom. This is the dual negative and positive function of the disciplines of abstinence. I explained this dual action of death and resurrection, putting off and putting on, vices and virtues, in earlier chapters (compare "the seven deadly sins" in chapter 9 with the disciplines of abstinence listed below).

In summary, the eight disciplines of engagement connect us with particular dimensions of *God's* Personhood in the kingdom already come. The eight practices of abstinence discipline a specific dimension of *our* personhood where the kingdom has not yet come. They plough up the hardness of our hearts and clear away the stones and rocks, weeds and entanglements, for fertile reception of God's kingdom come (Matt 13:18–23). Their purpose is *to free* our faculties of human need *from* their dependencies, attachments and sinful desires, and to release them *for* righteousness, leading to holiness, in training and service of God's rule and reign.

Solitude – People
Silence – Tongue
Fasting – Food
Chastity – Sexuality
Frugality – Wants
Sacrifice – Needs
Secrecy – Pride
Night Vigil – Sleep

Solitude – People

The discipline of solitude addresses our need for people interaction and daily activities, and all that we derive from that. By withdrawing into solitude, we abstain from this need in order to make space for realizing our need and desire for God, and satisfying our desire for his companionship, and all that results therefrom.

By *solitude* I mean being alone. Not alone for alone's sake. Not by chance. Not because we are tired of people, or to avoid responsibilities. Nor because we enjoy our own company. Merton says, "Solitude is not and can never be a narcissistic dialogue of the ego with itself... True solitude is the home of the person, false solitude is the refuge of the individualist."[346] Solitude is not an escape. Solitude is being alone on purpose: to be alone with The Alone. It is deliberate withdrawal from people and activities to be alone *with God*, to place our body, heart and mind *before God*. It is strategic disengagement from normal activities in daily life, at certain times for a decided period, to engage God in uninterrupted time and focused attention.

Solitude is going into your "closet" or private place, closing the door to pray and meditate, as Jesus taught (Matt 6:6).[347] It is withdrawing to a retreat centre, to the desert, to nature, to a quiet place. We have biblical examples in Moses, Elijah, Jesus, Paul and others. We can also withdraw into the anonymity of the urban crowd. Thus, solitude is a planned place of bodily quietness, *as well as* a cultivated inner state of constant stillness in heart and mind. The outer state, *solitude of the body*, enables and empowers the inner state, *solitude of the soul*, as the Desert Fathers taught.[348]

---

346 *New Seeds of Contemplation*, 52–53.
347 In Scetis, a brother went to see Abba Moses and begged him for a word. Moses said: "Go and sit in your cell, and your cell will teach you everything." Nouwen, *Sayings from the Desert Fathers*, 14.
348 "Solitude of the body is the knowledge and reduction to order the habits and feelings. And solitude of the soul is the knowledge of one's thoughts and an inviolable mind... an unrelenting power of thought which keeps constant vigil at the door of the heart and

This primary discipline of abstinence works hand-in-hand with the primary disciplines of engagement. Solitude creates the outer and inner space to engage God in study, worship and prayer in a qualitative manner. Solitude gathers our scattered thoughts, troubled emotions and tired bodies, in restful repose before and with God. In fact, without solitude it is difficult to practice most other disciplines, such as silence, fasting, service, giving, chastity, godly secrecy, and even fellowship.[349]

By the *discipline* of solitude, I mean the planned regular rhythm of *withdrawal* into God and *re-engagement* in public ministry with God in healthy detachment from people and activities. Solitude disciplines our need for people and activities where such needs are driven by unhealthy attachments to them; or where the kingdom has not yet penetrated *with death* to sinful tendencies and *with transformation* of legitimate needs in this regard. It is never good to be driven. God draws and leads us, he does not drive us. It is not good to hurry and rush. We ought to slow down and learn to live the unhurried life in the easy yoke of Jesus, as he daily paces us in his intimate knowledge of us and our needs, as he leads us according to his plan and purpose in his kingdom. In this way solitude restores true perspective of reality, of what is really important in terms of God, people and things.

More so, solitude frees us from people's need of us, and what they think of us. Who we are before God becomes most important. It frees us *from* being overly conscious of self and others *for* consciousness of God. To the extent we consciously lose ourselves in God, we unconsciously live our true nature in Christ – the person God created us to be. Hence solitude frees us from the need to uphold our reputation by wearing masks, performing, workaholism, and the drive for success. Our daily doings and people interactions push and mold us into the spirit of this

---

kills or repels the (bad) thoughts that come." John Climacus (579–649), in Maloney, *Pilgramage of the Heart*, 125–6.

349 Bonhoeffer says, "One who wants fellowship without solitude plunges into the void of words and feelings, and one who seeks solitude without fellowship perishes in the abyss of vanity, self-infatuation and despair." *Life Together*, 78.

world, into "patterns of feeling, thought and actions that are geared to a world set against God. Nothing but solitude can allow the development of a freedom from the ingrained behaviours that hinder our integration into God's order."[350]

There are, however, dangers to be aware of. People generally avoid being alone, let alone with God. Some withdraw to shut God out, or to switch off their thoughts and unruly emotions. It's impossible! So we drown our sorrows and numb our pain with people, busyness and addictions. Then when we are alone, unresolved issues come up. They demand attention. We can then bring them to God, who helps us process them. And if necessary, we need to seek help from those gifted and trained in healing. Solitude can have a restorative healing dimension.

We must be aware, therefore, of depression and other forms of darkness that can cloud us when practicing solitude. *Loneliness* is part of this – a massive issue in our day. Being alone and being lonely are different. "Loneliness is inner emptiness. Solitude is inner fulfilment."[351] Aloneness heightens loneliness, unless however, we turn – and even use – our loneliness for solitude *with God*.[352] Also, we must be aware of others, our family and friends, when we withdraw for solitude. If we are not wise about how we practice solitude, it can pain and threaten them in their own needs. And self-knowledge of our temperament and personality helps us to practice solitude in ways that work for us. Introverts get their energy from being alone, so solitude is easier. It's more of a challenge for extroverts who get their energy from being with people. All of this means that guidance and supervision is advisable, especially when practicing extended times of solitude.

---

350 Willard, *SD*, 160.
351 Richard Foster, *Celebration of Discipline*, 84.
352 See Nouwen in *Reaching Out*, moving from loneliness to solitude. Also Rolheiser, on loneliness and spirituality as "the torment of the insufficiency of everything attainable." He addresses five kinds of human loneliness: alienation, restlessness, rootlessness, psychological depression, and moral loneliness, in *Against the Infinite Horizon*, 49–68.

Silence – Tongue

The practice of silence disciplines our need to talk, to make room to hear God. By the discipline of silence, I mean closing oneself off from sounds as far as possible in our noisy world. Silence is more shocking than solitude; it strips us like nothing else to face reality. That is why silence is the close companion of solitude, as worship is of study – the two primary disciplines of engagement. Solitude frames and facilitates silence, while silence reinforces and intensifies solitude. To enter, let alone practice ongoing silence, without the discipline of solitude, is well nigh impossible.

The biblical examples of solitude mentioned earlier, from Abraham to the Early Church, imply the practice of silence. And Church history is full of examples. Why silence? To be silent is to wait on God, holding our tongue in order to listen, to hear God's word, to see his deliverance, to worship in holy awe. It's to surrender control and know God, to let *God* be God, as David says: "Be still, and know that I am God" (Ps 46:7). "Be still before the LORD and wait patiently for him" (Ps 37:7). Jeremiah says, "I say to myself, 'The LORD is my portion; therefore I will wait for him'... it is good to wait quietly for the salvation of the LORD... sit alone in silence" (Lam 3:24–28). Isaiah says, "In quietness and in trust shall be your strength... Those who wait for the LORD shall renew their strength... 'Listen to me in silence' (says *YHWH*)" (Is 30:12, 40:31, 41:1 NRSV).

To practice silence is to withdraw from outside noise to discipline our inside noise. We quieten the ongoing inner buzz of thoughts, emotions, restlessness and dis-ease. We come to peace. We become fully present to God in mind, emotions and body, as he is present to us in Spirit. Abstaining from talk, we silence our words, and the thoughts behind them. It disciplines our most unruly bodily member – the tongue – in all its attachments to destructive governing tendencies and unholy habits. The tongue has the power of life and death (see Js 3:5–12). Silence tames the tongue where the kingdom has not yet come, bridling it under God's controlling reign, training and directing "a well-instructed tongue, to know the word that sustains the weary" (Is 50:4). Indeed, we then "echo silence" in who we are, in what we think, write, say and do.[353]

Compulsive talkers who have no censors, who dump their "stuff" on others, and those who gossip, exaggerate, lie and curse, need the discipline of silence the most. Silence teaches us to be present to others, in deep respect, listening in silence. The ministry of presence, of listening, is greatly needed in our world. Then we speak only when we need to, with thoughtful words filled with grace that uplifts others (Eph 4:29). Silence frees us from the need to be convincing, to win arguments, to have the last say, trusting God's (silent last) word on each and every matter.

Silencing the tongue awakens the ear. Silence quickens our physical and spiritual sensibilities to sense and hear God. "He wakens me morning by morning, wakens my ear to listen like one being instructed. The Sovereign LORD has opened my ears" (Is 50:4–5). In silence we not only *hear* the voice of our Good Shepherd, but we learn to *recognize* and *know* his voice intimately, calling us by name. Then we follow his lead in all things. Silence teaches us how to distinguish Jesus' gentle and loving voice from all other incessant voices outside and inside of us that demand our attention, that falsely shepherd us, that seek to rob, kill and destroy (Jn 10:1–10).

In short, to hear the "still small voice" of God above all the (un)natural loudness in our lives, we need to practice solitude and silence as Elijah did (1 Kgs 19:12 KJV).[354] And it goes without saying, when we practice silence, we withdraw from and shut off technology that bombards us with

---

[353] Merton, *Echoing Silence*. Abba Isidore of Pelusia said: "Living without speaking is better than speaking without living. For a person who lives rightly helps us by silence, while one who talks too much merely annoys us." In Nouwen, *Sayings from the Desert Fathers*, 82.

[354] "A gentle whisper" (NIV); "a sound of sheer silence" (NRSV). Abbot Agatho is said to have carried a stone in his mouth for three years until he learned to be silent in order to hear God in the present moment. In Merton, *The Wisdom of the Desert*, 30.

constant communications via its multiple social platforms. Silence, in this regard, can literally restore sanity!

On the practicalities of how to enter and maintain silence see my discussion in chapter 9 on "the prayer of silence" (contemplation). Practice at least 15 minutes a day of silent contemplation for spiritual health. Extended periods of silence, as in a day or weekend retreat, is more challenging, and guidance is advised. When leading retreats, my wife and I often lead retreatants into silence by an exercise using the text, "Be still, and know that I am God". Once all are comfortably seated and silent, I repeat the phrase aloud in intervals of about three minutes, each time dropping a word. As the person repeatedly focuses in silence on the shortening phrase, they are drawn to stillness before God. It helps the mind to give it a thought or word, and to repeat it with our breathing in and out. This brings the mind to stillness before God. I often do this exercise in my morning devotions to simply "be"… with God:

"Be still and know that I am God"
"Be still and know that I AM"
"Be still and know"
"Be still"
"Be"

Fasting – Food

The discipline of fasting is to abstain from food, and possibly liquids, for certain periods of time, *for spiritual purposes*. By abstaining from the *specific* need for food, our appetites in *general* come under God's discipline.

In Matt 6:1-18 Jesus teaches three regular practices for his followers: *giving* addresses our relationship with *material* resources; *prayer* addresses our relationship with *spiritual* reality; and *fasting* addresses our relationship with our *body*, not just with food. Let me first elaborate on the body, then on fasting food.

Part Three: Praxis

Fasting confronts us with our body, teaching us about ourselves, our lack of self-control. The drive to satisfy normal bodily needs is so strong, enhanced by their sinful corruption, leading to gluttony, lust and greed (first three vices). By disciplining our appetites, we free them from addictive enslavement and retrain them for service in God's kingdom, in anticipation of our bodily resurrection. To be dominated by our corrupted appetites is to be "carnal", "fleshly" or "worldly" (1 Cor 3:1-3). For this, and other reasons, we struggle with our body, often rejecting, and even hating it.

A right view of and relationship with our body is vital for life, health and spirituality. We do not *have* a body as a burden we carry around. We *are* our body.[355] It is God's gift to us, his image on earth, designed for eternal living (death is but temporary separation till reunification in resurrection). Hence *our body* – spirit, soul, physicality – *is our greatest resource for the spiritual life*.

Fasting regulates a right relationship with it, teaching us to accept, respect and work well with our body in all its capacities, mortality and glory. Fasting brings our body and its appetites under God. It is the first constituent of earth where God's reign comes, where his will is done as in heaven, where the body becomes a willing servant resourcing us in kingdom living. We become restrained, moderate, content and self-controlled; being detached and indifferent to all created things, including our inner drives, using them only in service of our King. If we cannot, under God, rule over our own body, how will we rule over the (new) earth? If we allow the body to rule us, it becomes a tyrant. This is besides the plague of body-self-image issues in all its manifestations, such as eating disorders – as in anorexia and bulimia. Fasting directly and indirectly addresses all these issues.

Fasting food, and possibly water, is an act of self-humbling to seek

---

[355] Willard says (his italics and caps), *"Human personality is not separable in our consciousness from the human body. And that fact is expressed by asserting the IDENTITY of the person as his or her body."* SD, 84.

God. In Hebrew, fasting means "to grieve, humble and afflict oneself by denying our normal bodily needs". It is associated with repentance, mourning, crisis, intercessory prayer, service, justice for the needy, and ongoing spiritual health.[356] Fasting makes space for us to do all these things, and for God to encounter us and work in our situation. Fasting makes us depend on God, to keep him constantly before our minds, and to give extra time to wait on him (e.g. the time we use to prepare and eat a meal). By abstaining from food we humble ourselves to depend on God sustaining us. We feed on every word that comes from his mouth (Deut 8:3). Therefore, fasting is actually feasting on God!

However, there is nothing fast about fasting! It goes slowly, in weakness and battle, unless God gives special grace – which does happen. Each bodily weakness, headache, groaning of tummy and fantasy of food, or whatever we go through while fasting, reminds us *why* we are fasting. Then we cry to God for help, for strength. His power is made perfect in our weaknesses *as we pray*. As we groan, the Spirit groans in us, interceding for us according to the mind and will of God (Rom 8:23–27). To fast for no reason, or for the wrong reason and motivation, has no value.[357] God's people fasted mostly when faced with a particular need, issue, or crisis. Thus, we should decide on one or two or three specific reasons for which we fast, in order to focus our intercession, meditation and waiting on God.

In this sense fasting engages us in direct spiritual warfare. We experience the confrontation with the spiritual world in our body and mind. Fasting can unleash all sorts of forces, so be wise and practical (see below). However, fasting amplifies our prayers, or focuses them like a laser beam to penetrate the darkest heavens, piercing through unseen

---

[356] Ps 35:13–14, 69:10; 2 Sam 12:16–17; Is 58:3–12; Joel 1:13–14, 2:15–17; Jonah 3:5; Acts 13:2–3.

[357] Isaiah and Jesus warned (Is 58:3–11; Matt 6:16–18): do not fast to serve *your* interests in disregard of *other's* needs (justice for the poor), and do not fast for a show of spirituality; do it in secret with God. Fasting to punish the body is evil. Fasting for diet and health may have value, but is not biblical.

Part Three: Praxis

opposition. We participate in God's kingdom work and war. He responds by sending his angels to defeat opposing powers, though it may take persistent fasting with prevailing prayer as we see in Daniel.[358]

There are different kinds or types of fasting:

- A *regular* fast: like one day a week – a good spiritual discipline – assumed when Jesus said *"when* you fast…", not *"if* you fast" (Matt 6:16).

- A *needed* fast: when facing a particular need, to resolve a crisis or issue.

- A *full* fast: no food or water – a maximum of three days (Esther 4:16–17) or it will endanger health, unless God supernaturally sustains us (Ex 34:28).

- An *extended* fast: more than three days. It takes four days for the body to purge the toxins and stop craving food, then it enters a different dynamic.

- A *total* fast: forty days, more or less, depending on one's body – because this complete-body-cycle fast uses up all the toxins and fats, and eats muscle mass, till starvation pains set in (Lk 4:1–2).[359]

- A *partial* fast: fasting certain foods and liquids (Dan 1:12–17, 10:2–3) and/or "things" that dominate our attention – like TV, technology and social media.

Some practicalities. For novices in fasting, we suggest starting off small with what we have faith for – with what we can manage. Mastering such

---

[358] Dan 10:1–14. Daniel persisted in his fast for three weeks till God answered. His fasting and prayer caused war in the heavenlies. He mysteriously participated in the angelic defeat of the opposing powers – *without knowing it!* Daniel prayed *to God*, and *God* sent angels to defeat the principalities; i.e. he did not presume to directly address and rebuke heavenly powers, as Jude 9 warns against.

[359] *After forty days* Jesus was "famished" (NRSV), *then* Satan said, "tell this stone to become bread!"

fasts will enable us to train and condition our body into more serious fasting. Extended fasts ought to be done with spiritual supervision, and more so when breaking such a fast – restraint is required! If we are on medication, we should consult our doctor. Drink lots of water and/or diluted fruit juice. To do a *full*, or *extended*, or *total* fast, while working a full day job, is not advisable. We should tailor fasting to work with our rhythms and responsibilities. And depending on what kind of fast we undertake we ought to consider – and even consult – our family or those we live with, as the fast may require special arrangements.

Chastity – Sexuality

The practice of chastity disciplines our sexuality, as in our sexual appetite and awareness, freeing it *from* the corruption of lust, *for* right relating in love. If fasting addresses our relationship with our body in terms of food, chastity addresses our relationship with our body in terms of how we relate to others, in lust or love.

The classic order of the vices is gluttony (food – fasting), then lust (sexuality – chastity), and then greed (wants – frugality, the next discipline). Fasting undergirds chastity by disciplining desire, particularly sexual lust.[360] And fasting and chastity discipline greed, as in material covetousness; empowering frugality and simplicity. In fact, chastity, frugality and simplicity – properly understood – "refer to the *result* of a discipline under grace rather than to disciplinary activities themselves."[361]

Human sexuality is essentially about how we relate. God gave the fiery gift of sexual desire, in gender difference and complementarity, *to complete us in a union of love*. The two become one. And ultimately with God. We are created by relationship, in relationship, for relationship: for God and one another – not to live in isolation. Sex is psycho-social, not

---

[360] "He who cherishes his stomach and hopes to overcome the spirit of fornication, is like one who tries to put out a fire with oil." Isaac the Syrian (613–700), in Maloney, *Pilgrimage of the Heart*, 128.
[361] Willard, *SD*, 170 (his italics).

an individual pleasure. Our deepest yearning for completion can only be fulfilled in the love of authentic spiritual-relational intimacy. This can include but goes beyond genital intimacy – and is equally generative and life-giving.[362]

Sexuality under God's rule is the fire of his passionate love that relates and acts for the highest good of the other. However, sexuality as a sin-corrupted appetite under our own rule – or under its tyranny of wild fire – is the burning of lust that uses and abuses others (even God) for our pleasure and purpose, to meet our needs and achieve our goals. This substitute *false* intimacy can never satisfy our deepest longing for love. Lust enslaves, disintegrates and destroys us, *and* those we lust after. Only *true* intimacy with God and others – healthy sexuality as the passion of lust-free love – can satisfy, integrate and make us whole, ministering wholeness to those we love.

Therefore, by the practice of chastity I mean the conscious disciplining of our normal sexual need and desire, so that it does not rule us, so that it comes under God's order and purpose. Chastity means not dwelling on or engaging in the sexual dimension of our relationships to others. When aware of sexual attraction and/or erotic desire we yield our feelings to God by celebrating the other in their mysterious beauty as *God's* image.[363] This leads to true admiration and pure love of God and others.

Lust is unhealthy indulgence and/or suppression of our sexuality. Indulging sexual awareness and erotic attraction whenever we feel it – the permissiveness of "that's normal!" – turns us into animals driven by

---

[362] Sexuality is both *genital* (erotic passion/romantic love for/in the marriage covenant) and *social* (psycho-spiritual-affective intimacy of relational love). Corrupted by sin, *genital sexuality* clouds and drives *social sexuality* with all kinds of lust-full expression. Lust is undisciplined desire. Sexuality will be fulfilled in the coming age in the resurrection body that transcends procreation in gender differentiation, perfected in pure lust-free love, like the angels in heaven (Lk 20:34–36 cf. Gal 3:28).

[363] Beauty can fascinate, even bewitch, causing us to covet, to possess it. "A certain man, on seeing an extraordinarily beautiful body, thereupon glorified the Creator, and from that one look he was moved to the love of God and to a fountain of tears… what would have been the cause of destruction for one was for another the supernatural cause of a crown." John Climacus, in Maloney, *Pilgrimage of the Heart*, 211.

urges and instincts, not moral beings made in God's image. For many, sex is wringing every last pleasurable sensation out of our mortal bodies: an idolatry of pleasure and power. Giving license to unrestrained sexual feelings, corrupted by lust, leads to guilt, shame, addiction, violence and demonization. Chastity, however, is *not* the suppression of normal sexual desire. Such denial is equally a wrong view of sexuality, the moral legalism of "sex is sinful!" To cut off normal appetites is to demonize them. Then they drive us with lust. Sexual wholeness is healthy sexual integration into the whole of us.

Jesus said *outward adultery* – illicit sexual engagement outside of marriage – is *inward idolatry* of the eyes and heart (Matt 5:27-28). Chastity disciplines the lust of the heart and desire of the eyes with self-control for sexual character.[364] We celebrate sexual awareness *with God*, entrusting our needs and desires *to God*, to be satisfied in his time and way. That *sublimates*, not suppresses, our sexual energy into *sublime* intimacy with God and love of others.[365] The word sublime comes from sublimation, the Lat. *sublimare*, to "raise up" or "exalt" to a transformed state. To sublimate is to deny satisfaction of desire, holding it in waiting tension, diverting and channeling its energy for a greater good, resulting in sublime satisfaction of a higher order.[366] In short, what is pushed into darkness is demonized; what is brought into The Light is purified for passionate love and sexual healing in our broken world.

Chastity, from Lat. *castus*, meaning "pure" or "clean", is *self-containment in purity*. "Each of you should learn to control your own

---

364 "I made a covenant with my eyes not to look lustfully at a young woman" (Job 30:1). It's the second look, the gaze, that leads to lust. And it's not just young women, but all the permutations of attraction in sexual brokenness and gender dysphoria in our proudly self-identifying world.
365 "The essence of chastity is not the suppression of lust but the total orientation of one's life toward a goal." Bonhoeffer, *Letters and Papers from Prison*, 163.
366 "The sublime depends on sublimation… to have a great love, there must first have been a great chastity… the more soul-wrenching the sublimation, the more soul-exploding the ecstasy… we want the sublimity of deep sexuality, but we do not want the painful sublimation upon which it depends." Rolheiser, *Against an Infinite Horizon*, 66.

body in a way that is holy and honorable, not in passionate lust like the pagans, who do not know God" (1 Thess 4:4–5). This is not purity as in being prudish or prissy. Sexual purity, as in proper chastity, produces passion, as in true love; rehabilitating the corrupted passion of unbridled lust. Indeed, the greater the purity of chastity the greater the passion of true love. Like singles, married people exercise chastity daily in their relating (social sexuality) as part of their faithfulness in marriage (genital sexuality). They also abstain from the latter for agreed times for the purpose of prayer (1 Cor 7:5). Then "come together again so that Satan will not tempt you because of your lack of self control." Note Paul's realism – also in v.9 – "it is better to marry than to burn with passion."

Chastity, of course, is different to celibacy. Celibacy is a gift of grace (1 Cor 7:7) to abstain from all genital intimacy, with personal integrity, as a lifestyle. And/or celibacy is a naturally low sex-drive whereby one can live healthily without the need for genital sexual fulfilment. However, celibacy still requires the discipline of chastity to sublimate sexuality into psycho-spiritual-relational intimacy with God and others – our deepest human longing for love. Singles who seek to keep themselves celibate till the marriage covenant know what this means.[367]

To be chaste we need the support of community, as in affirming relationships across genders, with personal accountability in the trusted twos and threes. Isolation and rejection feed lust. Warm engagement from the healthy masculine and feminine – fathers and mothers, brothers and sisters – both in nuclear and spiritual family, is morally formative in early sexual development, and profoundly healing for sexual brokenness. Sexual character means wholeness, purity, self-control, trustworthiness in relationships, being passionate lovers of God and people.

---

[367] The doctrine of celibacy in the Catholic priesthood has tragically contributed to the horror of sexual abuse revealed in recent years. But it belies the reality in *all* denominations, and society in general, of lust in unrestrained sexual fantasy, addictive pornography and masturbation – the root *and* the fruit of all the manifestations of sexual brokenness and violence in our world.

Frugality – Wants

Frugality disciplines our body in relation to materiality. It disciplines our wants and desires for things in which we find comfort and security. In so doing it exposes and defeats greed and covetousness; it teaches us right management of material resources, clearing the way for us to discern and serve *God's* wants and desires in all the resources he has entrusted to our stewardship – a stewardship for which he holds us accountable.

God created all things good, to be enjoyed, even for our pleasure. Not to be despised as sinful, nor to be indulged as worship. God made us stewards of all his rich resources, *to be used* for the good of God, people and creation. However, materiality is deceptive: the more we possess possessions, the more they possess us. Hold them lightly! Our natural sin-corrupted desire for "things" to give us meaning, security and happiness, is to worship creation rather than the Creator. Materiality has a powerful seductive allure that leads to materialism: living by the lust of the flesh, desire of the eyes and pride of life (1 Jn 2:16). And so we quickly move from basic *needs* to normal *wants*, to selfish *desires*, and to outright *greed*. Let me distinguish between these.

Needs are the simple (material) things we need, not merely for survival, but for human dignity with fair justice of a shared quality of life under God's sun. We have basic needs for water, food, clothing, sanitation, simple housing, safety and work, i.e. *essential* "things". Beyond needs we have *wants* for more, for material wellbeing that makes us comfortable and relatively secure, lifting us beyond concern for basic needs. *Desires* go further than merely wanting more, to new, bigger and better, to excess, self-indulgent pleasures, status luxuries, self-serving lifestyle. All the above, of course, have mixed drivers: the fear of failure and poverty, or need for success and prosperity, or broken self-image, ego needs, pride, and so on.

Greed, however, is not class conscious. It works in needs, wants and desires without discrimination, finding its mature form in unbridled lust for wealth. The poor can be as covetous and materialistic as the rich. Greed is the drive for things as an end in themselves and covetousness is the desire for what others have and we want. Greed and covetousness corrupt character and lead to exploitation, stealing and social destruction. The practice of frugality disciplines our normal *wants* and *desires*, thereby exposing and putting to death their sin-corrupted elements of *greed* and *covetousness*. The next practice, sacrifice, disciplines our *needs*.

Frugality is the trained restraint of our wants and desires, bringing them, and all our material resources, under God's rule and reign. This requires thoughtful discipline of expenditure and acquisition of things, i.e. living within our means. Frugality is simplicity, which is not poverty. There is nothing good or saintly about poverty *per se*.[368] Simplicity is being content with basic things, living an uncluttered life, finding meaning, happiness and security in God and relationships, not in things. Furthermore, *we must learn to live simply so that others can simply live.*[369] Frugality is a matter of missional justice, not just personal spirituality. God's rich resources are there for all to share, not for a minority to possess. Hence frugality is not being stingy or miserly, examining every cent before we spend it. Rather, frugality is freedom for generosity.

Jesus taught the *regular* practice of giving – in fact, *generous* giving (Matt 6:2–4; Lk 6:38). Giving disciplines our wants and desires regarding material resources entrusted to us. OT giving, simply put, was tithes *and* free-will offerings: a tenth of one's income to God, and beyond that, giving to the poor and needy. Tithing was an act of worship as acknowledgement of God's ownership of us. Giving God 10% is to affirm he owns all we have and receive, including the 90%! Offerings were also an act of worship as faith in God's care, trusting his provision for all our *needs*. Tithes and offerings were not abolished, but included and fulfilled

---

[368] See Willard's chapter, Is Poverty Spiritual? in *SD*, 193–219. Correctly understood, the monastic vow of poverty was more missional as witness (Mother Teresa and her Sisters of Charity who live and work among the poor), rather than a means and measure of spirituality.

[369] The message of Ron Sider's book *Rich Christians in an Age of Hunger*.

in the NT. The coming of the kingdom means generous sharing of God's future rich resources now.

Jesus taught giving as a spiritual discipline that stores up treasures in heaven, securing our heart in God's kingdom (Matt 6:2f). Do not value possessions highly enough to seek them (vv.19-24), or to worry about them (vv.25-34). Building up treasures on earth to secure our own kingdom is of little value (see Js 5:1-6). We serve and worship either God or *Mammon* – Aramaic for money/possessions (Matt 6:24). Materialism addicts us to wanting more, to consumerism; driving us into debt, soul-destroying emptiness, and worry. The lost and lonely are often the rich. Money cannot buy love, life and security, in their true (eternal) sense. To have a "single eye" is to be generous, full of light (v.22), i.e. to seek first God's kingdom and his justice, trusting God's provision of "all these things" we need (v.33). To have a "bad eye" is to be stingy, full of darkness (v.23), i.e. to run after "all these things" ourselves, seeking our own kingdom that we have to protect, resulting in worry and anxiety.

Paul taught generosity as "the grace of giving" (2 Cor 8:7), based on a) *Jesus' grace* of downward mobility that lifts us from poverty to his riches – spiritual and material (8.9); and b) on *God's ability* to bless us abundantly, so that we, having all we need at all times, can abound in every good work (9:8). So we give time, energy and money cheerfully in faith, not reluctantly in guilt or obligation (9.7). Paul warns "those who want to get rich… (it's) a trap… of harmful desires". Money is not evil; it's a resource to be used for right or wrong. It is *the love of money* that is "the root of all kinds of evil", seducing us from "the faith" (1 Tim 6:9-10 cf. Heb 13:5). Money is an ultimate test of character because it corrupts the soul. The more you have the greater the test. God requires much from those to whom much is given (Lk 12:48).

The essence of frugality, for Paul, is *learning to be content* "whatever the circumstances… whether in plenty or in want", to be content with life's basics like "food and clothing". Such contentment is "great gain"

(Phil 4:11-13; 1 Tim 6:6-8). It means living a quiet and moderate life, minding our own business, working diligently so that we are not dependent on others (1 Thess 4:11-12). Thus, frugality includes having a good work ethic to earn money and get out of the spiritual bondage of financial debt (Rom 13:8), so that we can save *and* share with others.[370] There is the danger in frugality and simplicity of personal legalism and/or activist judgment of others in regard to lifestyle, wants and desires. There is also the danger of pride in our generosity, or in our humble lifestyle. Or of false guilt in what we have, especially if wealthy. We resolve these issues with God in a safe community where we can talk about money related to grace, justice, mercy.

In summary, *love* God and people, and *use* things for *that* end. Do not love things and use people – including God – to get the things we love. We detach from things to attach to God by becoming *indifferent* to all created things as Ignatius taught. We use things to the extent they help us pursue the end for which we are created: "to praise, reverence, and serve God our Lord." And we free ourselves from them to the extent they hinder us in that pursuit (see footnote 283).

Sacrifice – Needs

The practice of sacrifice disciplines our reliance on basic needs, connecting us to our *complete need* of God. Sacrifice makes us fully dependent on God *as God* in our lives. In reality, every breath we breathe depends on God and his merciful provision, whether we know it or not, acknowledge it or not. Many people live in utter presumption of God and his good grace, living in idolatry, seeking what they need from who or what they worship. Sacrifice strips us of idolatry.

The discipline of sacrifice is to abstain at certain times, on specific occasions, from using resources to meet our *need*. By denying satisfaction

---

370 As per Wesley's famous three rules: *earn* (generate) all you can, *save* all you can, and *give* all you can – detailed in White, *The Changing Continuity of Christian Ethics, Vol 2*. 271-2.

of a basic need we sacrifice that resource to God, giving it away as the need arises and as God so prompts. To sacrifice what we really need, what we value and even cherish as necessary for life, is costly worship. This goes beyond frugality – sharing what we want or desire – to total abandonment to God. The practice of sacrifice frees us for pure faith in God, stripped of reliance on things that secure our basic needs. We trust God's provision and care beyond all we have, knowing we ultimately need only God. In the coming age we will live completely by God, and God alone. We begin that now in Messiah Jesus. He embodied it in the ultimate sacrifice of his own life, in full faith of God's purpose. Sacrifice is *radical* faith, generosity and reliance on God.

Two biblical examples. In Gen 22 God tested Abraham's faith – his love and loyalty – by commanding him to sacrifice his beloved son, Isaac. He simply obeyed. But surely the three-day journey to the place of sacrifice was an agony of questioning faith? At some point Abraham's faith was purified with the peace and knowledge that "God himself will provide the lamb" in Isaac's place (v.8). However one interprets this story,[371] the point is that God can call on us at any time to sacrifice this or that, in faith and love of his greater purpose, often beyond our understanding. Jesus observed a poor widow putting "two very small copper coins" into the Temple treasury box (Lk 21:1–4). He commended her as giving more than the others, the rich included, because she gave what she desperately needed: "out of her poverty (she) put in all she had to live on." All the others gave from their surplus in varying degrees.

Both examples illustrate sacrifice as abandonment to God in faith of his provision and our ultimate need of him. Sacrifice ought to be practiced regularly in small ways in obedience to God, not only in the occasional heroic act of abandonment. It teaches us abandonment to the will of God in what we cannot control, and obedience to the will of God in everything

---

371 Historically, it's a polemic against the idolatry of child sacrifice, first born males, in the ancient near east. *YHWH* redeems the first born, including Israel *and* the nations, by providing his own sacrifice for sin – foreshadowing God's Lamb, Messiah Jesus – that leads to true love and faith in him.

that depends on our control. And this raises awareness of what prompts and motivates us in practicing sacrifice. To be impulsive, presumptuous, and even foolish in what and how we sacrifice, can be destructive. The need to prove oneself to God or others, or to be recognized and gain admiration, or to earn a blessing, or to test and even manipulate God into rescuing us, makes the sacrifice meaningless. God desires heart obedience rather than religious sacrifice. Hence we should, if necessary, seek discernment and spiritual guidance in the more significant and consequential acts of sacrifice.

Secrecy – Pride

The practice of secrecy disciplines our pride, freeing us *from* the need for human recognition and affirmation, *for* acknowledgement from God. The discipline of secrecy is to abstain from causing our good deeds and qualities, spiritual practices and other such information, from being known.

We are not talking about keeping things secret in a deceitful way. In teaching three core practices of piety (Matt 6:1–18), Jesus specifically instructed his disciples to do them "in secret" before God – for the audience of One. When we give, we do not let our left hand know what our right hand is doing. When we pray, we do it in secret with God. When we fast, we do not let others know. Jesus unashamedly contrasted it with the Pharisees, who practiced them to be seen by others, to impress with their display of spirituality. They looked for recognition and respect, wanting others to think well of them. Jesus called it hypocrisy: play-acting for people to see, performing for effect. Think about how much is done in our world with this motivation. Preachers and pastors are prone to performance. We "need" attention and approval, affirmation and appreciation. Unmet ego needs often drive leaders with the need to be needed, to save others, to be known – the hunger for success and fame.[372]

---

[372] "One of the greatest fallacies of our faith, and actually one of the greatest acts of unbelief, is the thought that our spiritual acts and virtues need to be advertised to be

Jesus' antidote is the practice of secrecy in a continuing relationship with God that meets ego needs and disciplines pride, making us independent of the opinion of others. God sees what we do in secret and backs us up publicly, mostly in ways we are unaware of – keeping pride at bay. We do not fish for complementary feedback, leaving the results of whatever we do with God. He alone is our public relations manager! Promotion comes from the Lord, not from the east or the west (Ps 75:6–7).

Traditionally, pride is chief of the vices, the original sin. There is the natural healthy pride of self-respect: to love, honor and take care of oneself. Corrupted by sin, pride is the self-love of self-worship, a devilish deception of the false self, the inflated needy ego. I have found there is little personal growth without the humiliation of my ego. We either humble ourselves, or God – and/or life – humbles us. God resists those who exalt themselves and promotes those who humble themselves (Js 4:6, 10). Building up a secret history with God in a long obedience in the same direction decisively disciplines pride, teaching us love and humility before God and others.

To be humble is to be spontaneously *un*self-conscious and *un*selfish, in total God-consciousness, secure in his affirmation and confident in his power. Humility frees us from selfish ambition, competition, and what others think of us. We then think the best of them, valuing their interests above our own (Phil 2:3–4). False humility is extreme self-consciousness in self-humiliation. It is actually self-pity masked as godly unworthiness, a form of pride. Humble people are not disturbed by praise; they gracefully accept and deflect it to God, the One worthy of *all* praise.[373]

There are other dimensions of secrecy as a discipline. Let me mention

---

known. The frantic efforts of religious personages and groups to advertise and certify themselves is a stunning revelation of their lack of substance and faith." Willard, *SD*, 173. See Henri Nouwen and Eugene Peterson, who penetrate the challenge of pastoral *integrity* – the *spirituality*, not technology, of leadership. Nouwen, *In the Name of Jesus*, and Peterson, *Working the Angles*.

373 "The humble man receives praise the way a clean window takes the light of the sun. The truer and more intense the light is, the less you see of the glass." Merton, *New Seeds of Contemplation*, 189.

two. The discipline of keeping secret what is confidentially entrusted to us tests how safe or trustworthy we are. We all know the excruciating pain of betrayal by those who have broken our trust with inappropriate disclosure. Also, the discipline of secrecy regarding our needs: "the needs that arise in our efforts to serve God can often be handled by looking to God only, not telling others that there is a need, but counting on God to tell them."[374] Our faith in God's care is greatly increased when he speaks to others to meet our need, knowing we have only spoken to God. Always telling others of our needs can be manipulative and reflect our lack of faith in God.

Night Vigil – Sleep

The practice of night vigil disciplines our body in regard to the need for sleep, training us in wakefulness to God. It is part of the practice of solitude and silence – the night hours are the most quiet and uninterrupted, the perfect time for listening to God. The discipline of night vigil, also called night watch, is to forego sleep for the purpose of prayer, to wait on God, to keep watch while resting in him.

There are seasons when God calls us to wait on him at night. Sometimes simply to spend a quality hour or two with him in meditation and prayer. At other times for a specific purpose. Or we wake and cannot sleep for whatever reason. We can then use it as an opportunity for prayer, perhaps resolving what is troubling us, with God's counsel. God does counsel us in the stillness of the night, if we listen (Ps 16:7). We can practice vigil-prayer at one or another hour of the night – at midnight as many monastic orders do – or in the early hours before sunrise: "He wakens me morning by morning, wakens my ear to listen…" (Is 50:4).

Jesus practiced such early morning prayer "while it was still dark" (Mk 1:35). He prayed through the night, at a very busy time in his ministry, before appointing his twelve apostles (Lk 6:12). At other times he prayed alone into the night (Matt 14:23). The evening before his crucifixion he

---
374 Willard, SD, 174.

took his apostles into a garden late at night. He challenged them to "keep watch" in prayer with him for one hour, though their bodies needed sleep. His reason: "watch and pray so that you will not fall into temptation. The spirit is willing, but the flesh is weak." (Matt 26:40-41). Night vigil disciplines our weak flesh into prayerful watching, to see what God is doing, to recognize and overcome the tests and temptations that come our way. It becomes an inner state of vigilance, a constant watchfulness of the heart.[375] And vigil trains us to draw from God what we need, bringing our body into submission to our spirit, willing to do *God's* will – "not *my* will be done." The apostles failed, whereas Jesus' training in vigil saw him through the greatest trial of his life – "*Your* will be done." If anyone needed sleep before his ordeal, it was Jesus. His weak, but trained body worked with his (the) Spirit, drawing on the grace he needed to endure and overcome.

Paul twice spoke of "sleepless nights" (2 Cor 6:5, 11:27). The context of both occasions is tests and trials in his ministry. KJV uses the word "watchings", which included the idea of night prayer – including when one could not sleep. After saying "many a sleepless night", Paul refers to the "daily pressure because of my anxiety for all the churches" (11:27-28 NRSV). Whether his sleepless nights were chosen vigils, or due to stress or insomnia, he used it all to pray for the churches.

The history of revivals is replete with stories of intercessors – individuals and small groups – who faithfully travailed in prayer through many dark nights, till God broke through in unimaginably powerful ways. My Pentecostal roots and years with the African (black) church taught me the value of night vigils. The half nights and whole nights of corporate prayer, at least once a month – mostly on Fridays – were very special experiences of supernatural grace. To do this on one's own is so

---

375 Isaac the Syrian said, "Do not consider that among all the practices of a monk there is anything more important than night vigil... If a monk keeps vigil of the mind with good judgment... (and) watchfulness of the heart... he will have the eyes of Cherubim, to keep them constantly raised on high and to contemplate heavenly visions." In Maloney, *Pilgrimage of the Heart*, 194.

much more challenging. I have fallen asleep in every posture of prayer known to human beings, including walking up and down!

Coming back to disciplining our need for sleep – as with other bodily appetites – we need to bring it under God's rule, lest it rule us. We need good sleep for psycho-emotional and bodily health. God indeed wills us to sleep well (Ps 4:8 cf. 127:2, "he gives sleep to his beloved" NRSV). We can, however, over-indulge sleep to escape pressure or responsibility. But there are times when we do need extra sleep (therapy) – mostly in certain kinds of recovery from sleep deprivation. For example, we can be deprived of sleep by simple insomnia, or sickness, among other reasons. Or we can unwisely deprive ourselves of sleep for whatever reason – although that catches up with us and we pay for it! Sleep research is uncovering the mystery of sleep, the dream state, sleeping disorders and the effects of modern life stresses on sleep, and why some people *seemingly* need more, or less, sleep.

Night vigils can address all these issues in one way or another, disciplining us into quality peaceful sleep, where we find our rest in God beyond the normal sleep response the body needs. We need not fear lack of sleep when correctly practicing night prayer because God indeed sustains us and renews our strength (Ps 3:5; Is 40:31). Unless, of course, we practice it excessively and foolishly. Any discipline becomes toxic when idolized, when it drives us, when we depend on it more than on God. We need to know ourselves, use common sense and be balanced in how we practice night vigils, and receive spiritual guidance if needed.

QUESTIONS FOR REFLECTION AND DISCUSSION

1. Reflecting on this chapter, on a purely personal level:
   a) What do you believe God has been saying to you? Isolate a few key things God has impressed on you. What are you going to do about them?
   b) What has been new for you, that you did not know before?
   c) What do you struggle with, or cannot agree with? Why?

2. How would you define, in your own words, the disciplines of abstinence? And why the eight classic ones – are the any others that you would add?

3. Why do these disciplines exist? What do you think is their reason and role in the spiritual life?

4. How would you describe, in your own words, their relationship to the vices, the classic "seven deadly sins" discussed in chapter 9?

5. Having read this chapter, which of these disciplines are you most familiar with and practiced in? Why is that the case?

6. Which of these disciplines do you need to practice on a more intentional basis? Why? What do you want it to achieve in you?

CHAPTER 13

PRACTICES III: OTHER CLASSIC TOOLS FOR SPIRITUAL LIVING

"Be diligent in these matters; give yourself wholly to them, so that everyone may see your progress. Watch your life and doctrine closely. Persevere in them, because if you do, you will save both yourself and your hearers."
Paul – 1 Tim 4:15–16

If one reads the context, Paul here instructs Timothy to prioritize his own spiritual formation and that of the Ephesian church he was pastoring. The idea of spiritual advancement in the eternal life of Messiah, both personally and corporately, was standard in those days. In fact, one's persevering progress toward perfection was strongly encouraged as an example and inspiration to others. Paul's exhortation to be diligent to "give yourself wholly" to spiritual formation clearly *applies to each of us*. And it applies specifically to our practice of the disciplines of engagement and abstinence, including the following tools and aids I now introduce.

When my own spiritual development took a decisive turn in 1984/5, due to a time of deep pain (see chapter 1), I encountered these extra practices for spiritual formation. They have significantly aided my psycho-spiritual healing and growth. The following supplementary exercises, from among others, have been practiced in the Christian spiritual tradition from the early centuries. This is not an exhaustive list, but they are those commonly used in spiritual formation. My intent is to simply introduce them, especially to the Evangelical, Charismatic and Pentecostal traditions. Some of these tools and practices may not work for the reader. We need not worry about that. The next and final chapter addresses how we integrate *personally appropriate* practices into living a balanced, vibrant spiritual life.

I normally include in this list two methods of contemplative prayer: *Centring Prayer* (Western tradition) and *The Jesus Prayer* (Orthodox tradition). Since I have already explained them in chapters 3 and 9, I omit them here.

Manual work, sabbath, recreation, nature and wonder

Manual work: In times past, it was normal to work with one's hands, earning a living from such work. Being close to the soil, working with tactile earthy elements, facilitated spiritual connection. Today, work is an all-consuming mind and people occupation; mostly pressurized, leaving us mentally and emotionally stressed. To break away from this by doing little projects of manual labour can be therapeutic. We all know that hand-work of various kinds can clear the mind and make space for spiritual mindfulness, giving us a sense of co-working with God in what we do.

Sabbath rest: In our ultra-busy world of work we need to renew the biblical practice of purposeful rest *in* God. Our spiritual life – let alone our psycho-emotional health – depends on regular times of disengagement to rest *with* God. Whether we do it on Sundays or other "holy-rest-days", *the Sabbath principle* is non-negotiable. We ought to take at least one day a week to cease work, stop doing what we normally do, and use the time to sleep, to worship God, and do different life-giving activities.

Recreation, hobbies and art: Recreation is to engage in activities, hobbies and interests that are not routinely obligatory – we choose to do them for joy and pleasure. They feed our soul, renew our strength, fill us with Spirit. We are re-created when we do re-create-tion. People without special interests and hobbies tend to overwork and burn out. Recreational activities may be forms of art; creative expressions of the multifaceted beauty and glory of God. Correctly understood, art is a means of spiritual engagement. All forms of art – from music to dance, to poetry, painting, pottery, and whatever gifts and interests God gives us – can be an experience of contemplation, an exercise in co-creation with the Spirit. We express God's image. It's like offering fragrant flowers for the Father's pleasure and for those exposed to our art form.

Nature: To make time now and again to be in nature, to detox from our busy lives in the concrete jungle, is a sure means of psycho-spiritual renewal. We can do this in many ways and places: walk on the beach, in a forest, visit a nature reserve, camp or hike in the mountains, or spend time in a garden (tend our own). God's story began in a garden where he dwelt with Adam and Eve and ends in a heavenly garden-city on earth, in which we will dwell with God forever. There is something special about being in nature in terms of being in God's presence.

Wonder: To enjoy nature is to wonder at God's beauty. We over-stimulate, condition, and even deaden our senses by preoccupation with daily technology and material living. We have lost the childlike sense of wonder, to stop and be surprised by the mystery of God in things (see chapter 9). To notice and be astonished at the ordinary – like the stark winter tree, the drop of water on a petal, the baby with a wet toothless smile – is to cultivate mystical awareness called wonder. Jesus marveled at the birds of the air, that they find food without sowing or reaping; was enthralled with the flowers of the field, astonished that their beauty surpassed Solomon's splendor (Matt 6:26, 29). Wonder is not a way of thinking, knowing or acting. It happens to us. We allow or disallow it. Wonder is a way of seeing and experiencing without words, images or understanding. It's a form of consciousness that spontaneously responds with awe and appreciation of God in moments of unknowing amazement.

Spiritual reading

Reading good spiritual writing is a godly discipline for spiritual health and growth. As a pastor I have observed the reading habits of people and seen the humiliation of *the word* by the triumph of *the image*.[376] We prefer to watch TV and video clips than read a book. Reading is active, requiring engagement to understand and learn. To watch is passive and entertaining. There are oral, literary and visual ways of learning, but clearly, the technology of the image now dominates. It's rewiring our brains with shortening attention spans, and an inability to think analytically and reason logically. The consequences are yet to fully manifest.

Besides reading itself, there is also concern about what is read – and watched – what is popular, the best marketed book, the latest fad or charismatic teaching. We read far less textbooks, spiritual classics and writings of substance that require mental effort. Biblical literacy, let alone spiritual intelligence, is dramatically in decline. We have raised a generation of Christians on feel-good quick-fix burgers, who are unable to stomach quality steak without serious cramping. Good reading habits, reading good spiritual writing, is essential for *healthy* spiritual formation.

When doing my academic studies, I quickly learnt that *who* I studied under was more important than *what* I studied. *Who* we read is more (in)formative than *what* we read. In terms of theological and spiritual books, I latched onto certain professors and saints, reading almost all they had written. It is like discovering a shimmer of gold, digging it out, and finding it's not fool's gold. Then returning to mine the entire seam till the gold runs out. The more we mine and process the real thing, the more we can distinguish between what is pure and trustworthy, and what is mixed, or fake.

---

376 See the important study by Jacques Ellul, *The Humiliation of the Word*.

Part Three: Praxis

I have also learnt that prayerful guidance from God and respected mentors, leads to the right book being read at the right time in one's life. It speaks to where we are at, answering questions, joining dots, nourishing us. I then re-read the book carefully, drawing all I can get from it. That is spiritual reading. Read fewer books – the substantial and seminal ones – and digest them properly.[377] Yes, one *can* read too many books, especially superficial and sensational ones. It can result in a mixed mess of unintegrated (apparent) knowledge. At worst it is slow poison. The same goes for an *indiscriminate* TV and YouTube diet. It's not about information and entertainment, but about formation of spiritual intelligence, true knowledge of God and life. But of course, there is a place for leisure reading, as in a good novel or biography.

My list of recommended *spiritual writers in Christian spirituality* from all traditions in Jesus' Church, who have been formative in my life, is obviously subjective.[378] Each will have elements with which one would not agree. All authors and mentors are recovering sinners and wounded healers, knowing only in part, so eat the meat and spit out the bones! And lastly, reading (auto)biographies of respected spiritual leaders has been a great inspiration in my own formation.

---

[377] I was so impressed with Dallas Willard when I first met him in 1987 at a pastor's retreat he led. At one point I asked him to recommend his top four seminal books that we should all read. He looked at me and smiled. Then said in his careful and deliberate manner, "Yes, my top four are: read the book of Mark, then Matthew, then Luke, and then John. And then read them again and again. Jesus said, 'learn of me.' We read too many books *about* Jesus and the Bible – read Jesus and the Bible!" See Peterson, *Eat This Book: A Conversation in the Art of Spiritual Reading*.

[378] My Bibliography has *some* of their titles: Dallas Willard, Eugene Peterson, James Houston, Richard Foster, Trevor Hudson, George Maloney, Henri Nouwen, Thomas Merton, William Barry, Ronald Rolheiser, The Philokalia, Reniero Cantalmessa, Karl Rahner, Morton Kelsey, Thomas Keating, Jean Vanier, Dumitru Staniloae, Kalistos Ware. This omits the classics like Augustine, Ignatius of Loyola, John of the Cross, Teresa of Avila, Julian of Norwich, and so on. Their underlying framework of spirituality is liturgical, ascetic and mystical. Some Evangelicals, like Willard, work with Jesus' kingdom paradigm, which I have articulated, reframing the liturgical, ascetic and mystical.

Keeping a journal

This, and each practice that follows, is a big subject, a book in its own right.[379] I started as a teenager making notes in my daily QT (quiet time), mostly on what I learnt in my Bible reading, on what/who I was praying for, and occasionally on what I was going through at the time. Over the years and many volumes later, I have learnt that journalling is a significant tool for spiritual and psychological growth. It has a range of applications and dimensions. My primary focus is spiritual.

Journalling is a writing tool for *the discipline of reflection*. Not all people write; some reflect by processing orally.[380] The issue is intentional reflection however we do it. Journalling connects us with our story, records our journey with God and builds up memory and meaning. We make sense of what God is saying to us, what is happening in us and how to respond. It is like a GPS (Global Positioning System) that tells us where we are, keeping us on track. By periodically reviewing our journal(s) we see from where we have come and the direction of God's guidance. A journal gives us a place to show up, no matter how we feel or what we are going through.

In terms of the purpose and value of journalling, it is a means of the following:

Prayer: Often when I come to prayer, especially when I struggle to pray, I begin by writing to God what I am feeling and thinking. This gets me into God's presence, expresses where I am at, and focuses me into meditation and prayer. It's like David's psalms: raw written disclosures to God, honest laments and appeals, joyful praises and thanksgiving. My journals are full of such prayer-psalms.

---

379 I recommend Kelsey, *Adventure Inward*. Payne, *Listening Prayer*. Virkler, *Dialogue with God*.
380 Video and audio journaling is popular, but is not quite the same. Those who do not self-reflect tend to process orally by dumping on others. This includes pastors: their pathology (causes and effects of unresolved issues) tends to leak in their preaching, if one carefully listens to them.

Part Three: Praxis

Hearing God: Prayer is dialogue, not monologue. Journalling helps us hear God as we record what we believe he says to us in our Bible meditation. We reflect on and record our encounters with God – the visions and "words" the Spirit gives us (e.g. Hab 2:1–2; Jer 36:4). We can explore "stream of consciousness" dialogue by asking God a question and spontaneously writing what God says via intuitive thoughts, feelings and spiritual senses. Or we simply do a review at the end of our prayer time to record a summary reflection of our experience with God.

Dream interpretation: We record and work with our dreams – another primary way God speaks to us, giving wisdom, guidance and healing (see next practice).

Processing thoughts and feelings: We can journal more broadly on a particular issue, on our day or week – what we are going through, why we feel alienated. This is a means of processing outside happenings and our inner reactions, as in perceptions, emotions, struggles and longings. This – together with dream interpretation – is an effective means of psycho-emotional therapy and personal growth. It leads to greater objectivity, self-acceptance and self-knowledge – marks of authentic spirituality. Spiritual progress and personal growth go hand in hand.

Creative and imaginative exploration: Journalling is creative writing and exploration, which includes drawing and sketching. We not only process our thoughts and feelings with God, we imaginatively explore God and ourselves, images and symbols, at both conscious and unconscious levels. Creative writing, prayers and dialogue with God, is free-flowing prose, poetry and drawing – mostly spontaneous stream-of-consciousness. Some written prayers are then reworked and structured into poetic form, rhythm and rhyme, like David's psalms – disciplined works of art.

To start journalling we buy a book of our choice, put our name in it, and mark it "Strictly Private and Confidential". We may add contact details so that if the book gets lost it can be returned. We ought to password the document if we journal on our smart phone or computer. No one should know what we write unless we choose to share. Date each entry, as this may be important when we later review our journal(s). We may want to record up front our sense of mission and/or vision, and some key texts or quotes that are dear to us and anchor us. And we quickly learn that journalling, as part of our devotions, takes extra time – but well worth it!

There are some dangers. We can get too involved and reliant on journalling, whereby it's no longer an aid but a dependence that blocks spiritual growth. Then we need to take a break from it. We can become overly subjective and introverted, and so misinterpret what is going on inside of us and what we hear from God. Or we hold our writings as special, even sacred, and withdraw from others in spiritual pride, no longer accountable and correctable. We can even end up deceived by evil. When we journal, we open ourselves to the unconscious, to repressed memories, hurts, moods and other "things" that come out. Discernment is needed.[381] Holding ourselves accountable to respected spiritual guidance in our journalling is advisable.

In closing, I thought of sharing an example of my prayer-psalms to encourage the reader to explore this kind of journalling practice. I randomly took one of my journals and it opened to 4 January 2014. That entry opens with this:

O Father, what a joy to be with you
Sitting in utter stillness in your presence
Deeply comforting, deeply therapeutic
Your faint whispers of love
Touching my face
On the cool breeze of the morning
Is it your breath breathing on me?

---

[381] For example, stream-of-consciousness writing, as we invite God's Spirit, is *not* automatic writing as in something taking over – another spirit or repressed part of our psyche. "Abandoning one's self to whatever spirit wishes to take over and control one is very dangerous business. It is my firm belief that human beings are meant to be *encountered* and not *possessed*", Kelsey, *Adventure Inward,* 96 (his italics).

O Father, I need your Spirit
I need your love
I wait for you
In silence
Held in your arms of love
Holding you in the womb of worship
I adore you

Dream interpretation

If we take note of our dreams and work with them, they can play a significant role in our spiritual and healing journey. I made my decision to give my life to Christ after a vivid dream (see chapter 1). Since then, dreams have instructed and encouraged me along the way, especially at critical points in my life. We all dream at night, but most of us do not remember them, unless it's a very vivid or recurring dream. In teaching on dream interpretation, I have seen that when people take their dreams seriously, by recording and working with them, they dream much more. In reality they have a higher recall rate due to a shift in consciousness – they now value their dreams.

Some dismiss dreams for various "rational" reasons, while others treat dreams like horoscope guides. Biblically, dreams are seen as part of a wholistic approach to the spiritual life. God created us to dream and he uses our dreams to instruct us in self-knowledge and prophetic guidance.[382] God is our guide, not our dreams! Dreams speak in the language of images and symbols that require interpretation. Discernment is required to correctly interpret what is a mystery to our rational mind. We can be deceived by wrong understandings that lead to misbeliefs and harmful responses. Those gifted in interpreting dreams can help us, like the biblical Joseph and Daniel, and other spiritual mystics and wise leaders. More importantly, they teach us to how to work with our own dreams; then we can help others interpret their dreams.

---

382 Gen 20:3–7, 28:10–17; Num 12:6; 1 Kgs 3:5; Dan 2:1–47; Matt 1:20, 2:12; Acts 16:6–10.

Dreams are a state of consciousness during REM sleep (Rapid Eye Movement), in which emotions, memories and whatever, bubble up from the subconscious and present themselves in symbols and images. There are various views on the types and sources of dreams, and on methods of interpretation.[383] In short, the majority are subjective dreams and the minority objective, with some overlap.

Subjective dreams concern us. They are an inner commentary that process and release worries, hurts, fears and repressed memories. Such dreams raise things for our attention, for self-understanding, healing and growth. They give us insight and wisdom as to what is happening inside us and how we can respond.

Objective dreams are about other people, churches, real-life situations and future things to come. God gives us such "prophetic" dreams, as some call it,[384] primarily for intercessory prayer, or to be shared, or to take some sort of action if God so prompts and wisdom confirms. There are, at times, objective elements in a subjective dream – recognized and distinguished by experience and discernment. All dreams, however, contain various elements such as instruction, warning, affirmation, promise, guidance, and so on.

Morton Kelsey integrated biblical understandings with Jungian analytic psychology in proposing different types and sources of dreams:

- From *bodily sensations* or "outer" stimuli, as in being hungry or thirsty (Is 29:8) – or commonly, the need to urinate!

- From *disturbed mind and emotions*, as in yesterday's events (Eccl 5:3).

- From *repressed memories and hurts*, from the recent and/or distant past.

---

[383] A good guide is Kelsey, and then Riffle. See my Bibliography.
[384] Strictly speaking *all* dreams are prophetic, meaning: God speaks to us in subjective *and* objective dreams; i.e. *all* are revelatory in some way. The dreams in the Bible are the significant ones. Millions of dreams were not recorded, through which God, we can be sure, spoke to people.

- When our *deepest instincts* – drives, motivations, needs – are aroused they present vivid imagery seen as universal symbols.[385]
- From our *personal unconscious*: inner projections of those "parts" of us that need to be faced and integrated, as in the blind, hidden or shadow self.
- From our *spiritual capacity*, either from God or another spirit: numinous dreams of God's presence or visitation, at times in the form of an angel; a clear message in a sentence or word; supernatural knowledge of a person, event or situation, or of the future; dreams – or elements in them – of consolation by the Spirit giving comfort, direction, wisdom, visionary overview of our lives, even glimpses of glory; or desolation and attack from evil in the form of fear, dark presence, nightmares, tormenting images, body paralysis, and so on.

With regard to *interpreting our dreams*: we first look for the subjective meaning as to what it's saying about ourselves, unless the objective interpretation is immediate and clear – the general nature of objective dreams. Subjective dreams require more work. The approach is to prayerfully ask questions and let the dream speak as we listen for associations and connections. The interpretation is meaningful to the one who dreams, and she/he will know when it fits – the "aha" moment. But again, be careful not to read into the dream what we want to see, or to impose our meaning on it. Not all dreams are significant. Not every image needs an interpretation. If a dream does not yield to meaning, do not be concerned – leave it. Recurring dreams and repeating symbols are important. They seek our attention and will continue till we work with them, integrating and putting them to rest as it were.

---

[385] For example, mother, father, child, friend, authority figure, wise man, warrior, clown-trickster. Jung called them archetypes of the universal unconscious. One has to be careful of Jung's assumptions and where they lead: the resymbolization of the (western) psyche with Gnostic pagan gods, away from the biblical Judeo-Christian symbolic worldview. See Satinover, *The Empty Self,* 19–34.

I conclude with some suggested steps in working with our dreams. At any or each of these steps the interpretation can unfold itself and "click".

1. Record the dream, and read it aloud, and ask God for its meaning.
2. Gain an overall impression. What is its basic sense? How did the dream make you feel? Is there an immediate intuitive sense of what it is saying?
3. Look at the setting of the dream: the real-life setting in which the dream took place, to which it could possibly refer; and the setting within the dream itself, the mood or overall sense that it communicates.
4. Then look at the dominant images and primary symbols in the order they appear. Ask what they mean to you. Start with personal meanings, then if need be, the cultural and/or religious, or universal associations.
5. Then look at the other details in the dream like secondary images – colours, people, animals, clothes, cars, actions, and so on – that may support the dominant symbols.
6. Write/journal what comes to you, looking for the meaningful connections that unfold the interpretation with "aha, that's what it's saying to me."
7. Check it out with a trusted friend or leader, and record any resolution of action in response to the dream – if it is needed.

Praying The Hours

Years ago, after our son spent six weeks with Coptic monks at St Anthony's Monastery in Egypt, he returned home with *The Agpeya* (see the Bibliography), the Coptic book used by the monks to pray the seven canonical hours. I devoured it! My Baptist, Assembly of God and

Vineyard church tradition had not exposed me to "Praying the Hours". I then acquired two books from the Western tradition and began reading and practicing what I read.[386] The Church developed this practice in the early centuries after Jesus.

"Canonical" in this context means biblical authority in reference to *The Hours* in the day of key salvation events that took place in Jesus' life. This is the strict focus of the Orthodox in *The Agpeya* that I follow below, with some additional comments. Western tradition, as in Merton and Tickle, is broader in its liturgical content in praying the hours. The ideal practice is with, and in, community. However, my personal pursuit in praying the hours has enriched my daily walk with Jesus. I strongly encourage the reader to try this practice for at least a year for it to become a natural part of you – if you are not doing it already.

In praying the hours, we stop what we are doing and consciously pray for a few minutes at each of the seven hours to recall and relive these events with Jesus. They are constant daily rhythmical reminders of intentional interaction with Jesus. It took me at least six months to get into this unforced rhythm of grace. I discovered that it's the spirit of the practice that is life-giving, not the legalistic enactment of the form. In other words, I did not always get up at 06:00 for "Prime", but my first thought on waking was of Jesus' resurrection, and thus to consciously live resurrection that day. And I did not always pray "Loads" (Night Vigil) at midnight, but on going to sleep I recalled Jesus' prayer in Gethsemane, praying with him, "Father, not my will, but yours be done."

Prime (or Mattins): First hour of the day, 06:00, morning prayer: *Jesus' Resurrection*. We commemorate the hour in which Christ rose from the dead (Lk 24:1–6). We pray his resurrection, and our rising from sleep to a new day, a new creation. We also then practice *morning prayer* as Jesus did, probably praying Psalm 5, in order to do his Father's will day by day (Mk 1:35 cf. Is 50:4–5).

Terce: The third hour, 09:00, mid-morning prayer: *Jesus' Crucifixion*

---

386 Merton, *A Book of Hours;* and Tickle, *The Divine Hours.*

and the Coming of the Spirit at Pentecost. We remember the hour of Jesus' condemnation by Pilate and him being nailed to the cross (Mk 15:25). We affirm that "there is no condemnation in Christ" (Rom 8:1) as we nail any uncrucified sinful tendencies to the cross. It also commemorates the hour of the Spirit's coming in power on the Church (Acts 2:1-4,15). So we consciously invoke and receive a fresh infilling of the Spirit – the power to endure and overcome with Christ.

Sext: The sixth hour, 12:00, midday prayer: *Jesus' Sufferings on The Cross.* We recall the hour in which Jesus suffered God's judgment for our sin. He drank the cup of wrath to the dregs in deep darkness from 12:00 to 15:00 (Mk 15:33-34). We also recall the thief on the cross asking Jesus to remember him in his kingdom (Lk 23:39-43). So we ask Jesus to pray for us in our need (Lk 23:34 cf. Heb 7:25).

None: The ninth hour, 15:00, afternoon prayer: *The Death of Christ.* We commemorate the hour in which Jesus cried out that God-forsaken cry in our place, then gave up his spirit and died. The Temple veil was torn, opening the way into God's holy presence (Matt 27:46-51). We pray our daily death to self in Christ and our confident and bold entrance into God's immediate presence (Heb 10:19-23).

Vespers: The eleventh hour, 17:00, sunset prayer: *The Washing and Anointing of Jesus' Body.* We commemorate the hour in which two old men took Jesus' body down from the cross and tenderly washed and anointed it, wrapping it with linen for burial (Matt 27:57-59; Jn 19:38-40). We pray for that same tender love for Jesus and others who suffer and die, that our devotion is equally a fragrant anointing.

Compline: The twelfth hour, 18:00, evening prayer: *Jesus' Burial in The Tomb.* We remember the hour in which Jesus was buried, laid to rest (Jn 19:41-42). His work for that day, for all his days, was over. In this *evening prayer* (Ps 4), we too lay down all our work, being buried with Christ. We are reminded of our death and judgment before Christ (Heb 9:27; 2 Cor 5:10), since sleep is the last hour of our day.

Loads (Night Vigil): The midnight prayer, 24:00, *Jesus' Three-Fold Prayer in Gethsemane*. We commemorate and relive the hour in which Jesus prayed three times in great agony in the garden, asking his disciples, "could you not keep watch with me for one hour?" (Matt 26:40 cf. Ps 119:62). In this hour we also watch and pray for Christ's second coming (1 Thess 5:2; Matt 24:42–44, 25:6).

Praying The Examen – The Ignatian Exercises

The examen is a daily practice – or twice a day – that originated with Ignatius of Loyola (1491–1556). It is an examination of conscience with its roots in similar forms in the early Christian tradition, going back to David's instruction in evening prayer, "when you are on your beds, search your hearts and be silent" (Ps 4:4 cf. 139:23–24). In other words, we search our hearts with the help of the Holy Spirit to see where we sinned during the day in our thoughts, words or deeds, and to make right with God.

Ignatius taught the examen as part of The Spiritual Exercises that he developed for every Jesuit priest (see Ganss in my Bibliography). He wrote them as four weeks of daily meditations for a thirty-day retreat. They focus on the birth, ministry, death and resurrection of Christ, and are conducted under the guidance of a spiritual director. Ignatius' 19th annotation allows for The Exercises to be done in daily life, an hour and a half each day. It takes ten or more months to complete, depending on one's progress as discerned by the director. Some years ago, my wife and I had the privilege of being conducted through The Exercises, each under the wise guidance of a Jesuit priest. The weekly accountability of seeing my spiritual director disciplined me into the daily rhythm of the meditations, prayer and journalling. The examen was introduced from the start and has been truly beneficial.

One need not have to do The Exercises in order to learn and practice the examen. I quickly learnt that it's not so much an examination of *conscience* for wrongdoing. Rather, an examination of *consciousness,* specifically *affective* consciousness as in positively reflecting on our experience of God. We review our awareness of God's loving presence during the day, identifying the gentle promptings and movements of the Spirit of Love in our thoughts, words and deeds. Therefore, the purpose of the examen is not for cleansing and perfection *per se,* rather for identity and co-operation. How did we experience the love of the Father drawing us to good this day? And how did our selfishness and brokenness, and/or evil spirit, lure us away from God and his love in subtle shifts of our consciousness?

So, we take five to ten minutes to review our day – or morning if we do it at midday as well – to become aware of the ways in which God invited us to deepen and develop this identity and co-operation, and the ways in which we responded, or failed to respond, to those loving invitations. In so doing we cultivate a consciousness of God in the present moment. We develop a discerning heart that recognizes and responds to the consolations of the good Spirit and resists the desolations of the bad spirit, in Ignatian terms. There are five steps to the examen:

Thanksgiving: We begin with thanking God for the generosity of his great love and his unchanging goodness to us in our absolute need of him.

Prayer of enlightenment: We ask the Holy Spirit to help us review our day and to point out what we need to see and learn in this reflection.

Examination: We do not rush into a detailed introspection of every thought, word and deed. Rather, we scan through what happened since we woke and let the Spirit highlight what we need to note. Where was God in this incident or that person? How was the Spirit working in my day? Were there invitations from within or without to respond differently? This grows sensitivity to our feelings and what happens inside of us so that we may respond to God. It is here in the depth of our affectivity that God encounters us, heart to heart, as we open up to him in trust. We become conscious of where we most need to converse and be entirely honest with God.

Contrition: The examination makes us aware of where we failed in the day, what we could have done differently, how we reacted instead of responding to God in the situation. We become aware of areas of brokenness and selfishness, how evil tempts us, how we are drawn away from the Father's longing for us to love him with our whole being. And so we ask for forgiveness, healing and transformation.

Resolution: This naturally leads to resolving with God what we need to do, changes we need to make, in order to face tomorrow with faith, hope and love.

Taking retreats

Retreating, or going on retreats, from time to time, is to facilitate certain primary disciplines such as solitude and silence, prayer and meditation. Retreat means to withdraw from – in this case, from daily work and regular activities. The purpose is to be with God for at least a full morning (anything less is not a retreat), or a day, or weekend, or longer. Jesus retreated for 40 days. Retreating is part of the regular rhythm of withdrawal and engagement in life, in order to recalibrate and refocus.

There are different understandings and types of retreat that I need to clarify. For many, retreat means simply having time in nature, going on holiday, or taking extended time out to do one's own thing. Or it may be called a retreat, but is really a conference, seminar, or think tank, which often leaves one feeling exhausted! All these may be, or have elements of, retreat in the broadest sense. This is not what I mean. I am writing about classic spiritual retreat, developed and practiced from the early centuries of the Christian tradition. It has proven to be an effective aid to spiritual advancement. Some struggle with the word or idea of "retreat" due to prejudice or misunderstanding. It is not going backwards, nor is it a negative withdrawal into self. Paradoxically, it is serious positive progress into God.

A spiritual retreat has certain key elements that distinguish it as a retreat in the classic sense. From study and experience I have come to understand there are three irreducible values and practices. I view it as the African pot with three legs. Remove one leg and it falls over. They work together as one.

Solitude and silence: A retreat is for withdrawal into solitude and silence with God. As mentioned earlier, solitude and silence cocoons us in God to hear his gentle voice. Even if we are on retreat in a group, being in solitude and silence *with* others for certain periods is still prioritized – however that may be expressed and practiced as decided by the retreat leader.

Rest and renewal: Retreat ought to facilitate and allow for the mind and body to slow down, relax and rest. To have some time just to do nothing, to sit and stare, to walk, to have a sleep, is to renew strength. Again, however this core element is facilitated in a group retreat, depends on the leader.

Meditation and prayer: A retreat without prayer and meditation is not a spiritual retreat in the true sense. The latter includes ongoing mental dialogue with God *and* formal prayer times in meditation on God's word. *Lectio Divina*, as described in chapter 3, is practiced: we read the Bible, meditate on what draws our attention, pray it through, then journal our experience in terms of what we believe God says to us.

Group retreats are always led – someone prepares the format and meditations and guides us. We can retreat individually by going to a retreat centre, or to a particular facility or place that lends itself to retreating. Such personal retreats can be led by someone we have asked to guide us. Or they can be unguided – we decide what we want to do or not do.

There are general-purpose retreats as per what I have already detailed – though the retreat may have a theme and set meditations. And there are specific-purpose retreats to address and resolve an issue in our lives, or to make an important decision. Certain times and seasons of change in one's life calls for retreat to wait on God for guidance. However, a regular rhythm of retreat for spiritual health is recommended. Over the years my wife and I have sought to facilitate a quiet morning or full day retreat, every six weeks or so, for our church. And also a weekend retreat at least once a year. Retreats that are led by Jesuits and other respected spiritual guides are highly recommended.

The dangers mentioned earlier in regard to the disciplines of solitude and silence apply here. Our moods can shift during a retreat. We can become too introverted and sink into a darkness or depression. The enemy may assail our mind in various ways. If we struggle, we ought to seek input from the retreat leader. It is advisable to do a few guided retreats before we take an unguided retreat on our own. An extended individual retreat requires a level of practice, of psycho-spiritual stamina and practical wisdom. An overly structured retreat with too many meditations and points of connection does not allow for rest and the easy flow of personal processing. Alternatively, too little or no structure can be daunting in terms of what we do with our time. Awareness of our temperament and personality and what works for us is helpful in making retreats meaningful. Ideally, there is the healthy tension of being challenged and stretched, yet not inappropriately imposed on.

Spiritual guidance

In my experience this, and the next tool (companionship), is really significant. Spiritual direction is now better referred to as *spiritual guidance*: to meet with a wise leader to help guide us in our spiritual life and development. It is one-way input. They help us. *Spiritual companionship*, however, is *mutual* engagement for encouragement and accountability between friends in the spiritual life. It's the qualitative difference between having spiritual mothers and fathers who guide us, and spiritual sisters and brothers who companion us. We need both.

Practices III: Other Classic Tools For Spiritual Living

Much has been written about the classic practice of spiritual direction or guidance.[387] In the Early Church, local leaders – pastors/shepherds – not only cared for their people, they purposefully guided their spiritual development; e.g. as in the text at the head of this chapter and my explanation thereof. Where this lacked, or fell away, the need for such guidance arose. The monastic movement particularly needed it for discernment and direction in religious vocation and ascetic practices. It became a specific vocation for which a professional formation was required. The danger then arose of the specialization and professionalization of spiritual direction divorced from local church and its elders. The renewal of classic spiritual formation in recent decades has, thankfully, entered the broader Church. With it comes the need to make local churches into families of formation where spiritual fathers and mothers equip and guide the community in spiritual living.[388] Such guidance in spiritual formation is not positional – because one holds the position of pastor or elder; it is purely charismatic, as in respect for genuine spiritual leaders in the community.

The role and boundaries of spiritual guidance must be defined. It is not psychotherapy, Christian counseling, healing ministry, or life coaching – though there may be minor overlaps. Mentoring has a large overlap with spiritual guidance, yet the latter's focus and purpose is more particular. It originally meant direction for the monks' *special vocation* in the graces of the Spirit and personal disciplines, to help them attain their vocational goal of lived union with God. The focus has broadened to guidance in our spiritual life, in our growth and formation with Jesus.

This does not mean that we deal with the spiritual "part" of us and not the

---

[387] See Barry & Connolly, Merton, May, and Leech, on spiritual direction in my Bibliography.

[388] Merton says of the Early Church, "The individual member of the community was 'formed' and 'guided' by his participation in the life of the community, and such instruction as was needed was given first of all by the the bishop and presbyters, and then, through informal admonitions, by one's parents, spouse, friends and fellow Christians." *Spiritual Direction & Meditation,* 11-12.

psychological, physical or relational. The spiritual life concerns the *whole* person: the mind, emotions, body, relationships and daily life activities are "spiritualized" by the workings of the Spirit. In dealing with our whole person, spiritual guidance seeks to penetrate beneath the surface of outer happenings and inner conditioning, to discern the deeper workings of the Spirit and guide us in recognizing such workings as invitations of loving grace. And to discern where selfishness, brokenness and desolations of "the bad spirit" keep us from responding to God. Hence spiritual guidance is an objective reinforcement of the daily examen. The goal of spiritual guidance is "to bring out his inner spiritual freedom, his innermost truth, which is what we call the likeness of Christ in his soul."[389] Blessed is the person who finds an elder-guide who is wise in the ways of the human soul, sensitive to the Spirit's stirrings, discerning of the devil's deceptions, and affirming of God's great love in our broken humanity.

Since 1985, I have had the privilege of journeying with four spiritual directors, each for years at a time. Our meetings, in which I often shared from my journal, gave me such a sense of safety, comfort and strength. The benefit I have derived is largely due to the spirituality, training, experience and ecumenicity of these leaders. Much depends on who we see – how they view and practice spiritual guidance. There is the good, the bad, and the mediocre. We bond with some and not with others; we have to find what works. Pray for a guide who listens deeply, discerns intuitively, asks probingly, feeds back and guides suggestively. It is up to us to seek and pursue such an elder-guide, and to "do the running" in setting the monthly (or more) meetings, and in working with their feedback and guidance. They are not there to chase us up.

I have seen, however, the danger of people running off to perceived expert or "professional" spiritual directors who are either unaccountable or far removed from the local church context. Outside objectivity can help, but separating such guidance – let alone direction – from pastoral care and responsibility is ultimately unwise. When one-on-

---

[389] Merton, *Spiritual Direction & Meditation*, 16.

one relationships become exclusive, dependent, even controlling, then abuse sets in – notorious in some "father-son" and "shepherd-disciple" practices. Again, our challenge is to build intentional, healthy spiritual formation in how we do church; and to equip pastors and lay leaders in this much-needed ministry. My journey has taught me that the Jesuits are making a significant contribution from their rich heritage of experience, training and resources in this regard. I am personally indebted to them.

Spiritual companionship

Some use "companionship" in reference to the above practice of guidance, i.e. a guide that companions us in our spiritual life. However, as mentioned earlier, the distinctive element of companionship is *mutuality* of spiritual care with one or two friends who "stick" closer than a sister or brother (Prov 18:24). We all need a mature spiritual guide as well as a faithful peer companion or two. Companionship is an intentional relationship of mutual disclosure and accountability in our journey with Jesus and practice of the disciplines for spiritual growth. We pursue this in regular weekly or bi-weekly connections for mutual sharing, encouragement and prayer.

Over the years, in the Spiritual Formation Ministry that we developed in our church, we taught these "twos and threes" companionships. Spiritual formation is a community concern. The lone-ranger pursuit of individual heroic spirituality is not biblical. Two are better than one, and a cord of three strands is not easily broken (Eccl 4:9–12). Spiritual companionship is intended in the marriage relationship, but each spouse needs what only friendships outside the marriage can give. We implemented the twos and threes as a subset of the home groups, men meeting with men, and women with women.[390] These micro-cells of mutual support have proven to be invaluable. I formulated five questions to be asked of one another in the micro-cell companionships. They strategically cover the basic areas of

---

390 One-way spiritual guidance works across gender lines, but it is unwise in spiritual companionship – the level of mutual psycho-emotional intimacy can lead to inappropriate (sexual) bonding.

spiritual life in regard to the whole relational person.

1. *Jesus and devotions:* How are you doing in your daily relationship with Jesus? In your spiritual disciplines? What is God saying to you?
2. *Marriage and family:* How are you doing in your marriage and family relationships? And in your spiritual family (small group)?
3. *Work and world:* How are you doing in your work life, in your finances, and in your daily engagement in the world as witness to Jesus?
4. *Renewal and recreation:* How are you doing in your overall lifestyle? Are you pacing yourself and balancing things? What recreation are you doing?
5. *Integrity and purity:* How are you doing within yourself? In your thought-life and emotions? In your sexuality and purity?

We go through them in a fluid easy manner, focusing on some more than others, depending on the need at the time, on what comes up, and how the Spirit leads. There is no fixed or proper way of doing it. My good friend, Bruce Boynes, added a sixth question when he felt it was needed: have you lied in any of your answers? Or told half-truths? That kept me fearfully honest! Such David and Jonathan friendships give you a real sense of safety and strength, a place where you can bare your soul in regular mutual disclosure and prayer. A true spiritual friend knows you and can read what's going on. Plus, you have given them permission to ask the hard questions, to "be in your face" if necessary, wounding you with truth and honesty. Such friends do not avoid confrontation – or at worst falsely flatter you, which is like the deceitful kiss of an enemy (Prov 27:6).

The aim of spiritual companionship, similar to that of spiritual guidance, is to penetrate beneath the surface of conventional responses and conditioning. We seek the deeper inner workings of the Spirit in self-honesty and spiritual formation, in all dimensions of our relational personhood. The goal is the inner freedom of mature self-knowledge, true knowledge of God, and predictable obedience to his will.

And as with spiritual guidance, there are dangers to be aware of, such as co-dependency and patterns of dominance and dependence; exclusivity and incestuousness; manipulation and betrayal of trust. It is safer to have two or three companions rather than only one.

QUESTIONS FOR REFLECTION AND DISCUSSION

1. Of all these extra practices and tools I have discussed, which is the stand-out one, or two, for you? Why is that so?

2. Which of these spiritual practices have you already engaged in? List them.

3. How have they benefited you in your spiritual development? Think about them one by one... how has it aided you... or not?

4. Of those you have not yet engaged in, what practice do you think you should try? Why do you feel drawn to explore it? What do you hope to get out of it?

5. Is there any particular tool in this chapter that makes you uncomfortable, that you perhaps cannot agree with? Why is this the case?

6. Have you had any significant dreams that you do not understand, that have not been interpreted? What do you need to do in order to work with your dreams so as to hear more deeply from God and learn more about yourself?

7. In terms of spiritual guidance and companionship, do you have anyone, or two, in each of these kinds of relationships? Who are they? How is the relationship(s) helping you in your spiritual journey? What do you think of the five questions I propose for mutual disclosure, support and prayer?

CHAPTER 14

CONCLUSION: LIVING THE INTEGRATED SPIRITUAL LIFE

> *"If you possess these qualities in increasing measure,*
> *they will keep you from being ineffective and unproductive in your*
> *knowledge of our Lord Jesus Christ…*
> *Therefore, my brothers and sisters, make every effort to confirm your*
> *calling and election. For if you do these things, you will never stumble,*
> *and you will receive a rich welcome into the eternal kingdom*
> *of our Lord and Savior Jesus Christ."*
> Peter – 2 Pet 1:10–11

This final chapter brings the book together. It summarizes the key points in presenting a practical way forward for us personally *and* as local church. How do we live a balanced, integrated, maturing spiritual life? I discuss the personal and then community formation, though they are interrelated and inseparable.

First a reflection on Peter's exhortation. Allow me to make these comments, and this entire chapter, more personal. Imagine growing to *your* full productive potential in Christ, into full spiritual maturity before you die? What would that look like? Imagine receiving a rich and rewarding welcome into the eternal kingdom of King Jesus? How will that become a reality in *your* life?

Peter's answer is clear: *if* we possess the virtues of Christlikeness in increasing measure, we become effective and productive in truly knowing Jesus. Therefore, we do not sit back, but we *make every effort* to add to our faith – by engaging in spiritual practices – the moral virtues that incrementally make us more like Jesus. We make every effort precisely *because* we have a new nature in Christ (1 Pet 1:23), and *because* we already participate in God's divine nature by the Spirit (2 Pet 1:4).

If we do these things, we will never stumble in the sense of being stunted, ineffective, mediocre, defeated. Rather, we will confirm our faith and identity as called and chosen by God to be conformed to the image of his Son. In other words, we begin to live *that* reality. By doing these things we work effectively with the transforming grace of the Spirit in a long obedience in the same direction toward Christlikeness.

Peter's emphasis on "doing these things" – and the number and nature of all the disciplines, virtues and practices discussed in the last three chapters – should not overwhelm us. Where do we even start? More importantly, it should not push us to one of two extremes mentioned in earlier chapters.

On the one hand this can lead to the idea that the spiritual life is all discipline and hard work. It's all up to us: a technology of spirituality that uses God and things to become spiritual; the humanist project of prideful achievement of the self-made person. It's the pragmatism of "don't bother with 'the theology', tell me 'the how to'; give me 'five easy steps'; 'just do what works'", and so on.

The overreaction, or the opposite idea, is that faith in God's grace unilaterally does "it" to us. "Just believe the Gospel and the Spirit will do it all for you, as you cannot add to the finished work of Christ." This is then set in false opposition to, and in negation of, Peter's "add to your faith… make every effort…" The result is a passive spiritual determinism, a presumptuous "faith" that borders on fatalism.

Paradigm of the kingdom and horizon of the Trinity

Here again is the pull of the binary either/or: over emphasizing either kingdom *now* in triumphalism and perfectionism, or kingdom *not yet* in tribulation and perseverance. To embrace both/and seems contradictory. Living in the overlap of two ages is not natural – we avoid kingdom-in-tension reality. The future kingdom is present in principle and power, not in fullness and finality. It is *not* all done and dusted! The nature of the future's presence is a mystery seen only by eyes of faith. The kingdom is like treasure *hidden* in the field of this age, like a tiny seed *planted* in the soil of our hearts, like yeast *working invisibly* in the dough of society.

The kingdom-in-tension view of spirituality is both/and. The kingdom *both* has a power in and of itself that is sovereignly at work; *and* yet its effect is dependent on the receptive condition of those to whom the kingdom comes (Mk 4:13–20 cf. 26–28). The kingdom already come means *God* changes us into the lived reality of Christ's rule and reign by the Spirit's power – the seed, the treasure, the yeast. The kingdom yet to come means that we – the soil, the field, the dough – wait in hope for God to change us, as we cannot change ourselves. However, the already *also* means faith is activated to assertively work with the Spirit's power by responding to transforming grace through daily events and planned practices – we plough up the soil and water the seed; we dig up the treasure and unpack it; we mix in the yeast and knead the dough. And the not yet *also* means we persevere in faith through sufferings and setbacks as hard-nose realists on a long obedience, doing the disciplines in season and out of season, finding God in the worst of events.

Indeed, kingdom people are planted like wheat side by side with weeds. We learn to live in that tension of warfare; knowing that brokenness, falsehood and evil, will only be finally separated from us at the end of the age. Therefore, we live faith-fully in the paradox of expecting kingdom breakthrough at any time, while pushing through all the time in hope of the coming kingdom and bodily resurrection.

Thus, kingdom now *and* not yet means that spirituality – transformation to Christlikeness – is a dance. A divine-human dance. It is fully divine and heavenly (the already) and fully human and earthy (the not yet) at the same time. The Spirit initiates and facilitates and we reciprocate and participate through our responsive efforts. We get better at it by dancing when aware of the Spirit's movements *and* through planned spiritual practices. The Spirit choreographs and leads the dance *uniquely to who we are* as persons and as local church: "All who are led by the Spirit of God are children of God" (Rom 8:14 NRSV). And we get better at it, more so, by training, which forms and fits us with exquisite sensitivity and readiness to respond to the faintest promptings of the Father and Son by the Spirit. Indeed, practice makes perfect.

We learn to blend and move as one in the Trinity, dancing in step with the Spirit (Gal 5:25) till our life is one continuous unaware dance of oneness in love with the Father, Son and Spirit. We become Being-in-Love as God is love. We love as the Father, Son and Spirit love – the essence of spirituality as God's mission in the world. All who watch lose sight of the dancers, seeing only the dance in its mysterious beauty and glimpses of glory. *This* is our witness, the Church's witness, to the world: by this love everyone will know that we are one with God and each other – that the world may believe (Jn 13:35, 17:21–22).

We are now full circle back to my preface where I summarized the distinctive heart of this book. *Christian spirituality is formation to Christlikeness by following Jesus in his kingdom. We are the Spirit's work of art at the still point of the turning world. There the Spirit carefully etches and creatively reveals on the canvas of our hearts and lives, stroke by stroke, the portrait of Jesus – the face of the Father. Each painting is a unique masterpiece, framed in the Rule and Reign of God that has come and is yet to come, set against the infinite horizon of the Eternal Trinity – the cosmic Trinitarian Dance of Love.*

And as T.S. Eliot penned…

> *At the still point of the turning world. Neither flesh nor fleshless;*
> *Neither from nor towards; at the still point, there the dance is,*
> *But neither arrest nor movement. And do not call it fixity,*
> *Where past and future are gathered.*
> *Neither movement from nor towards,*
> *Neither ascent nor decline. Except for the point, the still point,*
> *There would be no dance, and there is only dance.*
> *I can only say, there we have been: but I cannot say where.*
> *And I cannot say, how long, for that is to place it in time.*[391]

Living an integrated spiritual life through VIM

How do we dance *well*? How do we grow spiritually into full maturity?

This brings us back to chapter 5, to what Willard called "The Great Omission" of Matt 28:19-20. We make *converts,* bringing people to faith and baptism, but we do not make *disciples* – disciplined learners of Jesus – because we omit "teaching them to obey everything I have commanded you." Willard's question is: what workable and sustainable plan do we have *personally,* and as *local church,* to become the kind of person who routinely obeys all Jesus commanded? The emphasis here is not on *trying* as in external conformity of behaviour to obey, but on *training* as in internal formation of character for fitness to naturally do God's will as it is in heaven.

I share my own thoughts below, but it is difficult to improve on Willard's answer: VIM – Vision, Intention, Means (method).[392]

Vision: Have a clear vision of life in God's kingdom. We set a vision of our being and becoming in Christ – *God's* destiny for our lives in his kingdom. What is *your* life mission and vision? Without a vision people perish. We lose our way, our restraint, and give in to our lower nature. Vision gives direction and produces passion and motivation. Though we will be rewarded for the good we have done in Jesus' name, the only

---

[391] Eliot, *The Complete Poems and Plays,* 119.
[392] *RH,* 85–91.

"thing" we get out of our lives and take into eternity is the person we will have become. Doing and living expresses being. Our doing for Jesus is, or ought to be, the overflow of being-in-love with Jesus. So, who are you becoming?

Picture being Christlike. It's a matter of seeing Jesus and truly falling in love with him; our hearts captivated, and minds enthralled with his beauty, with the truth of who he was and is. Imagine having the complete character of Christ, the Spirit's full fruit described in Gal 5:22, that enables us to naturally obey all Jesus commanded? Imagine living as Jesus would if he were you, in every thought, word and deed? Living a life of love just as he loved (Eph 5:2)? Write out *your* mission and vision. Inscribe it in your heart. Hold it before God and make it your holy ambition. Before he died Jesus prayed, "Father, I have finished the work you gave me to do" (Jn 17:4 RAP). Paul said, "The time for my departure is near. I have fought the good fight, I have finished the race. Now there is in store for me the crown of righteousness" (2 Tim 4:6-8). A rich welcome into the eternal kingdom. Pray, trust and work for this kind of completion of your spiritual journey, for God's mission and glory.

Intention: Once we have this vision before us, within us, we commit to it. We set our intention, our will, to live by it. We count the cost of building our lives brick by brick into Christlikeness (Lk 14:28-30). We deny ourselves, take up our cross of death to self, and decide to do what it takes, with full reliance on God, to become "mature and complete, not lacking anything" (Js 1:4). It's a whole-life, life-long quest of being and becoming like Jesus. Vision forms and sustains intention. But without robust intention vision is a wishful dream. Do not underestimate the power of our God-given will, arguably our most God-like capacity as created in his image. More so when our will is aligned with God's will and empowered by his indwelling Spirit.

Means (Method): The most amazing vision with the greatest intention leads to nothing without the means to achieve it. If we do not have specific means, a strategic method, of working toward our vision, we meander and lose motivation. This is true not only of spiritual growth, but across all fields of human endeavor. Intention and desire are not only sustained but are deepened into godly passion by practices that reinforce and direct them toward an achievable goal. Such practices energize us for the long haul. The spiritual life is not a sprint: it involves the whole of our lives for the rest of our lives as the Spirit paces us step-by-step in the dance to eternity.

The means available to us are the spiritual disciplines, *both* daily happenings *and* planned practices, by which we keep in step with the Spirit. This is *our method of response* to the Spirit's work of forming the inner character and power of Christ in us: *his* vision, understandings, thoughts, feelings, words and deeds. Therefore, the means, the method, is not about performance: *trying* to be Jesus when we are on the spot. It's about ongoing formation: *training* off the spot till we spontaneously and unconsciously live and behave in Christ's character and power all the time.

What plan of strategic practices and diet of disciplines do you have in place to *sustainably* pursue your *intentional* journey to God's *vision* for your life? Respected elders and spiritual masters can guide us in such a plan – the norm in early Christian communities. Such a plan will lead to living a balanced and integrated spiritual life.

The temptation, again, is to look for the magic formula: "tell me exactly what to do." That will *not* do! VIM is not a cookie cutter but a broad framework in which each of us, with the guidance of the Spirit and those who know us well, work out the specifics for our lives. The vision, intention, and particularly the means and method of practices, must be appropriate to our spiritual development, personality, community and life context. If the VIM pattern is not implemented and held in place, Christ will simply not be formed in us. But if we do not work out and implement *what it means for each of us, specifically in daily, weekly and monthly living,* the pattern itself will fall away. This is the main reason for our failure to make disciples in contemporary Christianity. It's the main reason for the lukewarm mediocrity of multitudes of converted Christians made in the world's image.

Let us be clear, however, that the source of spirituality is God's eternal life which regenerates us. Without the Spirit's life in us, the best VIM can produce is a better version of the same old self. Only God's life, our new nature in Christ, changes us. Then VIM works wonders because it provides the right environmental factors and practical means of feeding the health and growth of God's life in us. All healthy things grow. Spiritual ill health is being "ineffective and unproductive" in our knowledge of Christ, in Peter's words. The goal of spirituality is not self-fulfilment, happiness, success, or sainthood. It is *health* – to grow to full maturity in Christ.

A kingdom spirituality of creative tension

The specifics of VIM for each of us, particularly the environmental factors and practical means, are worked out *within real life tensions*. We plan and decide and do them in a life of kingdom tension, whether acknowledged or not. *Kingdom spirituality* is in reality *a spirituality of tensions*.[393] Spirituality is our experience of and response to God as we follow Jesus in the eschatological tensions of the now and not yet of the kingdom – my consistent hermeneutic and interpretative approach. Kingdom tensions come through all of life's daily tensions, the various polarities that pull us in opposite directions. They are, by God's design, creative and life-giving tensions as we work with them. If we neutralize or escape them, they become destructive.

Below is a set of creative life-giving tensions between contradictory polarities in the spiritual life. They work best, paradoxically, when we

---

[393] Barry & Doherty, *Contemplatives in Action,* describe Jesuit spirituality as a spirituality of tensions. Their book so resonates with me as a kingdom theologian and Vineyard pastor.

feel the pull of both polarities. Opting out by choosing one over the other leads to dysfunctionality. We need to do both: *we live the contradictions*, allowing the tension to occupy the centre as we trust God for the wise use of time and energy to live in reasoned balance. We uphold the tension, integrating the polarities as far as is possible in one lived life. Parker Palmer asks and answers: "Why would anyone walk this difficult path? Because by doing so we may receive one of the great gifts of the spiritual life – *the transformation of contradiction into paradox.* The poles of either/or, the choices we thought we had to make, may become signs of a larger truth than we had ever dreamed. And in that truth, our lives may become larger than we had ever imagined possible!"[394]

We choose how we live and move; polarities do not simply overwhelm and pull us in their own direction. For example, in moving my arm, one muscle pulls my lower arm straight at the elbow as another pulls it up in the opposite direction. This creative tension of opposites is life-giving under one head – my brian – that governs and co-ordinates their cooperation for the good of the whole body. If one muscle (or more) has a mind of its own overruling the one will, the arm is "spastic" with uncoordinated movements or erratic jerks. The entire body functions organically through opposing tensions that are life-giving. This is precisely how we should view our personal lives and the way in which we apply VIM.

Biblical Hebraic wholism sees life as dynamic and relational, united under one God, lived as an integrated whole in the mystery and realism of contradictions in both/and tensions. Greek dualism separates life into "parts" logically prioritized for "tidy" management by either/or. Then life is planned, structured and lived in a static hierarchy of priorities: first God, then family, then church, work, recreation, and so on. We (try to) divide up time, energy and money accordingly.

The Hebraic view is like a bicycle wheel: our life is centred in God (the hub and axle) with multiple connections (the spokes) to every

---

394 *Promise of Paradox,* 19 (his italics).

aspect of one life (the rim, wheel); the unbroken circle of family, church, work, recreation and everything else. *Every* aspect of our life in all its polarities interactively touches and imprints (the tyre) the road of life as we travel to our destination in God. See the spokes as dynamic tensions that stretch, pull, absorb, contract, as and when the polarities of life are stressed. Centred in God means we experience and respond to him (our spirituality) as present, working for our good in every tension, in every aspect of life *and* condition of the road, no matter how polarizing, peripheral or painful it may be. VIM works well in this dynamic and fluid model.

These following seven sets of bi-polar tensions are not exhaustive or definitive. I chose them due to their value in guiding me in deciding and practicing the specifics of VIM. These *and other* tensions have been implicit, and some explicit, throughout this book.

Seven life-giving bi-polar tensions

1. Generic versus Tailored, Staple versus Appropriate. There is a difference between the generic or core disciplines we all ought to practice, as well as others tailored to our stage of growth, practiced and reevaluated as and when needed in our spiritual journey. What is the appropriate staple diet we all need? What "supplements" do *you* need for further growth, or to overcome an issue in your life? Look at the list of practices in the last three chapters and prayerfully answer these two questions with *your* menu of staples *and* the "extras" you need to address *your* current challenges and context? The tension of keeping the staples in place while taking on supplementary appropriate practices from time to time is important for spiritual health and growth.

2. Structure versus Spontaneity, Rhythm versus Freedom. We need both structure and spontaneity in our spiritual disciplines, in living the spiritual life. Too much structure can lead to rigidity, to guilt in failure, to legalistic performance, to mindless practice, empty rituals, monotony and boredom. Equally disastrous is too much freedom in the spontaneous practice of the disciplines, i.e. whenever we feel like it, when the mood takes us, when it's convenient, when struck by guilt, when things go wrong and we need help. Then our spiritual life goes in fits and starts and is a victim of our emotions and circumstances. However, *flexible* structures and *easy* rhythms lead to *disciplined* spontaneity and *responsible* freedom. And spontaneity and freedom in *the how* we do spiritual practices – creatively different ways at various times – strengthens structures and revitalizes rhythms. The body without the skeletal structure and the rhythm of heartbeat and breathing, cannot freely stand and spontaneously move and function. Their dynamic interactive tension is life-giving health and vitality.

What flexible structures and unforced rhythms of grace do *you* have for daily, weekly and monthly living? What would this entail? For example, *daily* devotions with God at a regular time and place, and The Examen before sleeping, among other daily graces; *weekly* church worship, home group and a one-day fast, among other weekly disciplines; a *monthly* meeting with your spiritual mentor and a Saturday morning or whole day retreat, among other monthly practices. Pray about it: God will show you the practices *you* need to pursue daily, weekly, monthly, even annually.

3. Context versus Consistency, Seasons versus Sustainability. Wisdom works with, not against, life context and seasons in how we pursue spirituality. We do not impose a forced consistency on evolving life contexts. Neither do we allow seasonal shifts to be *the* determining factor in spiritual practices. Yes, we commit to consistency in doing our disciplines, but it's more *sustainable* as we allow the rhythms of spring, summer, autumn and winter to influence *how* and *when* we do them. Even *what* we do. We do disciplines differently at various stages of spiritual growth *and* in seasons of life: as a teenager, or single adult, or married with young children, in a time of work pressure, when going through a divorce, when elderly, or terminally ill. Be consistent and persevering yet creatively adaptable.

4. *Temperament versus Character, Personality versus Discipline.* We all know the strong pull of our temperament/personality against the discipline of character growth in how we do life, let alone doing spirituality. *Temperament* is our hardwiring as in extrovert or introvert, or choleric, sanguine, melancholic, phlegmatic, depending on the temperament theory one works with. *Personality*, in my view, is a mix of nature and nurture, part temperament and part socialized development. *Character* is all nurture and choice as in moral/spiritual formation via virtuous disciplines and life practices. The 50/50 nature/nurture idea is a debate of false opposites if one does not include free will: the choices we make daily in what we believe, how we react or respond, how we behave. Who I am and become is thus a product of three elements: nature, nurture *and* free will. They dynamically interrelate; thus one element can have a greater formative effect than either of the others. For example, freewill – involving godly character choices – can have a greater impact on who I am and what I become, than nature and nurture can.

To take our temperament and personality seriously and see how they interact with character formation to Christlikeness is life-giving. However, to allow temperament and personality to overrun, or to separate from, discipline and character, is dysfunction and death. Therefore, self-knowledge, self-respect and wise realism are crucial in how we pursue spirituality. Extroverts get energy from being with people, while being alone energizes introverts. This informs how, in life-giving ways, temperament and personality types affect the spiritual quest; how we do our practices, and how to do them without guilt or judgment.[395]

---

[395] I cannot discuss the temperament/personality studies and theories of recent times. Though they have non-Christian origins we gain wisdom from these tools *if* we use them with biblical discernment, not as the whole truth that labels or defines us. Michael & Norrisey, *Prayer and Temperament,* is an insightful resource that integrates the Myers-Briggs Type Indicator with Christian spirituality. For another helpful personality theory see Rohr & Ebert, *Discovering the Enneagram.*

We do what fits and works for us. We cannot do spirituality exactly as others do, including Jesus! But we can learn from him how to do it as he would *if he were us*, in our body with *our* personality, in our context. So, we learn to do practices in keeping with who we are, yet *not* in selfish accommodation, but stretching our comfort zones with enough discipline for growth in character.

5. *Head versus Heart, Rational/Analytical versus Affective/Intuitive.* I have experienced myself as an intuitive introvert and an affective heart person – difficult to live with due to (self)rejection and inferiority. The Pentecostalism of my youth did not help, despising the head as "rational, humanist, theological" and valuing the heart as "prayer, Holy Spirit encounter, special revelation" (see Appendix 1 for such Gnostic dualism). But the pressure of socialization and performance, and many years of pastoral ministry and theological studies, pushed me to extroversion with a rational and analytical bent. However, in recent years a growing sense of burnout has made me face myself, my need for space and time to be alone with the Alone, to live an unhurried life, to echo silence, to (re) embrace and give permission to the affective and intuitive side of me, to live passionately from my heart, in honesty without pretence. Actually, to live with *my head in my heart*: spiritual emotional intelligence and intelligent affective spirituality.[396] To have the sharpest of minds matured in theological discipline, in the softest of hearts pumping with the mystery of God's love, is to be like Jesus. We seek a fully orbed, integrated, mature spirituality of the mind *and* emotions, spirit *and* body, relationships *and* creation, Word *and* Spirit, Church *and* world – discussed and diagrammed in chapter 3.

6. *Individual versus Communal, Personal versus Church.* We all feel the pull to either the personal or the communal. Extroverts tend towards spiritual practices that involve others, while introverts lean

---

[396] In rational passion and passionate rationale, moral/ethical intuition and intuitive ethics/morality, knowledged love and loving knowledge, wise theology and theological wisdom.

towards individual disciplines. Disengaging from community practices for individual spiritual pursuit is dangerous, despite reasonings such as: "I'm tired, church is hurtful, boring, irrelevant." Equally dangerous is to use others to do our spirituality. To depend (only) on church meetings, ministries and conferences for spiritual growth is to live vicariously via others. Again, look at the last three chapters and place all the practices into three categories: community practices, individual disciplines, and those that overlap in varying degrees. We need *both* personal *and* community practices, with the overlap of some by God's design. They dynamically interact and support, stimulate and feed each other, giving life to the person *and* the church.

I differentiate between "individual" and "personal". The Western value of the individual leads to *individualism* that detaches from, even destroys, community. It means "my right to do my thing my way", privately without interference, i.e. to be unaccountable. Personal means the individual *as defined by community*. That is, *both* individual *and* community practices are *personal* in that we do them ourselves, with or without others, but accountable to community – thus God. We do not exist for ourselves, but for God, the Eternal Trinitarian Community, and others. There is no such thing as a private individual spirituality in God's kingdom. Rather, kingdom spirituality is intensely personal *because* it is communal *and* missional.

7. *Being versus Doing, Contemplation versus Activism.* The age-old tension of being either an activist Martha who made the meal and served Jesus and the family, or a contemplative Mary who sat at the Lord's feet, listening to his word. Martha got fed up with Mary and Mary conveniently ignored Martha! To escape the tension, we either separate our being (Mary) and doing (Martha), choosing one over the other; or we enmesh our being in our doing. Either way is destructive. The better way, again, is to uphold the tension and be both contemplative and activist.

Natural "doers" lean to practices of action like church ministry, community service, practical work, justice activism, mercy and missions. They are vulnerable to finding their identity in their doing, more so if they have a need to be needed, to save others, to please (appease) God, to be praised by leaders. They are known for what they do and *not for who they really are*. What we do does *not* define us. God does. God identifies and defines us by love, for love, to love. We do practices that nurture our being-in-love with God – prayer, worship, meditation, silence, solitude, retreats – *and* practices of doing service to others. We uphold the tension by living in the rhythm of regular withdrawal into God for contemplation to nurture our being, to regularly engage in doing service with God for his people and world.

Developing spiritual formation ministry in the local church

What plan do we have as local church to teach and train our people "to obey everything I have commanded you"? Call it discipleship or spiritual formation, what *process and program* do we have in place for that purpose – no longer perpetuating The Great Omission? This responsibility under God falls squarely on local church leaders. Dallas' challenge in this regard led me to implement such a vision and plan for Spiritual Formation Ministry (SFM) in the churches I have pastored.[397]

First, I distinguish between *dimension* and *intention*. By nature, the church is a discipling community, so everything it does has (or should have) a discipling *dimension* to it. However, not everything that the church does has this discipling *intention*. There needs to be a ministry that intentionally initiates spiritual formation, or else it will simply not happen. That then "leavens" the whole church in the sense that spiritual formation becomes a dimension of every other ministry in *the way* they are practiced. Healthy spirituality is then "in the air", transmitted in all that we are and do as church. Leaders are responsible to build the discipleship formation intention (ministry) *and* dimension (environment) into local church.

---

[397] Guided by Willard's weighty chapter, A Curriculum for Christlikeness, in *DC*, 341–408.

We implement it by building discipleship into the church's DNA.[398] That means we develop a clear philosophy of ministry by "building from the bottom up", step by step, working out the mission and vision, values and priorities, practices, personnel and programs of the church.[399] For the church to become authentically spiritual in being *and* doing, we build spiritual formation into every step. Members then engage in the intentional plan and program of SFM while breathing the air of vibrant spirituality that fills the church.

It begins with the leader(s) having a genuine love for Jesus, with a passion to become like him. If leaders truly value spiritual formation, they *live* it and *model* it to the church. We can only make disciples to the extent we are disciples: exemplars of Jesus (see 1 Cor 11:1). We can preach and teach spiritual formation, but if we do not lead the way by our personal formation, we lack authority and thus fail to initiate our people into it. People catch who we are, not what we persuade them to believe. We only impart who we are, for better or for worse – a frightening thought! Hence Peter's challenge at the head of this chapter, and Paul's instruction to Timothy to prioritize his own spiritual formation for the formation of the Ephesian church he was leading – see my comments at the start of the previous chapter.

Leaders follow Jesus' pattern and process (clearly evident in the Gospels), in developing such a ministry in the local church:

a) He lived the kingdom, embodying kingdom-in-tension spirituality.

b) He publicly proclaimed and taught it.

c) He enfolded those who responded into his community of formation.

d) He continually modeled, demonstrated and taught it to them.

e) He initiated them into doing his kingdom practices, till they were ready.

---

398 Deoxyribose-Nucleic-Acid, the self-replicating material present in nearly all living organisms that determines its being and becoming – our genetic code.
399 Laid out in my book *Doing Church*, used by church planters, pastors and leaders.

f) He sent them out into the world with authority and power to do the same.

How then do we *practically* integrate Jesus' pattern with "building from the bottom up" to develop an *intentional* spiritual formation ministry?

The church planter or team leader (senior pastor), with the elders, takes time to set the spiritual DNA by modeling and teaching core *kingdom* values – discipleship included – on which the church is built. The spiritual authority to affect this foundational formation will depend on its incarnational reality in the lives of the leaders. They initiate and do SFM on a centred set basis,[400] *both* intentionally as a developing program *and* dimensionally as the environment in which they do church. It begins in the core team and moves inclusively outwards to home groups, to the newest member of the church, to irregular attendees who breathe the atmosphere of contagious Jesus spirituality whenever they enter the environment.

In short, the planter, or team leader, or an elder, initiates *intentional* SFM with a view to growing and equipping others to take the lead, as is done in all core ministries. The initiator-leader must clearly have a) the grace-gifting *and* availability to develop this ministry, b) modeled in their personal life, and c) having the leadership requirements, as in 1 Tim 3:1–13, which I have summarized as seven characteristics to look for in leaders.[401]

Practically, it means doing IRTDM, called "The Vineyard Mantra" in our circles: Identify, Recruit, Train, Deploy, Monitor.[402] The leader *identifies* those who respond to the kingdom discipleship vision and teachings that the leaders place before the people as a core value, in life and church with Jesus. Those so identified, including others who may volunteer, are *recruited* into a collaborative process of formation. The

---

400 Explained in *Doing Church*, 56–62.
401 *Doing Church*, 221–228.
402 *Doing Church*, 215–217. *Not* doing IRTDM is a primary reason why churches do not grow in strength and people participation, in its ministries and mission.

leader initiates them into certain personal and corporate practices for purposeful spiritual growth, with times of feedback, evaluation and adjustment.

This naturally leads to *training* the group and/or individuals for equipping in specific aspects of spiritual formation, with a view to them gathering and leading others into these practices. By this stage the leader will have drawn a core team around her/him[403] to work out the specifics of the SFM plan (below). At the appropriate time the leader *deploys* those who have been trained, to take the initiative and facilitate, even lead, aspects of the discipleship ministry. The leader *monitors* and coaches them into confidence and then encourages them to *prayerfully begin to repeat the process, i.e.* to identify other folk, recruit them, train them, deploy and monitor them – thus multiplying genuine disciple-making.

Based on the step-by-step approach to build from the bottom up in *Doing Church*, I developed and worked with a Ministry Planning Template in the churches I planted and pastored. Each ministry team, facilitated by its leader, prayerfully populates the planning template, then revisits, revises and updates it at the end of each year in planning for the next year. They do it in keeping with the overall vision and plan of the church – see Appendix 3 if you are interested in the detailed planning template. Briefly...

1. *Define the purpose* of SFM by stating its *mission* (reason for existence) and *vision* (future picture of its becoming).

2. *Clarify the values* and foundational principles of kingdom discipleship.

3. *Establish the priorities* and goals of this ministry; the few important things that must be pursued to grow into the vision

---

[403] I cannot here detail my philosophy/theology of leadership and ministry, but simply, every leader needs a team or they tend to autocracy, and every team needs a leader or they tend to democratic committee that goes nowhere fast. Leaders build teams and lead with, in and through teams.

and live the mission.

4. *Model the practices* that the team decides to work with, teaching and training team members and ministry participants, for their spiritual growth.

5. *Choose the personnel* that one works with: leaders, workers and learners.

6. *Implement the program(s)* of what needs to be done: when, where and how it is to be done.

The disciplines of engagement and abstinence, including other practices and tools I have discussed, can be prayerfully examined and some specifically chosen to work with as part of the SFM practices and program. For example, over the years the SFM team in our church, Following Jesus, has facilitated team meetings, regular quiet days and retreats, training times and basic discipleship courses, working with various themes and practices of spiritual formation, like prayer and meditation, silence and solitude, journalling, hearing God, dreams and interpretation, contemplative prayer, and so on. We have taught and encouraged the twos and threes spiritual companionships as well as spiritual guidance and mentoring. We have sought to equip and motivate home groups and ministries to build a spiritual formation dimension into *how* they do their ministry; e.g. the way in which Sunday services are planned and conducted can purposefully include aspects of SFM.

Stages of spiritual growth to maturity in Christ

Finally, what are the stages of growth in eternal life, in spiritual formation, from infancy to maturity in Christ? Some see Peter's progressive "adding to" as a pattern of growth to maturity in Christ (2 Pet 1:5–11). John clearly refers to stages of growth: spiritual children, then young adults, then fathers and mothers in the faith (1 Jn 2:12–14). I explained this when I detailed the threefold classic spiritual path of purgation, illumination, and union – giving it a full chapter due to its historical and contemporary importance. Yet, some will not relate to that path of growth. So I share Willard's simpler proposal, which is appropriate, because I have drawn so extensively on him. Then I conclude with my own view – a variation of Willard's.

As with the numerous temperament and personality studies and theories that have arisen, there are various theories and proposals on the spiritual/faith journey of growth to maturity. I cannot discuss them here. There is, however, James Fowler's "Faith Development Theory" that is really helpful from a different angle, which I have summarized in Appendix 4 for those interested.

Willard presents "Five Dimensions or Stages of the Eternal Kind of Life" in the growth of the disciple from here to forever![404]

1. It begins with *faith*, placing our confidence and reliance on Jesus.
2. This leads to a *desire* to be his apprentice in his kingdom life.
3. The abundance of life that it gives naturally leads to *obedience*.
4. Obedience leads to, and issues from, *pervasive inner transformation* whereby the Spirit's fruit (Gal 5:22) becomes the person's abiding condition.
5. Finally, there is *power to work the works of the kingdom*.

Though Dallas does not refer to Matt 28:18–20, it is implicit. From when I first heard his question in 1987 (what plan do we have to train disciples to obey all Jesus commanded?), The Great Commission has become a guiding Southern Cross in my spiritual journey – the North Star if you live in the northern hemisphere. Years of working with Matt 28:16–20 led me to see a progressive development in the text, as I laid it out in chapter 5. Here I adjust my earlier wording to frame the text in terms of the (biblical) pattern of spiritual growth. As with the threefold classic

---

404 In *DC*, 401–404.

Part Three: Praxis

spiritual path, these stages dynamically overlap – more simultaneous than statically sequential.

1. *Regeneration:* v.17, they saw Jesus and worshipped him, but some doubted. Our journey begins with a vision of and encounter with the Risen Christ that leads to faith in him, expressed in worship of Jesus as God and King. In other words, we are born again with his eternal resurrection life. Spiritual regeneration is a life of continual faith and worship in seeing Jesus for who he really is.

2. *Collaboration:* vv.18–19, Jesus has all authority in heaven and earth, therefore go in that collaborative authority to make disciples of him. However, we can only *make* disciples to the extent we *are* disciples who submit to the King's "*all* authority" in *all* aspects of life. Regeneration leads to growing collaboration with Jesus in all of kingdom life, authority and mission.

3. *Participation:* v.19, baptizing them in the name of the Father and the Son and the Spirit. We are, and make, disciples by being plunged into *the reality* of the Trinitarian God. Baptism is not merely immersion into Christ. It is participating in his death and resurrection, ongoingly, through which we participate in the divine nature of the Trinity. The life regenerated in vision, faith and worship, grows collaboratively with King Jesus in his kingdom authority and mission, leading to ever increasing participation in *real terms* in The Trinitarian Dance of Life and Love.

4. *Transformation:* v.20, teaching them to obey everything Jesus commanded. The above developmental stages – incrementally lived through both generic and appropriate spiritual practices *and* daily life events – progressively transforms our inner being to that of Christ himself. The formation into Christ's character, thoughts, words and deeds, is evident in the growing regularity of natural obedience to everything Jesus commanded.

5. *Maturation:* v.20, Jesus will certainly be with us constantly, to the very end, till we complete his kingdom mission. Jesus' abiding presence is the Spirit's power, the Empowering Presence, continually backing us up with all we need to live our transformed Christlike life and character, and to do the works and wonders of the kingdom till the job is done. Maturity is living entirely by grace – the enabling gift of the Intimate Trinitarian Presence – and by grace alone. Maturity is living naturally, without conscious effort, in the character and power of Christ in all we are and do. Maturity is consistently loving as Jesus loved, thus obeying as Jesus obeyed (Jn 14:15, 15:9–10), predictably and faithfully doing the will of God on earth as in heaven.

The mature fruit of regeneration, collaboration, participation and transformation – a long obedience in the same direction – is, "Father and Son, I have finished the work you gave me to do... I have fought the good fight, I have finished the race." And so, a rich and joyous welcome into the eternal kingdom for the person you will have become. Therefore, the best you can be, the best gift you can give, the best legacy you can leave, is to love each person in each moment as Jesus would if he were you. That is doing spirituality.

QUESTIONS FOR REFLECTION AND DISCUSSION

1. Begin once again by settling your heart and gaining an overall impression of this chapter. What has God highlighted for you? Specifically spoken to you about?

2. What training plan do you have to obey everything Jesus commanded?

3. Does your church have such a plan? Does it have a spiritual formation ministry?

4. Have you ever done the VIM exercise? You could do it by integrating the steps into the planning template of "building from the bottom up". *Why not do this exercise by recording the following?*

   a) Your life *mission* statement: your being, your reason for existence.

   b) Your life *vision* statement: your becoming; a future oriented picture of the person you would love to become in God.

   c) Your core life *values*: the foundational non-negotiables you seek to build your life on.

   d) Your *priorities*: the few things you need to do, and keep on doing, as goals or aims to grow into your vision and live your mission.

   e) Your *practices*: the menu of spiritual disciplines you need to implement, and adjust from time to time, to meet your priorities and achieve your vision.

   f) Your *personnel*: list your closest spiritual companions, and one or two spiritual guides and mentors, to purposefully connect with as helpers in the journey.

   g) Lastly, *intention and commitment:* now pause and pray. Count the cost of the plan you have just laid out, and then *decide* before God to engage and do it!

APPENDIX 1

UNDERSTANDING GNOSTICISM AND SPIRITUALITY[405]

Introduction and definition: Gnosticism is a belief system, a worldview that sees knowledge as key to salvation. Salvation is attaining higher levels of spiritual consciousness. Gnosticism is derived from *gnosis,* meaning knowledge, used frequently in the NT. Gnosticism uses *gnosis* as a special, revelatory and secret kind of knowledge that initiates a person into a level of enlightenment ("salvation") and thus into an elite group of "those who *really* know", those who are "spiritual".

Origin and influence: Gnosticism came from a mixture of Eastern mystery religions and Greek philosophy, used to reinterpret NT Christianity. It was incipiently present in the Early Church, refuted in John's Gospel, 1 John, Revelation 1 to 3, 1 and 2 Corinthians, Colossians, 1 and 2 Timothy and 2 Peter. The offer of personal spiritual experiences as opposed to rational explanations was Gnosticism's appeal. Secret rituals and intense experiences led to special knowledge that freed the person from problems and demons, making them more spiritual. It was a mix of beliefs from various sources – including Christian elements – becoming full-blown between 140 and 400 AD, when the "Gnostic Gospels" were written: *The Gospel of Thomas, The Secret teachings of John, The Gospel of Mary,* to mention a few. Today Gnosticism is represented in eclectic

---

[405] I have used Bible dictionaries; Morphew, *The Spiritual Spider Web* and *Different but Equal;* Satinover, *The Empty Self;* and Jones, *Spirit Wars.*

Appendix

New Age beliefs and elements of postmodernism, in a world traumatized by rapid change, tired of rational-materialism and hungry for spiritual experience. Throughout her history the Church has fought Gnosticism. It is no different today; Gnostic influence is a spiritual spider web in the church. .

Basic worldview and beliefs: Gnosticism manifests in a *dualistic view of reality,* the spiritual versus the physical. The former is inherently good, the source of all things. The latter is inherently bad – physical body and material world – because it is a fallen expression of the spiritual. The spiritual is mediated to us via descending levels of emanations, spiritual beings and revelations, to enlighten the "spark" – the "divine" spirit – in us from God/the gods. They all originate in and from a single *monad* ("that which is one and indivisible"), the source of divine being. This leads to a *monist* worldview, "all is one and one is all", a form of pantheism.

Gnosticism is a storied belief system most clearly articulated by Valentinus (100-160 AD). Briefly, the divine being unfolds from the monad (called Bythos), with more and more evolving emanations (called aeons). First there was a Trinity, then a Quadrupy, then emanations descending in goodness, till one at a lower level became evil. All the aeons are either male or female evolving from the original androgynous monad. The lower level female Sophia (wisdom) goes beyond the "one all" and aborts an emanation called the *demiurge* ("craftsman"), the male creator "God" of the Old Testament, *YHWH*. Corrupted by fallen desire, he creates the physical universe. Matter arose out of evil and is the cause of evil. However, there is the divine spark in human beings in varying degrees (the pneuma or spirit), with a neutral soul (the psyche), in an evil body (matter). Ultimate salvation is freedom from the body when the spirit is absorbed back into the monad in oneness with universal divine consciousness. As we enlighten and feed the spark through revelation knowledge, spiritual experiences and practices, we ascend the ladder of spirituality to become who we really are: "divine".

In practice this leads to pride and elitism. The dualism means we are "saved" in our spirit, *not* in our body. We will one day escape our body into the fullness of spirit. Because of this we either indulge and let our bodies go in licentiousness (we are saved in our spirit!), *or* we despise and reject our bodies in legalism and asceticism to free the spirit in spirituality. See Figure 12.

Figure 12. Gnostic Dualism

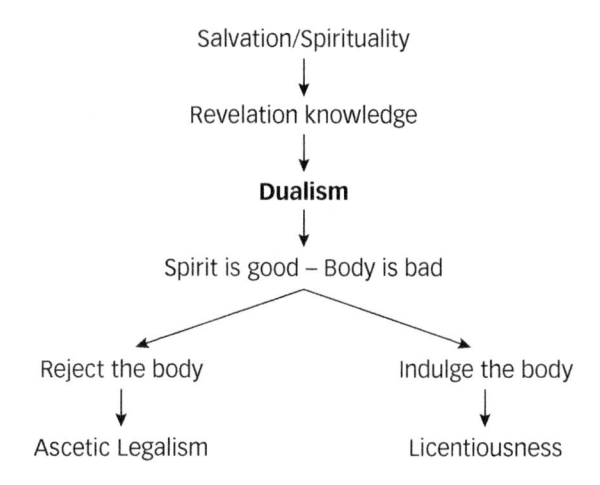

```
              Salvation/Spirituality
                       ↓
              Revelation knowledge
                       ↓
                   Dualism
                       ↓
           Spirit is good – Body is bad
              ↙                    ↘
      Reject the body          Indulge the body
              ↓                        ↓
      Ascetic Legalism           Licentiousness
```

Worldview confusion: Because the Gnostic worldview is *spiritual*, having elements that appear similar to a Christian worldview, it appeals to some Christians. Gnosticism has *pagan magical* elements, believing that knowledge and practices can harness spiritual powers – we can manipulate and control others through spiritual powers (1 Sam 28:3–25; Acts 8:14–24). Biblically, we are *not* to consult, invoke or use spirits; we are to seek and worship *only the God revealed in Jesus Christ – through his Holy Spirit* – no other spirit. We do not use spiritual practices and religious rituals for the purpose of experiencing and using spiritual

Appendix

power (God and/or angels) for others or ourselves. To do that would be divination and witchcraft. We are *always and only servants* of God and his power.

False spirituality: With regard to Gnostic influence on Christian spirituality, Paul warned Timothy: "Turn away from godless chatter and the opposing ideas of what is falsely called knowledge (*gnosis*), which some have professed and in so doing have wandered from the faith" (1 Tim 6:20). Gnosticism is preoccupied with special revelation, distorting the truth of God's revelation. Those who are "truly spiritual" receive revelation, secret knowledge. This "hearing from God" makes them special, leading to spiritual pride, placing them above correction: "You don't agree with me because you don't understand; God hasn't revealed it to you yet. If you prayed enough and heard from God, *then* you would understand and agree with me". They take any disagreement or correction as personal rejection, which often results in projection: "You don't understand because you're in the flesh"; or "you are under a controlling spirit", and so on.

Scriptural misuse: As Peter says (2 Pet 3:15–16), some people misinterpret and misuse Paul's (and John's) writings to teach forms of Gnostic thinking. Paul and John were Jews; they thought Hebraically but wrote in Greek. *Their method of correcting Gnostic ideas is important*: they directly refuted errors fundamental to Christian faith, as in Gnostics denying the human incarnation of Christ and his physical resurrection, but they did not *directly* attack distortions to Christian truth that the Gnostics claimed for themselves. Rather, Paul and John used terminology that Gnostics used to reaffirm Christian truth, thus correcting error. Consequently, some have misused this in support of Gnostic ideas. Here are some examples from Paul:

Secret wisdom and revelation: In 1 Cor 1 to 2 Paul speaks of "revelation" and "secret wisdom" that has been "hidden". This got the Gnostics salivating. Then he uses it against them by saying the revelation and wisdom of God is Jesus Christ, not a spirit revealed to the initiated elite, but a man revealed to the ordinary everyone!

The spiritual versus the natural (and carnal): In 1 Cor 2 to 4 Paul contrasts the "spiritual" person with the "natural" or "carnal". The spiritual are those who have received God's Spirit, not those who have great revelations. The natural live by worldly values and the carnal by their corrupted appetites – they are *not* those who are without revelation-knowledge. Paul says in effect: "If you can't understand God's revelation, it's because of your pride, disunity and conflict". True spirituality is relational, not revelational!

Body and worldliness: In 1 Cor 5 to 7 Paul deals with wrong views of sexuality, the body and worldliness. "Do not touch, do not eat, do not drink" type legalism leads to hidden immorality and even lawsuits against one another (see Col 3:13–23). Equally, "everything is permissible" leads to licentiousness. Both legalism and license are false spiritualities. True spirituality is to honor our bodies and material creation by honoring God and one another with our bodies, as indwellings of God's Spirit.

Knowledge versus faith and love: In 1 Cor 8 Paul contrasts knowledge with love. We are *not* saved by *gnosis*, which "puffs up", makes proud, but by faith in Jesus Christ, which leads to love and service – true spirituality.

Super apostles versus true apostles: In 1 Cor 4 and 2 Cor 11 & 12 Paul deals with Gnostic views of leadership. The real apostles are *not* those who have great revelations, are good orators, have title, position and power – called "Super Apostles"; Paul called them "false apostles". True apostles are those who suffer for Christ's sake, laying down their lives for God's people and God's world – true spirituality.

Spirituality and manifestation-gifts: In 1 Cor 11–14 Paul corrects Gnostic excesses in worship and spiritual gifts. The spiritual are *not* those who have dramatic revelations, gifts and manifestations, nor those who use the gifts for personal power and glory. It is those who love and edify the church. *All revelations and manifestations are accountable to community discernment and correction,* because we "see in part, know in part".

Appendix

The flesh versus the Spirit: Paul's usage of "the flesh" has been misused to mean *our bodies* as inferior and sinful; e.g. "you are in the flesh, not in the Spirit!" Thus, legalism and asceticism help to "crucify the flesh", i.e. punish the body. Paul never uses "the flesh" in that way, rather he uses it to refer to an attitude of "the self" in rebellion against God – our fallen nature, corrupted appetites (e.g. Rom 5:5–8; Gal 5:16–21. See footnote 231 for other usages in Paul).

Spiritual realm versus earthly realm: Paul's distinction of the unseen spiritual world and the seen physical world (2 Cor 4:16–18) is used to reinforce Gnostic dualism: the superior spiritual is eternal, and the inferior material will "pass away". The Hebraic revelation is that God's material world was created as "good" and "very good" (Gen 1:4–31); and God will recreate the material world, "making everything new" (Rev 21:5) after the resurrection of our bodies (Rom 8:19–23).

Fragmented versus wholistic human personality: People use 1 Thess 5:23 and Heb 4:12 to teach a "tripartite" understanding of the human person,[406] even dividing between soul and spirit, between thoughts and intentions, defining each "part". This leads to a Gnostic fragmentation of human personality into superior and inferior "parts", autonomous "selves". Paul and Hebrews do not teach this. They use these (Greek) categories to insist on the Hebraic wholeness and complex unity of the human person, which only God's Word and Spirit can understand, penetrate and heal.

Other Gnostic tendencies

The following "symptoms" in themselves may not be Gnostic, but a few of them in the same person would point to Gnostic tendencies. The purpose of this list is to make us aware, not to use it in negative judgment of others. *It must not cause us to react against hearing from God, to doubt*

---

[406] Captured in a (Gnostic) slogan by E.W. Kenyon, popularised in Pentecostal/Charismatic circles via Kenneth Hagin and Kenneth Copeland: "I am a spirit-being, I have a soul, and I live in my body". The biblical view is: "I am my whole body, soul and spirit, now and forever!"

passionate prayer and spiritual warfare, or to despise spiritual experiences and Spirit-manifestations.

- The obvious one: when a person despises and punishes their body through legalistic and ascetic practices in order to be more spiritual.
- It's opposite: the free indulgence of their corrupted bodily appetites without conscience, believing it does not matter because "God knows my heart!"
- An air of super-spirituality and elitism in hearing from God for everything.
- Language and mentality that reveals a "stepladder" spirituality, ever wanting to attain "deeper" experiences or "higher" levels of revelation and holiness.
- A sense of secretiveness, mystique, intrigue, withdrawal, keeping their own counsel, implying, "If you really want to know, you can ask me".
- An unhealthy preoccupation and fascination with revelation, angels, spiritual experiences and "words from the Lord".
- Forming a closed group of "like-minded" people, who engage in "deep spiritual warfare", revelatory experiences, intense practices and rituals. The give-away is when they are no longer accountable to others – especially leadership – being exclusive and elitist, above correction.
- Creating a sense of inferiority, guilt and self-doubt in others by the person's inferred superior spirituality and holiness, or "hearing from God" all the time.
- An implied judgment of others who do not understand or who disagree with the person's revelation, prophetic word, or expressed spirituality.

Appendix

- Judging, discrediting and disqualifying leaders who try to correct them, pointing to their "lack" of spiritual-savvy, Spirit-experiences and power.
- A critical or judgmental attitude based on measuring spirituality by outward criteria: how much we pray; how committed (intense) we are; how many spiritual experiences we have; how often we hear from God; how we dress; what we eat and drink, if we keep holy days and feasts.
- Using revelations, words, experiences and ministry to manipulate and control.
- The subjective, private and unaccountable nature of their experiences and revelations, and their inability to receive correction without being defensive.
- Repeated dualisms in their talk, whether overt or implied, because "out of the abundance of the heart the mouth speaks". It reveals the following divisions:

Spiritual reality	Material reality
Spiritual realm (superior)	*Earthly realm* (inferior)
Heart (good, the Spirit, passion, truth, intuition)	*Mind* (questionable, humanistic, rational, theological, anti-Spirit)
Spirit (strong, holy, Spirit-control, of God)	*Flesh* (weak, sinful, physical, human-control, worldly)
Spirit-led (free to do our own thing)	*Leader-led* (restricted and controlled)
Private (personal, unaccountable, subjective, in control)	*Public* (impersonal, objective, social construct, controlling)
Church (faith, the sacred, the spiritual, God's people)	*Society* (politics, the secular, worldly, "not my concern")

APPENDIX 2

COMPARING CATAPHATIC AND APOPHATIC APPROACHES

Read this list of contrasts in the context of my discussions in chapters 3 and 9 of the two ways of knowing God, *cataphatic* and *apophatic,* in the Christian spiritual tradition. It's my summary of these two approaches in experiencing God. The point I made in chapter 9 (see footnote 243) is crucial: we practice and blend both *cataphatic* and *apophatic* in doing spirituality. It is *not* either/or. This is *not* a list of (false, even Gnostic) dualisms – they are creative bi-polar tensions.

Cataphatic approach	Apophatic approach
Greek meaning "to affirm"	Greek meaning "to deny"
Positive way of engaging	Negative way of emptying
Human knowing via thoughts, images, feelings, words, senses	Human *unknowing* beyond thoughts, images, feelings, words, senses
Light of God, quickened senses	Darkness of God, darkened senses
Object-subject (objective encounter)	Inter-subject (subjective interaction)
Rational-logical	Intuitive-mystical
Affective-sensual	Spiritual-experiential
Pursuit of God's revelation (acquired)	Only God reveals himself (infused)
Purified Enlightenment	Ecstatic Union
Finding God in all things	Finding all things in God
Faith exercised by human faculties	Faith purified by love
Knowledge and Understanding	Wisdom and Love
Indirect mediated knowing of God	Direct unmediated gift of God himself
Meditation	Contemplation
Incarnation	Divinization

APPENDIX 3

MINISTRY PLANNING TEMPLATE

This template can be used to do spiritual formation ministry in church as discussed in the final chapter. I have kept Following Jesus (our church) details in this template as an example to be adapted to the local context. In 2014 we finalized our 2020 vision and plan. Each ministry and home group populated this template with their details, in keeping with the church mission and vision. There are annual planning meetings where each ministry revisits and revises their plan. The elders then use all the updated documents to integrate and finalize the overall planning of the church for the following year, to move cohesively toward the five-year vision and plan.

Following Jesus Mission Statement: *To follow Jesus and make followers of him, learning to live a life of love just as Jesus loved us.*

Following Jesus 2020 Vision: To be a healthy Jesus family that is *diverse, spiritual, healing, equipping* and *transformational* in and beyond our community:

Diverse: authentically reconciling genders, ages, cultures and classes.
Spiritual: intentionally growing intimacy with God and others.
Healing: wholistically restoring people to wellness.
Equipping: purposefully developing people for life and ministry.
Transformational: joyfully engaging the world through evangelism, social transformation, church planting and missions.

Ministry Planning Template

1. **Name**: The name of the home group or ministry?
2. **Mission**: Answers _who_ are we? The reason for the ministry's existence, its calling and identity, its sense of being. A mission statement is short, sharp, memorable.
3. **2020 Vision**: Answers _where_ are we going? Gives direction, a future oriented picture of becoming (5 years ahead, then 1 year). A vision statement is longer, listing the few essential aims of what we plan to grow into by 2020.
4. **Values**: Answers _why_ do we do what we do? Values are the foundational beliefs, principles, non-negotiables, on which this ministry is based. They are the criteria by which we evaluate what we do and where we are going. List the values.
5. **Evaluation**: Reflect on and record in a few points how this past year went, both strengths and weaknesses. What must we do next year for health and growth?
6. **Priorities** (2020 & next year's goals): Answers _what_ we are doing? List the key priorities the ministry or home group needs to do to fulfil its mission and 2020 vision. This annual evaluation will adjust the goals for the next year.
7. **Practices** (strategies): Answers _how_ do we do what we are planning and aiming to do in order to achieve our goals? List the required skills, practices and strategies to be implemented, modelled and imparted.
8. **Personnel**: Answers _with whom_ are we doing this home group or ministry?
Name of leader? And the assistant leader? An intern leader?
Names of the core facilitating team?
Names of participants, from regulars, to irregulars, to potential recruits.

Appendix

> Names of people resources to refer to and draw on for this ministry.

9. **Program** (structure): Answers *through* *what* do we do this ministry? Record the times, rhythm, place of meetings, i.e. the actual program for next year.

10. **Budget**: If this ministry requires funds to operate, attach a budget for next year and the elders will see what can be done.

APPENDIX 4

FOWLER'S FAITH DEVELOPMENT THEORY[407]

Here is another angle on spiritual growth discussed in my last chapter. James Fowler trained as a Methodist minister in the United States of America and has a Ph.D. in Divinity from Harvard University. He is known for his theory of *Stages of Faith,* applied to religious faith in general. It is an integration of developmental psychology and growth in faith – in spiritual consciousness. He wrote other books specifically on growth in Christian faith, pastoral care and the church (see the Bibliography). I have also used Creamer's insightful and helpful *Guides for the Journey* in this brief summary of Fowler's seven stages of growth.

Fowler understands "faith" beyond its typical usage as a noun, the *contents* of faith. He affirms the verb, the *action* of faith in trusting God, which leads to a certain kind of knowledge – knowing God – a relational faith of believing, interacting and growing, evidenced in deeds or works as James argued (Js 2:14–26). Hence Fowler uses faith as cognitive (what we believe as in doctrinal content), *and* affective-relational (heart trust that enables belief in God), *and* actional (living out that trust in daily life). It is dynamic and developmental, so the stages are not consecutive years – biological years are merely analogous – like climbing up steps to perfection. The stages are overlapping seasons or spirals of growth in the journey to maturity.

---

[407] The Bibliography has the details of Fowler's publications. See also David Creamer.

Appendix

Stage 0 – Primal Faith: This is the birth and infancy of spiritual regeneration into a world of immediate spiritual experience in seeing, hearing, smelling, touching and tasting. Primal faith "arises in the roots of confidence that find soil in the ecology of relations, care, and shared meanings..." in which we find ourselves.[408]

Stage 1 – Intuitive-Projective: Our world of immediacy enters a world mediated by meaning, with the emergence of words, language and enquiry. The early childhood stage of intuitive wonder and imaginative discovery sees (projects) God in those who have spiritual authority in our lives, more so when we are in need.

Stage 2 – Mythic-Literal: In the child stage (ages 6–12) we become more logical about our faith experience, distinguishing between fantasy and reality, seeing the pastor as God's representative, not as God. However, our spiritual world is black and white, ordered and dependable, with a God who rewards the good and punishes the bad. What is fair and right is important, so contradictions stumble us; e.g. the story of the labourers in the vineyard (Matt 20:1–16). If we remain in this stage, we become legalistic about law and sin, quickly judging others who are not like us.

Stage 3 – Synthetic-Conventional: "As one reaches adolescence (ages 13–20), the ability to think abstractly and reflectively provides a new awareness of oneself in relation to others."[409] Egocentric faith gives way to awareness of others in their beliefs and needs, including how they see us. We struggle with self-image, how to integrate and synthesize our identity with conventional beliefs and values that emotionally connect us with others. So we conform to their expectations and judgments. Many adults stay in stage 3 living faith "second hand", giving uncritical adherence to authority, not taking responsibility to grow up.

Stage 4 – Individuative-Reflective: This young adult stage (ages 21–35) is the movement from conformity to individuality, from unexamined faith to critical faith. We become our own person beyond conventional

---

408 Fowler, *Becoming Adult, Becoming Christian*, 53.
409 Creamer, *Guides for the Journey*, 144.

ideology to reflective and reasoned faith, integrated with personal responsibility and convictions in life experience. We begin to live first hand autonomous faith that is not dependent on others. The danger of course is a heroic *individualism* seen in those who are stuck in this stage.

Stage 5 – Conjunctive Faith: In the adult stage (ages 36–60) we come to terms with the *apparent* clarity and coherence of individual faith and face the mystery of paradox, i.e. of "conjunctive" faith, meaning God is revealed in the "coincidence and conjunction of opposites."[410] This pulls us to *inter*dependence in true community that defines our personhood, where we find ourselves by giving up ourselves in the pursuit of the common good. The adult stage is learning to live in the tensions of bi-polar opposites in life, till they "cease to be opposites; they lie down together peacefully like the lion and the lamb."[411] Here there is honest *dialogue* and heart exchange without the need to convince the other, able to live with paradoxes of people, truth and tensions that lift us to a mature fullness of being.

Stage 6 – Universalizing Faith: Fowler characterized this stage of maturity (60 years onwards) as "grace", saying few make this leap from conjunctive faith to living by God's grace alone, i.e. having a mature universalizing sense of God consciousness. "Universal" is *not* the universalist faith of a Cosmic Christ that ultimately saves and assimilates all into one universal spiritual consciousness. Mature faith is *universalizing* in the sense of seeing the whole world as God sees it, loving each and every individual as God's image, with compassion and justice, and acts accordingly with wisdom and grace.

---

410 Cited in Creamer, *Guides for the Journey,* 168 endnote 77.
411 Cited in Creamer, *Guides for the Journey,* 153.

BIBLIOGRAPHY OF SOURCES CONSULTED

Anthonisamy, F. *An Introduction to Christian Spirituality* (Bombay: St Pauls, 1999).

Augsburger, David. *Dissident Discipleship: A Spirituality of Self-Surrender, Love of God, and Love of Neighbour* (Grand Rapids: Brazos Press, 2006).

Augustine, Saint. John E Rotelle (ed.) *De Trinitate* (English Translation by Father Hill: published by New City Press, 1991).
The Confessions of St. Augustine (Modern English version. Grand Rapids: Baker Publishing, 2005).

Barclay, William. *And He had Compassion* (Edinburgh: Saint Andrew Press, 1975).

Barrett, David; & Kurian, George; & Johnson, Todd (eds). *World Christian Encyclopedia* (New York: Oxford University Press, 2001).

Barry, William SJ. *Paying Attention to God: Discernment in Prayer* (Notre Dame: Ave Marie Press, 1990).
Finding God in All Things (Notre Dame: Ave Marie Press, 1991).
Spiritual Direction and the Encounter with God: A Theological Enquiry (New York: Paulist Press, 1992).
God's Passionate Desire and Our Response (Mumbai: St Pauls, 1999).
With an Everlasting Love: Developing an Intimate Relationship with God (New York: Paulist Press, 1999).
A Friendship like No Other: Experiencing God's Embrace (Chicago: Loyola Press, 2008).

Barry, William SJ; & Connolly, William SJ. *The Practice of Spiritual Direction* (San Francisco: Harper, 1982).

Barry, William SJ; & Doherty, Robert SJ. *Contemplatives in Action: The Jesuit Way* (New York: Paulist Press, 2002).

Beale, G.K. *The Temple and the Church's Mission: A Biblical Theology of the Dwelling Place of God* (Downers Grove: IVP, 2004, in New Studies in Biblical Theology 17 series, ed. D.A. Carson).

Bibliography Of Sources Consulted

Beasley-Murray, George R. *John,* Word Biblical Commentary (Waco, Texas: Word Books, 1987).

Beker, J. Christiaan. *Paul's Apocalyptic Gospel: The Coming Triumph of God* (Philadelphia: Fortress Press, 1982).
The Triumph of God: The Essence of Paul's Thought (Minneapolis: Fortress Press 1990).

Benner, David. *Psychotherapy and the Spiritual Quest* (London: Hodder & Stoughton, 1988).
Surrender to Love: Discovering the Heart of Christian Spirituality (Mumbai: St Paul's Press, 2003).
The Gift of Being Yourself: The Sacred Call to Self Discovery (Downers Grove: IVP, 2004).

Bonhoeffer, Dietrich. *Letters and Papers from Prison* (London: Fontana, 1953).
Life Together: A Discussion of Christian Fellowship (San Francisco: Harper and Row, 1954).
Ethics (New York: MacMillan Publishing, 1955).
The Cost of Discipleship (New York: Macmillan Publishing, 1963).

Borg, Marcus. *Jesus A New Vision: Spirit, Culture and the Life of Discipleship* (San Francisco: Harper Collins, 1987).

Bosch, David. *Transforming Mission: Paradigm Shifts in Theology of Mission* (New York: Orbis Books, 1991).

Brown, Colin (ed.) Disciple, *The New International Dictionary of New Testament Theology*, Vol. 1 (Exeter: Paternoster Press, 1975).

Brown, Dan. *The Da Vinci Code* (New York: Doubleday, 2003).

Brown, Raymond E. *The Birth of the Messiah: A Commentary on the Infancy Narratives in the Gospels of Matthew and Luke* (New York: Doubleday, 1993).

Brueggemann, Walter. *Living Toward a Vision: Biblical reflection on Shalom* (New York: United Church Press, 1982).

Calvin, John, *John 1–10*, Calvin's New Testament Commentaries (Grand Rapids: Eerdmans, 1959 Translation, 1994).
John 11–21 & 1 John, Calvin's New Testament Commentaries (Grand Rapids: Eerdmans, 1959 Translation, 1994).

Bibliography Of Sources Consulted

Carnley, Peter. *The Structure of Resurrection Belief* (Oxford: Carendon, 1987).

Carrette, Jeremy; & King, Richard. *Selling Spirituality: The Silent Takeover of Religion* (London: Routledge, 2005).

Carson, D.A. *Matthew*, The Expositor's Bible Commentary, Vol. 8 (Grand Rapids: Zondervan, 1984).
The Gospel According to John. The Pillar New Testament Commentary (Grand Rapids: Eerdmans, 1991).

Chilton, Bruce. *A Galilean Rabbi and his Bible: Jesus' Use of the Interpreted Scripture of His Time* (Wilmington: Michael Glazier, 1984).
The Isaiah Targum: Introduction, Apparatus, Interpretation and Notes (Wilmington: Michael Glazier, 1987).
Rabbi Jesus: An Intimate Biography (New York: Image Books, 2000).

Christensen, Michael J; & Wittung, Jeffrey A. *Partakers of the Divine Nature: The History and Development of Deification in the Christian Traditions* (Grand Rapids: Baker Academic, 2007).

Coffey, David. *The Holy Spirit as the Mutual Love of the Father and the Son*, in Theological Studies 51 (1990), pp. 193-229. http://cdn.theologicalstudies.net/51/51.2/51.2.1.pdf

Collins, Gary. *The Soul Search: A Spiritual Journey to Authentic Intimacy with God* (Nashville: Thomas Nelson, 1998).

Cooper, John W. *Panentheism: The Other God of the Philosophers* (Nottingham: Appolos, 2007).

Creamer, David G. *Guides for the Journey: John Macmurray, Bernard Lonergan, James Fowler* (Lanham: University Press of America, 1996).

Cullmann, Oscar. *Christ and Time* (Philadelphia: Westminster, 1950).

Davidson, Richard M. *Flame of Yahweh: Sexuality in the Old Testament* (Massachusetts: Hendrickson Publishers, 2007).

De Caussade, Jean Pierre SJ. *Abandonment to Divine Providence* (1921; New York: Dover Publications, 2008).

De Gruchy, John W. *Icons as a Means of Grace* (Wellington: Lux Verbi.BM, 2008).

Downey, Michael. *Understanding Christian Spirituality* (New York: Paulist Press, 1997).

Dunn, J. *Spirit*, in Brown, Colin (ed.) *The New International Dictionary of New Testament Theology*, Vol. 3 (Exeter: Paternoster Press, 1978).
The Theology of Paul the Apostle (Grand Rapids: Eerdmans, 1998).
Christianity in the Making, Vol. 1, *Jesus Remembered* (Grand Rapids: Eerdmans, 2003).

Dupré, Louis. *Religious Mystery and Rational Reflection: Excursions in the Phenomenology and Philosophy of Religion* (Grand Rapids: Eerdmans, 1998).

Eliot, T.S. *The Complete Poems and Plays, 1909-1950* (New York: Harcourt Brace and Company, 1952).

Ellul, Jacques. *The Humiliation of the Word* (Translated by Joyce Main Hanks. Grand Rapids: Eerdmans, 1985).

Endean, Philip SJ (ed.). *Karl Rahner: Spiritual Writings*, Modern Spiritual Masters Series (New York: Orbis Books, 2004).

Fee, Gordon. *God's Empowering Presence: The Holy Spirit in the letters of Paul* (Hendrickson Publishers, 1994).
Paul, the Spirit, and the People of God (Massachusetts: Hendrikson Publishers, 1996).

Fiddes, Paul. *The Creative Suffering of God* (Oxford: Clarendon Press, 1988).
Participating in God: A Pastoral Doctrine of the Trinity (London: Darton, Longman & Todd, 2000).

Fischer, John. *Towards a Kingdom Theology of The Trinity* (Cape Town: Self-published, 2017).

Foster, Richard, *Celebration of Discipline: The Path to Spiritual Growth* (London: Hodder & Stoughton, 1978).
Streams of Living Water: Celebrating the Great Traditions of Christian Faith (San Francisco: Harper Collins, 1998).

Fowler, James. *Stages of Faith: The Psychology of Human Development and the Quest for Meaning* (San Francisco: Harper & Row, 1981).
Becoming Adult, Becoming Christian: Adult Development and Christian Faith (San Francisco: Harper & Row, 1984).

Faith Development and Pastoral Care (Philadelphia: Fortress Press, 1987).
Weaving the New Creation: Stages of Faith and the Public Church (San Francisco: Harper Collins, 1991).

Ganss, George SJ. *The Spiritual Exercises of Saint Ignatius: A Translation and Commentary* (St. Louis: The Institute of Jesuit Sources, 1992).

Gillet, Archimandrite Lev. *The Jesus Prayer* (New York: Vladimir's Seminary Press, 1987).

Green, Michael. *The Books the Church Suppressed: Fiction and Truth in The Da Vinci Code* (Oxford: Monarch Books, 2005).

Hart, David Bentley. *The Beauty of the Infinite: The Aesthetics of Christian Truth* (Grand Rapids: Eerdmans, 2003).

Hays, Richard B. *Echoes of Scripture in the Letters of Paul* (New Haven: Yale University Press, 1989).
The Moral Vision: A Contemporary Introduction to New Testament Ethics (HarperSanFrancisco, 1996).
The Conversion of the Imagination: Paul as Interpreter of Israel's Scriptures (Grand Rapids: Eerdmans, 2005).

Heschel, Abraham. *The Prophets* (New York: HarperPerennial, 2001).

Houston, James. *The Transforming Friendship: A Guide to Prayer* (Oxford: Lion Publishing, 1989).
In Search of Happiness: The Quest for Personal Fulfilment (Oxford: Lion Publishing, 1990).
The Heart's Desire: A Guide to Personal Fulfilment (Oxford: Lion Publishing, 1992).

Hudson, Trevor. *Signposts to Spirituality* (Cape Town: Struik Christian Books, 1995).
Invitations to an Abundant Life (Cape Town: Struik Christian Books, 1998).
Touched by Resurrection Love (Cape Town, Struik Christian Books, 2003).

Hughes, Gerard SJ. *God in All Things* (London: Hodder & Stoughton, 2003).

Hurnard, Hannah. *Hinds' Feet on High Places* (Wheaton: Living Books Tyndale House, 1975).

Jamison, Christopher. *Finding Sanctuary: Monastic Steps for Everyday Life* (Minnesota: Liturgical Press, 2006).

Jencks, Charles (ed.). *The Post-Modern Reader* (New York: St Martin's Press, 1992).

John of the Cross. *The Collected Works of St. John of the Cross*. Translated by Keiran Kavanaugh and Otilio Rodriguez (Washington DC: Institute of Cramelite Studies Publications, 1991).

Johnson, Luke Timothy. *The Real Jesus: The Misguided Quest for the Historical Jesus and the Truth of the Traditional Gospels* (San Francisco: Harper, 1996).

Johnston, William. *Mystical Theology: The Science of Love* (New York: Orbis Books, 2006).

Jones, Peter. *Spirit Wars: Pagan Revival in Christian America* (Mukilteo: Winepress Publishing, 1997).

Julian of Norwich. *Revelations of Divine Love*. Eds Halcyon Backhouse & Rhona Pipe (London: Hodder & Stoughton, 1987).

Kadloubovsky, E; & Palmer, G.E.H (trans & eds). *Writings from the Philokalia: On Prayer of the Heart* (New York: Faber & Faber, 1992).

Keating, Thomas. *Open Mind, Open Heart: The Contemplative Dimension of the Gospel* (Massachusetts: Element, 1991).
Intimacy with God (New York: Crossroad Publishing, 1999).

Keener, Craig. *The Spirit in the Gospels and Acts* (Peabody: Hendrickson, 1997).
Gift Giver: The Holy Spirit for Today (Grand Rapids: Baker Academic, 2001).
The Gospel of John: A Commentary, Vol. One (Grand Rapids: Baker Academic Books, 2003).
The Gospel of John: A Commentary, Vol. Two (Grand Rapids: Baker Academic Books, 2004).
The Hisotrical Jesus of the Gospels (Grand Rapids: Eerdmans, 2009).
Spirit Hermeneutics: Reading Scripture in Light of Pentecost (Grand Rapids: Eerdmans, 2016).
The Mind of the Spirit: Paul's Approach to Transformed Thinking (Grand Rapids: Baker Academics, 2016).

Kelsey, Morton. *Encounter with God: A Theology of Christian Experience* (Minneapolis: Bethany Fellowship, 1972).
God, Dreams and Revelation: A Christian Interpretation of Dreams (Minneapolis: Augsburg Publishing, 1974).
The Other Side of Silence: A Guide to Christian Meditation (New York:

Paulist Press, 1976).
Discernment: A Study in Ecstasy and Evil (New York: Paulist Press, 1978).
Dreams: A Way to Listen to God (New York: Paulist Press, 1978).
Adventure Inward: Christian Growth through Personal Journal Writing (Minneapolis: Augsburg Publishing, 1980).
Caring: How Can We Love One Another? (New York: Paulist Press, 1981).
Transcend: A Guide to the Spiritual Quest (New York: Crossroad Publishing, 1985).

König, Adrio. *The Eclipse of Christ in Eschatology: Toward a Christ-Centered Approach* (Grand Rapids: Eerdmans, 1989).

Kretzschmar, Louise. *The Importance of Moral and Spiritual Formation for 21st Century Africa*, in Ernst M. Conradie (ed.), *Africa Christian Theologies in Transformation* (Pretoria: Institute for Theological & Interdisciplinary Research, 2004).

Ladd, G.E. *A Theology of the New Testament* (Grand Rapids: Eerdmans, 1974).
The Presence of the Future (Grand Rapids: Eerdmans, 1974).

Lane, William L. *The Gospel of Mark,* The New London Commentary on The New Testament (London: Marshall, Morgan and Scott, 1974).

Laubach, Frank. *Man of Prayer*, The Heritage Collection (New York: Laubach Literacy International, 1990).

Leech, Kenneth. *Soul Friend: An Invitation to Spiritual Direction* (San Francisco: Harper Collins, 1992).

Lewis, C.S. *The Four Loves* (London: Geoffrey Bles Publishers, 1960).
The Weight of Glory (HarperSanFrancisco, 2001).

Lonergan, Bernard. *Method in Theology* (London: 1972).

Longenecker, Richard (ed.). *Patterns of Discipleship in the New Testament* (Grand Rapids: Eerdmanns, 1996).

Lossky, Vladimir. *The Mystical Theology of the Eastern Church* (New York: St Vladimir's Seminary Press, 1976).

Lovelace, Richard. *Dynamics of Spiritual Life: An Evangelical Theology of Renewal* (Downers Grove: IVP, 1979).

Maloney, George SJ. *Inscape: God at the Heart of Matter* (New Jersey: Dimension Books, 1978).
Invaded by God: Mysticism and the Indwelling Trinity (Bangalore: I.J.A. Publications, 1979).
Prayer of the Heart: The Contemplative Tradition of the Christian East (Notre Dam: Ave Maria Press, 1981).
Journey into Contemplation (New York: Living Flame Press, 1983).
Pilgrimage of the Heart: A Treasury of Eastern Christian Spirituality (San Francisco: Harper & Row, 1983).
Entering into the Heart of Jesus: Meditations on the Indwelling Trinity in St. John's Gospel (New York: Alba House, 1988).
God's Community of Love: Living in the Indwelling Trinity (New York: New City Press, 1993).
Alone with the Alone: An Eight-Day Retreat (Bangalore: Asian Trading Corporation, 1995).
The Mystery of Christ in You: They Mystical Vision of Saint Paul (New York: Alba House, 1998).
Abiding in the Indwelling Trinity (New York: Paulist Press, 2004).

Mangalwadi, Vishal. *In Search of Self Beyond the New Age* (London: Spire, 1992).

May, Gerald. *Care of Mind, Care of Spirit: A Psychiatrist Explores Spiritual Direction* (San Francisco: Harper Collins, 1992).

May, Rollo. *Man's Search for Himself* (New York: Dell Publishing Co., 1953).

Marsh, Robert SJ. *Looking at God Looking at You*, The Way, 43/4 (October 2004, 19–28).

McGrath, Alister (ed.). Spirituality – Christian, in *The Blackwell Encyclopedia of Modern Christian Thought* (Oxford: Blackwell Publishers, 1993).

Meier, J.P. *A Marginal Jew: Rethinking the Historical Jesus,* Vol. I: The Roots of the Problem and the Person (New York: Doubleday, 1991).
A Marginal Jew: Rethinking the Historical Jesus, Vol. II: Mentor, Message and Miracle (New York: Doubleday, 1994).
A Marginal Jew: Rethinking the Historical Jesus, Vol. III: Companions and Competitors (New York: Doubleday, 2001).
A Marginal Jew: Rethinking the Historical Jesus, Vol. IV: Law and Love (New Haven: Yale University, 2009).

Merton, Thomas. *Spiritual Direction and Meditation* (Minnesota: The Liturgical Press, 1960).
The Wisdom of the Desert (New York: New Direction Books, 1970).
New Seeds of Contemplation (New York: New Direction Books, 1972).
Contemplative Prayer (New York: Image Books, 1996).
A Book of Hours (ed. Kathleen Deignan. Notre Dame: Sorin Books, 2007).
Echoing Silence: Thomas Merton on the Vocation of Writing (ed. Robert Inchausti. Boston: New Seeds Books, 2007).

Michael, Charles P; & Norrisey, Marie C. *Prayer and Temperament: Different Prayer Forms for Different Personality Types* (Charlottesville: The Open Door, 1984).

Moltmann, Jürgen. *The Crucified God* (London: SCM Press, 1974).
The Trinity and the Kingdom (San Francisco: Harper Row, 1982).

Morphew, Derek. *Breakthrough: Discovering the Kingdom* (Cape Town: Vineyard International Publishers, 1998).
Different but Equal: Going Beyond the Complimentarian/Egalitarian Debate (Cape Town: Vineyard International Publishers, 2009).
The Future King Is Here: The Theology of Matthew (Cape Town: Vineyard International Publishers, 2011).
The Mission of the Kingdom: The Theology of Luke-Acts (Cape Town: Vineyard International Publishers, 2011).
The Spiritual Spider Web (Derek Morphew Publications, 2011).
Jesus Research and Kingdom Theology (Cape Town: Derek Morphew Publications, 2016).

Morris, Leon. *The Gospel According to John.* The New International Commentary on the New Testament (London: Marshall, Morgan and Scott, 1971).

Mother Teresa. *Words to Live By* (Notre Dame: Ave Maria Press, 1983).
Come Be My Light: The Private Writings of the 'Saint of Calcutta' (edited and with commentary by Brian Kolodiejchuk, New York: Doubleday, 2007).

Nathan, Rich; & Wilson, Ken. *Empowered Evangelicals* (Ohio: Vineyard Church of Columbus, 1995).

Neusner, Jacob. *A Rabbi Talks with Jesus* (Montreal: McGill-Queen's University Press, 2000).
Judaism when Christianity Began: A Brief Survey of Belief and Practice (Louisville: Westminster John Knox Press, 2002).

Niebuhr, Richard. *The Responsible Self* (New York: Harper & Row, 1963).

Nietzsche, Friedrich. *Beyond Good and Evil,* trans. Helen Zimmern (London, 1907).

Nolan, Albert. *Jesus Today: A Spirituality of Radical Freedom* (Cape Town: Double Storey Books, 2006).

Nouwen, Henri. *Intimacy: Essays in Pastoral Psychology* (San Francisco: Harper, 1969).
Reaching Out (New York: HarperCollins, 1975).
Behold the Beauty of the Lord: Praying with Icons (Notre Dame: Ave Marie, 1987).
In the Name of Jesus: Reflections on Christian Leadership (New York: Crossroad, 1989).
Beyond the Mirror: Reflections on Death and Life (New York: Crossroad, 1990).
Lifesigns: Intimacy, Fecundity, and Ecstasy in Christian Perspective (New York: Image Books, 1990).
Life of the Beloved: Spiritual Living in a Secular World (New York: Crossroad, 1992).
The Return of the Prodigal Son: A Story of Homecoming (New York: Image Books, 1994).
Can you Drink this Cup? (Notre Dame: Ave Maria Press, 1996).

Nyssa, Gregory. *The Lord's Prayer,* Ancient Christian Writers, Vol. 18 (Westminster: Newman Press, 1954).

O'Collins, Gerald SJ. *Jesus: A Portrait* (London: Darton, Longman & Todd, 2008).

O'Mahony, Gerald SJ. *Finding the Still Point* (Bath: Eagle Publishing, 2007).

O'Murchu, Diarmuid. *Quantum Theology: Spiritual Implications of the New Physics* (New York: Crossroad, 2004).

Pagels, Elaine. *The Gnostic Gospels* (Random House, 1979).

Palmer, G.E.H.; Sherrard, Philip; & Ware, Kallistos (trans & eds). *The Philokalia*, Vol. One, *The Complete Text* (London, Faber & Faber, 1979).
The Philokalia, Vol. Two, *The Complete Text* (London, Faber & Faber, 1981).
The Philokalia, Vol. Three, *The Complete Text* (London, Faber & Faber, 1984).
The Philokalia, Vol. Four, *The Complete Text* (London, Faber & Faber, 1995).

Pannenberg, Wolfhart. *Systematic Theology*, Vol. 2 (Grand Rapids: Eerdmans, 1994).

Palmer, Parker. *The Promise of Paradox: A Celebration of Contradiction in the Christian Life* (Notre Dame: Ave Maria Press, 1980).

Payne, Leanne. *Listening Prayer: Learning to Hear God's Voice and Keep a Prayer Journal* (Grand Rapids: Baker Books, 1994).

Pennington, Basil. *Lectio Divina: Renewing the Ancient Practice of Praying the Scriptures* (New York: Crossroads Publishing, 1998).

Peterson, Eugene. *A Long Obedience in the Same Direction* (Downers Grove: IVP, 1980).
Working the Angles: The Shape of Pastoral Integrity (Grand Rapids: Eerdmans, 1987).
Answering God: The Psalms as Tools for Prayer (San Francisco: HarperCollins, 1989).
Christ Plays in Ten Thousand Places: A Conversation in Spiritual Theology (London: Hodder & Stoughton, 2005).
Eat this Book: A Conversation in Spiritual Reading (Grand Rapids: Eerdmans, 2006).
The Jesus Way: A Conversation in Following Jesus (London: Hodder & Stoughton, 2007).

Polkinghorne, John. *Quarks, Chaos and Christianity* (New York: Crossroad, 1999).

Ponsonby, Simon. *God Inside Out: An Indepth Study of the Holy Spirit* (Eastbourne: Kingsway Publication, 2007).

Race, Alan. *Christians and Pluralism: Patterns in the Christian Theology of Religions* (London: SCM, 1983).

Rahner, Karl. *The Practice of the Faith* (New York: Crossroad, 1983).
Spiritual Writings (Edited with an introduction by Philip Endean SJ. New York: Orbis Books, 2004).

Ratzinger, Joseph (Pope Benedict XVI). *Jesus of Nazareth: From the Baptism in the Jordan to the Transfiguration* (New York: Doubleday, 2007).

Regan, David. *Experience the Mystery: Pastoral Possibilities for Christian Mystagogy* (London: Geoffrey Chapman, 1994).

Riffel, Herman. *Dream Interpretation: Biblical Understanding* (Shippensburg: Destiny Image, 1993).

Rolheiser, Ronald. *Seeking Spirituality: Guidelines for a Christian Spirituality for the Twenty-First Century* (London: Hodder & Stoughton, 1998).
Against the Infinite Horison: The Finger of God in our Everyday Lives (New York: Crossroad, 2001).

Rohr, Richard; & Ebert, Andreas. *Discovering the Enneagram: An Ancient Tool for a New Spiritual Journey* (New York: Crossroads, 1997).

Rutledge, Fleming. *The Crucifixion: Understanding the Death of Jesus Christ* (Grand Rapids: Eerdmans, 2015).

Sander, E.P. *Paul and Palentinian Judaism* (London: SCM Press, 1977).

Satinover, Jeffrey. *The Empty Self: C.G. Jung and the Gnostic Transformation of Modern Identity* (Connecticut: Hamewith Books, 1996).

Schnelle, U. *Apostle Paul: His Life and Theology* (Grand Rapids: Baker Academic, 2005. Translated by M.E. Boring from the German edition of 2003).

Sheen, Fulton J. *The Divine Romance* (New York: St Pauls, 1982).

Sider, Ronald. *Rich Christians in an Age of Hunger: A Biblical Study* (London: Hodder & Stoughton, 1977).

Siegel, Daniel. *Mindsight: The New Science of Personal Transformation* (New York: Bantam, 2011).

Staniloae, Dumitru. *Orthodox Spirituality: A Practial Guide for the Faithful and a Definitive Manual for the Scholar* (Pennsylvania: St. Tikon Seminary Press, 2002. Translated from Romanian by Archimandrite Jerome Newville and Otilia Kloos).

Stassen, Glen; & Gushee, David. *Kingdom Ethics: Following Jesus in Contemporary Context* (Downers Grove: IVP, 2003).

Stavropoulos, Archimandrite Christoforos. *Partakers of Divine Nature* (Minneapolis: Light and Life Publishing, 1976).

Tenny, Merrill C. *John*. The Expositor's Bible Commentary, Vol. 9 (Grand Rapids: Zondervan, 1981).

Teresa of Ávila. *The Interior Castle*. Translated by the Benedictines of Stanbrook (New York: Barnes & Noble, 2005).

The Agpeya: The Book of the Seven Canonical Hours (Cairo: Mahabba Publisher).

The Cloud of Unknowing, Introduction by William Johnston (New York: Image Books, 1973).

The Rutba House (ed.). *School(s) for Conversion: 12 Marks of a New Monasticism* (Eugene: Cascade Books, 2005).

The Way of a Pilgrim, unknown author, translated by Helen Bacovcin (New York: Image /Doubleday, 1978).

Thompson, J.W. *Moral Formation According to Paul: The Context and Coherence of Pauline Ethics* (Grand Rapids: Eermans, 2011).

Tickle, Phyllis. *The Divine Hours* (Oxford: University Press, 2007).

Trocmé, André. *Jesus and the Nonviolent Revolution* (Pennsylvania: Herald Press, 1973).

Van Ness, Peter (ed.). *Spirituality and the Secular Quest* (London: SCM, 1996).

Vanier, Jean. *Be not Afraid* (Dublin: Gill & Macmillan, 1976).
The Broken Body: Journey Toward Wholeness (New York: Paulist Press, 1988).
From Brokenness to Community (New York: Paulist Press, 1992).

Varga, Ivan. The Body – The New Sacred? The Body in Hypermodernity, *Current Sociology*. Vol 53/2 (London: Sage Publications, March 2005).

Venter, Alexander F. *Doing Church: Building from the Bottom Up* (Cape Town: VIP, 2000).
Doing Reconciliation: Racism, Reconciliation and Transformation in Church and World (Cape Town: VIP, 2004).

Bibliography Of Sources Consulted

Doing Healing: How to Minister God's Kingdom in the Power of the Spirit (Cape Town: VIP, 2009).
Praying the Psalms, Vol. One, *Learning to Pray* (Cape Town: VIP, 2012).

Virkler, Mark. *Dialogue with God* (New Jersey: Bridge Publishing, 1986).

Von Balthasar, Hans Urs. *Prayer*, trans. A.V. Littledale (New York: Paulist Press, 1961).

Von Hildebrand, Dietrich. *Transformation in Christ: On the Christian Attitude* (San Francisco: Ignatius Press, 2001 reprint).
The Nature of Love (South Bend: St. Augustine's Press, 2009).

Wakefield, Gordon (ed.). *A Dictionary of Christian Spirituality* (London: SCM, 1983).

Ware, Bishop Kallistos. *The Orthodox Way* (New York: Vladimir's Seminary Press, 1995, revised edition).

White, R.E.O. *The Changing Continuity of Christian Ethics*, Vol 2, *The Insights of History* (Exeter: Paternoster Press, 1981).

Willard, Dallas. *The Spirit of the Disciplines: Understanding How God Changes Our Lives* (San Francisco: Harper Collins, 1988).
The Divine Conspiracy: Rediscovering our Hidden Life in God (San Francisco: Harper Collins, 1998).
Spiritual Formation (Unpublished paper for Idaho Springs Inquiries, 1999).
Renovation of The Heart: Putting on the Character of Christ (Colorado Springs: NavPress, 2002).
The Great Omission: Reclaiming Jesus' Essential Teachings on Discipleship (San Francisco: Harper Collins, 2006).
Knowing Christ Today: Why We Can Trust Spiritual Knowledge (New York: HarperCollins, 2009).

Wise, Michael; Abegg Jr., Martin; & Cook, Edward. *The Dead Sea Scrolls – A New Translation* (San Francisco: HarperCollins, 2005. Revised Edition).

Wiseman, James. *Spirituality and Mysticism* (New York: Orbis Books, 2006).

Workman, Herbert B. *The Evolution of the Monastic Ideal: From the Earliest Times Down to the Coming of the Friars* (Indianapolis: Doulos Christou Press, 2007).

Wright, N.T. *The New Testament and The People of God* (Minneapolis: Fortress Press, 1992).
The Climax of the Covenant: Christ and the Law in Pauline Theology (Minneapolis: Fortress Press, 1993).
Following Jesus: Biblical Reflections on Discipleship (Grand Rapids: Eerdmans, 1995).
Jesus and The Victory of God (Minneapolis: Fortress Press, 1996).
What Saint Paul Really Said: Was Paul of Tarsus the Real Founder of Christianity? (Grand Rapids: Eerdmans, 1997).
John for Everyone, Part One Chapters 1-10, and Part Two Chapters 11-21 (London: SPCK, 2002).
Romans, in New Interpreter's Bible, Vol X (Nashville: Abington, 2002).
The Resurrection of the Son of God (London: SPCK, 2003).
Paul for Everyone: Romans – Part One Chapters 1-8, Part Two Chapters 9-16 (London: SPCK, 2004).
Paul in Fresh Perspective (Minneapolis: Fortress Press, 2005).
Surprised by Hope: Rethinking Heaven, the Resurrection and the Mission of the Church (New York: HarperCollins, 2008).
Virtue Reborn (London: SPCK, 2010. Published in the USA by HarperCollins, 2010, as *After You Believe: Why Christan Character Matters*).
The Kingdom New Testament (San Francisco: HaperOne, 2011).
Paul and the Faithfulness of God, Book I and II (Minneapolis: Fortress Press, 2013).

Yoder, John Howard. *The Politics of Jesus* (Grand Rapids: Eerdmans, 1972).

Young, Brad. *Jesus the Jewish Theologian* (Peabody: Hendrickson Publishers, 1995).

ENDORSEMENTS

"Alexander Venter has done it again. In his fourth book of the *Doing* series, we are presented with an invitation to whole-heartedly *engage* with the process of Christ being formed in us. The reality of this formation happening to us as pilgrims is unpacked in a profound yet clear and approachable way. This is one of those tomes that you will visit many times during your spiritual pilgrimage. So, dig in, go slow and see what actually happens to your heart." – *Phil Strout, National Director of Vineyard Churches USA.*

"*Doing Spirituality* is a widely informed, highly readable, textbook on Christian spirituality. It is grounded in the biblical theology of Jesus and the Kingdom of God, and set against the backdrop of the Trinity. Alexander Venter's sweep of the history of spiritual traditions in the Christian Church further enriches the theology and practice of spirituality – that is: faithful discipleship to Jesus in progressive character formation to become like him. *Doing Spirituality* will be valuable for all Christ-followers. Spiritual leaders, pastors and students will especially benefit from this insightful textbook." – *Craig S. Keener, F. M. and Ada Thompson Professor of Biblical Studies, Asbury Theological Seminary.*

"Alexander's works are substantial in content and have operated as textbooks around the world. But this one is the most-weighty of all. If I could use a metaphor, all his works are like a good full bodied red wine. If the earlier ones are like a merlot or a cabinet frank, this one is a robust, complex, weighty shiraz, not to be quaffed quickly but sipped slowly, savouring each mouthful (paragraph and chapter). Further there are flavours I have never tasted before. While reading the New Testament material I could rejoice in familiar flavours but then I found myself reading of deep subjects that I knew nothing about. I became the novice, tasting altogether new flavours. To leave the metaphor, it is also obvious to me, partly because I know him well, that none of this is purely theoretical research. Alexander lives and breathes 'doing spirituality.' Those who are serious about the spiritual life will be drawn into it, 'deeper still.' This work will again function as a textbook, but for pilgrims of the journey." – *Derek Morphew, Academic Dean of Vineyard Institute.*

"Alexander Venter in *Doing Spirituality* offers a reflective and practical text for both novice and seasoned Christians. He courageously and powerfully narrates his own

441

Endorsements

journey in an honest and open way. This lays the foundation for readers to do the same: examine their own journey and what it teaches them about their deepest longings, desires, meaning and purpose. Venter takes the reader back to their own experiences of life and God. He writes with clarity and conviction, helping us to overcome one of the most dangerous dichotomies of our time: the split between faith and daily life. The practical exercises at the end of each chapter keep the reader firmly grounded in the content and texture of their own lives. Venter draws from a great number of sources across the Christian tradition to ensure that the focus of his work is unashamedly Jesus Christ – the source and destination of all we are. This text is truly ecumenical, which is a great strength and gives it even more universal appeal. It challenges readers to re-examine their own long-held positions, reminding us that God is always more than we like to think or imagine. This is a wonderfully accessible and interesting book that will challenge anyone who enters into the journey it maps out. If you are truly searching and want to find God in all things, Alexander gives you what you need to begin doing just that." – *Fr Russell Pollitt, SJ. Director: Jesuit Institute South Africa.*

"A classic has been born! Alexander's book *Doing Spirituality* is set to be a major boost to the maturing and preparing Christ's Bride for his coming. Alexander has a way of grounding the most profound truths in the good soil of life lived in following Jesus. As I read this book I found myself praying, "Lord, help me to love, live, and lead like You do!" This book is aimed at the deepening and transforming of lives. Its theology is functionally relevant without compromising on academic integrity. It offers nourishment and tools to bring health and fruitfulness to the lives of believers. Supremely it extends the Trinitarian invitation to join the perichoretic dance as the New Humanity! It invites and inspires us – not obligates us – to new depths and heights of rapture in the celebrative release of a kind of spiritual oxytocin, a longing for more! This CLASSIC embraces both depth of insight and practical application. Alexander's questions for reflection and discussion at the end of each chapter help fuel us in applied benefits. They lead us beyond academia to a Hebraic grasp of lived wisdom. Every believer and seeker should read this book." – *David Pedersen, National Director of Vineyard Churches South Africa.*

"*Doing Spirituality*, the fourth in Venter's Doing series, demonstrates that the life of the mind and the Spirit are unified endeavours. A book for the head and heart, *Doing Spirituality* is personal, theological, and practical. One of the key contributions this book makes is laying out a biblical vision of the spiritual life that is rooted in the revelation of the Trinity and the Kingdom. Drawing from four Christian spiritual traditions, Venter illuminates the Trinitarian spiritual path, on which the spiritual disciplines of engagement and abstinence aid believers in their journey of growth into Christlikeness. Readers, as the book intends, will be encouraged to better understand and practice the spirituality of Jesus, become more like him, and follow him in the way of the kingdom. Whether you are a new or seasoned disciple, you will find transformative wisdom in these pages." – *Brock Bingaman PhD, Founder and Director of All Saints Centre for Theology, Spirituality, and Leadership. Pastor of Our Lord's Community Church, Oklahoma City.*

"This, the latest in Alexander's *Doing* series, is an enthralling piece de resistance – his magnum opus, the ultimate revelation of his soul. Every line of it is both inspirational and eminently practical, with multiple entry points for readers at every current level of spirituality, to be helped as well as motivated toward growth. And all written in Alexander's inimitable, passionate style. To read it is like listening to him preach it. And that, in turn, will leave you, the reader, hopeful of being a better you."
– *Costa Mitchell, retired National Director of Vineyard Churches South Africa.*

"Spirituality has become a white hot topic even among those who claim no allegiance to any religious tradition. When I read a book on spirituality, I want to know three things. First, does the author actually drink the water that they claim will quench my thirst? This is a question of authenticity. Alexander Venter has been a practitioner for decades of the type of spirituality that he's recommending to others. Second, what is the theological framework for someone's spirituality? Do they recognize life's suffering and bitter disappointments or is their spirituality escapist and unreal? On the other hand, have they experienced the radical inbreaking of God's future kingdom so that their spirituality is rooted in God's "incomparably great power for us who believe" (Ephesians 1:19)? Alexander frames his writing on spirituality in kingdom theology which carefully holds the tension of the already and the not yet of life. Finally, will the spirituality that's being taught work for me and for the people I pastor? I want truth to move from the abstract and philosophical to the practical and behavioural. *Doing Spirituality* actually enables the church to **do Christianity**. I highly recommend this book to anyone who is seriously pursuing the goal of looking more like Jesus." – *Rich Nathan, Senior Pastor, Columbus Vineyard in USA.*

"Alexander has provided us with a comprehensive, insightful overview of the history, theology and practices of Christian spirituality. He has masterfully weaved his substantial knowledge and life experience together to help us, as he puts it, become 'captivated by Jesus and his spirituality, to walk in his way and become like him, following him in his kingdom.' I firmly believe that if the insights and guidelines in this book are taken to heart and applied daily, they will be of eternal benefit to your life – this book is that significant!" – *Quinton Howitt PhD, Professor of Theology and Education, Vineyard Institute.*

"In his latest book *Doing spirituality*, Alexander Venter distils over forty years of faithful Christ-following within the South African context, continuous study of and reflection on Christian spirituality through the ages, and active pastoral ministry informing disciples within the local congregation. As a result, we receive in these pages an invitation to step into the deep stream of God's life that stretches our thinking and warms our hearts. In addition we are given wise and practical guidance with regard to the processes involved in the deepening of our own discipleship journey, that gradual transformation of our own characters, and the deepening of our life of prayer. Having had the special privilege of getting to know Alexander, both as a friend and as a teacher, I have witnessed first-hand the integrity of his own personal pilgrimage into the things that he so passionately writes about. His words whetted my appetite to walk more faithfully with Jesus Christ in the kingdom of God, and I am confident they will do the same for you."
– *Trevor Hudson, author, retreat leader, international teacher.*

"In *Doing Spirituality*, Alexander Venter offers us a wonderful and comprehensive overview of the spiritual life of Jesus so that we may take on the journey of becoming like Jesus. This book fills a gap by placing spiritual formation in the context of a theology of the kingdom of God, much like that of Dallas Willard's. What I found so helpful is how Venter shares from his experience, a life of doing, hearing, applying and obeying Jesus. Venter leads us down the road of with great care and clarity where we find companions in biblical characters as well church fathers and mothers who have gone before us. The result is a beautiful and insightful guide for becoming the kind of person who can live in the rule and reign of God, where we are permeated by his love just as Jesus did. There is no greater journey than this and Venter has written a book that is a must read for our time." – *Brandon Rickabaugh PhD, Instructor of Spiritual Formation, Truett Seminary, Baylor University.*

Printed in Great Britain
by Amazon